Contents

Cradles of Eminence

Second Edition

Childhoods of More Than 700 Famous Men and Women

The Complete Original Text by
Victor Goertzel and Mildred George Goertzel
with updates by
Ted George Goertzel and Ariel M. W. Hansen

Scottsdale, Arizona
Great Potential Press, Inc.
2004

Cradles of Eminence, Second Edition: Childhoods of More Than 700 Hundred Famous Men and Women

Cover and Interior Design/Layout: Lisa Liddy, The Printed Page
Copy Editor: Jen Ault Rosso
Indexer: Lisa Rivero

Published by
Great Potential Press, Inc.
P.O. Box 5057
Scottsdale, AZ 85261

Printed and bound in the United States of America
08 07 06 05 04 6 5 4 3 2 1

Library of Congress Cataloging-in-Publication Data

Goertzel, Victor, 1914-
Cradles of eminence: childhoods of more than 700 famous men and women: the complete original text / by Victor Goertzel and Mildred George Goertzel.— 2nd ed. / with updates by Ted George Goertzel and Ariel Hansen.
p. cm.
ISBN 0-910707-56-1 — ISBN 0-910707-57-X (pbk.)
1. Gifted children—Case studies. I. Goertzel, Mildred George, 1904- II. Goertzel, Ted George III. Hansen, Ariel. IV. Title.
HQ773.5.G64 2004
649'.155—dc22
2003018508

ISBN 0-910707-56-1

To the memory of Mildred and Victor Goertzel
and all those who have kept their concern for gifted children alive

Introduction

When Ted Goertzel inquired whether Great Potential Press would like to publish an updated edition of *Cradles of Eminence*, we were pleased. The book had been out of print for two decades, yet demand for it was still there.

The first edition of *Cradles of Eminence*, published in 1962, received substantial attention. The *New York Times* and *McCall's* featured it, and the authors were invited to speak to many groups throughout the country. There was much interest back then in helping children fulfill their potential, and these authors—through reading literally thousands of biographies—had studied the childhoods of more than four hundred eminent people to see what they had in common. Did the children have special opportunities? Were they educated or disciplined in a certain way? Were there aspects of their childhood environments that led to their later eminence?

The authors found that these 400 eminent people did have many childhood experiences in common. They grew up in homes where excitement and love of learning were present, though they often disliked formal schooling and some were schooled at home. The homes they grew up in were full of books and stimulating conversation and strong opinions, so that as children, they learned to think and express themselves clearly. They had at least one strong parent, usually the mother, who believed in them. These results and others in this book were—and still are—provocative and challenging, and make for fascinating reading today.

As you read this second edition of *Cradles of Eminence*—with an update at the end—you will no doubt find yourself thinking about its relevance for today. You may wonder, as we did, whether today's world will nurture and support the emergence of great potential to the same extent as previous decades. Are parents as involved in their children's lives and educational training as they were in previous decades? Have our schools improved in recognizing and encouraging children with high potential? Do schools offer opportunities for bright children to advance?

What is eminence after all? The Goertzels' method for identifying eminence was to study people who had at least two biographies written about them. Biographies are usually written about people who make a contribution to science, medicine, literature, world peace, the arts, sports, or politics, or in other ways serve as leaders A few of the famous people whom the authors judged as eminent by the fact that they had biographies written about them— for example, Hitler, Stalin, and Mussolini—were judged by history as evil for their particular contributions to history. Today, Idi Amin or Osama Bin Laden would fit this category. Their biographies remind us of the potential for harm when eminence goes awry.

But for the most part, when we speak of eminence, we think of the positive contributions of individuals who have served as inspiration for future generations. Most of the people described in this book are those positive eminent persons, though few lived trouble-free lives. We learn, for example, that Pablo Picasso, Louis Armstrong, Frida Kahlo, Will Rogers, Jack London, Eleanor Roosevelt, Charlie Chaplin, and Winston Churchill—all of whom made enormous contributions—experienced rather traumatic childhoods.

While human nature has not changed much, if at all, in the last century, society has changed remarkably. In the forty years since *Cradles of Eminence* was first published, the world has seen many changes— medical advances, computers, telecommunication, globalization, and others—that could enhance potential for developing eminence in many areas. With instant access to data, when inquiring minds want to know, information can be found. In one generation, we have seen routine acceptance of overnight deliveries, e-mail, Internet use, beepers, fax machines, cellular phones, satellite television, and CD-ROM discs capable of storing music, books, movies, encyclopedias, even whole libraries of information. Exchange of information around the world is rapid. Instant news from CNN, MSN, and the Internet is what we expect, and our world has become a much smaller, more interconnected place.

Cradles of Eminence gives readers a glimpse of family life and society in an earlier time. Have we lost some important things from that earlier time? Is it possible that modern information tools improve our lives at too great a cost? Does the resulting dramatically faster pace of everyday life handicap the development of eminence?

We remember the predictions, about ten years after *Cradles of Eminence* was published, that future technology would give us more leisure time to spend with our families and on hobbies, and that we would surely have a four-day work week. Yet instead of more leisure, most of us report having less free time, despite all our "timesaving inventions." When we do have free time, we typically turn to electronic equipment—TV, videos, computer games, or the Internet—to be entertained, rather than creating our own entertainment or interacting with family members. We entertain ourselves as individuals, but have less interaction with others; we touch keyboards and keypads more, but touch each other less. Are we losing touch—figuratively and literally—with each other and our families? Have technological advances become barriers to family communication, to relationships, or to creative thought and action? Have they distracted us from our concerns for larger world problems—environmental pollution, renewable energy resources—or concerns for the well being of humanity? Have we as a society sacrificed *love of learning* for less challenging *entertainments*?

Nearly all of the homes studied in *Cradles of Eminence* showed a love of active learning by one or both parents; these parents read literature to their children and discussed politics at the family dinner table. In fact, most parents of the later-to-be-famous children were highly involved in the daily lives of their children—even to the point of being pushy or dominating. They promoted educational pursuits like travel, study, practice, reading, playing board games, or making things. How many parents are there today who emphasize such things?

The majority of the four hundred eminent people in this book disliked school immensely as children; it was too slow for their quick minds. Many dropped out of school. Others skipped one or two grades—sometimes more—or were schooled at home by parents or tutors because school was not particularly challenging.

The Goertzels found that talented young people often were not recognized by their teachers as having great potential. In fact, some, including Thomas Edison, Karl Menninger, Marcel Proust, Albert Einstein, Sergei Rachmaninoff, Gamal Abdel Nasser, and Winston Churchill, were even seen by their teachers as "dull" or "slow."

Does the same condition exist today? Are the traits of bright, talented children well understood by most educators? Regrettably, much ignorance and misinformation still exists about talented, able learners. Many bright adults tell us they experienced little challenge in school (at least until they reached college). These same adults are now raising children who also experience little challenge in school. With a lockstep curriculum, where every child is expected to learn the same material at approximately the same age, this is inevitable. The rationale teachers and school administrators give for keeping all eight-year-olds in the same grade is that socialization of the child is more important in the long run than academic challenge. We wonder. We think the opportunity to make academic progress is at least as important as socialization. Many of the eminent persons described in this book became eminent largely because they challenged prevailing social customs.

As adults, we hope (and often assume) that bright, creative children will learn skills in schools that will challenge and develop their talents, intellect, creativity, and their desire to attain high levels of competence. But many education leaders note that the focus in many schools these days (except in athletics) is on basic minimal levels of competency that has had the effect of, "dumbing down" the curriculum content compared to that of earlier years. Though it is admirable to work toward all students meeting minimal competence, too much emphasis on this means slower students receive most of the effort and attention, which leaves bright students languishing with little or nothing meaningful to do. They know the material, but are forced to wait while others master the minimum standards for that grade. Some believe our society—at least in the U.S.—may be perilously drifting into an anti-intellectual mode where the emphasis is far more on mediocrity, conformity, and fitting in, rather than on innovation, excellence, and creativity.

What does happen for bright students? The last comprehensive nationwide survey of gifted education programs in U.S. public schools occurred in 1985—twenty years after the first publication of *Cradles of Eminence*—and the results of that four-year study were published in *Educating Able Learners.*[1] We have no reason to believe conditions have changed much since that survey. The survey found that over one-half of the school superintendents surveyed believed they had no gifted children in any of their schools and that almost 60 percent of the schools offered enrichment opportunities to gifted students for three hours per week or less. Where special programs did exist, schools selected services that were visible and easily identifiable to parents (such as a "pull-out" or "send-out" program), rather than programs that were more educationally substantive but less apparent. As part of their study, the authors of *Educating Able Learners* asked a sample of the MacArthur Fellows (who have received the so-called Genius awards from the John D. and Catherine T. MacArthur Foundation and who are considered to be promising future candidates for consideration as eminent) what educational programs were the most helpful to them. The MacArthur fellows described educational approaches far different from those being offered currently by most public or private schools. They listed early entrance, grade skipping, mentorship, and significant involvement by their parents in their education—all of which are similar to positive educational experiences listed by eminent figures in *Cradles of Eminence*. The

MacArthur fellows, like the persons studied in *Cradles of Eminence*, also typically disliked school but enjoyed being tutored or mentored.

Whether schools offer more these days for bright, talented, and gifted students is open to question. The answer seems to be uneven—some do, but most don't. A 1993 Task Force Report from the U.S. Department of Education stated, "The United States is squandering one of its most precious resources—the gifts, talents and high interests of many of its students."[2] Schools today offer more choices of academic and vocational subjects, and also extracurricular activities; however, the level of academic rigor is often suspect. One can find special schools for the arts, schools with Advanced Placement classes, schools with International Baccalaureate diplomas, and various kinds of advanced level charter schools and private schools that offer strong academic programs, but one has to hunt for them, even in large cities. There are special summer programs for talented students in many states. However, these programs reach a relatively small percentage of the students who need them.

Following the publication in the early 1970s of "The Marland Report,"[3] authored by the U.S. Commissioner of Education Sidney Marland, most states instituted at least some form of program and services for learners with high potential. About half of the states in fact have some type of legislative "mandate" requiring schools to serve the special needs of gifted and talented children, though less than half of the states require special training of teachers for gifted and talented students,[4] and there is wide disagreement as to what is appropriate. Sometimes, too, what is said on paper has little relationship to what actually occurs. Faced with budget cuts in recent years, schools do have a difficult time equitably meeting the needs of all children.

Despite the legislative mandates that may exist, today's educational system contains a widespread bias against programs for talented children, particularly the more "radical" approaches, such as early entrance, grade-skipping, and home schooling—all of which occurred with some frequency in the childhoods of the four hundred eminent people featured in *Cradles of Eminence*. The prevailing notion in schools today seems to be that talented children do not need special educational assistance because if they are truly bright, they will make it on their own—and besides, they need to learn to fit in with the rest of the children so that they can later fit into society.

Federal and state support for educational programs for talented students is lacking; for example, out of every Federal dollar spent for education, less than two cents goes to fund programs for gifted children.[5] State funding designated for these programs varies, but it generally supports only minimal services.[6]

Another recent change in public schools that has had a negative effect for bright students is that of mandated standardized testing. Many states now require students to pass written tests at third grade, sixth grade, etc., in order to progress to the next level of schooling. Of course there is no problem with bright students passing these tests. The problem is that with so much emphasis on basic minimal standards, quick learners are left without suitable enrichment or academic challenge. Perhaps, along with minimum standards testing, we should also consider testing to what extent students are advanced relative to their age and grade, and work to ensure that their programs match their ability levels.

Today's teachers are pressured to prepare all students for yearly achievement tests to measure whether or not students have reached "grade level competency." With school ratings and teacher evaluations becoming more dependent on the results of these standardized tests, teachers spend more time each year "teaching to the test" and therefore less time modifying curriculum for individual students, particularly those students who are advanced. A primary thrust in schools these days is toward "heterogeneous grouping"—that is, grouping many different abilities together—and "cooperative learning," in which a mixed group of students work on a project together and help each other complete it.[7] But *Cradles of Eminence* points out that to be eminent, one must learn to function independently and be self-directed, something George Betts and Jolene Kercher[8] call the "autonomous learner."

Peer pressure in today's world is another factor that handicaps the development of individual identities. High population densities, combined with extensive media exposure, shape what our youth think and how they behave. Marketing departments are quite skilled at promoting the latest fads. It takes a very strong adolescent to resist intense peer pressures, yet many areas of eminence—particularly those involving creative endeavors—require non-traditional behaviors and a strong sense of personal identity.

We have observed that it is for reasons such as those above that parents of gifted and talented children are turning to home schooling.[9] Like parents described in *Cradles of Eminence*, home schooling parents today tend to hold strong and often unconventional opinions; they do not want their children subordinating themselves to peer pressures of conformity and mediocrity, and they themselves have a strong love for learning, a keen sense of values, and a personal mission.

But do we even want our talented children to be eminent? We were pleased to see that Ted Goertzel and Ariel Hansen, in their update of *Cradles of Eminence*, give attention to the personal costs often associated with eminence. The single-mindedness required to achieve eminence in many—perhaps most—fields implies a selective neglect of other duties. The few studies of creative and talented adults have noted that eminent adults are often eccentric and/or difficult to live with. Spouses, children, coworkers, and supervisors can become quite irritated with the eminent person when their needs are being ignored. Similar to the persons described in *Cradles of Eminence*, today's most innovative and influential adults, eminent or not, are often criticized for being "intense," "driven," "too creative," "too sensitive," "too different," too "non-traditional," or too "self-absorbed."

It is our hope that the publication of *Cradles of Eminence, Second Edition* will spark a resurgence of interest in finding and then nurturing—or at least tolerating—persons who may be on their way to potential eminence. Our world, with all its complexity and difficulties, needs eminent persons to emerge as leaders in many fields. We need individuals who want to work to preserve the environment, who will solve problems of hunger, who will discover new cures, who will find new energy resources, who will lead us in social justice causes, who will guide us in exploring outer and inner space, and who will help us learn to live peacefully together on this planet earth. We must nurture today's children as tomorrow's future eminent leaders so that they will have the dispositions and tools that they need in order to pursue their achievements in ways that promote and celebrate humanity, rather than destroy it.

James T. Webb, Ph.D.
Clinical Psychologist
Former President, American Association for Gifted Children
President and Publisher
Great Potential Press, Inc.

Janet Gore, M.Ed.
former Gifted Education Specialist
Arizona State Department of Education
Developmental Editor
Great Potential Press, Inc.

Foreword to the Second Edition

by Ted George Goertzel

When my parents did their original research and then published *Cradles of Eminence*, parents, educators, and the media all eagerly received it. The *New York Times* and the *Herald Tribune* picked up the story when my father first presented their findings at the annual meeting of the National Association for Gifted Children held at New York's Henry Hudson Hotel on April 20, 1961. The *Times* headline was "Learning Found the Key to Fame," and the story reported that "a study of the childhood of about 400 outstanding persons of the twentieth century has shown that one of the most common qualities was love of learning, although not necessarily formal, organized learning."[1] The *Herald Tribune's headline was "'Madness' Rare Mark of Genius," and the story led with "geniuses are not mad, but those who acquire fame do so in spite of their surroundings, upbringing—and schooling—if there is a love of learning in the home and sufficient drive."*[2]

The newspaper stories coincided with the publication of an article my parents had written for *McCall's*, a leading women's magazine. The *McCall's* article led with five key points:

- ▲ A survey of 400 eminent men and women shows that none of them had an easy time of it in childhood.

- ▲ Almost all of them had at least one parent who was striving and driving in his or her own ambitions.
- ▲ Most of the fathers and mothers were highly opinionated.
- ▲ Many of the parents held unconventional opinions that were shocking, sometimes even antagonistic, to people around them.
- ▲ Many of the parents—this was true especially of the mothers—dominated their children's lives.[3]

The *McCall's* article also reported that "as children, almost none of the 400 liked school. Very few liked their teachers. Yet by today's accepted tests, nearly all showed the characteristics of gifted children." This finding struck a nerve with many readers. In 1961, many parents and teachers were rethinking the conformist norms that had predominated in the 1950s. They were concerned about children who seemed to "march to a different drummer" and who did not fit easily into the mainstream culture of their neighborhood or school. Should these children be helped to "adjust," as many psychologists and educators had advocated? Or should their differences be respected and perhaps even encouraged?

The book sold well when Little, Brown published it in 1962, finding its readership among parents, educators, and others who were simply curious about the childhoods of famous people. My father was listed as the first author because he had a Ph.D. in psychology and it was thought that this might help sales. The lion's share of the work was actually done by my mother, a high school English teacher who had quit working when she had her first child at 37. She had the time and interest to tap into a rich source of information that had been almost completely ignored by professional psychologists: published biographies.

Biographies are a rich source of information, but not an easy one to assimilate into a scientific study. No psychologist had ever taken the time to read hundreds of biographies and analyze them for common patterns. Fortunately, most biographers cover the subject's childhood in a few chapters, and most provided the essential information my mother wanted. She enjoyed spending her days at the library or taking library books home, reading about the childhoods of important and accomplished people.

Readers found *Cradles of Eminence* inspirational and recommended it to others. Little, Brown kept it in print for many years and issued a paperback reprint some twenty years after it was published. When they finally allowed it to go out of print, the interest did not die. A Google Internet search for *Cradles of Eminence* in 2003 produced 905 links, many from people inspired by its message. In remarks that are frequently quoted on the Web, Dr. James Dobson summarizes the findings and says that the application of *Cradles* "to your own family should be obvious. If your child has gone through a traumatic experience or is physically disadvantaged, don't give up hope. Help identify his or her strengths and natural abilities that can be used to overcome the handicap."[4] Dr. Dobson is the founder of Focus on the Family, a nonprofit organization that produces radio and television programs. His website says that his commentaries are heard by 200 million people every day.[5]

Murray Peters, Gifted Education Resource Teacher of the Coquitlam School District in California, writes in a March 6, 2003 *Newslette*r that "my concerns about 'underachieving' gifted students have recently been enlightened" by reading *Cradles.* He urges parents to read one of several copies he has placed on reserve in the library. He says, "One cannot read *Cradles of Eminence* without being challenged to embrace those students who show so much promise, yet struggle to fit our system of education.[6]

Suzy Red of the Little Red School House website says, "I found the book in a search on Amazon.com, but the cheapest I could find was $50. I hope you can find it in the library! It is really eye-opening!"[7] The April, 2002 "Padre's Corner," published to provide inspiration, humor, reflection, and insight to the United States European Command, quoted the key findings from the book under the title "Successful People and Suffering" and suggested that the people in the book most likely went on to outstanding accomplishments by compensating for their weaknesses in one area by excelling in another.[8]

Cradles of Eminence is listed on a great many reading lists for parents, especially for parents with gifted children or for those interested in home schooling or other educational alternatives. But the book has been hard to find. Usually there are a few copies listed on Amazon.com and with other used book dealers, but these are often quite expensive. I checked as I was writing this paragraph, and the least expensive was $92.00. A copy with the dust jacket signed by Victor was offered for $200. I decided to post a brief excerpt from the book on my website, and I got occasional inquiries from people looking for copies. One woman had been unable to find the book in local libraries and was eager to read it because "I have one very young child of my own, would very much like to learn all that I can from this book...as it may (or may not)...some day apply directly to my own child."

A reader in the Great Britain wrote, "The only copy I can find in the United Kingdom is in the British Library. Why is no one reprinting such a valuable book? Who has the publishing rights? Is someone sitting on it? If enough of us make a noise perhaps someone would bring out a new edition."

An American woman asked, "Who is the holder of the copyrights to the books *Cradles of Eminence* and *Three Hundred Eminent Personalities*? What is the possibility of them ever being back in print?...I see a possibility of many thousand being sold, given the market I deal with, which is the home school market."

My parents are now deceased, and neither had thought it necessary to name a literary executor. My brother John, however, as their executor, agreed that it would be fine if I could arrange to have the books republished. Little, Brown released the rights, and Jim Webb, President of Great Potential Press, has enthusiastically accepted my suggestion that he issue a new edition.

In addition to reissuing the original text of *Cradles*, I thought it would be good to update it. A great deal has happened since 1962, and readers naturally will want to know if the findings of the earlier studies still hold. We had done some follow-up work, including a sequel I helped my parents to write in 1978, titled *Three Hundred Eminent Personalities: A Psychosocial Study of the Famous.* I had also published a third comparative biography book, *Turncoats and True Believers: The Dynamics of Political Beliefs and Disillusionment,* in 1992. There have been studies by other authors as well, two of whom did a wonderful job of replicating the statistical findings in *Cradles of Eminence* (these are discussed in the Chapter 12).

There have been important social changes since these books were published. Gender roles and relationships between men and women have certainly changed. Many of the people in *Cradles of Eminence* had mothers who devoted their entire lives to their children's careers, even after the children were grown. In today's world, more mothers have careers of their own. Schools have changed, giving at least lip service to creativity and diversity. And many parents choose to school their children at home, using curricula readily available through the Internet and other sources. As shown repeatedly in *Cradles of Eminence,* parental involvement is critical for bright students to reach their potential.

Perhaps today's eminent people will have a better time in school than those in *Cradles,* most of whom found formal schooling to be unpleasant. Indeed, *Cradles* itself may have contributed to some changes in how gifted and talented children are treated, and this update will, we hope, contribute more.

Completely updating *Cradles of Eminence* with a new sample would require reading the first few chapters of hundreds of biographies, which would take several years. This would certainly generate enough material for a new book, and it may be one that we do in the future. For now, however, we decided to reprint the full text of *Cradles of Eminence* as it was originally published, with some editing for clarification. Then we added a new 2003 update (Chapter 12) discussing trends since the first edition was published.

Fortunately, I was able to persuade my step-niece, Ariel Hansen, to help with the project. Ariel is a recent graduate of Haverford College and was eager to find a job in journalism. Her particular interest was in science journalism, and she had the talent and enthusiasm to help me continue my parents' work. With her help, the last chapter includes key findings from a new sample of biographies published between 1995 and 2003. Thus we bring the story up-to-date for the twenty-first century.

Foreword to the First Edition

by Victor and Mildred Goertzel

Sit down before fact as a little child, be prepared to give up every preconceived notion, follow humbly wherever and to whatever abyss nature leads, or you shall learn nothing.
– T. H. Huxley

Curiosity about the training of that most valuable human resource, the capable child, led us to attempt this survey of the emotional and intellectual climate in which eminent people of the twentieth century were reared. Some of these men and women have been as eminently wicked as others have been productive of good. Most of them, however, have devised new social groupings, set people thinking in a different frame of reference, or added to the sum of human culture. We use the term "eminent" to describe them because they became important enough to their contemporaries to have books written about them. This is the only basis on which Hitler and Schweitzer, Dalí and Steinmetz can be on the same list. They are all eminent, in the dictionary sense of "standing high in comparison with others."

To know why people differ as well as why they have common characteristics, it is necessary to have a large number of subjects to examine. Do dictators have similar backgrounds? Where do famous people come from—the country, a village, a city? Do celebrities grow up in warm, permissive homes? Were they usually happy as children? Were they usually healthy?

The list of individuals that we compiled (see Appendix A) may very well be amusing to the critics and scholars of the year 2065. Traditionally, the men of any given age have not been clever at recognizing those of their own contemporaries whom future scholars are going to value. This list of the eminent is, in a sense, everybody's list. Into its compilation went the judgment and preferences of countless other persons—all the people who read, write, and buy books; the critics, authors, editors, and publishers.

The research plan finally used for the selection of subjects was as follows: "Include each person who has at least two books about him in the biography section of the Montclair, New Jersey Public Library if he was born in the United States and all persons who have at least one book about them if they were born outside the United States. Include only those who lived into the twentieth century and are described in a standard reference work."

This plan often frustrated us, as it must anyone who has strong likes and dislikes for the outstanding men and women of his or her times. Ralph Bunche—African-American U.N. diplomat who won the Nobel Peace Prize in 1950—is not included because there is no adult biography written about him. William Cody (Buffalo Bill) is included. Like Einstein, he has five books about him in the biography section of the Montclair Public Library. That is not the fault of the book buyer at the library. It represents the lack of biographical books about scientists in general, and it also evidences a public interest in William Cody. Einstein, to be sure, has twenty-one non-biographical books about him in the same card file; Cody, none.

We have been invited on several occasions to speak about our research before neighborhood groups. Men, in general, have treated us well during the question period. They may like being told that there are many fathers who have failed to achieve their own goals but whose sons have not seemingly been harmed.

The mothers in our audiences enjoy hearing about the troubles of the O'Neills and the Wolfes and the Chekhovs, then rebel against our recital of woeful facts and assume falsely that we advocate mistreatment of children as a way of stimulating creativity. All we can then do is to reiterate that we are reporting a survey and that we have no intention of becoming ogres at home on the off chance that one of our own three sons may become a playwright or a novelist. It may be currently possible to be both creative and comfortable. We suspect it isn't, but our suspicions are not scientific data. We emphasize that we had nothing to do with the child-rearing practices of parents who lived decades ago. They did it; we didn't. Mothers are, in our experience, more likely than fathers to apply every statement made by a speaker to their own children, regardless of its relevance.

We do not consider all of the persons we write about equally eminent, and we rely on the weight of the published material about the person to decide that for us. Time alone can sort out the truly great, and still people will disagree. This is not a matter of great concern to us. Some of the least well-known people write with the most insight about what went on in their homes and give the best clues as to the things parents and teachers can do to teach and nurture all bright, curious children, regardless of talent.

The people who had the most biographical books about them catalogued in the Montclair Public Library are as follows: Franklin D. Roosevelt, 28 books; Mahatma Gandhi, 21; Sir Winston Churchill, 20; Albert Schweitzer, 17; Theodore Roosevelt, 17. The top five in the circulating department of the New York Public Library at Forty-Second Street are: Churchill, 27; Franklin D. Roosevelt, 26; Gandhi, 20; Schweitzer, 16; Theodore Roosevelt, 16. Within limitations, most sizable libraries have much the same biographical collections.

We used the Montclair Public Library because it was the nearest adequate library and has a fine collection of thousands of biographies on open shelves. It was, incidentally, the first library in the country to use a computer system to record its circulation. Montclair is a prosperous suburban residential town of 40,000 with a large percentage of professional and business people.

Once a person was included in our list of eminent persons by virtue of the card catalogue in Montclair, we were free to read about him or her from books found anywhere. We have used the New York Public Library, the Newark Public Library, the Indianapolis State

Public Library, the Toledo Public Library, California public libraries in Santa Barbara, Ventura and Los Angeles, our personal library and our friends' libraries, as well as bookstores and commercial circulating libraries. We usually used *Books in Print* to find out what material was available and also to be sure that no really significant person was omitted.

Sometimes we regret not extending our coverage to Americans with only one biography, but a list of "one-biography" American celebrities would include dozens of minor politicians, athletes and actors. Biographies of the foreign-born that reach the U.S. are less likely to have only topical interest. Therefore, we required only one volume for such individuals. We did, however, exclude persons whose biographies are published because of their inherited positions—kings, queens, princes, and so forth.

"Do you think these famous people are like the children who are called 'gifted' today because they test very high on intelligence tests?" is a question often asked us.

Many of the children of the past who were to become eminent, like the intellectually gifted children of today, tended to possess superior ability in reasoning and in recognizing relationships. They showed intellectual curiosity, had a wide range of interests, and did effective work independently. They showed their greatest superiority in reading ability; many read at the age of four. Almost all were early readers of good books. They were original thinkers and had scant patience with drill and routine. They were likely to be rejected by their playmates and had parents who valued learning. The majority of them came from middle-class business and professional homes. Their brothers and sisters were capable. Most of those children who became eminent would probably have tested high on today's intelligence tests.

Admittedly, there are those who will question the reliability of the autobiography or biography as a source. We cannot be sure that the authors we have used are telling the truth; we can only report what they say. To check the reliability of what a person says about himself, or of what his biographer says of him, is not part of our self-imposed task. We can only hope to be accurate in reporting what they say and sensitive in the selection of material chosen to report. But it is not so easy to be untruthful or misleading as may be believed.

Henry M. Stanley, the man who found Dr. Livingstone in Africa, tried to conceal both his nationality and the fact that he was illegitimate. When his true identity became known, the consequences were disastrous for him. He told the true story of his life in his autobiography in his old age. So far as we know, Stanley is the only one of our subjects who ever attempted a major deception. Misrepresentations, when they occur, are more often the result of omission than of commission.

In pre-Freudian days many felt free to make statements comparable to the one Carnegie made about his mother: "After my father's death she was all my own." Then came a period when stories that might be subject to psychoanalytic interpretation were omitted by wary writers who did not wish to seem naive or to betray fundamental weaknesses. We are now in an era of self-conscious revelations made in full awareness of the significance in Freudian terms of the behavior described. It is in omission and selectivity that we get the half-truth, which is different from untruth. By taking statements as fact from many sources, we hope to approximate reality. Thus, when Thomas Mann says, "I loathed school," we record him as one who strongly disliked school, relying on forthright statements such as these.

There is a tendency for biographers to pass on the cliché type of observation, with scant reference to the homely but candid statements by the subject and his relatives. In family accounts, the mothers of Clemens, Freud, and Churchill emerge with personalities more unconventional and dynamic than the versions of them in biographies by writers who pass on accepted stereotypical images or those who support a preconceived theory of personality development.

When we can, we report from the subject's autobiography or from accounts written by family members, neighbors, or close personal friends, corroborated by detailed descriptions of events and behavior expressed in simple, colloquial terms.

In the 1950s, we wrote a chapter on "The Gifted Child" for a college textbook, *The Clinical Psychology of Exceptional Children*, edited by the late Professor C. M. Louttit. Since that time, we have had a heightened interest in the gifted children selected by Lewis M. Terman in the 1910s on the basis of tests of teacher-nominated California school children; those 1500 children with intelligence quotients of 140 or above have been studied since that time. These studies appear in the series *Genetic Studies of Genius*. The fifth volume of the series, *The Gifted Group at Mid-Life*, published in 1959, presents these individuals as comfortable, solvent, conservative, well-functioning citizens. Their principal achievements have been in science. Three men have been elected to the National Academy of Sciences. There has been, however, a lack of outstanding accomplishment in aesthetic fields.

We have ourselves seen a number of intellectually gifted youngsters grow up and fit themselves competently into suitable and remunerative positions that offer them little intellectual stimulation or deep satisfaction. These same children had financial and emotional security in their childhood homes and received the best of schooling. When we turn to biographies and autobiographies of eminent people, however, we find exciting, experimental, creative men and women who in their childhood experienced trauma, deprivations, frustrations, and conflicts of the kind commonly thought to predispose one to mental illness or delinquency. The inexplicable difference between the bright child in the classroom who becomes the competent, unimaginative adult, and the academically unsuccessful child who later makes his impact felt on a whole generation, continues to challenge our attention with increasing force and persistence.

We decided to study the life histories of men and women who were more creative than the Terman group. We sought a group of persons who were more deeply involved in politics or social reform, more likely to be musical or artistic or literary and/or to challenge the usual in our culture. If there are Edisons and Einsteins and Thomas Manns among the younger generation, we want to anticipate their coming and to help accelerate their progress.

Since 1957, we have had occasional reading sprees in the biography section of the library and have used the resultant data in lecture rooms where, ironically, graduate students in education were more vulnerable than PTA audiences to the following hoax. We asked several groups to listen to these descriptions of children and to predict the children's future development. In five years, we asked, would they be functioning as gifted, average-normal, psychotic, neurotic, delinquent, or mentally deficient persons?

> *Case 1.* Girl, age sixteen, orphaned, willed to custody of grandmother by mother, who was separated from alcoholic husband, now deceased. Mother rejected the homely child, who has been proven to lie and to steal sweets. Swallowed penny to attract attention at age five. Father was fond of child. Child lived in fantasy as the mistress of father's household for years. Four young uncles and aunts in household cannot be managed by the grandmother, who is widowed. Young uncle drinks; has left home without telling the grandmother his destination. Aunt, emotional over love affair, locks self in room. Grandmother resolves to be more strict with granddaughter since she fears she has failed with own children. Dresses granddaughter oddly. Refuses to let her have playmates, puts her in braces to keep back straight. Does not send her to grade school. Aunt on paternal side of family crippled; uncle asthmatic.

> *Case 2.* Boy, senior year secondary school, has obtained certificate from physician stating that nervous breakdown makes it necessary for him to leave school for six months. Boy not a good all-around student; has no friends, teachers find him a problem, spoke late, father ashamed of son's lack of athletic ability, poor adjustment to school. Boy has odd mannerisms, makes up own religion, chants hymns to himself, parents regard him as "different."

> *Case 3.* Boy, age six, head large at birth. Thought to have had brain fever. Three siblings died before his birth. Mother does not agree with relatives and neighbors that child is probably abnormal. Child sent to school—diagnosed as mentally ill by teacher. Mother is angry—withdraws child from school, says she will teach him herself.

When Eleanor Roosevelt, Albert Einstein, and Thomas Edison (the three case studies above) had been categorized by our audience as delinquent, mentally ill, and retarded, respectively, we then spoke to them of the danger of making snap decisions on superficial, incomplete evidence and emphasized the need for objective examination and adequate case study in making proper judgments. The audience, in turn, frequently retaliated by making us confess that we could not account for the high achievement and resilience of these children from troubled homes.

The completion of the survey and the writing of this book were interrupted by other concerns and duties. In the normal course of things, professional research in the Goertzel family is confined to the rehabilitation of mental patients. An opportunity to present a preliminary paper at the annual meeting of the National Association for Gifted Children provided an outlet for our extra-curricular interest in the emotional and intellectual climate in the homes that produce eminence. The motivation was our own unsatisfied curiosity—and an audience.

Leonard Buder, education writer for the *New York Times*, reported the preliminary findings. The quick public response at home, and even abroad, persuaded us that there were many other persons who shared our curiosity about the child-rearing practices of parents whose children later became famous; so we set to work to complete the survey and to write this book.

We deliberately chose to make this a homework assignment. We wanted to read for several weeks without choosing the specific items to be looked for. We decided that at least one person should read all the material about each of our subjects to get the full flavor of the emotional and intellectual climate in the homes. It was not, for example, until several hundred books had been read that the impact of the recurrent father-failures made itself felt. This item, we feel, would have not been noticed had the task of reading been delegated to a number of readers. This extracurricular, self-initiated project has been in a very real way a labor of love and a source of real enjoyment.

Consequently the only persons hitherto admitted to the close, two-year relationship between us and the Four Hundred have been Alan D. Williams, our patient, prescient editor at Little, Brown, and Anita Kramer, a personal friend, who took time from her own family duties to volunteer as typist and research assistant.

In the process of satisfying our curiosity, we have found a few answers and have raised a whole new series of uncomfortable queries.

Chapter 1

Homes that Respect Learning and Achievement

Einstein continued to work hard at his physics until the end. The curious thing was, he worked in complete disagreement with almost all of his contemporaries.

—C. P. Snow, *New Statesman*, March 26, 1960

A strong drive toward intellectual or creative achievement is present in one or both parents of almost all of the four hundred men and women of the twentieth century who are under investigation here. The parents of these celebrities are curious, experimental, restless, seeking. They are physically driving, intellectually striving; they respect learning, and they love truth and sometimes beauty.

There is no geographical center for giftedness, no racial or national or cultural monopoly. To find these families, we must seek out the farms, villages, and small towns where most of them live. They come from the North, South, Midwest, East, and West in the U.S.A.—from Blue Hill, Maine; Diamond Grove, Missouri; Elwood, Indiana; Fresno, California. They come from places like Dean's Marsh, Australia; Graves County, Kentucky; from Munchenbuchsee in Switzerland; Oologah, Indian Territory, U.S.A.; from Pokrovskoye, Siberia; Nagyszentmiklos, Translyvania; Zapotlan, Mexico; Tienghua, China; Gorcum, Holland; and Nkroful, Africa—indeed, from every continent on the globe. A minority comes from the metropolitan centers, and many of the city-dwellers have to be sought in the green fringes at the outskirts. The common ground for these scattered families is the driving need to be doing something, learning something, changing something, or going somewhere to better themselves.

This respect for learning should not be confused with a love for the classroom. By conventional standards, the attitude of the family toward formal schooling is often careless or even negative. A few boys and girls never went to school at all. Parents of these future well-known individuals are prone to withdraw the children from school, to teach them themselves, to take them on trips, or to let them go to work. Thomas Edison and Guglielmo Marconi were home-taught boys. Wilbur and Orville Wright tinkered and traded and never went to college. The scientist, the doctor, the teacher, the lawyer—all of whom perform specialized services and must be licensed—do manage to reach the good colleges and are usually happy there, but not without having given their parents many anxious hours.

The parents try hard to make the most of their children's capabilities. Harvey Cushing, eminent brain surgeon, was a very poor speller in his youth—also as an adult—but then it did not matter. His letters home from Yale and Harvard reveal such boners as: *priviledge*, *definate*, *sacarafice*, *pharsical*, *cronicling*, and *amatures*. When he was in grammar school, his mother, Betsey Maria Williams Cushing, who was never one to let time hang on her hands, drove this youngest of her ten children back to school after his noonday lunch. During the half hour in which the horse ambled and Harvey chafed to play ball, she taught him spelling. When he was in high school, she helped him with his Latin and Greek. This was no more than she had done for her older children or for the half-brothers and sisters she helped to rear—or for anyone else who needed her for any reason whatsoever. When her husband, Dr. Henry Kirke Cushing, told her that he had brought home an aged woman for her to care for, an abandoned woman without any arms, she was immediately sympathetic and rushed out to welcome...a plaster cast of the Venus de Milo her husband had purchased as a household decoration.

This mother's recreation was to read from a propped-up book while she knitted useful garments for her family. Her son says of her, "Her day was planned to get the most out of it, and often, singing at her tasks, she went at them from early till late with untiring enthusiasm."[1] These are the women who rock the cradles of eminence.

When communication and understanding are good between an adult and a promising child, the relationship is rewarding for both. Mothers achieve this happy state more easily than do fathers, who are sometimes carried away by over-enthusiasm and a desire to be experimental when they have such receptive students right at hand.

William and Henry James (who later became well-known as a psychologist and author, respectively) and their brothers and sister were always in and out of schools, always traveling here and there with their father, a wealthy Swedenborgian of cosmopolitan interests. His eagerness to have the children know many cultures and countries well had varying consequences—not the least of which were two eminent sons.

Norbert Wiener, mathematician, son of Leo Wiener, professor of Slavic languages at Harvard, was put through a grueling course of study by a father who professed to believe that each pupil is capable of learning more than he is ever taught and that it is the skill of the teacher alone which determines what is learned by the pupil. No boy was ever so rigorously tutored by a father as was Norbert Wiener, but even he cannot bring himself to say that he would like to have had it be otherwise. The advantages of not being bored made up for the disadvantages of being driven.

Woodrow Wilson, who was to become President of the United States, did not learn his letters until he was nine or learn to read until he was eleven because his father read to him. His father could not wait for Woodrow to learn to read the books he himself enjoyed and wanted his son to enjoy. The brilliant and verbal minister kept the boy home, read to him, explained the meaning of what he read, then asked for young Woodrow's reaction to the ideas of the book.

Another experimental parent was California rancher and lawyer George Patton III, who believed that ontogeny recapitulates phylogeny—that each boy lives out the history of the human race and must start life as a savage enjoying fire, water, earth, the simple speech rhythms of the native chant and the nursery jingle. He did not believe in teaching children to read until they were adolescent and could read history books for themselves. George Patton III kept George Patton IV home on their isolated ranch and read to him. When his father went to work, his mother and an aunt took over the storybook. They read nursery jingles, then graduated him to stories of witches, to animals that speak, to goblins, and to legends. When George IV went away to boarding school at age twelve to be tutored for West Point, he was an authority on epics and could write script but could not read print. To say that he was unhappy at school is an understatement.

In homes that cradle eminence, there are strong tendencies to build directly on personal strengths, talents, and aims rather than to assume that there is a large, specific body of knowledge that everyone should possess. A family, or some member of the family, is likely to take off wholeheartedly on a course of investigation or action that differs from one's contemporaries.

This nonconformity is not self-conscious or forced. It seems to happen because the individual is unable to do otherwise. When parents permit a child to be different from his playmates or involve her in an unusual learning situation, they may be acting from what they feel is weakness rather than strength. They are often self-critical and argue among themselves. They can become guilt-ridden and anxious. Relatives and neighbors contribute to parental ambivalence by being critical. For example, there are letters from relatives who thought it odd that young Woodrow Wilson was so dull and backward, and they expressed sorrow for his parents.

The fathers and mothers in these Four Hundred homes are not prescient. The road to eminence is not paved with plaudits or even scholarships. Boys and girls who are to become famous are not often "all-round," competent, conforming students. To parents who love good books and respect learning, this is frequently frustrating. There is a personal involvement with ideas in these homes. There are few who uncritically accept whatever they are told as passive receptors of fact.

That this stress on learning is a part of the pattern of producing eminence is verified by a study done by the psychologist Anne Roe, in which she reports, in part, the testing and interviewing of sixty-four outstanding physical, social, and biological scientists in the United States. Because of the very personal nature of these interviews, the names of the sixty-four persons were not revealed. [We do know that chemist Linus Pauling was one of the scientists studied, and we obtained permission to have his Rorschach test analyzed. The results are in our book *Linus Pauling: A Life in Science and Politics* (Goertzel, et al, 1995).] Learning was highly valued in these sixty-four middle-class, low-income, professional homes, as was true in families of the Four Hundred. Generally, the fathers and mothers showed overprotection and also firm control. These children also pursued their rather independent paths and followed their own particular interests with more than usual intensity.

Like the Four Hundred men and women under survey, many of the children in the Roe study, though from learning-centered homes, had school problems. A few, who were thought retarded by their teachers, were kept back in school. A famous psychologist had a "hell of a time in kindergarten."[2] A scientist's mother was always after him for reading too much. A physicist led a stink-bomb attack on the faculty. One boy overate because he had no other pleasures. A biologist says he was always lonesome; the other children did not like him, but he never knew why. Another youth was always in flight from two or three overgrown louts who liked to catch him and twist his wrist. The work to which they were individually committed became their chief pleasure and continued to be so in adulthood. They were not good scholarship material in the sense of being good all-around students, leaders, versatile. Many of them had to work their way through college.

In 1929, Paul Witty,[3] psychologist from Evanston, Illinois, also found that parents of gifted children were engrossed in mathematics, music, reading, travel, invention, religious work, sports, politics, dramatics, or lodge work. P. F. Brandwein,[4] in 1955, studied a group of New York high-school students who had won Westinghouse Talent Awards. They, too, came from homes that had substantial libraries;

they had parents who wanted their children to become professional men and women.

Dael Wolfle,[5] who directed an extensive study of American sources of specialized talent, estimates that about half of each year's gifted high-school graduates come from homes where the parents have no particular interest in schooling or in learning, and that the talents of this half tend to become wasted. A rule of thumb for predicting success is to know the number of books in the home and the father's occupation. Until we learn to motivate an enthusiasm for learning when it is not found in the home, economically valuable human potential is wasted yearly.

They Have Hard Driving, Striving Parents

Leslie Stephen, father of the English novelist Virginia Woolf, was a champion walker with an enthusiasm for twenty-, thirty-, fifty-mile hikes. He was president of the Alpine Club, was the first man to climb the Schreckhom, and as the indefatigable editor of the *Dictionary of National Biography*, often worked at his desk until he was exhausted and ill.

Captain Samuel Edison, Jr., who stood six feet one inch in his stocking feet, could outjump any man in his township at the time he was forced to flee for his life. For two and a half days, he ran from a spot in Canada to the United States border eighty miles away while the King's men, Indian guides, and bloodhounds followed in hot pursuit. Had he been captured and punished for his part in the abortive Mackenzie uprising, which aimed to effect separation of Canada from England, he might never have lived to be the father of Thomas Edison, whose own physical stamina enabled him to cut his sleeping time to five hours daily.

Leonard Jerome, grandfather of Sir Winston Churchill, was an active, exuberant man, a gambler, diplomat, newspaper editor, and also the first man to drive a team of horses four in hand down the streets of New York City. The father of H. G. Wells was a professional cricket player.

The mothers of many eminent men and women were not prone to faint or flutter after the manner of the Victorian lady. The eighty-one-year-old mother of Edmund Allenby, military hero, thrust her head out of a window a few hours after an appendectomy and frightened a laggard gardener with her expostulations. Adelaide Nansen, mother of the arctic explorer Fridtjof Nansen, was a tall, vigorous woman who went skiing even though the other women in her neighborhood thought such activity unwomanly. She dug in her garden like a man, and she tailored the suits of her sons and stepsons until they were eighteen. For a hobby, she read history. Jennie Jerome Churchill, mother of Sir Winston Churchill, encouraged Englishwomen to wear comfortable outdoor clothing. An admiring reporter called her the "panther woman," and the Englishwomen ascribed her exuberant energy to her one-eighth Iroquois Indian ancestry.

In the parents of Wendell Willkie, one time candidate for President of the United States and author of *One World*, we have what might be called a representative family among the sample—a driving, striving family, physically vigorous, intellectual, dynamic, and bookish. It is typical in that the mother is more driving than the father.

As a small-town lawyer in Elwood, Indiana, Herman Willkie made bitter enemies as a crusader for reform. The town was wide open, with thirty saloons and a red-light district. But this six-foot man could lift an office safe without assistance and was not someone to be lightly challenged.

His wife, Henrietta Trisch Willkie, was the first woman ever admitted to the bar as a lawyer in the state of Indiana. Her only sister was the first woman doctor to be licensed in the United States. Their mother, an emigrant girl, had fled from the South because she was nearly mobbed when she expressed her views about the sale of African-American children in a public square. Henrietta Trisch Willkie was a big woman with strong features. Each day she went out to work and played a man's role as a lawyer. At home, she painted delicate designs on her china plates, cups, and saucers, or she played the piano. The five children were never as close to her as to their father. On her tombstone is written, "A woman driven by an indomitable will."

The Willkie children ran about unattended except for the casual supervision of the housekeeper during the day, and they were combed, scrubbed, and dressed in proper clothes by their mother when she came home from work. After supper, the family gathered in the library with its six thousand volumes to hear the father read from Dickens or R. L. Stevenson or George Eliot. When the first child dropped off to sleep, Herman Willkie would carry that child tenderly upstairs to bed. The father always returned to the library to continue reading to the other children until the last sleepy child had been carried to bed. As they listened half-awake from the upstairs bedrooms, the splendid sounds of piano music played by their mother filled the big old rambling frame house that still stands at the end of A Street, half in the country, half in town.

In another striving and driving, middle-class lawyer's family in England, during approximately the same period, small Clement Attlee, one day to be Prime Minister of England, was experiencing another type of bedtime ritual. Both his father and mother were strongly concerned with their children's academic achievement. Each evening, the children sang songs their mother had taught them while they marched about the room. While their mother played the piano and the children sang, a nurse took the younger children off to bed, one by one, as each became exhausted. The older children then had dessert with their parents in the dining room, and there was conversation with both parents about the happenings of the day. (The children were cautioned to be very kind to a new governess. She was still quite upset over her experiences with her last charge, that incorrigible little Winston Churchill.)

Ellen Attlee was not a mother to let any one of her three daughters or five sons be uninstructed in letters or morals. When three-year-old Clem, the youngest, had temper tantrums, she was stern about his behavior. As a result, he hid his head in a pillow and called out when he saw her coming, "Clem 'penting" (repenting). He had adopted the quiet meditation that his mother enforced upon him. The father took a keen interest in the education of both his sons and daughters and set them to writing essays on such subjects as "How to Govern England" and "How to Bring Up a Family on a Fixed Income a Year."

There is frequently a dreadful urgency in the driving nature of these parents, which made them difficult for the children to endure. Langston Hughes, the African-American poet, was rebellious and angered by his father's compulsion to keep busy and to keep everyone else busy. He says in *The Big Sea*:

> *"Hurry up!" was his favorite expression in Spanish or English. He was always telling the employees under him at the electric light company, the cook at home, or Maximiliano, or me, to hurry up, hurry up and do whatever we were doing—so that we could get through and do something else he always had ready to be done.*

His father, impatient with racial prejudice directed toward him in the United States, went to Mexico and became successful there as an expatriate American businessman and rancher. He expressed to his son complete contempt for persons who were slothful and indifferent, and he was often out of bed at three in the morning, ready for a long, exhausting day. He was reluctant to spend money, but quite willing to give his son money for college expenses.

The father of Karl Flesch, the violinist, was a physician in general practice in the small Austrian town of Wieselburg and regarded his profession as a mission rather than as a means of earning money. He often gave free treatment to the poor and was reluctant to press any patient for fees. His attitude toward money was one thing; toward work another:

> *Work was his credo. In no circumstances did he tolerate idleness. His stereotyped question used to be, "What are you doing now?" I owed it to his systematic education that, in later years, I felt an insatiable need for activity, which almost mounted to a vice; "pleasure trips" were not only repulsive to me, but actually resulted in attacks of neurasthenia* [fatigue, worry, and irritability].[6]

His father's essential loving kindness did not shield the boy from being sent away from home at age nine. Karl had no particular love for the violin. It was not he who chose the instrument; he might even have preferred playing the piano, but his two older brothers and sister took piano lessons, and it was more convenient for the family if he played the violin. The piano was always in use from 4:00 to 7:00 p.m. by the older children. Karl spared no trouble to shorten his practice hour, cut or break his strings, or put the big clock ahead a quarter of an hour. Despite his indifference, it soon became obvious that the boy had exceptional ability. To the family, this indicated that he should develop this ability. Neither the kindly father nor the fiery mother, who was still boxing Karl's ears when he was sixteen, hesitated to send the talented nine-year-old boy to Vienna, where he could have the best of teachers. Aunt Regi, an unloving egotist to whom he was nothing but a source of extra income, took him in as a boarder.

Unhappy Karl, returning to the city of Vienna after a too brief holiday in rural Wieselburg, often shut himself in the lavatory of the train to cry unnoticed. At eleven, he contemplated suicide, stood on a bridge that crossed the Danube, stared into the cold, black water, then decided it would not be best to jump. The desire of the family to have the talented son make good use of his musical gift outweighed consideration for his personal happiness.

Anna de Mille—mother of Agnes de Mille, the American dancer—was the daughter of Henry George, wife of film director William de Mille, and sister-in-law of renowned film director and producer Cecil B. de Mille. Anna never permitted herself—or her children—to waste time; she required her daughter to say prayers in French for the dual purpose of communication with the Deity and for practice in a foreign language. Anna had a favorite phrase that her daughter describes:

> *"Don't just sit there, dearie," she would say coming into a room. "Do something!" To this hour I find it impossible to read a book before sundown unless it has some immediate connection with my work.*[7]

The mother's drives were by no means merely physical. Agnes continues:

> *As the daughter of Henry George, Mother had early settled for herself the causes of war, of economic depression, of unequal distribution of wealth, and so on, and she naturally found it a matter of no great effort to reach definite conclusions on hats, dresses, interior decoration, manners, painting, music, plays, cooking, the rearing of children, and sex.*

William de Mille, father of the would-be dancer, was a physically vigorous man. At seventy, he could wallop young players on the tennis court. William—known as "Pop"—was considered the intellectual in a learned family. His interests were not confined to his work on the movie lot:

> *In the tradition of his father, Henry de Mille, Pop was a liberal and a free-trader. He never hesitated to speak out for what he believed in, even buying space in the reactionary* Los Angeles Times *and more reactionary* Examiner *to argue the case for the people. His political articles were brilliant.... Pop's outstanding characteristic was his wit. Language was his delight and tool.*

The drudgery of becoming a dancer was faced by the daughter with an attitude appropriate to the household climate:

> *My well-filled curriculum—classes, homework, tennis, piano, editing—was ordered with first one thought: to make room for the dance practice. I rose at six-thirty, and I studied and practiced at breakneck concentration until six in the evening when I was at last free to put on dancing dress and walk—to Mother's bathroom.*
>
> *All through the lonely, drab exercises beside Mother's tub, without music or beat, proper floor or mirror, I had the joy of looking forward to dinner with Father, to hearing him talk about his scenarios and what was going on at the*

studio.... Sometimes after dinner he sang and I accompanied him.... These evenings my cup ran over. I went to bed early planning next day's practice, praying to do better in class. And as I lay waiting for sleep, breathing in the moist garden smell with my fox terrier slowly pressing me from the comfortable center of the bed, I used to dream about dancing on the stage with Pavlova, dancing until I dropped in a faint at her feet so that she would notice me and say, "That girl has talent."

A composer, a writer, or an artist may postpone her "practicing" years, but the dancer or musical performer must make good use of the prepubescent years if he or she is to develop skills. Since the musician almost invariably shows his talent early, his parents are faced with early decisions. The child who shows musical talent is particularly vulnerable to parental pressure if she is to be a performing artist. In these families, it is usually the parent who urges the child to practice, thereby making it possible for the child to achieve success as an adult. There is probably no family that was so fragmented by one child's unusual talent as that of Pablo Casals, the cellist.

Pablo was born in Vendrell, a little Catalan town about seventy kilometers west of Barcelona, the second in a family of eleven children. His father, the church organist, was a modest man, a remarkable musician, a true artist. It was he who gave his children their initial musical training. When the boy was eleven and a half, his mother insisted that he go to Barcelona to undertake advanced study. "He must go to Barcelona, and I shall take him there."

Take him she did, and until Pablo was twenty-two, the home was fragmented, burdened, impoverished by the weight of the mother's consuming drive to see the talent of her son actualized and recognized.

My father thought that all these schemes did not make sense and attributed them to what he called my mother's "folie des grandeurs." They argued with such bitterness that it pained me terribly and I felt very guilty.[8]

When Pablo left the village of Vendrell where he had experienced a happy, carefree childhood, he had no dreams of becoming a great artist. It was his mother who dreamed for him. He never lost his love for his native village and often returned there as an adult.

Initially, his mother installed him in Barcelona with relatives. After a year passed, his mother joined him, leaving his father at home with the other children. The family ties of affection were not broken by the mother's decision to divide the family by coming to Barcelona to make a home for Pablo. Pablo's father bought him a full-sized cello, came to Barcelona, and rode with him to the hall by tram when Pablo gave his first concert, reassuring the frightened boy all the way. Pablo was always to love his father, but he appreciated his mother also and credited her with his ultimate success.

As time passed, there were no spectacular gains, and Pablo, while going through a period of religious mysticism, had thoughts of suicide, which he did not describe to his mother for fear of making her unhappy. When seventeen-year-old Pablo finished his school at Barcelona and graduated from the Municipal School of Music, his mother took him and his two youngest brothers and moved to Madrid. They rented a garret in a slum dwelling, where the hall porter's two mentally defective children were disturbing, and the neighbors were noisy and dirty. The Count de Morphy became interested in Pablo but wanted him to become a composer. Pablo's mother thought differently! The cello must come first. Relations with the Count became strained, and thus part of the Casals family went on to Brussels, where they had prospects of financial assistance. Throughout several long, lean years, Pablo's mother remained supportive, optimistic.

Pablo and his mother went to the Conservatory of Brussels, where he had been offered a scholarship. A sarcastic teacher's first reaction was to ridicule Pablo before the class because the boy said he could play certain selections. When the new student demonstrated his skill, the teacher was abashed and begged the boy's forgiveness, but Pablo would not stay. The day after this humiliation, the family left for Paris, where they lived in a hovel, dieting to save money, until

Pablo became ill with enteritis, dysentery, and hemorrhage. His mother cut her hair and sold it to get money; his father sent money until his own savings melted away.

In despair, Pablo and his mother and baby brothers went back to Barcelona, and Pablo's luck changed. He found his first adequately remunerative employment as a teacher in his old school, the Barcelona Municipal School of Music. A former teacher, Garcia, had vacated a post to go to Argentina and recommended Pablo to fill the post. When Pablo was twenty-two and went again to Paris, his mother stayed home with her husband and the younger children. Her son says of her:

> *She was an exceptional woman! Just think of what she did in Madrid: she studied foreign languages and more or less did the same lessons as I did, partly because she thought it would help my work, but mostly because the deep feeling we had for each other should not be affected by any difference in our education.*[9]

The question of what happens to the other brothers and sisters in such a family is forced upon us by a consideration of the Casals. We were sensitive throughout our study to this query and made notes about the careers of the brothers and sisters in each instance where that information was given.[10] In general, the siblings fall into a category familiar to those who do studies on the brothers and sisters of gifted children. The same striving, driving parents who produce one child of extraordinary ability generally produce other children who are capable and intelligent. For instance, a brother of Pablo's also became a musician and stayed in Spain at the time Pablo left because of his rejection of the Franco government.

The Baden-Powell family, which once lived at 6 Stanhope Gardens in Paddington, London, was perturbed when the sixth son in the family of ten children was considered too academically inept to follow the family tradition of going to Oxford. The father, Professor David Baden-Powell, was a lecturer in mathematics at Oxford and an insatiable seeker of knowledge. He was such a busy man that he usually managed with only five hours' sleep each night. He lectured to his classes and wrote learned articles on the need to liberalize religious thinking, on labor relations, and on natural philosophy. He maintained intimate contact with the learned men of his day—Benjamin Jowett, Dean Stanley, John Ruskin, Robert Browning, and his wife's cousin Charles Kingsley.

The professor found time to take his children on nature hikes, encouraged them to make collections, drew amusing caricatures for them, and taught them to make playthings from discarded possessions. They did special experiments and art projects in his study, where he could be on hand to give advice and encouragement. They were paid a penny for each four errors they could find in the articles he was writing. Since he had been teaching at Oxford for thirty years, he was not a young man when his sixth son, Robert Stephenson Baden-Powell, was born.

Professor David Baden-Powell also founded the Royal Geographic Society. He was the first editor of the *Manchester Guardian.* In addition, he found time to lecture before many audiences about health, religion, and education. His third wife, Henrietta Smyth Baden-Powell, married the professor, who already had three children, ages eight, five, and three. She bore him ten more children, seven of whom lived to be adults. She also found time to do volunteer work for hospitals that housed the indigent, and she was a member of the Central Committee of the Woman's Education Union, which in 1872 founded the Girls' Public Day School Company. She was also an accomplished artist.

When Professor Baden-Powell died, Henrietta's youngest son was one month old and her oldest stepchild twenty-two. To the best of her ability, she continued to rear the children as her husband would have wished. David Baden-Powell had had a horror of learning by rote and rule and believed that children learn best when they learn happily. His wife developed theories about inductive reasoning which she applied to her own home-grown laboratory of boys and girls.

Robert Stephenson Smyth Baden-Powell, who later founded the Boy Scouts, did not observe the proper barrier between master and student when he went to Charterhouse as a redheaded, twinkly-eyed lad. His classmates could not understand this overeager boy who was so ready to assume a father-role, to keep his fellow students amused, and to be useful to the teachers. When the school moved from the city to a new location farther out, "Ste," as he was called, was of much help to the school administration. The teachers liked him; the students thought him "odd."

He became a member of all committees, chairman of none. He did impromptu imitations, drew amazing caricatures, reproduced bird calls, and imitated animal sounds. He took the comic roles in the school plays. He worked with all his heart to keep his classmates happy after the manner of a father as a four-year-old boy remembered him. At that age, he had not been capable of noticing his father's devotion to science and mathematics and philosophy.

When it was time for "Ste" to go to Oxford, he was not accepted by the old friend of the family, Benjamin Jowett, who said the boy was not "quite up to Balliol form." His father had taught there; his older brothers had achieved there. That very year, his half-brother George Baden-Powell had won the Chancellor's prize. But "Ste" was rejected.

Haig Brown, headmaster of Charterhouse, said that his faith was shaken in Jowett's judgment of men and that mother wit truly triumphed when Robert Stephenson passed second place for cavalry and fourth for infantry in an army examination taken by seven hundred candidates.

The brothers of Baden-Powell were to make the kind of adjustments that the majority of the fifteen hundred gifted children studied by Terman made. They were competent to a degree far beyond the average person on the street; although they achieved highly, they did not make any original contributions. Even so, they were well-recognized in society. The oldest half-brother became a judge. The half-sisters married well. The oldest full brother was knighted for his work as a geologist. George Baden-Powell was knighted for his services as an administrator and was a Member of Parliament. The next living brother became a competent artist and barrister. Another became Astronomer Royal of Scotland. The youngest, an experimental balloonist, was knighted as an aeronaut. A sister was married to a man who was knighted for his services as director of the Natural History Museum. There are many such outstanding siblings in the homes that produced the Four Hundred.

The originality and imaginativeness, rather than the intellectual qualities, of Robert Stephenson Baden-Powell were what set him apart and made him eminent. He was always a good-natured, boyish fellow who could not compare his definitive treatise on *Pigsticking* with the scientific and scholarly contributions of his brothers who were better educated than he. Yet it was his drive to perpetuate the child-rearing habits rather than the intellectual interests of his opinionated parents that made him famous.

David Baden-Powell did not live long enough to know that each of his sons became catalogued as distinguished, and that each daughter married a man of ability—except the youngest, Agnes, who remained a spinster. She helped her older brother, Robert Stephenson, to use their memory of their father (although they lost their father when they were four and three years old) as a model for the ideal "Scoutmaster." There is no other family among the Four Hundred that produced so many sons and daughters who may be found in encyclopedias and other reference books.

Most of the parents who so loved learning created a home climate that produced eminence—and also competence of a high order. Not all parents were as altruistic and patient and unselfish as was the lovable Professor David Baden-Powell or the long-suffering father of the famous cellist Pablo Casals. There were mothers as well as fathers who were too intent on their own careers to do much more than be an example of industriousness. They were too busy to be bothered by the special needs of a son or daughter.

A son can sometimes build upon the career of his father, despite being rejected by him. Douglas Fairbanks, Sr., the star of silent Hollywood movies who had been deserted by his own failure-prone but energetic father, had, while a boy, been hyperactive, forever bounding, climbing, leaping, out of pure animal spirits—brilliant, but inattentive in school. When he married and later divorced the mother of Douglas Fairbanks, Jr., he did so without any special regard for the feelings of his pudgy, unattractive boy. Douglas, Sr. failed as completely to develop paternal feelings as had his own father. Beth Fairbanks, mother of Douglas, Jr., described the situation:

> *Senior was perfectly tender and nice; he just did not have the instinct of being a father. All through Douglas' youth he paid no attention to him. He used to come into the house, day in and out, and he wouldn't know the child was there.*[11]

The father was frantic with rage and anxiety for his own hard-earned career when his son, whom he had never liked, starred at age thirteen in a picture under the direction of a rival producer, Jesse L. Lasky. Douglas Fairbanks, Sr. insisted that the boy instead should prepare for college. Junior's inevitable failure as an actor would surely shame the boy and ruin the father.

The film was a flop, just as Douglas Sr. had predicted. Instead of admitting defeat, however, Douglas Jr. started at the bottom of the industry and made a new beginning, supporting his improvident mother and her clinging Southern female relatives. Meanwhile, he became an assistant cameraman, lugged heavy supplies, spent tedious hours in the cutting room. It was Mary Pickford, his tactful step-mother, who was sympathetic, who understood in both son and husband the implacable push to create and the need for self-expression through acting. She helped them to become friends when Douglas Jr.'s growing success made him more acceptable to his ambitious father. Douglas, Jr. never did get to college. When received public acclaim for his role in the John van Druten play *Young Woodley*, his father was quoted as saying, "Have you seen my boy's play? I guess I was wrong. He shouldn't be doing it at seventeen, he should be in college, but pay no attention to me; he's an independent cuss, and by God he's gotten away with it."[12]

It had taken the father fifteen hard years to fight his own way up to stardom. He was not inclined to let his son, so opposite from him in temperament, threaten his status in the industry. The son, although alienated from his father, continued the father's drive for achievement.

Isidor Schnabel, wool merchant, was also not inclined to subordinate his career to that of the son in his family. The family business was in the small Austrian town of Bielitz. When the son Artur showed musical talent beyond the family's ability to subsidize, the mother found patrons for the boy who enabled the family to move to Vienna. The father was to find new customers for the wool business in Vienna; the son was to study classical piano there. The arrangements were satisfactory to everyone except the father.

> *Business there had not come up to expectations. ...he must have disliked the family's partial dependence on the patrons of his young son. ...he turned the agency over to an old established Vienna firm. In the following year, the entire family, without Artur, returned to Bielitz.*[13]

This new move was a fortuitous one, since it left the father and son each free to develop his own abilities in his own way, and the stormy weekly scenes between mother and son were ended. Ernestine Schnabel was so grimly determined to see her son become a great artist that his tendency toward laziness exasperated her. She was always eager to display his talent. She once infuriated his teacher by arranging a concert for Artur when he was eleven in his hometown during his holiday period. More than a thousand persons attended, crowding into Bielitz's largest hall. Mother and son both enjoyed the affair, but the crusty teacher considered it premature. The teacher was prone to humiliate Artur to tears by demanding more of him than of the adults in her class.

Artur, turned loose in Vienna and commissioned to fulfill his talent by his family on his own, enjoyed himself completely. He chose his own boarding places; when the Nelkens bored him, he moved in with the lively Frau Husseri, a widow with four student sons and a pretty daughter with whom the precocious Artur fell in love. Artur was a popular guest in sophisticated homes where children of his age were sent to bed while he played for the adult guests and joined in the conversation. At twelve or thirteen, he was enjoying all the privileges of an eligible young bachelor in wealthy and cultured circles. His ambitious mother, back in Bielitz, had to be content with the continuing reports of adequate progress. There was, nevertheless, an incomplete satisfaction in this situation for Artur. "Life in this atmosphere was not always pleasant. I was not always happy there." Despite his unhappiness, his need for training kept him away from home and on his own.

The Love for Learning Can Persist into Parents' Old Age

One of the unexpected observations we have been able to make while doing this survey concerns the number of parents who stay intellectually and physically active long past middle life—until they are eighty or even ninety. There is frequently a love for learning and achievement in many parents who are aged, which is more commonly associated with impetuous and ebullient youth.

John Butler Yeats, Dublin artist, author, and philosopher, felt so strongly about playing second fiddle to his son, the famous poet William Butler Yeats, that he became a self-exile in New York at the age of sixty-nine and enjoyed a personal renaissance there. He had no ill-feelings for his children and grandchildren, whom he was never to visit again. His personal relationship with his children was always that of a contemporary. He wrote to them often and sometimes corresponded with his son William Butler three times a day. In New York, he enjoyed an income and adulation he had never known in Dublin, where he had been sensitive about being introduced to men who had more fame than he, where he had deliberately submerged himself among the failures in the artistic set. In contrast, his paintings sold well in New York; he began to read and to write with vigor and enthusiasm, and his extraordinary conversational ability was valued in literate circles. For thirteen years, until he died at eighty-two, he was the old man who ran away from home and made good.

An old man who stayed home and made good just to show that "if my son can write, anybody can,"[14] was the acrimonious impossible Dr. William Gilbert, whose arguments with his equally unpredictable son, Sir William Schwenck Gilbert, were good theater within the family. Dr. Gilbert, contemptuous of the praise given his son's plays (primarily Gilbert and Sullivan light operas), set himself to write a number of novels. He proved his point to himself, if not to posterity, when *Shirley Hall Asylum* and *Dr. Austin's Guests* became best sellers.

The dependence on books and the urge to be creative can survive sickness, penury, disappointments, tragedies, and the infirmities of old age. To all of these points, the Beveridge family can bear witness. The Beveridge children as described by the parents, long before the traits of the gifted were compiled by scholars, show the traits catalogued by contemporary students who select such children by means of standardized tests. Their story is told by one son, William Beveridge, a sociologist and the father of English social security, in his book *India Called Them*. This account makes these parents the most intimately known to us of any of the Four Hundred.

Like many other parents of the gifted, Henry and Annette Beveridge were not in early youth when they bore their children. Annette was a schoolteacher and social reformer in India. Her good intentions for the fourteen young Indian women whom she was teaching to be independent and modern were being lost in a drab battle over spoons, forks, filters, absconding servants, and drunken landlords, when she met and married a shy widower, Henry Beveridge, who proposed to her on their fifth meeting. He was a colonial administrator in the Indian Service. She was thirty-two, he was thirty-eight when they married. Agnostics both, they were married at the Registry, rather than at a church.

The contemporary ideal home is economically stable, emotionally calm, and the children grow up in a familiar neighborhood with a competent community health department and child welfare clinics. Journeys, if they must be made, are quickly carried out. The Beveridges enjoyed none of these advantages. They were burdened with financial problems, serious illnesses, deaths in the immediate family, and disappointments in their professional and social lives. During the children's early years, they were constantly moving and traveling.

India was dotted with the graves of English children. Thus, every dish of food was prepared under close supervision by Annette, but this care did not suffice. She suffered from cholera. Then their youngest child, Herman, was stricken at eight months with a high fever and was thereafter speechless, hyperactive, destructive, and out of contact with reality. When the remaining son, Will, almost died from a similar undiagnosed fever, Annette took all four children to England and bought a house there. She was cheated in its purchase—the drains were bad, the cook got typhoid, and inept sanitary inspectors dug up the fine old lawn. A dear relative, Aunt Bessie, who came to help, was killed in an accident. The school chosen for Will turned out to be a sham and facade. He was beaten after school by a big boy who resented the new boy's precocity until Annette challenged this bully and threatened to have him arrested if he ever touched her son again. A knighted physician was no more able to help Herman than the bungling doctors they had seen in India. Henry Beveridge, who had never won preferment in the colonial service in India because of his views about Indian home rule and other matters, was hard put to keep the divided family afloat financially. He had other dependents—a sister and a mother who at seventy-seven was a giddy, helpless woman—and yet it was Will's father, so prone to bankruptcy, who was vital and aggressive.

These parents were never distracted from their books and learning by misfortune. The happiest year of their married life was one they spent in an isolated post to which they were sent as a disciplinary measure by a bigoted superior. While there, they enjoyed the opening minds of their growing young children, their books and papers, and each other, whereas in the previous area, they had been deeply involved in the petty intrigues of the station.

The four children they bore were a daily pleasure and excitement to these parents, who, when separated, wrote intimate, tender letters about their dreams for the children. On furlough in Scotland, Annette wrote a two-thousand page "Memorandum" about her three oldest children. Although they had flopped on the street in London to peer curiously through gratings and had embarrassed her, she was not too weary of them to catalogue their beauties, virtues, and talents. In a document which is a discriminating observation of three gifted children, she foreshadows studies made years later.

Psychologist Leta S. Hollingworth, in *Children Above 180 IQ,* describes the gifted children whom she isolated for study by test as being taller, stronger, and handsomer than other children. Hollingworth's New York children were sensitive to injustice, emotionally moved by reading about man's inhumanity to man. One child cried when reading about the treatment of the South by the North after the Civil War. They were, like the Beveridge children, likely to be pedantic, painstaking in expression, and impressed observers as being quaint, old-fashioned, overly adult children.

Decades before, Annette Beveridge described these same qualities in her own English children. Letty, at age six, was tall, slender, had hair the "color of a chestnut hulk," was an excellent walker, and was "bookish." At six, she could read both German and English. She cried when Annette read to her about the death of a poor collier's boy. "She cried most naturally and would not be comforted." Letty then made the interesting discovery for herself that it did not move her to tears to read the poem silently, and she discussed the probable reasons for this reaction with her mother.

Willie, at four years and nine months, was slim and compact, with fair hair and loving blue eyes. He spent much of his playtime writing a series of arithmetical and multiplication statements very neatly. "One of the distinct traits of Willie's character is his accuracy of statement. He speaks deliberately and requires it of others. He allows no one (not even sister Tutu) to lapse into mistake." When his mother mispronounced a German word, he corrected her, not in a dictatorial fashion, but as one who had the right to make an observation. He read German better than English, although he loved to be read to in English and spoke it well enough.

Tutu, at three and a half, was a curly-headed child with a piquant face and rotund figure. She did lessons for about twenty minutes daily and could read about two pages from a German reading book. Since coming to Scotland, she had given up her stately dance in which she "used to don a sari and move slowly before my bedroom fire in Bankipur to the music of Bogmonia's song. She now dances jigs with tremendous energy." Annette makes reference to the children's refusing to talk Hindustani in Scotland. The children were at this age trilingual. Annette and Henry in their letters used as many as four languages easily and learned others for pleasure.

The Beveridges were willing travelers. Annette never minded trains, however many children she had with her, and she turned journeys into sightseeing tours, purposely taking the long way around to see new sights. She triumphed over everything, crossing Europe with her retinue. She sailed the sea from Genoa to Bombay, traversed India by train, stopping off at Bankipur, changing at midnight at Allahabad. Once in India, the family delighted in excursions to remote and difficult areas. They went down to the valley of the Runjit River, five thousand feet below Darjeeling, and became giddy on the swinging cane bridge that hung across the water.

Annette was quite aware that her children were exceptional in ability. The English relatives often referred to them as prodigies. As time passed, one of them, William, surpassed the others. This too, is usual. They were also typical in that it was Willie who had the problems in school adjustment. Boys more than girls among the gifted are prone to problems. The girls soon made friends when they came to England, but Willie did not, and his mother characteristically met his attackers head-on in argument, then set about seeking friends for her son. Annette was the more aggressive of the two parents—which is also customary.

William Beveridge, both as a child and as a man, was capable of long, self-initiated problem solving. To a marked degree, this was present in both of his parents, whose love for books and learning persisted to the end of their days. Henry retired at fifty-six and came home to Annette and the children:

On January 14, 1893, he stepped out of India's service all but unnoticed—as quietly as he had stepped into it thirty-five years beforehand—on the night when he heard the jackals howling on the tiger-haunted island of Saugor.

Annette and Henry now had time to read—histories, travel, biographies, novels, philosophy, poetry. Each became absorbed in a task of translation from Persian to English—Henry working on the Abul-Fazl, "The Owl," and Annette on the Gul-Badan. Annette learned Persian after Letty died in adolescence. Henry suggested this activity as a way of keeping his wife from devastating melancholy. She later learned Turki in order to translate the Babur Nama.

Henry finished his translation in 1921. At eighty-four, he occupied himself with errata, index, and addenda. Annette published her translation of the Babur Nama in four volumes in 1922 when she was almost eighty—despite deafness, operations for cataracts, and a major abdominal operation at seventy-seven. Henry moved down to the country cottage with a servant at eighty-eight, but Annette would not join him except for weekends because she needed to be near the library in order to work on her revisions. They both died in 1929. Annette, the first to go, was working on her books the day before she died. A passion for learning was there until the end.

Prolific novelist and poet John Cowper Powys came from a curate's household that produced four novelists and other men and women of distinction. His morbid and melancholy mother, a descendent of John Donne, had a contempt for success and for good health and happiness. God's ways were sad ways. She liked the shade, feared the sun. John remained her favorite son only because his self-deprecating ways kept her from knowing that he was really celebrated. John takes notice of the drive that makes for fame, but gives no credit to the stuff of which the driver is made, when he says of the successful:

The majority of eminently successful men, such as the "vulgar" call great, are successful because they want to be just that—above everything else. Mistakes do happen, as when some

> *quiet mathematicians are suddenly hurled, like meteoric projectiles, into notoriety. But as a rule it is those with energy and will and the desire to be at the top who are at the top.*[15]

The "bookish" and driving quality of these homes which cradle eminence lasts through the years and has no relation to money, as is evidenced in this statement about his father's will by William Beveridge, who says:

> *By the time he ended, he had parted even from most of his books, except those with a family association. His will was sworn at eighty-two pounds. He went out of the world with almost as few possessions as those with which he entered it.*[16]

There are only two of the Four Hundred, both politicians, who flatly say they had no early love for learning. Al Smith, the Democratic Party nominee for President who opposed Republican Herbert Hoover, professed a scorn for books, saying that in his lifetime he had read only one book, a biography of a famous prizefighter. He does not credit his father, an Irish-immigrant truck driver, with learning or status or power drives. His mother, always a driving woman, blamed his father for not being willing to buy a farm in what was then the outskirts of New York City, but which later sold for fabulous sums as city lots. Al Smith's talent, developed early, was in leadership, a quality not yet measurable by a standardized test. At ten, he won a prize for oratory, and his speaking and interpersonal skills enabled him to become Governor of New York.

Nikita Khrushchev, who was to become leader of the Communist Party of the Soviet Union, described his father as a man who had no use for schools or learning. It was not until Nikita left home to live with relatives who were deeply involved in reading and revolutionary activities that he became a hungry reader. His father, a blacksmith, was, as a man of physical vitality, a great eater and drinker. There was music, dancing, singing, and physical exuberance in the parental climate. The mother had a shadowy role in the scanty data—a widow driven by necessity. It was relatives who communicated a love for learning to the adolescent boy. The physical driving and striving he seemingly found at home.

Only one parent among the seven hundred-plus is described as a physically lazy woman, but her husband was driving enough for two. This was the mother of the writer Konrad Bercovici.

The Family Value System

It is, then, the family value system that seems to have the strongest impact on the child with ability. If the child's parents respect ability and have strong intellectual and physical drives, the child is evidently more likely to become outstanding among his or her contemporaries.

A willingness to let a young man or woman leave home to further his or her achievements is seen as a factor making for achievement by Fred L. Strodbeck, one of a group of four scholars whose four-year study of identification of talent is reported in their volume *Talent and Society.*[17] Among the Four Hundred in the present study, there are young children sent away from home to seek training that the local community does not offer. There are husbands and wives who endured unwelcome separation in the interests of their children's development.

The love for learning is seen as a lifetime trait. It continues despite illness and frustrations, and even after reasonable and satisfying success. It is not particularly associated with a desire for material gain. Along with the drive for knowledge and achievement, there is often also a physical vitality in both the parent and the child. These intellectually striving, physically driving parents and children are likely to enhance, if not advance, the status quo. Only one person in the family may become eminent, but the entire family is likely to be competent and useful.

Over 90 percent of these Four Hundred families show a love for learning and achievement.

Chapter 2
Opinionated Parents

In those days young people, unless invited to speak, were seen and not heard. But as soon as father considered us old enough to have opinions, we were given full scope to express them, no matter how adolescent.... He hated the slavery of pattern and following of examples and believed in the equality of the sexes...fought for free libraries, free education, free books in the public school...took single tax in his stride....

—Margaret Sanger, *An Autobiography*

Recent fashion in parental attitude favors the neutral parent who is warmly supportive, provident, nondirective. Fathers and mothers discipline themselves to patience, especially for the critical adolescent, because they do not want to be responsible for delaying his maturity or stifling her creativity. If, despite their best intentions, they express themselves blatantly and embarrass their child with statements of opinion that run counter to the opinions commonly held by most of the neighbors, they are defensive and guilt-ridden. If they persist in any kind of nonconformity, they do so under the deep burden of conscience and are painfully aware of the social problems to which they subject their child.

Most parents today act on the premise that the child has a right to do what others do and to have the things that others have, and to feel a part of the common culture of the neighborhood. Parents try to stay in the background of the child's life. To this end, they relinquish much that they might like to see established as a family tradition.

The neutral parental attitude was practically unknown to the families in this study. Two hundred twenty-seven families among the Four Hundred espoused strong political attitudes, held sectarian views about religion, were religious liberals with equally strong feelings, were atheists or agnostics, espoused unpopular causes, worked in reform movements, or expressed controversial views in print or on the public platform. These parents with strong concerns we chose to call opinionated.

Among them were partisans of Charles Darwin, Henry George, and Robert Ingersoll—parents who rejected the theories of infant damnation and predestination, and parents who believed that science and religion could and should be reconciled. Some worked for the abolition of slavery and for civil liberties, or were involved in civic reform movements in their communities. Better housing, better public health, and better schools and hospitals were popular causes. There were few extremists; only one family was a member of a communal group that withdrew from society at large. One father was a Populist, another a Chartist leader. Two mothers were mediums. Four fathers were Swedenborgians. A number were socialists.

Most of the causes to which they committed themselves would raise no eyebrows today. In their own times, however, fathers—and less often, mothers—found themselves in conflict with the established order and accepted mores. Contemporary parents who would self-consciously emulate them have an almost insurmountable problem. They must first make a choice among the "far-out" causes of their own day and choose one which, although it is a minority cause today, will make them admired as its exponent decades later. Their involvement in this cause must be sincere, altruistic, and without regard for possible negative repercussions that will affect the economic welfare or social status of their children or their spouse. They must feel that their dedication to principle is a spontaneous reaction to environmental stimulus.

Rebellion in the Homes

The children in these opinionated homes are more likely to emulate the parent than to be rebels. Over one-fourth of the boys and girls adopt the parental attitude and make it the springboard of their own fame, or they fulfill a family daydream or enter the family profession. They are like Charles Darwin, whose grandfather preceded him by writing a poem on evolution.

The brash, critical adolescent who quarrels with his parents or disagrees with them violently about cultural or political matters is not often found in these families. He or she is more likely to be tagging along after opinionated parents, trying to find out what the excitement is all about. This child is much more likely to be expelled from school than to run away from home. Patterns of rebellion in adolescence may have changed, however, with the adoption of compulsory education. It is the teacher, in these biographies and autobiographies, who is the butt of hostility. Today's parents—rather than the teachers—being a less retaliatory target, may have accommodated themselves to the need of the adolescent to be critical and rebellious. This is a point for speculation.

The boys and girls who rebelled against parents were few—twenty-four—and their rebellions were often short-lived. Jules Verne ran away at eleven to be a cabin boy, but was relieved when his father, a lawyer with a poetic streak, brought him home to his affectionate mother, who was prostrate with anxiety. It was the school, rather than the home, from which he fled. He had a definite hostility for school, and he filled his books with designs for ships and flying machines. He was punished for running away by being put on a bread and water diet; in a repentant mood, he said to his mother, "After this I shall travel only in my imagination."

Harold Laski, the phenomenally brilliant political theorist, at eighteen threw his ambitious Orthodox Jewish family into complete confusion by coming home from a summer cultural conference with a twenty-eight-year-old Gentile bride, a highly opinionated young woman interested in genetics and politics, herself a rebel. They were immediately separated by his parents, and Harold was sent along to college. The bride went back to Scotland to wait until Harold was out of school. When he graduated, the marriage was resumed, and the parents became reconciled when a grandchild was born. When their son became well known and it was obvious that his wife had a good influence on his professional career, they lost most of their hostility for her.

Arnold Bennett, future novelist and playwright, refused to be a clerk in his father's law office and went off to London to be a writer the year after he had graduated with honors from secondary school. His mother took money budgeted for groceries to finance his rebellion. Norwegian dramatist and poet Henrik Ibsen cut himself off completely from his entire family after he left home at seventeen. He rejected the family's religious fundamentalism and was ashamed of his father's financial failure.

One rebel who was communicative about his rebellions is psychiatrist Ernest Jones, best known as a biographer of Freud. His father was a Liberal in politics, an agnostic, and a self-made man involved in community activities, the school board, the parish and district councils, and the like. Ernest was deeply attached to both of his parents, and he justifiably regarded himself as the bond of the union between them. They were warm and supportive, liberal and opinionated, but his father had difficulty admitting he was ever in the wrong. However, Ernest Jones says he never knew his parents to be angry with each other. When he was thirteen, his own sharp tongue and outspoken ways led him into an acrimonious argument about a siphon pump, which caused a rift between father and son for a period and hurt his father's feelings.

Composer Frederick Delius rebelled against entering his father's wool business and fled to Florida on a pretext that left him time for music. Unlike most of the other parents, his father never forgave him for his rebellion.

Children Who Extend Parental Opinionatedness

The number of instances in which the child becomes an extension of the parent, if described, would of themselves fill many volumes. The clearest examples are those in which the parents are involved in humanitarian or reform movements and the children express similar concerns. Children who did not reject their parents' unconventional ideas but used them to advantage in their adult lives were often not conformists at school.

To the Hicksite Quaker father of Jane Addams, who later would found Hull House, no cause that his daughter ever undertook was contrary to his convictions. A close friend of Abraham Lincoln, he valued a letter from him inquiring as to the direction in which the Quaker conscience was pointing on a specific issue. He was always concerned about questions of peace and brotherhood and conditions among the poor. His daughter Jane was to win the Nobel Peace Prize in 1910. She was also known for her social work and reforms in labor relations.

Jane used to creep downstairs in the night to talk to her father to ease the fears that came to her so often because of a recurring nightmare. In her dream, everyone in the world was dead except herself. Upon her alone rested the responsibility of making the world resume its course again, and this mission could not be accomplished unless Jane could make a wagon wheel. She was all alone in a deserted world. The village street looked as it always looked, except for the lack of people. The blacksmith shop was in the usual place with the anvil near the door, but there were no human beings in sight. In her dream, Jane had the overwhelming responsibility of having to start the world moving again, of having to do this before all of the lost people could ever come home again.

She was never able to tell her father this particular nightmare. Over and over again in autobiographies, subjects tell of fears and persecutions they endured without ever once telling any adults about them. The inarticulateness of childhood, even of verbally gifted children, is frightening and places a tremendous responsibility on adults.

Jane's father, a widower, enjoyed these nighttime visits from his delicate youngest daughter. She asked him about her anxiety in feeling less knowledgeable than her playmates, who completely understood the meaning of "predestination." Jane confessed that it was all a puzzle to her.

Her father replied, "You and I do not have the kind of minds that will ever understand foreordination, Jane. But it really isn't very important.... It is very important not to pretend to understand what you don't understand and you must be honest with yourself inside.... Mental integrity comes above everything else."[1]

The need that these gifted young children have for communication with adults was met (in part) for Jane by her father. She was reluctant to complain about her village school except to indicate that it did not meet her needs. Her father supported her educational decisions, allowing her to withdraw from her boarding school when she could not accept its emotional evangelism.

Another girl who had school difficulties as a result of being influenced by her own opinionated parents was Pearl Buck. Until she went away to Miss Jewell's School in Shanghai at seventeen, Pearl had previously studied most of her lessons with her dynamic and imaginative mother at the dining room table. The school did not have much to offer her scholastically, but she liked being assigned to help the girls at the Door of Hope, a rescue home for Chinese girls who had cruel mistresses. Since Pearl spoke colloquial Chinese, they talked with her freely about having been raped by adolescent boys in the homes of their masters, of being beaten with whips by bad-tempered mistresses, or of being burned with coals from pipes or cigarettes.

Pearl's missionary parents had deliberately chosen to live among the Chinese people and had not restricted themselves to a compound. Pearl played with her Chinese playmates in the tall pampas grasses or under the verandas where the brown earth was cool and dry. When she went walking and strange children called out, "Little foreign devil," she struck them dumb by replying (in Chinese), "Little turtle!" She knew this meant "You bastard!" but her parents did not. The children did not resent her yellow hair and blue eyes so much when she could answer them in their own street language.

Her parents did not restrict her from fighting the dogs away from the bones of dead children lying on the hillside. She met lepers on the street and saw starving people during the famine year. Her mother sought Pearl's companionship and assistance in trying to bring comfort and help to their neighbors. Consequently, Pearl found it difficult to be companionable with the students at Miss Jewell's School, since their parents had not allowed them to associate so intimately with the distressed Chinese population. Because of her parents' views about the level of association with Chinese people, she felt that she was Chinese, not American.

Her ideas about religion made her an outcast at school. She quoted to the girls in her dormitory from her father's monograph on the similarities between Christianity and Buddhism. He also believed that Jesus and Confucius had both formulated the ideas associated with the Golden Rule. He advanced the theory, in a monograph, that Jesus himself might have visited the Himalayan Kingdom of Nepal when he was a young man during the unrecorded years of his life. Her father had read about this idea in the Vishnu Purana, an ancient Hindu scripture, and he often discussed these theories with Pearl.

When the girls relayed Pearl's account of her father's views to Miss Jewell, the shocked headmistress took Pearl out of the dormitory and put her in a little room alone, which did not displease Pearl because she could then read after the lights went out in the other rooms. She did not like school, with its prayer meetings, moans, sighs, grovelings, or the talk of infant damnation about which her mother also felt so negatively.

There were other parents whose zeal for good works led them to acquaint their children early with poverty and disease and man's inhumanity to man. Among these was another humanitarian and writer, Pierre van Paassen, who is sometimes called the non-Jewish Zionist, who describes his childhood in *Days of Our Years*.

This boy, brought up in the small urban town of Gorcum, Holland, had three opinionated persons in his household—his mother, his Uncle Kees, and his father. His mother was drawn into the relief activities that the Protestant community set up for Jewish refugees fleeing from Russian pogroms. At his own dinner table, Pierre heard a weeping man tell how his wife had been forced to watch her two children thrown into a burning furnace before she was granted the mercy of a like fate.

In addition to Jewish relief activities, Pierre's mother was interested in assisting the ill and poorly housed in their own city. She took young Pierre with her to call on families where destitute children lay dying of tuberculosis. On his way home from school, he stopped by the slum section where she had organized a cleanup campaign. The street was so narrow that he could stand in the middle of it and touch the walls of the houses on either side with his outstretched hands. They crawled with vermin.

His father took him all the way to Utrecht to hear the statesman Oom Paul Kruger talk of the unspeakable horrors of the Boer concentration camps, and he heard Kruger say, "England told them to shut the door in my face and all of them obeyed." Exiled and intransigent Boers became his heroes, and with shivers of horror, he heard them tell how Lord Horatio Kitchener, British Chief of Staff in the Boer War, had said falsely in one of his communiqués that Boer women were totally bereft of the normal maternal instinct, and how these women were subsequently given over to the lust and cruelty of a whiskey-crazed soldiery.

It was Uncle Kees, a bachelor landscape painter, who was his favorite teacher. With him, Pierre roamed the countryside searching for landscapes to paint, staying away for weeks, camping, returning home suntanned and weatherbeaten. From Uncle Kees he learned more history than from all his schoolbooks combined. Uncle Kees, who foretold a coming bloody war, described at length upon the significance of the Franco-Prussian War, the era of Napoleon III, and the Commune of Paris. He told Pierre of his personal acquaintance with such brilliant persons as artist Vincent van Gogh, writer Tolstoy, theologian Ernest Renan, and political anarchist Mikhail Bakunin. As they walked the countryside, he spoke of Irish independence or

Macedonian nationalism, and Pierre drank in his words as if he had been born in Cork or in the Balkans, such was the spell of his uncle's oratory. Uncle Kees was a liberal, and he acquainted the boy with Voltaire, Rousseau, Saint-Simon, Proudhon, and Goethe.

The elders in Pierre van Paassen's family, with all their opinionatedness, seem to have closed their eyes to what went on in their son's school. Of his headmaster, Pierre says in his autobiography:

> *His face was a mask of deep wrinkles, his bony fingers tapering off into nails as long as those of a Chinese mandarin, he inspired me with so much more terror than respect that I still see his ghost at times... in a blaze or anger, his lips curled in a tigerish leer that revealed his yellow stumps of teeth... pounding upon a fellow pupil* [of Pierre's], *beating the boy until he sank fainting to his knees.*[2]

The headmaster had once found a sentence in this pupil's copybook that infuriated him. The incident made such an impression upon Pierre that even as an adult he remembered the phrase that offended the headmaster: "snowflakes fluttering from a pitilessly gray heavenly roof."

When a younger brother died and his mother's reason was consequently feared for, and when his father's business failed, Pierre was happy enough to postpone college, and his surviving brother was willing to forego attendance at a military academy in Holland. The whole family emigrated to Canada, where schooling was less rigid. Pierre's first work in Canada was with religious exiles—the Russian Doukhobor and the Dutch Hernhutters—and his mother was delighted with this assignment given her son by the dean of theology at Victoria College in Toronto.

Children Who Adopt Related Causes

Ernest Bevin, English statesman and labor leader, had a mother who did day work in the kitchens of wealthier people and who was the community midwife. When she received her fee, she always asked the head of the household for a few extra pennies for the Methodist

Chapel. She was a strong temperance worker and a fanatic Protestant Dissenter. For years, she devoted her spare energies to the raising of money for a chapel to be built on the road to Dover. There was only one cemetery in the community, and it was Anglican, which raised a serious consideration among the Anglican authorities when she died. There were those who objected strongly to her being buried in the village graveyard, and her coffin was at the church door before the rector and churchwardens gave consent.

Her youngest son Ernest was seven when she died. At age three, he had passed out hymn books at the chapel. When he was five and his mother lay very ill, he went to church alone, then came home and told her what the minister had said in his sermon. At thirteen, the orphan boy ran away from the farm of William May, where he had been scaring birds, following the dibble (a planting implement), hoeing, and cutting up mangels (beets) and turnips for the cows. There were harsh words over the chores. Ernest was whipped, but then he frightened the punishing farmer with a sharp tool and ran off to Bristol with his clothes and savings. It was at the Methodist Sunday School that he first became interested in learning and in the problems of labor.

Maxim Litvinov (born Meer Wallach), Russian diplomat, had parents who were among the Jewish intellectuals of Belostok. His father, Moses Wallach, a produce merchant, and his mother, Anna Wallach, made their home a center for book-loving Belostok intelligentsia. Moses was a bright and inquisitive man, interested in contemporary literature, especially Turgenev, Dostoevski, and Tolstoy. People were always dropping in to borrow a book and talk over the latest news, and discussions lasted until late at night. Five-year-old Maxim was deeply affected when secret agents came and took away his father and held him incommunicado for six weeks. A rival in the produce business had given false information about Moses, but the matter was happily resolved. Upon his release, he was welcomed by his townsmen.

Another child reared in a home that was turbulent with opinion who also did not adopt the parental cause but found a tangential cause upon which to expend her energies was Margaret Sanger. This protagonist of Planned Parenthood was one of eleven Higgins children, who were used to being called the "children of the devil" because of their father's admiration for evolutionist Charles Darwin and agnostic lawyer Robert Ingersoll. Higgins once rented the biggest building in Corning, New York in order to present Robert Ingersoll to the public. The building happened to belong to the Roman Catholic Church, and when an indignant mob drove the speaker and his audience to a field behind the Higgins' house, his daughter was tagging along. Her subsequent quarrels with the Roman Catholic Church were over birth control and planned parenthood. She, too, was a school rebel and expelled herself from her eighth-grade class when the teacher was insulting and sarcastic.

On another family tree, Bertrand Russell, English philosopher, mathematician, teacher, writer, and iconoclast, found a variety of opinionated ancestors. His father, Amberley Russell, willed his sons Bertrand, four, and Frank, ten, to the custody of two agnostic friends. The British public was offended and the children became wards of the court, which placed them in the custody of their paternal grandparents instead. Their grandfather, a dynamic reformer in his day, was old and ill, sat in his Bath chair and ignored their noise. But Lady Russell, who had been known as the "Deadly Nightshade" by the members of her husband's cabinet during the period he served as Prime Minister, was still exceedingly active. At seventy, she quit the Presbyterian church in which she was reared and became a Unitarian. She openly opposed Imperialist Wars and the government's attitude toward the Irish. The boys' own father had not done well in politics because he had introduced a bill in Parliament to make legal the giving of secular lectures and debates on Sunday. Bachelor Uncle Rollo, who also lived in the home, read them his poems about "contending atoms." Frank ran away from home and was subsequently sent to boarding school, but Bertrand was educated for college at home. When he was fourteen, he thought of suicide because of his torments over religion, but once he had resolved that matter by becoming an agnostic like his father, he was relieved of his burden.

The influence that Daniel and Lucy Anthony had on their daughter, suffragist Susan B. Anthony, was early, direct, and lasting, and it turned her toward a desire to be politically effective. As mill owners, they exercised a paternal jurisdiction over the young factory girls who worked for them, housing them in model cottages with flower gardens. The men employees were not allowed to have liquor on the premises. Each Sunday, all of the workers were invited to the owner's house to hear discussions of world affairs. Daniel was an abolitionist, a worker in the temperance society, and as a Quaker, he accepted the equality of women. Susan was having difficulties as secretary of the New York Women's Temperance Society because the New York Men's Temperance Society thought it improper for women to organize. Susan's parents attended a meeting where they heard Elizabeth Cady Stanton speak. Her father's enthusiastic letter about this woman prompted his daughter to seek her out; it was the beginning of a long and fruitful association.

The Anthonys were an independent family. Daniel Anthony was not perturbed to have a daughter who wanted to take part in politics. In a Quaker business meeting, the weight of a woman's decision is as strong as a man's, and if any one person expresses disagreement with the sense of the meeting, no action is taken.

Even among Friends, Daniel and Lucy were unique, because Lucy was a volatile outsider brought into membership in the quiet Meeting by her husband. The Meeting was reluctant to accept the vibrant girl with a voice that resounded in the hills when she sang outdoors.

Daniel's business failed during a national panic, and Susan was delighted to be withdrawn from her restrictive school. There was almost nothing in her career that was not the natural flowering of the family influence upon her.

Father's Boys Among the Opinionated

A statement by George Bernard Shaw to the effect that mothers' boys have a "narrow-minded wisdom" and fathers' boys a "broader humanity" would seem true in many of these families. Fathers' boys are more likely to be social rebels or revolutionists or philosophers. Mothers' boys more often turn to the arts.

A look into some of these father-centered homes that were highly opinionated will show how boys often act out the paternal daydream. Among the Four Hundred, one-fourth extend the parent in vocation or in ideology. Although several of the boys were rebels in the community, they were often heroes to their fathers. Labor activist David Dubinsky's father did not object when his son went on strike to get higher wages for bakery employees, even though his father owned a bakery shop. He bribed a jailer to get his son released from imprisonment as an agitator.

The mother of newspaper editor William Allen White was an abolitionist Republican. She was a Yankee schoolteacher who lost her job because she insisted on admitting black children to the white school she taught at in Council Grove, Kansas, a town with a nest of Southern sympathizers. The tall, thin, thirty-year-old spinster attracted the attention of a pudgy, middle-aged storekeeper and sometime physician, a Democrat during the Civil War who was called a Copperhead because he believed in a negotiated peace and thought that Lincoln should have insisted on a peace conference even after Sumter. (Robert Frost's father was of the same opinion.) He was not only a Democrat in a town where 80 percent of the men were in the Union Army, but he was also a freethinker who was castigated in the press because he cut wood on Sunday.

Their son, who loved them both profoundly, says:

> *Never had a child more strongly minded parents who were so different in their ways of thinking.... I am amazed that they lived together with an approximation of peace and amity for something more than fifteen years.*[3]

David Ben Gurion, the first Prime Minister of Israel, did not disappoint his father, Avigor, when he was arrested for leading a street meeting in Warsaw that extolled Zionism. David (whose boyhood name was David Green) was jailed and had to send for his father to get him out. Avigor was not surprised and had quite expected this to happen when David left home and went to Warsaw to matriculate at the University. Avigor arrived, top hat and all, the efficient, practiced lawyer used to getting clients out of petty scrapes. Since the police-adjunct also had the surname "Green" and felt avuncular toward the boy, the formalities were soon over.

"This boy of ours will be known all over the world some day," Sheindal Green used to say.[4] Only six of her eleven children survived infancy, and "Sheindal the Righteous," as the mother was known, tended to overprotect David. Under her care, he was withdrawn, sickly, and introverted. He sat among the visitors, listening to the talk of Zionism that went on about him; he played chess with the men and was spoken to as an adult. After his mother's death when he was eleven, he became active, strong, and aggressive.

The town of Jiquilpan, where Lázaro Cárdenas, who was later to be President of Mexico, was reared was, in the days of his youth, an active center of revolutionary thought and activity. Most of the householders of Jiquilpan were engaged in light industry, making scarves or sandals. The young men in the town went away to work in Mexico City and came home periodically to report the new ideas they learned there. Señor Carreón, the most influential man in Jiquilpan, was not only the tax collector, but also the editor of the liberal periodical *La Popular*, published every fifth day.

Domasco Cárdenas, father of the precocious Lázaro, was also a respected civic leader. Domasco had a strong desire to raise the health and living standards of the town. Since there was no physician or hospital, he read medical books and treated his own and the neighbor's children. None of his eight children died in infancy; this made the family unique. Domasco valued education for all children. When Lázaro and a friend played truant, he whipped both children impartially.

This driving and opinionated man was a freethinker, responsive to the new ideas about the need to improve the living standards in Mexico. He tried hard to improve his own lot. When his loom was unprofitable and confining, he started a soap factory that failed. His billiard hall was more successful, but his oldest son Lázaro disliked the drinking and gambling of the men who frequented it. The father was sympathetic and apprenticed his eleven-year-old son, after graduation from the only school the town afforded, to his own close friend, the revolutionary editor of *La Popular*. It was here that Lázaro Cárdenas was really educated. He learned to read Victor Hugo instead of buccaneer fiction and was taught revolutionary techniques.

When President Lázaro Cárdenas raised health and educational standards to a new level in Mexico, and when he established federal education, nationalized the oil industry and the railroads, and abolished the parochial schools, he was extending—not rebelling against—his home training. Sons among the Four Hundred often accomplish what the fathers wish they might have done. In his own personal life, Lázaro Cardenas showed the strong paternal drives of his forthright father. President Cárdenas required his own family to live simply and added eight orphaned children to his household.

In 1815, a wealthy young Unitarian liberal, Richard Potter, married a "strange, introspective, mystic, wayward 'creature,'" whose empathy with the rejected and despised made her identify with them and "be them." She called herself a Jewess and dreamed visions of taking the Jews back to the Holy Land. She also sometimes called herself a gypsy. It is thought that she really was an English girl of Celtic origin. Mary Sedden Potter and Richard Potter's only son married Laurencina Heyworth, daughter of a Liverpool merchant who was associated with the Anti-Corn Law League and other radical activities in his area. Laurencina, a learned and charming woman, and her husband had nine learned and opinionated daughters, each of whom married an outstanding man, four of whom were at one time or another Members of Parliament, each of whom had a specialized talent, and almost all of whom were highly opinionated. Two descendants of Mary Sedden and Richard Potter are among our Four Hundred eminent men and women: their granddaughter Beatrice Webb, an important socialist leader, and their great-grandson, British statesman Sir Stafford Cripps.

Stafford Cripps was a boy who identified strongly with his pacifist father, Charles Alfred Cripps. Stafford had the freedom of action and affection that many pre-politicians enjoy, and he was the intellectually superior child in his family. Like most people who become involved in politics or in some phase of political science, he found this vocation late in life. His first goal was to be a scientist.

Stafford was nicknamed "Dad" or "Dadialissimus" because of his persistent habit of offering unsolicited information (a frequent habit of the gifted child) and advice to his elders. He was the youngest in a family of five children. When Stafford was a year old, his mother, Theresa Potter Cripps, identified him as the "rising genius" in the family. By the time he was three, the rest of the family had to acknowledge that "Dad" had unusual intellectual powers.

Theresa Potter Cripps died when her youngest son was four. As a legacy, she left messages to her husband and children: "I should like the children to be brought up as much as possible in the country, and to be educated in much the same style as their father was. I should like their living to be of the simplest, without reference to show or other follies.... I implore my children to stand by each other through thick and thin." Her sister, Beatrice Webb, described Theresa Cripps as "a born artist with an intense sensitivity for people and a power to seize the really significant facts about a person or event."[5]

Stafford's early potential was recognized by the whole family. There were many traditions he could follow, but his father, who became the first Baron Parmoor, wished him to be free to make his own choices. Baron Parmoor was the eighth in four generations of his family to be elected to the House of Commons. He also served as Vicar General of the Archdiocese of Canterbury. Three paternal uncles, a grand-uncle, and his great-great-grandfather were Members of Parliament.

The maternal side of Stafford's family was equally distinguished. Aunt Kate Potter Courtney acted as a maternal figure to Stafford after his mother's death. She was the wife of Leonard Henry Courtney, a political economist, a leader-writer for *The Times*, and a Liberal Parliamentarian. Blind for many years, he was still a great British statesman who pursued a liberal-pacifist line, as did Baron Parmoor.

Stafford Cripps had an early acquaintance with other highly opinionated relatives and family friends. His aunt, Margaret Hobhouse, another of the nine granddaughters of Mary Sedden, was a Quaker and a pacifist and the wife of Henry Hobhouse, a member of Parliament and of the Royal Commission on Secondary Education. Stafford's youngest aunt was Beatrice Webb, who, with her husband Sidney Webb, was a leader of the Fabian Socialist group. Stafford's mother, before her marriage, did volunteer work in improving housing conditions for the indigent under the direction of Canon Barnett, the founder of Toynbee Hall, which became a model for adult education of the poverty class.

Stafford's life was never entirely bounded by his family, although the family had the most important impact on his thinking. He was also influenced by an adult Quaker, William Sturgis, a family friend with whom he spent time on a holiday, and later by his Quaker stepmother, Marian Ellis, and by his principal at Winchester, the Rev. H. M. Burge.

Whatever the family climate of opinion, being treated as an adult is incomparably important to a young child who is intellectually capable. When he receives an audience and can speak and be spoken to, he is emotionally, as well as intellectually, satisfied by the experience. Other children may find him difficult, as is evidenced by the nickname "Dad." Teachers and parents who have the confidence of an exceptionally able child in important formative years have a tremendous and exciting responsibility. At school, Stafford Cripps was a scientist, did well and acquired knowledge, but was not particularly aware of social or political issues.

There are wide divergencies in this family, but a central tendency toward social concern operates within the wider framework. A cousin, Stephen Hobhouse, refused to inherit his father's property and, while in prison as a conscientious objector, wrote *English Prisons Today*, a valuable sociological document.

Various contemporary members of this opinionated family are presently concerned with freedom for colonial peoples, the furthering of the United Nations, agricultural advances which will help to feed world citizens in underdeveloped areas, town planning, rural housing, vagrancy, footpaths, and national parks. Among the descendents of

Mary Sedden Potter are the children of a distinguished African diplomat, Joseph Appiah. A great-great-grandson, Col. Richard Meinertzhagen, who is a military hero as well as a scientist, shows the family strain of individuality by naming as his recreations in the current *Who's Who*: "biology, geography, solitude and space."

Eccentric and energetic ancestors, however opinionated, should not be underestimated. The "neutral" parent who flattens his own affect in order to be the colorless background against which his child can appear with distinction may find that his children are also colorless and mediocre.

As boys and girls, the Four Hundred enjoyed the intimate companionship of stimulating persons who spoke to them as if they were adults. John Galsworthy, whose parents were not congenial, felt that his mother's limited approach to life made such a formidable barrier in their mother-son relationship that he could never enjoy her company. She bored him with her closed mind. No famous person surveyed said that he or she is sorry to have had an opinionated parent, but often says that he or she liked having had parents with something to say and who were not afraid to be outspoken. Even when the adult child repudiates the conclusions to which they came or rejects the causes for which they labored, he or she tells anecdotes about them to illustrate something about which he or she cannot openly boast—an inheritance of intellectual capacity and curiosity and vitality of expression.

Parents Who Suffer Death, Prison, or Exile

Certain offspring, however, although they approve of their parents, seem wary about actually extending the parental pattern when the statement of a strong conviction or a rebellious action has caused an ancestor to be exiled, imprisoned for an appreciable period, or to meet an untimely death. They turn, perhaps unconsciously, not to the cause for which the parents labored, but to artistic expression.

Polish pianist and composer Ignace Jan Paderewski was only three years old when his father was imprisoned for thirteen months because of anti-Russian activities. The stories he heard of his father's imprisonment affected Ignace deeply. He turned to music, but espoused the cause of Polish freedom in his later years with equal intensity. He had psychological difficulties in both careers and turned to farming for a period when he was physically unable to play the piano. He was never easy or relaxed in either of his vocational roles. To what extent his father's imprisonment was related to his own problems is not at all clear.

Joseph Conrad, the Polish-born boy who wrote his novels in English, was never to tell a story more tragic and tender than that of his father, Apollo Nalecz Korzeniowski, and his mother, who was born Evelina Bobrowsky. Their marriage was postponed for six years by the bride's family because the handsome fiancé did nothing but sit in the mansion on his father's estate and write poetry and plays which were never published. It was only because Evelina became physically ill with frustration that her brothers finally consented to the marriage when she was twenty-five and Apollo was thirty-six. They considered themselves among Apollo's best friends but demurred against his marriage to their sister.

To the consternation of the relatives on both sides of the family, Apollo, who had taken a position as an estate manager to please his in-laws, soon lost his own inheritance and also the money from his wife's dowry. Evelina loved him nonetheless, and both became involved in the cause of Polish freedom. When Apollo Korzeniowski was sentenced to exile in Siberia, he was fortunate, since it was only because of his distracted relatives that he was spared execution.

Evelina demanded that she be permitted to be considered a political prisoner also. The authorities consented, and the delicate wife and four-year-old boy (Joseph) joined the caravan of prisoners on a rugged three-month coach trip to Siberia. No other woman or child was in the group. When she was a maiden in her own home, Evelina had not even dressed herself. Joseph nearly died on the terrible journey; and Evelina, near death when the journey's end was reached, never fully recovered. Conrad watched his parents die lingering, painful deaths; first his mother when he was seven, then his beloved father when he was twelve.

At seventeen, he refused to go to college, and his affectionate but puzzled relatives let him have his way. The orphaned boy wanted to find the sea, about which he had only read—the warm, faraway South Seas. Secondary school had been an obnoxious experience to him despite his brilliance. During the long Siberian winters, Apollo Korzeniowski had been his son's tutor, and no classroom teacher could ever take his place. Joseph Conrad, as he is known to the English-speaking world, never espoused the cause of political freedom that his parents adopted so passionately. Nature was the enemy that preoccupied him.

Another boy whose father suffered persecution is the writer Konrad Bercovici. In the Bulgarian community in which this Jewish boy was reared, there was only one citizen who treated the gypsies like human beings—Konrad's father. Young Konrad had a gypsy nurse to whom he "belonged." She was so much like a mother to him that she was permitted to take him away from the home with her for long periods of time.

Konrad was not fond of his own mother, who lived in a fantasy world where the novels she read incessantly were more real to her than her husband and children. Konrad Bercovici was his father's boy, and when he found school unbearably dull because it did not challenge him, his father enthusiastically tutored him at home. Both father and son enjoyed the rapid academic progress Konrad made. They were kindred spirits, both volatile and quick of understanding.

This domestic tranquility was abruptly ended when the father was fatally beaten in a pogrom directed against the Jews and gypsies in the community. When his father died, Konrad ran away with the gypsies. He never became a community leader like his father, but he won fame as a writer about gypsy life.

William Cody, better known as Buffalo Bill, always felt that the abolition movement took his father from him. Isaac Cody set up a store near Salt Creek in the Kansas Territory and was a member of the Topeka legislature and an officer for the New England Emigrant Aid Society, which brought in abolitionist settlers. Isaac was well on his way to achieving both economic security and political status when, after being stabbed by pro-slavers, he was forced to hide in a cornfield to avoid further attacks; he was overworked by the demands of this tent city of emigrants who were bogged down in the mud. His death from a respiratory infection was attributed by his family to his abolitionist activities. Bill Cody, at eleven, took a man's job as a rider for Russell, Majors, and Wadell of the Pony Express in order to support his widowed mother and sisters. He was never deeply concerned with politics or reform movements as his father had been.

Clovis Gauguin, father of artist Paul Gauguin, was an ineffectual journalist for the *National*, a liberal Republican paper. When Napoleon III came into power, he fled France and was en route to Peru when he died of a heart attack.

To Aline Marie, the pretty and flirtatious wife of Clovis Gauguin, her husband's death was merely another calamity in a long series of adverse events. In her childhood, she had once been kidnapped from her school by her father, who was later sentenced to twenty years hard labor because he shot and seriously wounded her mother, the beautiful and dynamic Flora Tristan Chazal. Flora had left her husband to go about Europe preaching the doctrines of the Comte de Saint-Simon: socialism, sex equality, and free love of a noble sort. Her husband, Paul's grandfather, had obtained custody of their son through the courts. For twenty years, Chazal grieved because his lovely young wife had left him to lecture and to write books and pamphlets, each more inflammatory than the last. When he shot her, she was seriously injured and never fully recovered. All of France was titillated over the trial.

To young Paul Gauguin, an exiled child in Peru, these family stories were a familiar part of his heritage. He always spoke well of his grandmother when he was an adult, calling her a "deuce of a woman, a true blue socialist, a pretty and noble lady."[6] In his middle years, Paul Gauguin was not opinionated like his father and grandmother, but a painter who turned to a re-creation of the life he lived in Peru at the time he lost his father.

Claudio Toscanini, father of the Italian conductor Arturo Toscanini, made a vocation out of being a follower of Giuseppe Garibaldi, the father of modern Italy, and took part in three campaigns. On one occasion, he was sentenced to be shot. Claudio watched his comrades die, was placed against the wall to be executed, teased, and taunted, but then was reprieved and sentenced to three years' imprisonment.

When he came home to his family, which was in poor financial circumstances, Claudio could not bring himself to work for long in his tailor shop. Instead, he roamed the streets, seeking citizens with whom he could argue about politics. When his adolescent son Arturo assumed the support of the family, Claudio was not sorry. In his old age, he still buttonholed citizens and made them listen to his speeches, but the content was changed. He talked of the incomparable skills and infinite glory of his son Arturo. Arturo Toscanini did not extend his father's interest in politics, but neither did he accept fascism when it came; he became a voluntary exile and refused to perform in Nazi Germany.

Status and Opinionatedness

Families with wealth or inherited status, for whom there are multiple listings in standard reference works and who also have a representative among the Four Hundred are: Adams, Baldwin, Balfour, Byrd, Cecil, Chamberlain, Churchill, Cooper, Cripps, James, Kennedy, Nehru, Rau, Rockefeller, Roosevelt, Russell, Sitwell, and Taft. In these families, the contribution is commonly in the field of political action. Accumulative opinionatedness in the family, an expectation of achievement, and a habit of speaking out and making definite decisions are inherent in the total family climate of opinion.

Low-income families less often contribute multiple names to fame. When they do so, the honors frequently come for shared achievement. This, too, speaks for the power of family cohesion, the value of pooling ideas, and the need for support in working out difficult problems. Wilbur and Orville Wright, sons of a strong-minded, small-town, United Brethren minister, were looked upon with affectionate feeling and were respected for their right to work out their ideas in their own way. They sorely needed the support that they gave each other. Disbelieving major newspapers would not report the news of their accomplishment at Kitty Hawk in 1903.

Among the other famous brothers who came from opinionated families with comparatively low incomes are the medical Mayos and Menningers. Those who knew Walter, Victor, and Roy Reuther in their young manhood could not conceive of the contributions of any one of the brothers having been as readily accomplished without the support of the others. Each Sunday, their father, a union official in a Wheeling, West Virginia brewery, gathered the three Reuther boys together in a back bedroom upstairs for a discussion on labor reforms, politics, and women's suffrage. He took them to see the famous socialist leader and future presidential candidate Eugene V. Debs in prison. Their grandfather, a German socialist leader, was a family hero.

Politics, Religion, Race, and Nationality

Politics and religion, in that order, were the subjects about which parents of the Four Hundred were most likely to be opinionated. Abolition of slavery, women's suffrage, colonialism, reforms in education, and world peace were topics that the children heard discussed at dinner. They were concerned with the reconciliation of science and religion, the single tax, the Boer War, the special problems of India and Ireland, civic reform, and education for the masses. Only twenty-seven of the families were strictly sectarian in religious practices and tried to restrict their children's participation in the larger community of ideas and beliefs. Political views were most frequently described as liberal.

Forty-four parents were partners in interdenominational or international marriages. Winston Churchill, Thomas Mann, and William Carlos Williams are among those who spoke favorably of having parents who represented two nations. George Santayana had the most involved national background. Marcel Proust, Fiorello La Guardia, and Stephen Spender each came from homes where one parent had been reared Jewish, the other in a Gentile tradition. Norbert Wiener, Erica and Klaus Mann, and Charlie Chaplin had both Jewish and Gentile ancestors. Diego Rivera and Paul Klee had ancestors representing both dark- and light-skinned races.

There is no evidence that ability or achievement must be confined to any nation or race or mixture of nationalities or races. There is no way of determining to what extent provincialism or prejudice inhibit expression of talent in the past or present. Terman, in the 1920s, found only one family on the West Coast of the United States with more than one intellectually gifted child. This family had four Eurasian children. Leta Hollingworth found only one family in New York City with more than one child who had an IQ of 180 (Binet) or more. These children had one white and one black parent.

Among the newer biographies that are not included in this survey (because in each instance there is only one volume about the person) are indications that children born of interracial marriages are beginning to enter the ranks of the eminent. There are excellent biographies of Harry Belafonte and Catherine Dunham (both children of black-white marriages) and of Eugenie Clark, an American-Eurasian ichthyologist married to a physician of Greek ancestry.

Although there is a drift toward more unconventional marriages among the parents of the Four Hundred, most of them married persons of their own race, nationality, and religion. Among the Four Hundred themselves, there is an increase in the less conventional marriages. David Daiches, Enrico Fermi, Harold Laski, Abraham Flexner, Virginia Stephen Woolf, Artur Schnabel, and Bernard Berenson are among those who made Jewish-Gentile marriages. Kwame Nkrumah is married to a young woman from Egypt. Syngman Rhee married a Westerner. Author and journalist Lafcadio Hearn, the son of an English father and a mother from Malta, married a Japanese girl. Santha Rama Rau, a writer from India, married an American. Samuel Clemens' only granddaughter has a Jewish father.

The plain listing of the religious backgrounds of the children reared in these cradles of eminence might seem to be a simple though tedious detail. In practice, it was a complex and frustrating task. In one out of eight families, it was not possible to find any description of religious preference—not in accounts of births, marriages, or deaths, nor in the indexes of many books thumbed through, nor in reference material, nor in the thread of personal narrative in an unindexed autobiography.

Naming of religious background is not to be confused with indicating the religious preference of the eminent adult who comes from this family. Writer G. K. Chesterton, reared an Anglican, became a famous protagonist of Roman Catholicism. Psychoanalyst Alfred Adler, a member of the only Jewish family in his Roman Catholic community, became Protestant. The drift in the families, as well as it can be estimated, is toward nonsectarianism or agnosticism. It is often the work that is the absorbing goal of the famous man or woman. Education and science tend to replace religion as the pathway to what is thought good.

In an age when even to read Darwin was daring, there were many agnostics or freethinkers or avowed atheists among the parents.[7] Among these was the "freethinker" Moses Carver, foster father to a slave boy whom he bought back from kidnappers who had stolen the child in order to resell him. Moses Carver played an important role in giving the talents of George Washington Carver to the world. Not holding the conventional attitudes toward established religions of the place and time in which they lived makes these parents particularly opinionated.

A highly opinionated group at the other end of the ideological scale was composed of the twenty-one ministers,[8] two rabbis, and one Greek orthodox priest who fathered eminent sons and daughters. Ministers' sons have been observed to be exceptionally competent. In the 1921-1922 volume of *Who's Who in America*, according to Stephen S. Visher,[9] the clergymen of all denominations were represented by one son for each 20 fathers; the professional men in *Who's Who in America* by one son for each 46 members; farmers by one son in 690; skilled laborers by one child in 1600; and unskilled laborers by one in 48,000. Among the clergymen, Unitarian ministers, known for their love of learning and opinionatedness, were the most frequently represented, with one son for each seven of the fathers.

It is one thing to be exceptionally competent and another thing to enhance or disturb the status quo sufficiently to become the subject of a biography. There are no sons of Unitarian ministers among the Four Hundred, unless we include lawyer Clarence Darrow, whose father left the ministry before his son was old enough to know him in that role. There are, however, sixteen sons of Unitarian laymen among the Four Hundred. Writer David Daiches and magician Harry Houdini were both sons of rabbis, and physiologist Ivan Pavlov was the son of a Greek Orthodox priest.

Roman Catholic parents, internationally, are not often involved in controversial social issues and do not often produce scientists or humanitarians. They do become involved in revolutionary or political movements. The non-opinionated families are often engrossed in business or in the arts. Almost none are described as reactionary in politics, few as fundamentalist in religious beliefs. The seven persons[10] who became eminent as representatives of a specific religious organization had interests that reached far beyond their own sectarianism. They were involved with trying to further peace, or with the problems of displaced persons and migrants, or with furthering cooperation between Christian and Jewish groups, or with the problems arising from racial prejudice, hunger, and disease.

It is the non-Catholic families, internationally, that are highly opinionated and that contribute to the world pool of talent in science and in humanitarian and reform movements. Knapp and Goodrich,[11] in a study of the origins of American scientists, found that "a disproportionally large number of scientists are produced in the U.S.A. by Protestant middle-class backgrounds and are trained in the small liberal arts colleges that mirror these values." All of the sixty-four eminent scientists studied by Anne Roe[12] were Protestant in childhood background except for six Jewish members of the group. Jewish families are well represented in all major fields of endeavor.

One-half of the Four Hundred come from highly opinionated families. It is these homes that produce most of the scientists, humanitarians, and reformers.

Chapter 3

Failure-Prone Fathers

The family ruin seems to have been the lifting of the dam upon their creative potentialities.... Within two generations they gave four names to the National Biography. Father's name was the fifth.

—Sir Nigel Conan Doyle (son of Sir Arthur Conan Doyle)

Approximately one-half of the fathers in this study turn out to be failure-prone in the routine of everyday life. Since it is impossible to know whether they were more or less addicted to failure than their male contemporaries in the geographical area and in the times in which they lived, we can only conclude that bankruptcy or professional failure on the part of the father does not preclude success on the part of the offspring. A child can make the most of him- or herself in a home where the economic basis for subsistence is insecure and variable. Seeing a father try and fail does not seemingly inhibit the child's striking out into untested areas of achievement.

An examination of the emotional climate in these homes affected by father-failure finds that there are two types of fathers who have difficulties in their professional careers and in their business ventures. First are the fathers who are given to daydreaming and to scholarly retreat from the mainstream of life. Second are the fathers who are impractical, grandiose—who leap before they look. Both groups are inclined to believe that good times are just around the corner.

Abraham Maslow,[1] in observations of "self-actualizing people," uses descriptive terms that are found repeatedly in characterizations of fathers of eminent sons. The fathers of the Four Hundred are often not successful, although they are willing to be reasonable adventurers and take calculated risks—qualities necessary in those self-actualizing persons who do make significant contributions. The inference is that a son with these traits may succeed even though his father failed.

Maslow has observed that the famous man often has a "second naiveté," that he is frequently childlike in his spontaneity, is unfrightened by the unknown, and is attracted by the mysterious and the puzzling. He finds that men who have achieved highly can be "comfortably disorderly, sloppy, anarchic, chaotic, vague, doubtful, uncertain, indefinite, approximate, inexact, or inaccurate," which he defines as being desirable qualities at certain moments in science, art, or life in general. He finds that great men have less need than other people to be pleasing to other men, and that they are commonly indifferent as to what people think of them.

Cursory examination of the adult lives of the Four Hundred would tend to support Maslow's observations. We can certainly cite a high frequency with which individuals of this type are the fathers of eminent men. Nor is Dr. Maslow the only scholar who makes the observation that naiveté is a characteristic of the creative. The eminent psychoanalyst Ernest Jones has observed that great men can be gullible and credulous and often have characteristically receptive natures. He cites Goethe, Copernicus, Newton, and Darwin as his examples. Nobel Prize-winning author Thomas Mann observes that in some human beings, there can be the union of the greatest intellectual gifts with the most amazing naiveté.

Novelist, social philosopher, and political activist Arthur Koestler, in discussing the characteristics of his own father, an ebullient, erratic man who was sometimes a business failure and sometimes very wealthy, says:

> *The financial heavyweights who have crossed my path, publishers, art dealers, bankers, movie producers—have been without exception idiosyncratic, eccentric, irrational and*

> *basically naive individuals.... Apparently the shrewd, cold calculating type is mainly to be found in the light and middle-weight categories of business.*[2]

Psychologist Erich Fromm says that creativity requires the courage to let go of certainties. Certainties are let go with abandon in these families, often before the new course is charted. Norbert Wiener, mathematician and founder of cybernetics, ended his career as a professor of languages at Harvard. He is an American citizen because his Russian father got stranded in New Orleans on his way to join a communal colony in South America where the elder Wiener could practice vegetarianism.

In a good number of these families, the father is prone to flights of fancy, is restless and experimental. Richard Nixon's father was restless by nature, was extroverted, argumentative, and gregarious. He frequently decided to sample job opportunities in various places, and was, at different times, a glass worker, potter, grocer, a painter of Pullman cars, a potato farmer, sheep rancher, pioneer telephone lineman, motorman, roustabout in the oil fields, carpenter, and a labor agitator who organized the streetcar motormen after he froze his own feet standing in an open vestibule. When he finally settled down to his fruit store and gasoline station in California (where the warmth was kind to his tender feet), his store became a kind of neighborhood club where he, the proprietor, talked politics, and his wife soothed the ruffled customers. Had not illness struck the family, he would probably have achieved some security in his old age.

Major George Whistler, a onetime army engineer, was the father of the erratic bachelor painter James McNeill Whistler. It was the Major who made the decision that the family go to Russia, where he was commissioned to build a railroad from St. Petersburg to Moscow. His wife, always a foreboding woman, did not want to go and never quite recovered from the shock of having a child die in her arms en route. Major Whistler did not find it easy to get employment. His work changes in the United States had been frequent, and he had little ability in handling his own financial affairs. As an engineer, he was apt at cutting roads through difficult terrain; he enjoyed solving technical problems, but his employers were prone to mistrust his judgment. The Tsar, however, was excited by the ebullient American and gave hundreds of reluctant peasants orders to help him build a railroad through four hundred miles of swamp. When cholera broke out in the labor camps, Major Whistler died. The Russian Tsar offered to give the two oldest boys, James and William, positions as pages in his court, but the family, left in straitened circumstances, instead sought refuge on a Connecticut farm.

Morris Gershwin, father of composer George Gershwin, a man who seemed to specialize in business failures, created a folklore of Gershwinisms based on his spontaneous and childish reactions. His sons once counted twenty-eight flats in which they had lived while moving about to be near their father's latest business. Morris tried his hand at restaurants, Russian and Turkish baths, book making, bakeries, a cigar store, and a pool hall.

Milovan Djilas, a Montenegrin-born politician and author of *The New Class*, had an incapable farmer father who set his stone house high on a windy hill where the chimney could be seen for miles around. The family lived on the second floor so that the animals, below, would be warmer. His overworked wife cursed the wind and cared little for the view. Milovan's father was a tireless worker, but he built irrigation ditches where no water was ever to flow and planted seeds in barren soil. His children knew their mother was right; the house should have been built in a sheltered valley, but they were always glad to see the house on a hilltop when they returned from afar. "So men are divided. Some are for the useful, some for the beautiful. I placed myself," says Milovan, "on the side for beauty."[3]

Amadeo Modigliani's mother was in labor when the bailiff called to cart off the family's household goods. Her son was born amid valuables hidden in his mother's bed to save them. Fortunes were made as well as lost in this family. They were never really poor; they merely experienced catastrophic reverses.

An engineer, Joseph Ravel, father of composer Maurice, won no acclaim for the two-cylinder horseless carriage he built and patented in 1866. Instead, he was fined for disturbing the peace. Nobel

Prize-winning author Anatole France, whose father rose from peasant to bookseller—only to find that he had more chair-warmers than customers—was torn between his cold, withdrawn father and his weeping, smothering, neurotic mother. François Zola, who died while involved in a scheme to build canals, left his young son Emile and his helpless wife destitute. Sigmund Freud was just plain irked when his gentle father told him that he could no longer support a twenty-six-year-old scholar. Dr. Freud was his mother's boy and had a mild contempt for his father.

An extreme example of compensating the mother for the business failure of the father is found in industrialist Andrew Carnegie. This was not accomplished without trauma, and the influence of the dreaming, idealistic father emerges strongly in the life of this adult financier.

Through no fault of his own, William Carnegie lost his means of livelihood, and it was his wife, Margaret, who became the head of the household and made plans for them to sail from Scotland to America when Andrew was ten and his brother Tom was five. There was no work for William Carnegie in Dunfennline, Scotland; in all Great Britain, the new textile mills had replaced the hand-loom weavers. The family might have starved, as three hundred thousand workers in Ireland had already done, had not the wife opened a shabby grocery store and mended shoes while William unsuccessfully peddled his hand-woven tablecloths from door to door.

William Carnegie had never been a good provider, even when there was a steady market for his work, so the family had no resources for an emergency. William was an incorrigible dreamer, an idealist, a man unconcerned about money unless an acute need for it threatened his wife and children. He turned to Swedenborgianism for his religion, but his wife confided to her oldest son that she preferred the old-fashioned Scotch Presbyterianism in which they had been reared.

Andrew's "Uncle Tammie" Morrison, the Chartist political party organizer, was known from one end of Scotland to the other. Uncle Tammie, his mother's brother, tramped from one village to another carrying a huge cudgel, whiskers flying in the wind. He was a forceful speaker, so much so that he was even jailed for a week because of his oratory. William Carnegie also was a Chartist, and Andrew planned to be a Chartist like his father. Once when William was speaking to a big crowd, Andrew tried to push through to the front to hear his father. The undersized boy was lifted to the shoulders of a strong man in the audience and sat there trembling with pride to hear his father speak while other men listened.

Later, when Andrew became rich, he lived with his mother in a succession of hotels. He longed for a home, but she preferred to flit from hotel to hotel. Andrew was devoted to her, and after his gentle father died, he had his mother all to himself. She made him promise never to marry and to make her rich. She used to say, "No woman is good enough for my Andra." At forty-four, he fell in love with a girl of twenty-two but did not marry her until he was fifty-two and his mother had been dead a year.

Boys who dislike their fathers, who have poor peer relationships and mothers who are self-centered and socially withdrawn are often hostile and unfriendly adults, but Andrew Carnegie had a gentle affection for his father. He became a generous and kindly man to those he met in person. He responded to begging letters, had a long list of pensioners, and immensely enjoyed returning to Dunfennline, Scotland as a rich man. He never forgot his family's arrival in America, nor his own employment at twelve as a bobbin boy operating a spindle in a cotton factory. In business, however, Carnegie could be ruthless, if not completely thick-skinned; during the Homestead strikes, he hired an army to put down a union strike, but the strikes upset him, and he went to Europe until they were over.

Andrew required his wife to sign a marriage agreement promising not to be his heiress, although he endowed her generously so that she would never fear want or dependency. His gifts to libraries, research projects, and world peace totaled $330,000,000. His booklet outlining the social responsibilities of rich men became a bestseller in the United States and Europe for a brief period. The personal debt he felt he owed his mother was paid in full; most of his personal wealth he gave away.

Tom Carnegie, his younger brother, was never burdened by a compulsion to "make it up to mother." He married a young woman of his own age, had a houseful of children, and always worked for his brother, who took a paternal attitude toward him. But Andrew Carnegie was always torn between his father's idealism and his mother's materialism. As he grew richer and older, the sight and touch of the money he earned offended him. He could not carry money on his person and was once put off a London tram because he had no coins in his pocket. Similarly, Henry Ford and Charlie Chaplin, other poor boys who later became rich, also had a distaste for the actual handling of money.

Another boy whose father experienced spectacular ups and downs was John D. Rockefeller, who was born on a farm near Richford, New York. His father, William Avery Rockefeller, was a traveling vendor of quack medicines. He was a charlatan who sold a cancer elixir by the bottle and offered treatments for twenty-five dollars each. The signs he posted outside the village hotels promised to cure all cases of cancer, unless they were too far gone—and even then they could be greatly benefited. "Big Bill" was a flamboyant, good-looking giant, racing sleek horses with never less than a thousand dollars in his pocket. He doled out five-dollar gold pieces to his children.

Big Bill cheated his own sons whenever he could, just to teach them to be clever in handling money. He gave them early responsibilities; he sent John D. to buy cordwood for the family when he was ten, and a little while later commissioned him to build a house. The boy employed an architect, let out the contracts, and saw that the house was built. During the long intervals when Big Bill was not at home, however, the family had lean living; on one occasion, James and William could not have their pictures taken with the class at school because their clothes were shabby. Young John D. used to sit by the road waiting month after dreary month for his father to come home.

The father-failure in this instance was that of periodic, drastic nonsupport. The ups and downs of life are harder on children than poverty, which is unrelieved by riches. Unless there is actual hunger, children like future Vice-President Alben Barkley, whose father was a sharecropper on many poor Kentucky farms before he could buy his own small farm, are not affected by the consistently low standard of living experienced by the family.

Even when a family is actually very wealthy, the children can experience strong anxieties about money if the father frets about business matters. Diana Cooper, daughter of an English lord and House of Commons member Duff Cooper, was a girl who lived in a castle with parents who were wealthy; yet she developed real fears about poverty because of her father's way of speaking about taxes. John D. Rockefeller's daughter Bessie, during a period when her father was under public censure, lay physically stricken in France and was also deeply disturbed, sure she would die penniless.

Being rich does not mean the children have no experience with failure, which can be based on more than just financial factors. The succeeding Rockefellers have been concerned at times with the failure of their ancestors to win universal public acclaim and respect. When John D. Rockefeller's wife, Cettie, died, her body could not be taken home to Cleveland for burial because Cleveland tax assessors said John D. owed the city money and they were waiting to serve him with papers if he brought his wife to the family plot. John D.'s brother, Frank, disinterred his two dead children from the family burial plot as a protest against his brother's business practices.

John D. Rockefeller, Jr. was never permitted to feel rich as a matter of parental principle. Away at school, John Jr. pressed his pants under music books. His own children had only one tricycle so that they could learn to share. A penny was the fine for coming late to prayers.

When John D. Rockefeller, Jr.'s family went on a trip, each child had a job and a salary. Each child had an allowance, and each child's financial books were closely scrutinized. The children helped with baggage, cleaned shoes, hung up clothes. When they were home, they swatted flies, weeded gardens, shined shoes, and raised rabbits for sale to a laboratory. When sons Nelson and Laurance spent a summer with a Grenfell group in the northern wilds and the cook became ill, the two boys were able to take over the sick man's work and do it better than he.

According to William Manchester, author of *A Rockefeller Family Portrait,* the tradition of simple living and sticking to a budget persists:

> *When a Rockefeller allowance is gone, it's gone. Nelson was talking to a visitor in his Seal Harbor home not long ago when one of his sons came in. "Dad, I've got five dollars left," the boy said. "If I just had five more I could go to the dance." Nelson looked sympathetic. "Gee, that's too bad," he murmured, and went on talking.*

The energy and imaginativeness of the picturesque old medicine man who told amusing stories and lived to be a spry one hundred has not been dissipated in his great-grandsons. Nelson Rockefeller has an impulsiveness and physical energy that has been known to send him mountain climbing in the evening after he has exhausted his fellow workers during the day. Manchester says, "Nelson's talent is for action, for plunging ahead.... [His] brothers lack his impulsiveness, but they all have something of his physical energy."

There are other failures. Caitlin Thomas, wife of poet Dylan Thomas, in her book *Leftover Life to Kill,* says of her father-in-law:

> *...that most unhappy of all men I have ever met; who did all the spade work of casting off the humble beginnings, bettering himself, assiduously cultivating the arts; and finished up a miserable finicky failure; while passing on to Dylan, on a heaped up plate, the fruits of all the years of unrewarding labor.*

To F. Scott Fitzgerald, the failure of his father to make an adequate living for the family as a wholesale grocery salesman was the catastrophe that turned him into a boy who was alternately crawling in front of kitchen maids and insulting the great. When F. Scott was sent to a school for wealthy Roman Catholic boys by his aunt, it was not only his feminine prettiness but also his habit of debating and contradicting the boys who had more money than he that made him a social failure. He was always a "poor relation" among the rich.

A boy can be ashamed of his father's failure and try to conceal the family's low status. Henrik Ibsen never forgave his father for the sudden failure that impoverished the family, moved them from the well-to-do section of town to the impoverished outskirts, and required Henrik to be an apothecary's assistant rather than a college student.

Albert Berenson, the immigrant peddler, was once greeted in the kitchen of a customer for whom he was displaying his wares with the news that a certain young man, the important Bernard Berenson, a scholar, art historian, and critic, was in the house as a guest.[4] The abashed father hastily gathered his wares and left before his own close familial connection with the honored guest could be known. Albert Berenson was modest and unsuccessful. His relatives did very well in the liquor business, and his wife and children resented being poor relations. Albert could talk beautifully about French history, philosophy, Voltaire and Rousseau, but his "dreadful laugh" annoyed his son; they did not get on well together. No one talked much to the man, not even his wife, who placed her hopes on her son; so the lonely old fellow went about speaking to himself.

Paul Ehrlich, famous bacteriologist, had such a father—an innkeeper in the small town of Strehlen in Upper Silesia, a kindly, eccentric man who sat talking to himself while his wife ran the tavern. Two expedients are common in homes where the father is not a good provider—keeping a boarding house or tavern, or keeping a private school.

One of the families that made a good adjustment to an early catastrophic experience was that of President Dwight David Eisenhower. His parents, before they had finished their freshman year, quit college to marry. Within two years, they lost the two thousand dollars and 160 acres of Kansas farm land near Abilene which David Eisenhower had been given as a wedding present by his well-to-do and thrifty father, an important dignitary in the local Church of the Brethren congregation. David had not wanted to be a farmer; he had intended to be an engineer. His dynamic young wife, Ida, an orphan girl who had been overworked on a farm owned by inconsiderate relatives, had spent her own small inheritance on her schooling and a fine piano. She was a music student.

The young husband and wife mortgaged their land to David's older sister Amanda, and they bought a small general store at Hope, Kansas. An absconding partner robbed the till and left the country. Bills that he had said were already paid were presented for payment. Customers who had been given credit could not pay what they owed because of a drought and a drop in the price of wheat. The distracted young husband put his affairs in the hands of a lawyer, who also cheated David and kept the remaining money. A subsequent move to Denison, Texas was also a mistake and disappointment. Relatives coaxed David and Ida to come home.

When the family was reestablished, with David as foreman of the Belle Springs Creamery in Abilene, Kansas, there were no scenes, no recriminations. To Ida, their early misadventures were as much her responsibility as his. She once bought law books to try to find out how they might get some returns from the lawyer who cheated them, but soon gave up the lost cause. The children never heard their parents quarrel, and it was always David who was deferred to as the head of the household—but it was Ida who was the more dynamic and could make a decision in a minute. She never worked outside the home, even when times were bad, and spent her spare energies on her embroidery and her music. She made the boys do their chores over and over until they did their work right. She supervised the selling of vegetables from the three-acre garden tract upon which their home was situated in the "wrong" part of town. The children were busy but never poverty-stricken. Their neighbors were not more wealthy than they.

David was a dreamer and seeker. Religion was his hobby; he read all books on religion that came his way and once occupied himself trying to correlate Bible history with the building of the pyramids by drawing diagrams and making computations. Ida Stover Eisenhower was a Lutheran, and when she and David were first married, they attended the Lutheran church. Later, for a time, they went to Methodist services. Mostly, they attended the Church of the Brethren, the denomination in which David had been reared. Eventually, he broke from the River Brethren Church and met, in his own home and in the homes of others, with a group that called themselves Bible students. David had an inquiring mind, but he never found an answer to his religious doubts and left this last organization because he could not go along with the dogma.

The sting of his early failure kept him from accepting the law as an honest profession. He had little admiration for soldiers or lawyers; he felt even more sorrow over having a lawyer son than a soldier son. The doctor son he wished for, he never had. To David Eisenhower, the physician was always the most admirable of professional men.

The Alcoholic Fathers

The alcoholic, failure-prone fathers of the Four Hundred present some unusual findings, which are corroborated in part by sociological studies. A convincing relationship between subsistence anxiety and insobriety was found by D. Horton,[5] who analyzed fifty-six primitive societies and found that the greater the anxiety concerning drought or flood or crop failure, the greater the consumption rate of the available alcohol. He sees alcohol as a means of reducing anxiety. The amount of alcoholism in a culture also depends on the degree to which the culture operates to bring about acute needs for adjustment or inner tensions in its members, the set of attitudes toward drinking which the culture produces in its members, and the degree to which the culture provides suitable substitute means of satisfaction.

A great many of the alcoholic, failure-prone parents in the Four Hundred are caught in anxiety-producing situations. An unexpected and provocative observation, not previously noted, is that twenty-one alcoholic fathers in this survey produced fourteen children who became actors, singers, or writers with an exceptional sense of humor.

George Bernard Shaw's reasoning as to this relationship between a drinking father and a clowning son is as follows: "If you cannot get rid of the family skeleton, make it dance."[6] He explains that a boy who has seen his father, with an imperfectly wrapped goose under one arm and an equally unwrapped ham under the other, butt at the garden wall with his tall hat and crush it into a concertina will not become a boy who makes tragedies of trifles instead of trifles of tragedies.

His own father, George Carr Shaw, was a failure as a clerk and government civil servant and made a bad investment when he bought a corn mill that was always near bankruptcy. Impending failure set the elder Shaw giggling; funerals drove him to helpless laughter. His own tippling shamed him, however, since he did not believe in drinking. He gave talks to that effect, which his son sincerely believed—only to find out later with consternation that his father was a secret drinker.

When George Carr Shaw's wife, Lucinda Elizabeth Gurly Shaw, left him and went to London with a fellow music teacher, he began drinking less and started calling on old friends. He reformed almost completely as to drunkenness but never gained in competence as a businessman. It was not love but rather a need for income and a revulsion for her husband's drunkenness which prompted Mrs. Shaw to go away with Vandaleur Lee, an older man who had shared a house with the Shaws in Dublin, so that they could both have an impressive studio for their pupils.

George Bernard Shaw always described the separation of his parents in terms of financial straits, not passion. He said that anyone who could have seduced his mother could have seduced the Virgin at Nuremburg, that she could have boarded and lodged the Three Musketeers and D'Artagnan and would have taken no notice of their sex—unless they smoked in the living room.

Shaw could jest of his boyhood, but his descriptions are essentially tragic. Pearson describes the house as cold with penury and rejection. Lucinda Elizabeth never liked her son, who may have reminded her of her husband. To her daughters, she was somewhat less rejecting. She worked hard at her music and thought the ill-paid servants were "unfit to take charge of three cats, let alone three children." The meals were of stewed beef and badly cooked potatoes. Tea was left on the hob until it was pure tannin. When Mrs. Shaw went to London with her daughters, she left the boy with his father, and for six years she did not write to him. There was no picture made of him. No one valued his personality or his abilities or planned for his future. He disliked himself and felt that he was correctly regarded as a disagreeable "little beast." For his father, he had such contempt that he would not volunteer to help when the man struggled for hours over accounts that the son could have done quickly. The father was too proud to ask the boy to assist him.

"The way we were brought up, or rather not brought up, doesn't bear thinking of," Shaw said when he was eighty-six. He was more neglected than ill treated, which gave him a dreadful self-sufficiency but delayed his emotional development. He says, "It left me a treacherous brute in matters of pure affection." At his own mother's interment, he entertained himself and his one companion with a witty monologue as to the dead woman's probable reaction to the scene she was missing.

Joshua Cobb, father of the American humorist Irvin S. Cobb, was a little bantam of a man who injured his eyes while he was a Confederate soldier. While leaning over a campfire to light a cigar, he ineptly let fall a pistol cartridge from his belt. The explosion injured his tear ducts so that he was forever tearful and his lower eyelids were inflamed and painful.

As a tobacco merchant, and as a steamboater, he was a failure. But he was a proud little man who wore the finest of starched shirts; his tiny feet were shod in expensive handmade boots, and he smoked the very best cigars. He loved the sound of children's laughter and bought their respect and affection through gifts. When the circus came to town, he took not only his own children but the neighbors' children as well, and he brought them home at nightfall stuffed with red popcorn and parched goobers. A whole week's salary was not too much for him to spend on an outing for the children.

This red-eyed little man, Joshua, who was the poor son of a rich father whom the Civil War ruined financially, was a failure as an in-law. When he married into the Saunders family, he had no chance to prove excellence in that distinguished circle. His father-in-law, Dr. Reuben Saunders, who supported him and his family during frequent periods of financial crisis, was known internationally for his discovery of the effectiveness of atropine in treating cholera. The Cobbs were always "poor relations," and the situation was both irksome and humiliating. Joshua Cobb had not finished college when he was given medical discharge out of the Confederate army, but he could not go back to school because of his eyes.

His oldest daughter, Reubie, named for her grandfather, took his wife's time and most of her affection. They could have left Paducah, Kentucky and gone where job opportunities were better had it not been for neurotic Reubie, a pocket-sized Cinderella whose niece described her as a female Jonathan Swift. She was the spoiled first daughter. Her grandfather bought her a diamond ring for Christmas the same year he bought the tone-deaf Irvin a violin. When she was disappointed—about what, no one ever knew—she became a young recluse, pulled the shades of the windows, and would not go outdoors. She dressed carefully each day, tripped from window to window in her size one shoes, peered out at passers-by, and made clever and caustic comments about them. Her mother was completely absorbed in Reubie and her problems, leaving her son Irvin always feeling rejected by her, even though he loved her.

Joshua lost his job with the steamboat company when it changed hands. His sizable insurance policy had a suicide clause, so he set himself, his son later felt sure, to deliberately drink himself to death. Joshua was a strong, healthy man except for his sore eyes, and it took him four painful years to die. Irvin Cobb wrote in his autobiography: "They were a hard four years on my mother, too. The memory of them is still like a scar burnt on my brain."

Irvin Cobb married an out-of-town girl and went off to New York to be a newspaperman and a humorist; Reubie eventually came out of retirement. She was gay and competent in her old age, took tender care of her mother, and had a charming, important man of Paducah as a steady suitor. Each evening for forty years he came to dinner. Each evening they went for a drive. Three days after her mother died, Reubie married her sweetheart. Both were dead within the year.

Stephen Leacock, the Canadian humorist, came from a troubled home with an alcoholic father who was failure-prone. Like the senior Eisenhowers, the Leacocks married very young. Peter Leacock was a handsome, likely lad, born to wealth and a good family in England. He led a casual life, sailed his boat, and attended school irregularly. At the age of eighteen, he courted and secretly married a poor girl, Agnes Emma Butler. Because Peter was a Roman Catholic, her Protestant family would not have him in their house.

The immature husband and wife were sent to South Africa to farm. The locusts ate their crops, so they were sent to Kansas to farm, where grasshoppers ate their crops. They moved to Canada and lost a third farm. Grandfather Leacock sent money for a special tutor for the children when he was told about the poor schools.

As Peter Leacock grew older, he became abusive to his wife and children. The two oldest boys left home, and it was seventeen-year-old Stephen Leacock who took his father to the railway station, brandished a whip, and threatened to use it unless his father left home and never came back. For fifty years, Peter Leacock lived in Nova Scotia under the name of Captain Lewis, and he never came home. His wife lived in perpetual indebtedness until the younger children were old enough to help her. Thanks to the kindness of wealthy relatives, the Leacocks were never actually indigent. Stephen was the one among the eleven children who resented his father most, and he was also the family member who was to win fame as a humorist.

A whimsical writer whose father became alcoholic and deserted the family when his wife died was Kenneth Grahame, author of *The Wind in the Willows*, who was the oldest child in his family. The children were turned over to the indifferent care of the maternal grandmother, who had no affection for them and considered them an intolerable burden.

Actor Maurice Chevalier was glad when his father, a house painter, deserted his mother and three brothers, because his father was abusive when he drank—which was often. Maurice tried to help support his mother as soon as he left school at fourteen, but he hurt his finger while laboring in a tack factory, then spent the unexpected "time-out" getting his first professional job as a singer. When Maurice was a famous man, his father came to see him in his dressing room, but Maurice sent the old man away in anger. Remembering the sadness in the eyes of the hesitant, shabby fellow, he was somewhat sorry later, but he never saw his father again. His mother was always the most important person in Maurice Chevalier's life. "There was a quiet and a sweetness about Mama and the beauty of simplicity.... Her smile when it came was like a light.... She seems always close to me now, just as [when] she was alive.[7]

The father of Charlie Chaplin died of alcoholism. Charlie's father, who was his wife's third husband, was a popular singer of sentimental ballads in England and also in the United States, and his wife was a successful singer and dancer who sometimes played in Gilbert and Sullivan shows. It was she who taught Charles to mimic and to note bodily posture—she had an intuitive knack for knowing a stranger's personal problems by observing his posture. Charlie's parents taught him to jig and sing as soon as he could toddle. His mother soon began to develop symptoms of mental illness, which were never to leave her; she withdrew from reality and sometimes did not recognize her own sons. It was Charlie's alcoholic father who gave him his premiere by pushing him on the stage when he was five to sing a streetseller's song, "Jack Jones," as a substitute for his mother, who had suddenly become ill.

Charlie spent his years from five to seven in an orphanage where there was never enough to eat, where the children were treated like criminals, flogged, and put into solitary confinement. At the age of ten, through the management of his thirteen-year-old half-brother, Sidney, who acted as his agent, Charlie was playing a good role at the London Hippodrome. He toured the provinces in an appropriate role of boy hero in a rags-to-riches play, became quite the successful young actor, enjoyed his success, dressed well, and sported a cane. Charles and Sidney were soon able to take their mother from sordid surroundings and put her in a good nursing home. The Chaplins had drifted apart before the husband died of alcoholism.

The tragic stories of humorists with alcoholic fathers is not complete without the story of Alexander Woollcott, author, radio personality, and drama critic for the *New York Times*, whose life story has been so candidly told by Samuel Hopkins Adams, who knew and loved him well. Alexander Woollcott was brought up in the Phalanx, a socialist-communal colony in New Jersey. It was made up of Unitarians, Universalists, Congregationalists, Jews, Presbyterians, Quakers, Swedenborgians, and a leavening of agnostics who found a common denominator in a lofty Fourierist thesis. Frances Bucklin, daughter of the founder of the Phalanx, against the advice of her elders married a visiting Englishman, Walter Woollcott, whose alcoholism and erratic ways made him an extremely poor provider. The destitute wife and children spent so much time at the Phalanx and so little time with the husband and father that some of the Bucklin relatives caustically remarked that Walter's function was for "breeding purposes only."

Walter Woollcott became very rich at one time—when he struck up a friendship with a stock market plunger named Gibbs. The whole family moved into a mansion for less than a year. When failure struck hard, Walter Woollcott said that he was very tired and took to his bed for two years. Alexander Woollcott described himself as the son of a crazy father and a doting mother. He rejected his father severely, although the unhappy man was essentially kind and never abused the boy. When the elder Walter Woollcott dropped dead on the streets of New York, his son Alexander interrupted his card game for an hour to arrange for a cremation and then returned to the card game.

The part that rejection of the alcoholic, failure-prone father played in Alexander Woollcott's difficulty in sexual adjustment is probably considerable, however. His sister Julie and her best friend may also have contributed by making a pet of the youngest boy in the family, who was so delicate and precocious. They sheltered him from rough contacts with other boys and dressed him as Puck in a neighborhood tableau. When he went fishing, Alexander took a hat along to decorate. Another feminine influence was his first public school teacher, Sophie Rosenberger, who made him a devotee of Louisa May Alcott and her works. In his early teens, he loved to dress up and pass himself off as a girl, and he had a girl's name, Alecia, which he used while doing his female impersonations. A case of mumps in his early adulthood is thought to have almost neutralized his sexual capacity. He was never described as a homosexual, but a friend who knew him in early manhood attested to a "private life which even the straitest-laced Puritan would have admitted was blameless. The more honor to him."

Alexander was apparently uncomfortable with marriage; he was not able to have a husband and wife as guests at the same time, although he could entertain either if the other were not present. All of the Woollcott children adored their mother, and all of them except Alexander liked their father, whom they regarded as "an amusing, if somewhat irresponsible crony." In this family, it is the boy who felt the greatest antagonism to the alcoholic, failure-prone father who later made the family skeleton dance in the most effective fashion with his wit and caustic wisdom.

Joseph Stalin's mother was described as being pleased when her abusive alcoholic husband died. Had he lived, her son would have been expected to be a shoemaker. When he died, she was able to plan for her son to be a priest, which he studied for a while before joining the Marxist revolutionary group. Both Josep Tito of Yugoslavia and the early-orphaned monk Gregory Rasputin lived in the squalor of rural slums made the more untenable by their fathers' frequent drunkenness. Tito's father was amiable, and the boy's school adjustment was superior. The hypnotist and scheming charlatan Rasputin had an abusive father and had lost his mother, sister, and brother when he was young. There was no friendliness in his home community for him or his family, no teacher who recognized his ability and his drive to rise above his station.[8]

No humorist, actor, or actress in this study had a serene, happy life with well-adjusted parents, but not all of the parents of humorists or actors were alcoholic. Samuel Clemens, Harry Lauder, Eddie Cantor, and Ring Lardner had failure-prone, but not alcoholic, fathers.

Psychologist Lewis Terman noted that a teacher is ordinarily a proper, middle-class individual with middle-class mores. The child from the "good family," the child who is clean, proper, and well brought up, is bound to have, in the thinking of most teachers, more possibilities for achievement than is the neglected son of the town drunk. Children from broken homes or homes where the parents are immoral, alcoholic, or eccentric are likely to be downgraded in the minds of the community and school and are expected to be problem children. A Yale University sociologist, A. B. Hollingshead, tells of this attitude in *Elmtown's Youth*, an excellent study of a typical Midwestern small town.

> *This denigrating attitude faced Sherwood Anderson in the small town of Camden, Ohio, where he was reared. Sherwood was late thirty-two times one semester, but the school authorities did not notify his mother because of the unusual home circumstances. Everyone in Camden knew that Sherwood Anderson, or "Jobby," as he was commonly called, was a hard worker, was always on the search for a new job—hence the nickname. There was nothing honest he would not do. He sold innumerable copies of the Cincinnati Enquirer; he helped his mother by gathering her customers' dirty wash and bringing it home to her and by delivering the clean laundry.*

Sherwood always had a book in his hand. When he went fishing he took a book, and while acting as manager of the baseball team he read between innings. He showed no special talent like his sister Stella, who recited verses nicely, or his brother Karl, who drew well.

Jobby's industry was in contrast to his father's inactivity. After his harness business failed, his wife had to take in washings. He drank and was unfaithful to his wife. Jobby knew all this and was defensive of his mother.

The school authorities did not consider him a potential scholar and decided that it was permissible for him to stay out of school to help his mother.

Elliott Roosevelt, father of Eleanor Roosevelt, was a child of "sun and fortune." When he married, he was tall, aristocratic, tanned—and heir to two hundred thousand dollars. He had just returned from a tiger hunt in Africa. To Anna Hall, the lovely, spoiled, oldest daughter in a well-to-do family, he was a romantic figure, just the playboy husband she needed to join her in her amateur drama club and to accompany her in a fatiguing round of social activities to which she was committed. The marriage began to break up when he decided to work in New York like any other man and began commuting from their home in Long Island each day. When she wanted to have fun, he wanted to rest. When they had a homely little girl, the father was enchanted with his daughter and preferred to play with her in the dirt of the back yard rather than accompany his wife to social functions. Anna Hall Roosevelt related well to her two sons, born subsequently, but could never bear to have her daughter touch her. She called the child "Granny" and ridiculed her in front of guests for her quaint, old-fashioned ways.

When Eleanor was five, her father broke his leg and began to drink to alleviate the pain. He became alcoholic, and the family went with him to a sanitarium in Italy. Eleanor was put in a boarding school nearby where she was very unhappy. She swallowed a penny to gain the sympathy of the nuns, and was shamed by everyone but her father for her behavior. By this time, she had developed habits that made her mother think her an impossible child. During this same period, she also began to show her empathy for others. She came back from a pony ride one day walking instead of riding. The boy who had been hired to lead the pony had sore and bleeding feet, so Eleanor insisted that he ride and she walk. Her parents separated while her father was still in the sanitarium in Italy, and mother and the children went back to New York.

Anna died of diphtheria, and her youngest child, Ellie, whom this mother had never reprimanded and who was so beautiful, did not long survive her. Young Eleanor and her brother, Hall, were left in the care of their maternal grandmother in accordance with Anna's will because she did not want their father to have their legal custody.

Some time after Anna Hall Roosevelt died, Elliott came to speak to Eleanor and took her for a long drive. During this visit, he promised her that some day she could come to live with him to be the mistress of his household. He then went away, and she was left to live with him in a dream world where she was the heroine and he the hero. In her autobiography, she says, "Into this world I retired as soon as I went to bed, and as soon as I woke in the morning, and all the time I was waking, and when anyone bored me."[9]

Having failed to gain control over her own four adolescent children, Grandmother Hall was determined to be very strict with her grandchildren, especially with Eleanor, who was "a Roosevelt." Thus, Eleanor was never permitted to have much to do with the Roosevelts of whom her grandmother disapproved, not even her kind great-aunt Gracie, whom even her mother had loved. Aunt Gracie had taken Eleanor to the wax-works, told her stories, and had gone with her to the dentist, but Grandmother Hall said that the father's family was a bad influence. There were no more trips to see the crippled children in the special hospital set up for them by her Grandfather Roosevelt, whose life was filled with charitable activities.

Apparently, Grandmother Hall never said "Yes" if she could say "No." Eleanor was invited to go see the Old West, but her grandmother refused and gave no reason. When she was not reading, Eleanor daydreamed of her father. She remembered how he took her to help serve a Thanksgiving dinner in a newsboy's clubhouse that his father, Theodore Roosevelt, Sr., had started. Elliott had explained that all of the ragged little boys had no homes; they lived in wooden shanties or vacant lots or slept in vestibules of houses or public buildings. Elliott was always thoughtful of poor children and, when he was only seven, had given his good coat away to a shivering child. Eleanor knew, too, that he gave dolls to poor children and that he told them about his little girl whom he saw so seldom.

When she was ten and was told that her father was dead, she cried bitterly, then went on living with her father in daydreams even more than when he was alive.

Eleanor's relatives were not happy with her. She lied, she stole sweets, and she was poor in spelling and arithmetic and grammar. She bit her nails; she had a great fear of burglars and the dark; she was shy and awkward. She was dressed in short skirts when other girls her age had their dresses down to their ankles, and she wore heavy flannels from November 1 to April 1, regardless of the weather.

A neighbor, Mrs. Henry Parish, who was friendly to the Roosevelt family, was kind to Eleanor and let the lonely girl play with her own small children. The washerwoman, Mrs. Overhalse, was a cheerful woman, and Eleanor spent many hours with her. Governesses, French maids, German maids—all of them were walked off their feet by energetic Eleanor. As she walked, she daydreamed, always of her father.

The only time she ever saw boys was when she was permitted, at Christmastime, to go to a party at her Aunt Corinne's home. Aunt Corinne was her father's sister and had nursed Elliott during his last illness with great devotion. The girls at these parties were not kind to gawky Eleanor in her odd clothes. Her ankles were weak and she fell down when she tried to skate with the others. It was there that she met a handsome boy, also a Roosevelt, a fifth cousin named Franklin, who was kind to her. Her own father had been this boy's godfather.

Grandmother Hall said there was too much gaiety in her own home for a girl going on fifteen, and she feared that Eleanor might get as unmanageable as were her young aunts and uncles. When she was sent to the Allenswood School at South Fields, near London, Eleanor took with her the memories of her father. When he had died, the Abingdon, Virginia, newspapers had described him in an editorial as a young man whose name was a byword among the needy for his abundant and unostentatious charities. In this family, the alcoholic father, whose acquaintance with his daughter was brief and infrequent after she was five, surely played a positive and definite role in channeling her sympathies and future concerns.

Louis Armstrong, deserted by his alcoholic father and neglected by his mother, who was usually "out on the town," was lucky when he was picked up for firing a pistol on the streets and was sent to a home for "colored waifs." He learned music there, and he appreciated the food and comfort of the humble institution.

Writer Thomas Wolfe, who turned the sad story of his own childhood into literature, had teachers, Mr. and Mrs. J. M. Roberts, who recognized his talents and helped him. His brothers and sisters used to tease him at the family table about his love for Shakespeare. From his mother, he inherited an indomitable will and a dogged persistence. This odd-looking boy with a little head on his big body used to spit in people's faces when he stammered. He had two roofs and no home, for his mother ran a boarding house, while his alcoholic, book-loving, artistic father lived in the family homestead with his daughter as housekeeper. One of Thomas Wolfe's best known books, which probably reflects his own experiences, is entitled *You Can't Go Home Again*.

John Stanislaus Joyce, the colorful father of James Joyce, ran through a modest fortune while becoming the father of either sixteen or seventeen children in eighteen years. The drama of a life that involved family moves played itself out so frequently that count was lost. Yet the family always maintained an address in the right part of town. John was a man who diddled his life away with song and story and gay companionship. As long as he had the money that he inherited, he was popular in the bars and restaurants and racecourses. But he lost his fortune by investing it unwisely. John had many positions, none of which he filled well, but at one time he was secretary to the National Liberal Club in Dublin. He never felt like a poor man, but instead thought of himself as a rich man experiencing bad luck. His children and his wife, however, often felt very poor, and James Joyce disliked his father intensely.

Contributions of the Failure-Prone Father

A willingness to take risks is a distinguishing characteristic of fathers of many of the Four Hundred. Lillian Smith, author of the controversial novel *Strange Fruit*, was born in the small town of Jasper, Florida to a father who was opinionated, learning-centered, and also experimental. The daughter was willing, as an adult, to "burn bridges behind her" by discarding the racial prejudices of her family and her Southern community long before the days of Civil Rights in the South. She says in *Killers of the Dream*:

> *We knew we were a respected and important family of this small town, but beyond this knowledge we gave little thought to status. Our father made money in lumber and naval stores for the excitement of making and losing it—not for what money can buy nor the security that it sometimes gives. I do not remember at any time wanting "to be rich" nor do I remember that thrift and saving were ideals which our parents considered important enough to urge upon us. Always in the family there was an acceptance of risk, a mild delight even in burning bridges, an expectant "what will happen now"! We were not irresponsible; living according to the pleasure principle was by no means our way of life. On the contrary we were trained to think that each of us should do something that would be of genuine usefulness to the world, and the family thought it right to make sacrifices if necessary, to give each child adequate preparation for this life's work. We were also trained to think learning important, and books, but "bad" books our mother burned. We valued music and art and craftsmanship but it was people and their welfare and religion that were the foci around which our lives seemed naturally to move.*

Cartoonist Bill Mauldin, son of a daydreaming, improvident farmer, also had childhood experiences that made it easier for him to risk personal failure by expressing himself uniquely in his cartoons. Mauldin describes his irrepressible "Pop" and his many projects in his *A Sort of a Saga*:

> *When he talked about a new scheme, he went on for hours, painting a glorious picture and giving all the objections and then batting them down, as if six or seven people were discussing the matter instead of one. Sid [Bill's brother] and I never got over being entranced when Pop sold himself on something new. But as time went on, my mother's eyes became less and less starry....*

Pulitzer Prize-winning author and literary critic Van Wyck Brooks says that it was his father's failure to fit into the business world that made him seek another kind of expression for himself, made him critical and observant of the social scene. His father was a scholarly man who owned a nickel mine in Nevada, but the nickel was too far down to be easily worked, and the mine was too far from the railroad. Worry over his investment destroyed the father's gaiety and wit. In *Scenes and Portraits,* Van Wyck says:

> *The irony of it is that he had once owned a world famous mine and traded it for this chimera in the Nevada mountains.... I felt my father never should have been a businessman. I was melodramatic, no doubt, in my view of the case. I hated business and saw it as a Moloch that devoured whatever was best in the American mind.*

Among the Four Hundred, the end result of having a father who experiences failure is not the child's withdrawal from action or conservatism, but his release from fear of innovation. The wife of the husband who does not do well may turn for comfort to a son, who frequently tries to make her happy by his own success. In most instances, however, he does not achieve fame by a conservative, cautious approach to problems, but instead puts his imaginative, creative qualities to better use than did his father.

The men and women who are able to produce a novel product or add to the knowledge or pleasure of mankind seem almost to depend for their creativity upon their fathers' childish eagerness for new experiences, their naiveté, and even their inefficiency.

Chapter 4

Dominating Mothers, but Few Dominating Fathers

When she herself [the poet's mother] was unable to fulfill her desires for personal accomplishment, she transferred her ambitions to her children. That she loved her children goes, perhaps, without saying. But that an uncompromising stubbornness toward an ideal preceded that love is nearer to the truth. There was little softness in her.... That long purpose, outside of herself, made her a difficult person to live with.... The excuse for domination seems valid.

—William Carlos Williams, *Yes, Mrs. Williams*

Among the parents of the Four Hundred, the dominating mothers are those who would today probably be career women. Today they might be leaving their children to the casual companionship of the television set and be completely engrossed in vocations, adult education, or community betterment activities. We studied mothers of the Four Hundred because they lived in a different era and often seemed to find that the best outlet for their own drives and abilities was through capable sons and daughters. The pendulum in child nurture today has swung through a wide arc, and devotion to a child's career is not now so frequently a mother's principal source of satisfaction.

If the dominating mothers keep their tendencies for decision-making and for planning ahead within reasonable bounds, they may ultimately be honored by famous sons or daughters and receive credit for their children's successes. Annette Beveridge and Ida Eisenhower were two such women. Many aggressive women who dominate their households have philosophical husbands. This has been observed to be a common pattern in Jewish homes, which are known to be excellent cradles of eminence. Dominating mothers are apt to keep a close eye on the pantry, on new branches of the family tree, and on the inscription of the family name in some hall of fame.

The dominating mother who oversteps reasonable boundaries, however, makes it hard for her captive child to rebel, since she is the focus of both love and authority. If the child does not progress, she can withdraw affection. If she has a husband who is failure-prone, as 90 percent of the dominating mothers do, the child often resolves to make her so proud of him or her that she will forget her disappointment in her husband.

The child who rebels against domination makes an easier adjustment in courtship and marriage than does the one who is sorry for his or her mother and identifies with her. The man who was a "mother's boy" is frequently uneasy with his male contemporaries. He is apt to quarrel with professional colleagues, and if a soldier, he is likely to consider human life expendable. He is wary of democratic procedures and may become dictatorial, mistrusts mankind, thinks he—and mother—know best. He needs to have women around him who approve of him; and he gets along best with older women, children, and animals. He may marry only after his mother dies, or he may remain a bachelor. If he marries, he expects his wife to play a secondary role to his mother or to reenact her supportive role. If the mother bears down too heavily upon him and he tries to rebel, he may become highly introverted and creative, but he is seldom happy in his personal relationships.

At least eighteen of these dominating women were the young wives of men old enough to be their fathers. Others seemed deliberately to choose husbands whose only function would be to father sons and daughters and then leave their wives free to guide the children.

The dominating father, despite the place given to him in the novels of the Victorian days, is comparatively rare. When he does overwhelm his family, he is critical, irritable, driven by compulsions he cannot resist. He seldom has grandiose plans for his child and is more likely to retard than to block his children's ambitions.

Sometimes he wants a son to repeat his own career by staying in the family business or profession. It is the mother whose daydreams are more often infinite. The parental daydreams do not so often encompass the daughter, and the family may actually be disturbed by the daughter who wants to be a career woman.

Certain groups such as the Quakers and Unitarians were more likely to accept the woman who wanted to work, but they accepted her more easily in the role of a social reformer. When a girl did become eminent, she most often did so out of a deep personal concern for the ills of mankind or out of a need to use a talent. Two only daughters, actress Maude Adams and educator Marie Montessori, experienced mother domination, but it is ordinarily male children who are driven to succeed by the intense desires of their mothers.

Some Homes Are Matriarchal

Some of the homes are not only mother-dominated but also tend to be matriarchal in composition. Nobel Prize-winning microbiologist Selman A. Waksman, born in the bleak town of Novaia-Priluka in the Russian Ukraine, lived in what was essentially a matriarchal society. His mother, already a dynamic businesswoman at twenty-one, was urged into marriage by female relatives who feared that she was likely to be an old maid.

Soon after the wedding ceremony, her husband, a coppersmith, left for the army and did not return for five years. When he came home to his bride, he found that she had made a home for her mother and for those of her seven sisters and her nieces and nephews who needed a roof. She and her widowed mother had been very successful with their thriving dry-goods business. She was more than a businesswoman; she arranged dowries for poor girls, she loaned money without interest, and she was interested in every citizen of the village who had a problem.

The death of his small sister turned young Selman's thoughts toward medical research. The household was a friendly one, but the middle-aged father played only an incidental role in the boy's life. His mother's interests were so scattered that he escaped being overwhelmed by her. When she died while he was in late adolescence, he was helped by people who had been helped by her.

Edwin Jones, father of Quaker educator Rufus Jones, a poor farmer from near North China, Maine, wore his overcoat the year round; in winter to keep the heat in, and in the summer to keep the heat out. He was prone to moods, neglected his work, then finished it quickly in a burst of energy. He kept no hired hand, and he worked alone. His youth was disturbed by seizures. In Friends' Meetings, his message seldom varied in content and had to do with "making a little heaven on the way to Heaven." He was a kind man, silent and self-effacing.

When his wife, the energetic, nineteen-year-old, redheaded Mary Hoxie, moved into the already woman-dominated home, she became the new mistress of the household in fact as well as name. Her energy, humor, tact, and understanding made her a good hostess to the stream of guests who visited the home—often one or two a week, each of whom brought news of the outside world and spoke dynamically of world concerns.

Already in the household was Edwin Jones' mother, Susie Jones, a rugged pioneer woman who smoked her pipe three times a day and was an elder in Meeting, as well as a competent cook, dairymaid, weaver, tailor, gardener, soapmaker, and nurse—and a woman with great breadth of mind and depth of heart. A maiden aunt, Peace Jones, a mystic and woman of remarkable culture, also lived in the household and had a fanatic faith in her young nephew's potentialities.

On the periphery of the household was Sibyl, the wife of Eli Jones, the much older brother of the inarticulate Edwin. It was because of Aunt Sibyl and Uncle Eli that the little town of North China, Maine, was well known to Quakers all over the world, and it was due to them that the small rural Meeting had so many international visitors. Aunt Sibyl had a voice like the wind in the pine trees and had spoken in Nova Scotia, England, Liberia, Sierra Leone, Europe, Greece, and the Holy Land.

Four strong women made up this matriarchy.

Kwame Nkrumah was the only son of one of the several wives of a man who lived in what was then the Gold Coast—now, largely through his efforts as an adult, the independent country of Ghana. His mother's will, he says, was not to be disregarded. All of the mothers were responsive to the needs of all of the children. These women did not quarrel among themselves, and his older half-brothers tended to spoil Kwame Nkrumah, as did his mother. She used to coax him to eat by wrapping food in plantain leaves and hiding it under his pillow. It was she who persuaded his father to educate her only son.

When she became a widow and Kwame's uncle became his guardian, her drive to see her boy educated was not lessened. When he returned to her after his college years in the United States, she did not know him because of his maturity—and also because of dental work he had had done. No man in her experience had ever come home with a gap in his front teeth so miraculously filled in, and she was bewildered by the inexplicable change in his appearance. Since she was illiterate, communication with her had been through letters read to her by a friend of her son who sometimes journeyed to her village.

Despite his close involvement with his mother, Kwame Nkrumah believed that wives impeded the progress of men bent on achievement. He delayed getting married until he was forty-five.

Children with Special Talents

It is, however, the child with a special talent who brings out the most dominating traits in the mother. This mother, then, may disregard other family members in her zeal for the most talented, as did the mother of cellist Pablo Casals.

Another performer who owes his career to his mother is playwright Noel Coward. It was his mother who guided him in his career and who read an advertisement in the *Daily Mirror* asking for the services of a talented boy of twelve for an all-children's play. During his second engagement, Noel and his mother had real problems with a magistrate who passed on the applications of children of school age who wished to work at the theater. The judge was inclined to believe that his parents were trying to profit by the two pounds a week the boy was to earn. Noel's mother dramatically described the emotional breakdown the boy was sure to suffer if he were deprived of the pleasure of acting; she would herself, to avoid that catastrophe, bring the judge four pounds a week if he would let the boy act instead of going to school. The courtroom spectators were amused; the judge hastily dismissed the case and let the boy and his mother have their way.

When he was sent to school during periods when he was not acting, Noel used to be truant and wander about the city "acting." He pretended to be a poor waif with an alcoholic, brutal father. In reality, his father was a kind and gentle man, but even in fun Noel did not tell tales about his mother.

When Payne's Piano Company failed, Noel's father had no employment. His mother then took over a boarding house in London. She cooked meals, rushed up and down the stairs, and dealt sternly with tradesmen. Noel's father made model yachts to sail in Clapham Common pond—beautiful, delicate boats, exquisitely made in every detail. The youngest son, Eric, who was rather sickly, played with his father. Eric was his father's boy; Noel, his mother's.

Had Mrs. Coward been willing to reliably enlist the aid of her husband, she might never have had the near collapse that she suffered as the mistress of the boarding house. When Noel went with his mother for a holiday at the seashore, the much more sociable Mr. Coward then ran the boarding house quite successfully. He had a grand time chatting with the boarders and went "hopping in and out of rooms with breakfast trays." Noel never did marry, though he had a series of male lovers, and he continued to center his life around his mother when he was an adult.

Some mothers planned careers for sons not yet born. Anna, mother of architect Frank Lloyd Wright, believed in prenatal influence. Even before her son was born, Anna decided that he should be an architect. She framed ten full-page wood engravings of old English cathedrals and hung them in the nursery. She never doubted that her child was to be a boy and also an architect.

When the rural schoolteacher Anna Lloyd Jones was twenty-nine, she married a forty-six-year-old itinerant music teacher, William Gary Wright, who visited her community. She knew that he had already given up medicine because it was not a true science and had also quit law because he became disillusioned with its practice. He had turned to the teaching of music and to the Baptist ministry. Since her husband was seventeen years older than she, the dynamic Anna with the long free stride was not able to change his life patterns appreciably—although she tried hard. She did influence him to turn from the Baptist ministry to Unitarianism, which cost him employment. At the time when she told him gently but firmly that he should leave the household, her son was eighteen, she was ill, and they were poverty-stricken. The irritable, unhappy husband had not turned to alcohol in this instance, but to the teachings of Sanskrit and the reading aloud of "The Raven" while pacing the floor of his study. Anna Wright did not actually expect William to leave her, but he went, and for fifteen years, until he died, she always expected him home again.

Louis Bromfield, the Pulitzer Prize-winning novelist, also had his career chosen for him by his mother. Her husband, Charlie Bromfield, was always an easy touch if a friend was broke; his humble farmhouse was always full of indigent or ill relatives. If he earned a little extra cash, some "wild, romantic scheme would siphon it off almost as soon as it had appeared." What he had to give his children was his love of land, for animals, and his endless enjoyment of friendly contact with his fellow man.

Annette Bromfield decided that her first-born son was to be a writer. Shelves were stocked with the classics, and Louis was made to read for a definite number of hours each day while his sister Marie practiced at the piano. Annette had wanted to be a musician when she was young, but there had been no money for lessons. During her married life, she collected responsibilities like a sheep collects burrs. After she married, she had to go back to her old home twice each week to cook and clean for her father, a widower. She also nursed various ailing relatives who came to visit and to die. All of her personal ambitions had to be extended through the lives of her children.

Had Louis Bromfield not loved reading, her domination might have irked him to rebellion as it did her second son, Charles, who became a businessman and a professed nonintellectual. Louis's sister, Marie, died before she could fulfill her talent. Annette Bromfield's drives did not lessen with age. At eighty, she was still determined to dominate her children, and there were stormy scenes when she came to live at Malabar Farm in Ohio with her novelist son, Louis. All of her days, she sought to possess her children by a pathetic pursuit of them.

Dominating Mothers

The tendency to dominate is not racial, national, or cultural. Wealthy mothers and poor mothers apply their will with identical intensity. The child who is talented in musical performance is the most vulnerable, since his talent is evidenced early. Pablo Casals is not the only musician with a dominating mother, although few of them are as determined as the mother of the nineteenth-century composer Anton Bruckner, whose mother stopped on the way home from his father's funeral to enroll him in music school.

The mother of Yehudi Menuhin did not expect to be the mother of musicians, but when her son showed exceptional talent, she isolated him from his contemporaries and included her daughters in the edict, presumably so that all of the children could share their isolation together. She was quick to withdraw her affection if any one of them deviated from her exacting ideas of good behavior. Her daughter Hepzibah says of the way in which they were reared, "It made awful fools of us all when we faced our first life situations."[1]

When Giacomo Puccini's father died, his mother looked among her children for a boy to carry on the family tradition. A Puccini had been the village organist in Lucca for four generations. She needed the older boys to help earn a living for the big family, so six-year-old Giacomo was her arbitrary choice, though he did not want to be an organist. His father had been a kindly man, but the uncle who assumed the unwelcome task of teaching the recalcitrant pupil was abusive and kicked his student in the shins when the young musician made an error. Giacomo Puccini subsequently developed a muscular tic, which made him jerk his leg whenever he heard a wrong note being played.

The dominating qualities of Sara Delano Roosevelt have been documented in numerous volumes written by the family and by the many biographers of her son, Franklin D. Roosevelt. She extended her rule for two generations. Of this grandmother, James Roosevelt says:

> *This* [Hyde Park] *was Granny's home and we all knew it. She laid down the rules, and all of us—even Father and Mother—accepted them. We "chicks" quickly learned that the best way to circumvent "Pa and Mummy" when we wanted something they would not give us was to appeal to Granny.*[2]

When Franklin D. Roosevelt was an adult, he paid no attention to his mother's comments on public affairs, but he was always vulnerable in terms of his personal and family life—because it was Sara Delano Roosevelt who held the purse strings, and she was miserly. James says that his father rarely exploded, but that he seethed under the drip-drip of maternal advice. Franklin never ceased resisting his mother's attempts to tell him what to do, what not to do, how to ensure the regularity of his digestive tract, and how to manage her grandchildren, whom the family agrees she spoiled woefully.

Sara Delano Roosevelt used to say, "My son Franklin is a Delano, not a Roosevelt at all!" She was twenty-six when she married the fifty-two-year-old James Roosevelt, whose son James by a first wife was exactly her own age. Young "Rosy," as he was called, was one of the flamboyant playboys of his age. Sara's step-grandson was already at Groton when she sent her son Franklin to school there.

Sara's father, the adventurous Warren Delano II, had given his daughter acquaintance with financial insecurity and world adventure by the time she was ten. Warren Delano lost his wealth in the crash of 1857, and he sailed for China to recoup his fortunes by engaging in the opium trade, a legitimate enterprise aimed at supplying medical needs. The whole family joined him there; his wife, the servants, and six small children made a 125-day journey halfway around the world on the square-rigged clipper *Surprise*. The sea adventure was so successful that Sara eventually inherited $1,338,000 from the father she admired and whom her only son was to resemble. She was stingy with her money and would never touch the principal, resolved to hand it on intact to her son at her death. She doled out money to him and was slow to pay bills.

Sara's father had objected to the marriage because of the age of the bridegroom, but the imperious Sara had her way. Opinionated James Roosevelt, her elderly husband, in his own youth served for two months with Garibaldi and went on a walking tour through Italy with a mendicant priest. Three times in his business career he gambled for high stakes in money and power, and all three times he lost. He was voted out of control of a company that took heavy losses in the 1873 panic. He failed when he tried unsuccessfully to get control of a railroad in the South. He also helped form a company that attempted to dig a canal across Nicaragua, for which he raised six million dollars, and then had to give up the project when the depression of 1893 dried up his funds.

This husband was not dominated by his wife, by all accounts, but Franklin was not so fortunate. Franklin admired his father, who controlled his mother, who in turn controlled the boy. James Roosevelt taught his son many skills—hunting, fishing, and boating. Until he was fourteen, Franklin studied at home, his education supervised by his mother. The family went to Europe each year after Franklin was three years old, taking with them tutors, with whom Sara often quarreled. Among the governesses was a liberal and discerning Swiss woman, Mlle. Jeanne Sandoz, who taught the boy to be aware of such human factors in history as the plight of the Egyptian workers sacrificed to the Pharaohs, who built the Pyramids. The relationship was a continuing one; Mlle. Sandoz still corresponded with her pupil when he was an adult in public life. She advised and admired him.

From the beginning, Sara Delano Roosevelt was confident that her only child would be a great man. She saved every scrap of paper upon which he wrote school exercises, and she bundled and labeled his baby clothes for the reference of future historians. His indifferent career at Groton and his equally undistinguished career at Harvard did not shake her aplomb as to Franklin's superiorities. There is no record of her feeling a need to lecture him when he failed in Greek or made C's in his major subjects.

In this attitude she was probably justified; as John Gunther says of the boys who were Franklin D. Roosevelt's classmates at Groton:

> *The boys who were the best "Grotties" usually turned out to be nonentities later; the boys who hated Groton did much better.... The boys who became successes were not conformists; hence they were apt to be excluded from the compact group that made the core of each class.*[3]

Gunther quotes international diplomat Sumner Welles to corroborate the observation. When asked if he had had a good time at Groton, Welles once replied, "Oh Lord, no, I was a worm."

Franklin D. Roosevelt went unnoticed at Groton. He was not liked or disliked. He was called "Uncle Frank" because his nephew "Rosy" was in the grade above him. He was not "boxed" (shoved into a locker too small to hold a boy in comfort) or "pumped" (taken to the lavatory and half-drowned by basins of water poured over his head) as were the boys who were really "odd." But he was hazed by being made to stand in a corner and dance while other boys struck at his ankles with hockey sticks.

He debated, and in his last year, he developed an interest in lessening social discrimination against Jews and African-Americans, of whom Groton then admitted none. This represented a rebellion against his mother, who was, according to Phyllis Bottome, not inclined to accept Jews as social equals. But this did not mean that he did not love her deeply or fail to write her frequent letters that began, "My Dearest Mummie." His father died during Franklin's freshman year at Harvard, and Sara Delano Roosevelt moved to Boston to be near her son.

Once a boy among the Four Hundred has known the unshakable faith and admiration of a mother, he needs the continuation of that homage from other women. The younger James Roosevelt says of this trait in his father:

> *Father was a man who enjoyed feminine companionship. He was at his sparkling best as a conversationalist when his audience included a few admiring and attractive ladies; this was an entirely natural circumstance, for Father was a great show-man who enjoyed being the center of attention.*[4]

His wife was not always able to give him the uncritical adulation to which his mother had accustomed him. Eleanor Roosevelt says:

> *He might have been happier with a wife who was completely uncritical. That I was never able to be, and he had to find it in other people. Nevertheless, I think I sometimes acted as a spur, even though the spurring was not always welcome. I was one of those who served his purpose.*[5]

The Roosevelts frequently speak frankly about themselves and each other. James closes his lengthy comments on his grandmother as an authoritative figure by saying:

> *Eventually, Granny lost out when Mother began to grow in other directions—and to build for herself a life larger than the one bounded by "Ma-ma," the "chicks," the sewing circle and social obligations. Mother became a personage in her own right, not to be dominated by anyone, not even by Father.*[6]

The Roles of Wives and Mothers

These Four Hundred complicated individuals sometimes made significant personality changes as adults. It is not possible in this survey to go beyond the childhood period in a discussion of all of the

Four Hundred persons, and it is only with the most eminent that it becomes expedient to note the possible effects of childhood experiences upon adult attitudes, particularly regarding attitudes toward marriage or other close relationships. It is also seldom possible to adequately discuss the contributions that wives or other adults have on the development of the eminent men, although Lewis Terman found that the gifted young men in his group were more likely to succeed when they married women who were themselves interested in learning.

Had it not been for the role played by Eleanor Roosevelt after her husband's polio attack, he probably would not have tried to continue his career. Other women who played definite roles in their husband's careers include the wives of artist Salvador Dalí and musicians Edward Elgar and Antonín Dvorák. These women are mentioned to recognize the influence—positive or negative—that others have on the ability of the intelligent, sophisticated adult if he is to continue to mature past his childhood. In today's world, it is likely that the same could be said of husbands who are supportive of eminent wives.

In 1898, General Arthur MacArthur was ordered to the Philippines. His wife went to Milwaukee instead, took an apartment there, and hired a tutor to coach her young son Douglas for the West Point examinations. A doctor was set to work to treat a slight curvature of the boy's spine, which might conceivably have stood in the way of his proposed Army career.

In June of that same year, Douglas passed his tests with the highest score ever received by an applicant, a score of 99. His nearest competitor scored 77.9. His mother had been his only teacher until he was thirteen. A goal desired by both parents had been achieved.

Until she died at the age of eighty-two, Mary MacArthur lived for her gifted son. Like Sara Roosevelt, she outlived her husband by many years, and like Sara Roosevelt, she stayed on to be near her son while he was at school.

A classmate reported that young MacArthur was "arrogant from the age of eight." Fellow plebes at West Point were not inclined to be gentle with the young man whose mother lived so close and so obviously regarded her son as a child of destiny. The upperclassmen made young Douglas do knee bend squats until he passed out.

The cadets at West Point had only a brief period during the day when they could be completely free, the half hour between dinner and the call to quarters. When the weather was fine, mother and son strolled along Flirtation Walk. If he ever walked with a girl there, the incident is not recorded. On stormy days, he talked with his mother at the hotel, told her of his day's adventures, and received contraband fruit as a gift. He sometimes overstayed his limits and on one occasion had to be sneaked out through the coal chute when the Commandant of Cadets came to call on his mother.

In 1935, when President Roosevelt asked General Douglas MacArthur to go out to the Philippines to build up the native defenses, the General debated as to whether or not he should go, because his mother did not seem well enough to make the trip with him. Knowing that he wanted to go, she accompanied him despite her dislike of the sea and a progressing cerebral thrombosis. By the time they reached Manila, she was very ill, and she died before medicines flown out to her could be of any use. General Douglas MacArthur, in his middle years, married a young woman whom his mother met on shipboard, recognized as the perfect wife for her son, and introduced to him.

A mother who used her beauty, her ill health, and her femininity to dominate was Isabel Mackenzie King, whose son later became Prime Minister of Canada. As a child, she suffered hardships and humiliations as the daughter of the exiled rebel William Lyon Mackenzie.

Isabel King decided early in the life of her most promising child that he should reestablish the family's fame and fortune. Her husband, a gentle and scholarly man, was not capable in the sense that her son, Mackenzie King, was recognized to be by all of the family. It was she who kept the family accounts, made decisions, and used her feminine wiles to direct the destiny of her son.

Isabel was a vivacious and lovely woman who romped with her four children during their early years as a companion rather than a parent. All of the children deferred to her. When there was not enough money for new dresses for all of the women in the family, the mother had the new dress; the daughters did without.

Away at school, Mackenzie King kept five photographs of his mother in his room and read Barrie's *Margaret Ogilvie* aloud with his mother's picture in his hand. The whole family was patient with the episodes of nervous indigestion that followed her top-speed activities. Her husband joined in the adulation and wrote to his son describing Isabel as being pretty as a picture in her new dress and lovely little bonnet.

When Mackenzie was doing his work toward his degree in Chicago and fell in love with a nurse, his mother pled her age and grief and begged him not to marry—at least until she was dead—and if he must marry, please, not to a nurse—a woman beneath his station in life. He wrote twenty-one thousand words of apology to her for his unfortunate romance and never married. In his old age, he turned to spiritualism to keep in touch with his dead mother and also with other persons from whom he solicited advice, including the deceased Franklin D. Roosevelt. In his isolated study stood a huge oil portrait of his mother. He lived aloof from society in his latter years.

A mother-dominated girl was delightful little Maude Kiskaddin of Salt Lake City, who became better known as the actress Maude Adams. James Kiskaddin was not happy when his wife and daughter left home to become actresses, but there was not much he could do about their activities except to ask that the daughter not use the family name. He worked in a bank in Virginia City and eked out his small salary traveling with mule trains between Denver and Pueblo. James was non-Mormon, but his wife, Annie, was a Mormon who had been reared in Brigham Young's household. Had their first children, twin boys, not died, the family might not have scattered.

At age four, little Maudie was singing "Somebody's Coming When the Dewdrops Fall" to San Francisco audiences. She played the mining camps with her mother's troupe, was Little Eva in *Uncle Tom's Cabin*, Little Paul in *The Octoroon*, and Alice Redding in *Kit, the Arkansas Traveler.*

Periodically, mother and daughter returned to James Kiskaddin, who welcomed them. James was a dashing horseman; he was lovable, lighthearted, and never let work get in the way of a good time. He stormed a bit when his wife and daughter made a wild goose chase trip to New York, only to be stranded when the star of their show ran off with the box-office receipts. He died when his daughter was twelve. The schoolteachers begged Maude's mother to let their favorite student stay in school, and they advised that she be trained as an elocution teacher; however, both mother and daughter preferred the stage. In her old age, Maudie's mother was very smug about her spinster daughter's lifelong indifference to men. It was a mother-dominated girl from Salt Lake City and a mother-smothered boy from Kirriemuir, Scotland named James Barrie who delighted a generation of theatergoers with *Peter Pan*, a play about the little boy who never grew up. Neither did the author or the star.

Literary critic Ludwig Lewisohn speaks of the "unrelenting mother dominance" in the life of Theodor Herzl, Zionist leader whose family was self-sufficient and "lived in a state of hot and brooding intensity." Jacob Herzl, the father, a clothier in Budapest, had his financial ups and downs, lost one fortune, then gained another. When the daughter, Pauline, died in late adolescence, it was the one remaining child, Theodor, who was left to compensate and to reward his mother, Jeannette Diamant Herzl. According to Dr. Alex Bein, it was his shattering relationship with his mother that ruined Theodor's marriage.

Dominating Fathers

The father who is dominating is not often concerned with the talents of his son or daughter. He is more concerned with his own potential than with his children's, and he struggles to maintain his position as head of the family or to assure his own comfort and well-being. His goals are more immediate than are the mother's long-term dreams of fulfillment through her children and grandchildren. He frequently wants his son to be like him, but not necessarily better than he. He is too proud to live only for his son's or daughter's success.

Quick-tempered, impatient parents are not necessarily dominating, and they do not always interfere with a child's choice of career, or censor his ideas or choice of friends. Of his father, who was loving and permissive where major matters were concerned, Jawaharlal Nehru says in his autobiography, "His temper was indeed an awful thing, and even in after years I do not think I ever came across anything to match it."

Sir William Eden, father of the English statesman Anthony Eden, First Earl of Avon, was an overwhelming—and overwhelmed—man. He could be overcome by the sight of red flowers in a garden, the yelping of a dog, or the smell of whiskey or tobacco. His son describes him as being in a state of perpetual internal combustion. Sir William had a sharp and critical tongue, and his son learned early to avoid his father and to believe that any show of strong emotion was undesirable. The father made life somewhat easier for his family by leaving home during the children's school holidays to seek a spot where he could enjoy doing delicate water-color landscapes without distraction.

Sir William was not discriminating in his emotional outbursts, and he included children, servants, and friends in his storms of temper. Only his wife, Lady Sybil, a woman whose rare beauty had attracted him, seems to have been exempt from his rages. Randolph Churchill says of Lady Sybil, "His [Anthony Eden's] mother, like many great beauties, was a spoiled woman." He says it is a family belief that Anthony's resentment over his mother's indifference motivated him to try to succeed. Anthony seems to have been more rejected than dominated. His reaction was to withdraw. At Oxford, even his tutor was not close to him.

In his autobiography, J. Middleton Murry, the English critic, said of his dominating father, "My manifest purpose in life was to be what he wanted me to be. The idea that a small human being might have needs of its own would have been confusing to his simple soul: therefore it gained no lodgment in it." John Murry, J. Middleton's father, worked from eight in the morning until twelve at night and saw no reason why his son should not study at his lessons with the same persistence. It was the only way for the boy to escape from the squalor and futility of the poor working-class families from which his father and mother came. John Murry had taught himself all he knew; he was a clerk at a hotel by day and a cashier in a Penny Bank at night. His wife kept lodgers. She was ten years younger than her driving husband and was at times also rebellious. A warm, gay young girl, she once admitted to her son that she daydreamed of running away to join a gypsy caravan.

J. Middleton Murry read well at two, and at two and a half could do his tables to 12 x 12. At seven, he did quadratic equations, and he was a prodigy at remembering dates. The family had Sundays together, and on Sunday afternoons, J. Middleton was set to doing interminable sums with his father. If any were wrong, it was a calamity since it upset John—and the whole household was perpetually mobilized to keep the father from being upset. J. Middleton was subject to recurring nightmares, which he tried to evade by ritualistically taking a knotted towel to bed with him. In the nightmare, there were great circles of light that bore down on him, circles swifter than light, which narrowed and grew intense as they came.

The father of Konrad Adenauer, Chancellor of the Federal Republic of Germany, gave up an army career to marry a pretty little woman who sang all day at her work; he never fulfilled his own ambitions and was a minor civil servant. He taught his children to read before they attended school, and he once raged when one of his sons stopped his homework to run after the firemen who passed the house en route to a fire. Konrad became a "lone wolf" at school, was perpetually engrossed in his studies, and kept much to himself.

"You made me lose all possible self-confidence and exchange a boundless guilt for it," stated Franz Kafka, son of a wealthy merchant of Prague whom the writer detested as much as he loved his exotic, eccentric mother. Two brothers, who were born after Franz, died, and there were three much younger sisters. Kafka's complaints are bitter but nonspecific, and we have no family accounts to give the father's point of view.

Lieutenant Colonel H. H. Kitchener, father of Horatio Herbert Kitchener, who became eminent as a military leader, did not believe in blankets, although the family lived in a dark, damp house in a famine-stricken corner of Ireland where he was an administrator. The Lieutenant Colonel taught his children that they, the English, were of a master race and must not accept the Irish children about them as equals. His wife, a delicate, sickly woman twenty years younger than he, objected to being covered by newspapers sewn together, so he tacked them to a frame set about the bed to keep out drafts. She tried, while she lived, to protect her delicate, withdrawn son. When she died, Lieutenant Colonel Kitchener married music teacher Emma Green, but she did not stay married long to the eccentric disciplinarian.

Rules for the children were stringent. They lived by a code that required them to punish each other sadistically for minor infractions of an unintentional sort. No real naughtiness was permitted. Herbert, the son, was once found spread-eagled on the lawn—hat on his back in the hot sun, pinned to the ground by his arms and legs, which were roped to croquet hoops. Herbert was a timid, silent boy who never defended himself and once crawled under a bed and hid like a sick animal when he hurt himself badly.

As an adult, according to Brigadier C. R. Ballard, "Kitchener could not unbend. If he cared anything for personal popularity, he certainly never stooped to court it." He discouraged advice, avoided discussion; it was his "driving power which crowned his plans with success." His men did what was considered impossible when he drove them hard enough. He was displeased if a man on his staff married; he was never known to be interested in a woman himself.

H. L. Mencken, (Henry Louis Mencken), a rebel in adolescence and in adulthood, is one of the fifteen boys among the Four Hundred eminent persons who had a strong conflict with his father over his choice of vocation. August Mencken was a hard-headed businessman, the owner with his brother of a thriving tobacco business. He was a pronounced agnostic, a loyal Shriner, an expansive, genial practical joker, a strikebreaker, an opportunist, and a man tolerant of corruption as long as "corruption was harmonious with his self-interest," according to his son's biographer, William Manchester.

In his own view, he was a permissive and devoted father to his two sons and daughter. He played active romping games with his children, set up a photographic darkroom for Henry, took the children on trips, bought them a pony, and devised endless adventures and entertainments for them. He gave them piano lessons, bought Henry a printing press, and sent him to the YMCA for special setting-up exercises to straighten his shoulders—rounded by poring over the books he read so omnivorously. August Mencken rewarded Henry with a hundred-dollar purse when he stayed at the top of his class at the Polytechnic Institute. He hired a tutor to teach the boy good Spanish so he could be of more use in the tobacco business. When August forced the boy to spend two and a half years in the family business, Henry's bitterness toward his father increased. But Henry would not accept the alternative of being sent to Johns Hopkins to be trained as a lawyer.

H. L. Mencken commences his autobiography, *Newspaper Days*, by saying:

> *My father died on Friday, January 15, 1899, and was buried on the ensuing Sunday. On the Monday evening immediately following, having shaved with care and put on my best suit of clothes, I presented myself in the city room of the old Baltimore Morning Herald.*

The animosity that evidences itself in the first words of the autobiography is pathetic, in view of what seems to have been the headstrong father's good intentions. The widowed mother consented to Henry's plans to sell the family business and made no objections to his becoming a journalist.

"There were two parties in my family," Mao Tse-Tung, Chinese Communist leader, told journalist Edgar Snow. "One was my father, the Ruling Power. The Opposition was made up of myself, my mother, my brother, and sometimes even the laborer."[7]

The family lived in a simple cottage, although the father was a successful rice trader. One day when there were guests, thirteen-year-old Mao quarreled violently with his father, cursed him, and left the house. His mother ran after the boy and begged him to come back, while his father followed hard on the boy's heels, shouting and cursing. At the edge of a pond, Mao threatened to jump into the water if his father came one step nearer. After demands and counter-demands, there was a compromise. Young Mao promised to make his father one knee bend if his father would promise not to beat him.

Mao's mother is described as a warm, generous woman whose husband scolded her for giving rice away to the poor. Mao once ran away for three days and wandered in the woods because his father had punished his mother for her generosity. He returned only because he thought his mother might need him. He was a Buddhist when he was young because his mother was Buddhist, and at eight he contemplated burning the temple of Confucius because his father was a follower of Confucius. His mother wanted her son to be a teacher; his father wanted him to keep the family books because the family had lost money using the abacus. Mao could read three times as fast as any other student in his class and was accelerated in all of his subjects.

Those close to him say that they cannot remember a time when Mao was not writing martial poetry. He wrote verses as a boy; he wrote verses all during the Revolution. At conferences, he "doodled" poems, and his followers often picked them up from the floor to save as mementos.

Like seven others who loved mother and hated father, Mao combined a military career or a fascination with violence with an interest in martial poetry. How overprotective his mother was and how much of his father's ire was justifiable are difficult to determine. In his old age, the father mellowed and did not evidence an authoritarian attitude.

There are 109 mothers who can be readily categorized as dominating, but only twenty-one fathers who meet this description. The most common adjectives used to describe these traits in the men and women are: dominating, overwhelming, adamant, strong-willed, and determined. In old age, the mothers become more domineering and the fathers much less so. The fathers "mellow" and often become quite charming and companionable to their adult children, as did the dominating father of Pearl Buck, whose aggressive middle years she describes in *The Fighting Angel.* By the time he was eighty, daughter and father enjoyed each other.

The mothers tend to be right at their gifted children's elbow until the day they die, as was the mother of horticulturist Luther Burbank, a persistently controlling woman. Dominating mothers are more likely to have sons who never marry—or who have marital problems if they do—than are dominating fathers.

Sons rebel at being father-dominated, but are often lifelong victims of mother-domination. Luther Burbanks is a typical example, "Mother was of a very intense nature," says her daughter, "walking with a firm step and speaking with a falling accent." Mrs. Burbank had black hair and sparkling eyes at sixty-four, and she was at her son's elbow until she was ninety-seven, encouraging him in all that he did. Like many other such mothers, Mrs. Burbank was much younger than her husband, who was fifty-four years old when his son was born. She fought bitterly with Luther's first wife and was happy when her son's marriage ended in divorce.

The love for learning and achievement, the physical vigor in the parents, plus the dominating qualities in a parent often pay off in eminence, though not necessarily in personal satisfactions.

Fred L. Strodtbeck, in *Talent and Society,* published in 1958, reports a four-year study of home situations which make for the efficient use of ability and finds that the combination of a father who relinquishes power, either through weakness or as a matter of principle, and a mother who has strong ideas about achievement is favorable to the son's development of talent. If the father is a strong, dominating man who believes he can control his own destiny, the son is frequently convinced that there are forces beyond his control and acts accordingly. He is fearful of leaving home and is overdependent on his father's guidance.

Both mother and son are better able to express their own talents in a family climate in which the father is not overpowering. *Talent and Society* also reports that the mother who has high but realistic expectations for her young children in regard to such matters as being sent to the store alone, taking care of their own personal needs, dressing themselves, and so forth has children whose sense of value is high and who do better at work and at school than do children of mothers who expect less from them. The mother's high expectations and performance are presumably not seen as competition by the son; but the son of the very capable father is often less sure of himself than is his father.

These reactions from a large group of families in ordinary neighborhoods would seem to indicate that the dominating mother, although sometimes overwhelming at close range, plays a positive role in developing talent of her children. If she overplays her role, the child is not the less creative but may have serious problems in his interpersonal relationships, especially in courtship and marriage.

Chapter 5
"Smothering" Mothers

I didn't know until I was fifteen that there was anything in the world except me.

—F. Scott Fitzgerald

Smothering parents demand their children's affection and demonstrate their own love for the child by caresses and sacrifices. Dominating parents are those who concentrate on their children's careers. The smothering mother, as opposed to the dominating mother and her ambitions for her child—usually her son, draws a circle about herself and lets no one inside except her son. He is the center of her universe, and both mother and son act on the premise that the world revolves about the boy. The mother and son see the whole of society as a force to be manipulated to give happiness and honor to the son.

Such a boy tends to become precious. He is frequently frail and sickly, and the mother fears that he will not live to be an adult. She has a profound admiration for him and for everything he does, but unlike the dominating mother, she is not constantly driving him toward a goal of her own choosing. He fulfills her by his very existence, which to her is a daily miracle.

Boys of the lad's own age find it hard to accept his mother's evaluation of him; hence, he finds peer relations difficult as a boy and as a man. He is often, although not always, restricted to easy relationships with pets, with children, and with women of his mother's generation.

If the mother is basically a kindly woman, he, too, is kindly. However, he seldom loses his feeling of being invulnerable, and he finds democratic processes irritating, although he may give lip service to them. A smothering or overpossessive attitude in the mother by no means precludes her son's becoming a creative or capable person, but it seldom increases his chances for personal happiness.

To the degree that the mother is hostile or fearful or feels perpetually abused, the son is likely to be inhumane or fearful. The sons of women who dislike their husbands tend to have few friends and also to have problems in sexual relationships. They sometimes enjoy the excitement of battle, feel invulnerable in the midst of carnage, and are moved by martial music and war poetry. They like the rhythm of marching feet and the waving of flags. Presumably, they are always proving to Mother and to themselves that they can whip the boy down the street who would not play with them.

A need to bolster a dubious masculinity is suggested in a study by Terman and Miles,[1] in which city firemen and policemen unexpectedly rated with the lowest in masculinity among the occupational groups studied. The researchers, believing that an error had been made, sought a second group of policemen and repeated the test. The results were similar, leading them to conclude that these occupations may attract men who need the security of the civil service appointment and the authority of the uniform to strengthen their confidence in themselves as aggressive males. On this same test, engineers, bankers, and lawyers scored highest in masculinity.

A need to prove maleness and a clinging to the mother's world and her sense of values are persistent traits of mother-smothered sons. The smothering mother tries to delay the maturation of her son, and unless he is strongly rebellious, she may make him effeminate. Anatole France says of his own mother, "She would have preferred that I should not grow, so as to be able to press me to her bosom.... Everything that brought me a little independence and a little liberty offended her."

Gabriele D'Annunzio, dictator, poet, and military man, illustrates the pattern of behavior that tends to repeat itself among the mother-smothered boys who dislike their fathers and turn to war or poetry or both. His father, who was mayor of Pescara, was physically repulsive to his son, who described him as a corpulent, full-blooded, fiery-eyed man with a huge neck that bulged over his collar. He was notoriously unfaithful to his wife and is said to have made mistresses of the daughters of his concubines. He avoided his son, left the boy to his doting mother, and did not attempt to discipline him. He was generous with his money, however, and paid for the publication of a book of poems written by the talented adolescent. His wife, no matter what her son did, found no fault with Gabriele either as a child or as an adult. She was the one woman in Gabriele's life whom he ever truly and profoundly loved. Tom Antongini, who was his biographer and male secretary, quotes him as saying:

> *I am yours; I am the blood of your blood. I have remained united to you by a strong tie which still emanates from the center of my being. You go on feeding me.... I still feel myself palpitating in you as when I was about to be born.*

Gabriele was unable to feel sincere affection for women of his own generation. At thirteen, he was as sophisticated sexually as are most men of sixty. The poet's physical relationships with a series of women meant nothing to him emotionally. It was only his mother to whom he expressed devotion in letters and conversations all of his life. D'Annunzio did marry a rich woman who was useful to him in the early days of his career, but he left her soon after their third child was born. He ignored the sons born of the union. Women's tears meant nothing to him. Eleonora Duse, the actress, left the stage and went into retirement when he described her in *Fuoco* as his aged, discarded mistress.

Gabriele had poor relationships with male contemporaries, but he liked animals, and he minutely described the personalities of several of ninety-one pets. So reluctant was Gabriele to admit men of his own generation to his intimacy that he was unable to write if a man were in his room, although a woman sitting at his feet did not bother him. Gabriele called his mistresses "brother" or "sister." This did not reflect affection for his own brothers and sisters, with whom he had unsatisfactory relationships. Pet names given to his mistresses were so indiscriminately allocated that a telegram announcing the imminent arrival of a woman who described herself with one of these diminutives left the sender unidentified and caused confusion in the household. Tom Antongini, his secretary, knew as well, or perhaps better, the identities of the various mistresses; D'Annunzio often became confused in this respect.

Like other mother-smothered boys, he felt invulnerable from threat by other males. World War I gave the famous poet an opportunity for eminence as a warrior. The women of Italy, who had been remunerating his barber for clippings of hair from the almost bald head of the poet, found it exciting when the great lover became a military hero at the age of fifty. "Spilling blood," he wrote, "is just like spilling sperm."[2] He had no personal fear of injury on the battlefield.

> *Life is a dreadful bore without the fever of war.... I fly [a military plane] and I wander about beneath the shrapnel, but I am invulnerable....*
>
> *Life is for me only a game to be put off from one day to the next and delicious in consequence. I frequently fly over the enemy three or four times in twenty-four hours.*[3]

He looked forward with dismay to the day when the conflict might end. "What shall I do? Another war? I'm always ready to fight."

Mother's boys are often sickly, and Gabriele was no exception. His seeming eagerness to risk himself among the shrapnel did not lessen his lifelong hypochondria. Even in battle he was concerned about his baths, his foods, his appearance. He once made himself ill by overdosing on patent medicines. He took them all, even when he did not have the symptoms they professed to cure. He often sent for Doctor Duse, his personal physician, but the doctor injected him with harmless drugs—which had the placebo effect of morphine because that's what D'Annunzio thought he was receiving.

Despite his fears for his health, his principal ailment was the common cold. He hated to have to blow his nose and thought it sad to see the brains of a genius blown away on a handkerchief. The "mother's boy" often regards his body as his mother's and is guilt-stricken if he does not care for it properly.

He kept his house stifling hot, sprayed himself with perfume day and night, and surrounded himself with symbolic objects that represented "black magic" to him and could ward off evil. After his mother's death, his preoccupation with his own survival and doubts as to his invulnerability grew to psychopathic proportions. His neurotic traits did not preclude his literary productivity. He worked hard to the end of his days, and he died with his pen in his hand.

The relationship between eighteen-year-old Adolf Hitler and his mother was so close that family friends felt intrusive in their household, where Klara Hitler lay dying while her only son attended her. "Never," says August Kubizek, author of *The Young Hitler I Knew* and Adolf's constant companion during adolescence, "have I come across this same peculiar spiritual harmony between mother and son."

At the time when Klara Hitler was stricken with breast cancer, her son had just returned from Vienna where he had failed to be admitted either to art school or to architectural school. Adolf said nothing of this disappointment to his boyhood friend. Instead, Kubizek says, he lost himself in the nursing of his mother.

> *His unbounded love for his mother enabled him to carry out this unaccustomed domestic work so efficiently that she could not praise him enough for it. I found him kneeling on the floor,... wearing a blue apron... scrubbing.... The kitchen cupboard had been moved into the living room and in its place was a couch on which Adolph slept so that he could be near her at night as well. The little sister slept in the living room.*

The spiritual harmony between the mother and son was not so complete that Klara did not find an occasion to speak in secret to August Kubizek. She confided in him her fears for Adolf's future and begged August to influence Adolf to learn a trade or to train himself to become a civil servant, as his father would have wished. She also spoke to the young man of her own marriage: "What I had hoped for and dreamed of as a young girl was not fulfilled in marriage, but does such a thing ever happen?"

It is true that her marriage did not have an auspicious beginning. Klara was already pregnant when she became the third wife of her cousin, a surly customs official twenty-three years older than she. She must have been familiar with his marital history when she became his wife. Franzeska, his second wife, a hotel cook who was also young enough to have been his daughter, had already borne him a child when his first wife, who was fourteen years older than he, died without giving birth to any heirs.

Vocationally, Adolf's father Alois Hitler had done well enough. For the illegitimate son of a working-class girl to become a customs officer was a satisfactory adjustment, and he was proud of his status. At work, however, he often antagonized the other men by his dogmatic statement of his liberal views, and he was said to be a touchy man who flared up over trifles. His regular drinking companions found him difficult. At home, he was apt to give his adolescent son a stern whipping when he thought the boy needed punishment. Their quarrels were frequent and bitter.

It was not until he was fifteen that Adolf Hitler found a constant companion in a boy of his own age in Kubizek, the sixteen-year-old son of an upholsterer, whom he met at a concert which each had attended alone. For four years the boys were often together. Both of them were smothered by mothers who had seen their other sons die; both boys were frail, socially isolated, and were attracted to cultural pursuits. August wanted to be a musician, but his mother wanted him near her and his father needed him as an apprentice in his upholstery shop. Both boys had made poor marks in school. Adolf was the talker, August the listener.

August was attracted to the pale Adolf, who was so meticulously dressed, who carried his black ebony cane with a flair, who talked and gesticulated like a volcano in eruption as he strode about the town of Prinz, planning its architectural revision, speculating about the proper use of this and that vacant lot. August appreciated Adolf's interest in his own desire to be a musician, especially when Adolf was able to convince August's father and mother that they should let their son study music seriously.

Adolf had no interest in ordinary recreational pursuits. It was not because of parental pressure that Adolf did not smoke or drink or use tobacco. He had no interest in games or sports but instead talked, drew pictures, and wrote poems.

The mother-smothered boys whose mothers dislike their husbands resent ordinary boys of their own age. Adolf and August were strolling down the Landstrasse when a well-dressed, friendly young fellow recognized Adolf as a former classmate at the school from which Adolf had been withdrawn because of failing marks. The youth took Adolf familiarly by the arm and asked him in the friendliest fashion how he was getting on. Young Hitler exploded in rage, pushed the young man aside and strode off down the street complaining that he had once had to sit in class with such fellows, all of whom were surely going to turn out to be "civil servants." He angrily denigrated the students for laziness and said that school was a place where teachers taught children to be idle, even though he himself had been idle and failed. He examined the school exercise books of his little sister Paula and then led her to her sick mother's bed to make her swear that she would always be a good pupil in school and do her work well.

He also had an unusual reaction to a girl of his own generation. As the boys walked about the city, Adolf orated to August about Stephanie, a charming and proper girl a few years older than he. Stephanie was not especially aware of his distant adoration. She did not know that he wrote poems about her in the little black notebook he always carried in his pocket as other boys carried tools.

When Stephanie did not smile at Adolf as he passed, he contemplated suicide and planned that Stephanie should be made to jump from the bridge into the river with him. He demanded, in seeming seriousness, that August engage her mother in conversation so that he could kidnap Stephanie, but August was not cooperative.

"Our friendship endured because I was a patient listener," says Kubizek. "He too had no other friends besides me." Adolf was jealous of August's attention, scolded if his friend was late to an appointment, once accompanied him to the funeral of August's deceased teacher rather than be left alone; in short, he was extremely possessive.

As a little boy, Adolf had had scant opportunity to form friendships with other children. Although he stayed on the same job, Alois Hitler found it difficult to live in the same house very long. Adolf attended five different elementary schools, in all of which he was lost and unnoticed. His teachers remembered him only as a quiet, good boy, and a passable scholar. His mother did not form attachments to the women in her neighborhood. She was withdrawn from everyone except her son. Although the mothers of August and Adolf both approved of the intimacy of their sons, they themselves did not become close friends. Klara was difficult to know and was not close to her daughter.

On the day of Klara Hitler's funeral, her son was not too lost in grief to watch for a flutter of the curtain as he passed Stephanie's house. To him, a slight movement meant that Stephanie was watching him as he passed and was grieving with him. August was noncommittal but unbelieving as he listened to the wishful thinking of his friend. After the funeral, Adolf was bitter, distracted, and melancholy. He quarreled with his guardian and his brother-in-law, who tried to apprentice him to a trade. Nor would he be a "civil servant." He soon went back to Vienna, alone and without much money, and he terminated his adolescent friendship with August Kubizek abruptly. There were no letters, no return visits. When they met as adults, they differed in their political attitudes.

"If my mother had not died," says António Salazar, dictator of Portugal, "I would not have become even a Minister. She could not have lived without me. I couldn't have worked, knowing she was troubled." His sister Martha, one of two spinster sisters, describes her brother's relationship with his mother:

> *Our mother...was called Mariado Resgate Salazar. She was exceptionally intelligent. I told you she was particularly fond*

> *of our brother. He was always absolutely devoted to her. When he was a student at Coimbra, he did some tutoring on the side so he could afford the trip home to see her each Sunday.*[4]

He was restricted and uneasy with the boys at school. As a student, he could not bring himself to enjoy the easy familiarities of school life. When he was asked to enjoy delicacies sent from home to another boy, he ceremoniously asked the permission of the school authorities before he could enjoy the treat. Even then, he stood in the doorway to eat, not wishing to disobey the school rules about entering another student's room. As an adult, he was said to have enjoyed children and older women, but he was stiff and formal with other adults.

In speeches, he extolled the virtues of family life, but he never married or was known to be attracted by a woman. He lived with his two adopted daughters and a housekeeper. Like Hitler, he nursed his mother through a long illness. He followed her coffin to the grave on feet so swollen he could scarcely stand.

Another boy who adored his mother was the Arab leader Gamal Abdel Nasser, who also hated his father.[5] His father, a postmaster, is described as "stubborn, proud, fatalistic." It was his mother, so curious and romantic and affectionate, whom the boy loved.

As a boy, Nasser was prone to emotional disturbance. At the age of six, he attempted suicide because he wished to escape going to hell. If he died before he was twelve, he reasoned, he would be safe, since he would not have reached the age of accountability. He failed at school and was in one elementary grade three years. When he was sent away to live with a bachelor uncle, his homesick letters to his mother brought no response. He returned after a year's absence and found that she had long since been buried. He refused to accept a stepmother and was very unhappy with his uncle, who lived in a Jewish section of the city. Gamal Abdel was the only Arab boy in the neighborhood. A foster son of his uncle's accepted some Jewish neighbors very well, but the younger boy refused to make friends and also continued to dislike his father. In secondary school, he became a fearless leader of a group of students who were in rebellion against English domination. It was poetry and drama that appealed to him at the school, where teachers gave him grades in order to appease the rebel, who was known to have a strong following among other students.

George Seldes says of Benito Mussolini in *Sawdust Caesar*: "He was whipped and bullied by his father, pampered and kissed too much by his mother.... He never loved deeply, never had a true friend."

At sixteen, Mussolini contracted a venereal disease; at eighteen, he stabbed his mistress in the thigh. At the same time, he was afraid to walk in the dark alone. He loved poetry about the days of chivalry, and at seventeen, he recited martial poems while standing alone on a hilltop.

When a woman loses other children, remaining children must often bear the brunt of a mother's overpossessiveness. Soon after three sisters died of scarlet fever, poet Vachel Lindsay's mother nursed him through an illness which was nearly fatal. She carried him about on a pillow for more than a year and "breathed life into him." During Vachel's childhood, he was kept apart from other children who might be rowdy or dirty. His curls were uncut, he wore immaculate white pique suits, and he played with two sisters who had also survived their childhood illnesses. His mother wrote a children's play in which Vachel was cast in the role of Cupid.

As a twenty-year-old college student, Vachel complained of being treated as if he were a "premature, brilliant, inspired baby" by his mother, who responded by reminding him of the time in his infancy during which she had willed him to live.

Vachel disliked his physician father, whom he described as a man with a queer, baffling savage streak, a man with restless energy who would rather kick open a barn door than push it. The poet depicted his father as an unconquered Ishmaelite who took diabolical delight in driving at three o'clock in the morning at top speed down a muddy road in pelting rain, whipping his frantic horse straight into the thunder and lightning.

Despite the husband's virility, it was the wife who ruled in this household. She dominated her circle of acquaintances, threw herself into church and public affairs with ardor, and organized and taught a class in the principles and achievements of Christian civilization. She was a mystic, given to moments of insight and to hearing voices. She had room in her life for other concerns than her only son. He was desolate when she died, however, and found nothing worthwhile without her to report to. Three years after she died, when Vachel was forty-six, he married a young woman of twenty-three. In a paranoiac episode shortly before he poisoned himself with cleaning fluid, he talked himself into a fury, recalling the days when the other boys at school would not play with him. He also accused his wife of having taken his most precious possession—his virginity. He adopted his mother's sympathy for mankind, but his relationships with the men and women of his own generation were difficult and painful.

When Oscar Wilde was convicted of homosexuality and was separated from his wife and two sons, his wife used to say to them, "Try not to feel harshly about your father. All his troubles arose from the hatred of a son for his father." It was true that Oscar Wilde hated his father, the physician Sir William Wilde, who was publicly pilloried in a sensational trial for his unfaithfulness to his wife. He also had a smothering mother who grieved deeply when her daughter Isola Francesca died at the age of ten. Since the time of her birth, Isola Francesca had been the pivot around which the family's affection revolved. Jane Franceses Wilde, the mother, then turned to her fat little boy and tried to substitute him for his sister, even dressing him in girl's clothing.

As a girl, Jane had embraced the cause of Irish freedom and written inflammatory articles under the name of "Speranza." When Gavan Duffy was tried for sedition, she rose dramatically in court and took the blame for a seditious action ascribed to the prisoner. She became a tragedy queen in her old age and lived in semidarkness, a terrifying, severe woman. When she died, her son Oscar was in Reading Gaol, an English prison about which he wrote his famous poem of the same name.

David M. Levy,[6] in a study of maternal overprotection, found that husbands of these overwhelming mothers were often passive or were unable to intervene in the relationships that developed between mother and child. Such fathers are frequent in the homes of the mother-smothered among the Four Hundred.

A pint of champagne and a mutton chop was the unheeded prescription made by a prominent doctor on behalf of his small son, Duff Cooper. The boy was chronically delicate and debilitated, had no pleasure in the outdoors, sat by the fire, read poetry, and looked at picture books. He memorized much of Macaulay's *Lays of Ancient Rome,* and he recited Poe's *The Raven* and whole sections of Aytoun's *Lays of the Scottish Cavaliers.* At school, he began to lose his fragility, but not his aloofness.

When Duff was called home from Eton because his father was dying, he was not moved by his parent's illness. Although he had never been spoken to crossly by the physician, he never felt close to him. Yet his father had not neglected him; each week, Duff had received from Dr. Cooper a letter that described the week's events and gave the family news. It was, however, impossible for Duff to speak to his father about his deepest thoughts. When Duff had a poem published in the *Saturday Review,* his father looked into *Whitaker's Almanac* to discover the salary of a poet laureate and said dryly, "The appointment's not worth the having."[7]

Duff's mother was a solitary woman who had few friends and did not care to make more. It was she whom Duff adored. She ran away from her first husband because she wanted to be with a man she really loved. When her second husband died, she married Duff's father, who had loved her in vain since she was a young girl. Her family always thought the doctor their social inferior.

Duff enjoyed debating but found no foeman worthy of his steel, and Eton did not permit debate on controversial subjects such as religion or politics. He had few close friends and was eager to be done with Eton because he felt he had outgrown the society of boys.

Had his father lived, Duff Cooper might have become a poet in rebellion. Instead, he went from Oxford to the foreign office, to the Brigade of Guards, to the War Office, and on to the Admiralty.

In the Rilke family, the father was unable to communicate with his son. Sophia Rilke, the mother of the poet Rainer Maria Rilke, was a foolish, emotional woman, full of whims and flights of fancy. In her eyes, Rainer replaced a sister who had died before he was born. His mother pretended that he was a girl, let his hair grow long, kept him in girl's house frocks, taught him to dust and clean, and called him "Sophie." His playmates were charming little girls with whom he shared his dolls and for whom he left nosegays under garden seats. He lived in an emotional climate of piety; his mother prayed, he said, as other people took a cup of coffee.

Both parents were fearful lest the delicate boy catch cold, and they coddled him through innumerable illnesses. The father, Josef Rilke, was a soldier who never won the preferment he desired. Even so, he considered leaving Prague and taking a less desirable post so that his son could have a better climate. But Rainer's parents were not congenial, and they separated. Josef could never accept his effeminate son as a poet. Since the family had a military tradition, he insisted that Rainer be sent to military school to be away from the influence of his mother. So at age eleven, the boy was taken from his mother and put in uniform; his hair was cut short. There were five hundred boys—fifty to a dormitory—at the Military College at St. Polten. Brutality was the order of the day. Rilke was teased and beaten. He found no place to be alone except the school infirmary, where he spent a substantial portion of his five years of schooling at the college.

Another father who failed to make his son an out-of-doors boy was an eccentric French count. On the flyleaf of a book on falconry, Count Toulouse-Lautrec wrote to his son:

> *Remember that an outdoor life under the light of the sun is the only healthy life. Everything deprived of freedom deteriorates and dies quickly. This little book will help you to enjoy the open-air life. If, later on, you happen to taste life's bitterness, you will find faithful companions in dogs, falcons and above all in horses who will help you to forget a little.*[8]

The Count's marriage, which produced the painter Henri-Marie Raymond de Toulouse-Lautrec, was not a love match and never became so. It was arranged for two cousins to marry so that the family fortune could be preserved. Their second child, a beautiful, normal, healthy boy, died suddenly and mysteriously when he was a year old. Their older child was frail, thick-lipped, exceedingly homely, and small. His mother, a dogged, unimaginative woman, set herself to protecting the unfortunate first son from unpleasant experiences and physical danger. He was frequently ill. The only two reasonably healthy years he enjoyed were years when he was away at school. Although he was undersized and homely, he had good friends there, and at home he enjoyed his father's company and that of dogs and horses and ponies.

Two falls which broke his fragile legs also checked his growth and made his appearance even more grotesque. Children on the street thought him a circus freak and ran after him in ghoulish excitement. His mother moved closer and closer to the boy, but she made no protest when he enjoyed himself at bars and brothels.

His father had long since escaped into the world of his own eccentricities. He often wore a fancy vest and hose and carried a falcon or rode a white mare, milked her, and drank the milk while strollers in the park watched in snickering fascination. The unconventional Count once lived in a tent on the Cathedral grounds and once shut himself in a tower of his own estate, hoisting his food to his quarters by means of a pulley.

Henri's mother was with him when alcohol and syphilis, given him by attractive Rosa la Rouge, combined to ruin the health of the talented painter. His mind was affected. He saw microbes everywhere. He flooded the floor of his bedroom with kerosene to destroy insects that were never there while his distracted mother feared that he would burn himself alive. He died at the age of thirty-seven.

Count Toulouse-Lautrec had wanted his son to enjoy horses and falcons and dogs, but Thomas Church, an English mail-sorter, held out for the benefits of bicycling. In two autobiographies, *The Golden Sovereign* and *Over the Bridge*, Richard Church, poet, novelist, and literary critic, chronicles the life of a mother-smothered boy with sensitivity and a literary finesse that make the two volumes valuable to the clinician who is interested in this area of relationship between mother and son.

Richard's parents were simple people; his mother was a schoolteacher and his father a postman. Richard's relationship with his musically gifted brother Jack was excellent. He never heard his parents quarrel until the day when the father, who believed in the therapeutic effects of fresh air and exercise, led the family on an exhausting bicycle excursion. Through two autobiographical volumes, Richard Church cannot forgive his father for an interest in bicycles and cars.

Young Richard's universe was centered on his mother's fragrant person. As she took off her garments, her apron, her handkerchief, he would touch them with rapture. The farther he was removed from his mother physically, the darker were his days and nights. His vitality lessened, his confidence in the strength of his own flesh and blood ebbed.

When he was nine, Richard was hospitalized as a result of an undiagnosed, debilitating illness. He was sent to the Yarrow Convalescent Home at Broadstairs and stayed there for six months. His stomach was distended, his limbs thin. When the wind was in the north, his limbs felt numb, his belly full of lead, his vision askew. He was a slave to rhythm; moving objects hypnotized him. Every sound, every color overstimulated the boy, who fainted with excitement when he first glimpsed the evening sky through glasses which corrected his extreme myopia.

Richard had never been able to separate his identity from that of his mother. He was very homesick at the hospital for a few days but soon relaxed in the warm, comfortable, friendly place. He was left to his own devices and, while the others went off to town or to the beach, he spent hours just lying on the couch by the open window surrounded by his favorite dog-eared books. He was now able to think of his mother as someone apart from himself, to feel all around her personality, to observe her with detachment, with the humor and sympathy he used when he looked at his brother or his father.

Richard's father completely failed to enter into the charmed mother-son circle. This circle was not broken until his mother's death from bronchial asthma, a sickness through which her adolescent son, Richard, nursed her devotedly.

"All of his life Syngman Rhee [President of South Korea] has been more influenced by women than by men," says his biographer, Robert T. Oliver.[9] His mother, Kim-Hai Kimsio Rhee, was his closest companion during childhood. A period of blindness caused by the aftermath of smallpox made the child, born to the mother in her fortieth year, even closer to his doting, worshiping mother. A previous son, who had been "sickly" since birth, died soon after Syngman was born. He was her first healthy son. His elderly father, absorbed in a study of genealogy, in which his son was uninterested, was inclined to leave the boy to his mother's care and supervision.

Widows Are Often Overpossessive

One-third of the fifty widows in the homes that produced eminence can clearly be called smothering. The least likely to be overprotective are the widows who are left in straitened circumstances. Politicians Aneurin Bevan, Ernest Bevin, George W. Norris, and Al Smith, physician Abraham Flexner, and singer Marian Anderson—all were children of such women. They experienced no coddling, maternal anxiety for their survival, or restrictions of normal behavior. There is apparently a considerable advantage in being the child of a poor but respectable widow. On the other hand, children of well-to-do widows are sometimes subject to an all-encompassing maternal concern.

Although Friedrich Nietzsche was the son of a deceased minister, there was enough money in the family to free his mother and grandmother and two maiden aunts to spend their full time overprotecting, caressing, and overruling the docile boy, who was a model of propriety until he was eighteen and began drinking. His sister also shared in the adulation of the gifted boy. It was they who invented the imaginary world of the Kingdom of King Squirrel in which miniature toys played a part.[10]

Professor Paul Gide, who died when his only son was eleven, was a well-to-do lawyer who made a practice of never accepting a client of whose innocence he was not convinced. Young André, who became a Nobel Prize-winning author, was not only mother-smothered, he was women-smothered. The three excessively proper women who brought him up hovered over him, and they were shocked if he betrayed himself by any expression of boyish spirits. The wealthy, precious boy was moved about from place to place, to the Riviera, to Montpellier. If he trampled on a playmate's sand castle or was obstinately aggressive or bit a girl playmate's bare shoulder, he was speedily removed from temptation by a change of scene. Occasional male tutors taught him little except the intimate details of their personal lives—which André found both edifying and stimulating.

One poor widow who centered her life about her son was the mother of Joseph Stalin, the fourth child of Ekaterina and Vissarion Djugashvili, who lived in Gori, a little Georgian village in Russia. Ekaterina was only fifteen when she married. Her first three children died soon after they were born. The fourth, a wiry, strong-willed boy they called "Soso," almost died of smallpox. He suffered an infection which left his arm twisted. His toes were webbed. He attended the ecclesiastical school at Gori because his mother wanted her boy to succeed, although his father had failed. Vissarion Djugashvili closed his shop when it did not pay, but he became irritable when he went to work in the Anelkhanov shoe factory.

His father died when "Soso" was eleven, and Ekaterina immediately made plans to have the boy trained for the priesthood. At fifteen he entered the theological seminary of Tiflis. There are two versions of his leaving school before graduation. His mother says she withdrew him because he was sickly from overwork and she feared he might come down with tuberculosis.[11] His official biographers say that he was reading revolutionary literature.

An English widow's son, Arthur Balfour, who was later a conservative Prime Minister of England, was fortunate in his mother's choice of a preparatory school. The Rev. C. J. Chittenden, housemaster at a school in Hoddesdon in Hertfordshire, discovered that the only way to teach him the subjects necessary for Eton was to help him constantly to see the general principle in everything and not try to get him to remember isolated facts beyond what was absolutely necessary. Arthur's biographer, Blanche Dugdale, quotes from a reminiscence written by the Rev. C. J. Chittenden: "He had an uncommon power for a boy, of taking in the purport of a number of connected facts and seeing quickly any apparent inconsistency between them."[12]

Teaching eleven-year-old Arthur Balfour was difficult because of his lack of vital energy. The school doctor advised that the boy lie down in the afternoon when he felt tired and try to sleep. He enjoyed this activity if someone played the piano softly in the hall below. He walked with his headmaster while the other boys played at cricket, and he conversed with the intellectual ability of a boy of at least eighteen.

Arthur's father, James Maitland Balfour, had died of tuberculosis when Arthur, his oldest son, was seven. Arthur could never remember his father well, and he had only a vague notion of the man's personality.

Lady Blanche Balfour was a woman with a very powerful personality. When her husband died, she forsook society and concentrated her dominating personality and powerful mind upon her children. In the days of Arthur's grandfather, the drawing room was hung with yellow damask and filled with French furniture and Sevres china, and the house was filled with guests. When Lady Balfour became a widow, the dust covers were never removed from the furniture; the nurseries and the schoolroom became the heart of the house. A friend of Lady Balfour wrote of her in the early days of her husband's illness: "To know her slightly—you would never suspect the intense funds of feeling, dashing and flashing and bursting and melting and tearing her at times to pieces."

At Oxford, Arthur collected china, spent hours resting in his rooms, and was called "Pretty Fanny" by his classmates. In later years, Winston Churchill described him as an implacable politician who was fearless in the internal battles of politics and who looked blandly through his pince-nez at battlefield carnage when he was taken on a tour during World War I.

Churchill says in *Great Contemporaries* that there was no way of getting at Balfour. When he was threatened physically by an irate fellow politician in Parliament, he looked upon the disturbed man as if upon the contortions of a rare and provoked insect. Churchill believed that had Balfour lived during the French Revolution, he could have consigned an erring colleague to the guillotine with complacency, but in a thoroughly polite and completely impersonal manner.

This bachelor first Earl of Balfour lived in an aura of nieces. His political friends found it hard to break through the closed feminine family circle in order to communicate with him.

A minister's widow in Newark, New Jersey, novelist Stephen Crane's mother was a woman of strong principles. When a young girl in the community was bearing a baby out of wedlock, it was Mrs. Crane who took the girl into her home, housed and defended her. Soon after his mother's death, Stephen published his first book at twenty-one and titled it *Maggie, Girl of the Streets* after his experiences. He married a woman ten years older than he who was the proprietor of a hotel of dubious reputation. He turned to poetry, to the excitement of being a war correspondent, and to a prose outpouring, such as in *The Red Badge of Courage*, concerning the fascination of the horror and fear of spilling blood. Crane annoyed his friend Joseph Conrad by making the assumption that he knew better than Conrad about the language and desires of the Conrad children. Stephen Crane was an affectionate and devoted uncle, but he could never relate warmly to his male peers, though with older women, children, and dogs he was quite comfortable. In a perverse way, he was always his mother's boy and moved in her generation rather than his own, even when he defied her and her smothering, dominating ways in personal habits. For his father, he had contempt but never hatred.

Crane's mother was the daughter, widow, and sister of clergymen. "You might as well argue with a wave as mother,"[13] said Stephen. Her voice was deep and strong, and Stephen said that she spoke slowly as the clock ticks. She wrote articles for Methodist papers and church news for the *New York Tribune* and the *Philadelphia Press.* "It isn't that I dislike books," Stephen protested when she spoke with him about his grades. "It is the cut and dried curriculum which does not appeal to me."

Mrs. Crane tried to rear her youngest son properly. Since she had lost five babies before he was born and he was so delicate and frail, Stephen was not sent to school until he was eight. When he learned to read, she took his paperback Westerns away from him, but she let him pore over Harper's picture history of the *War of the Rebellion.* He occupied himself for hours playing at the strategy of war with buttons from her mending box. War was his favorite game. He almost smothered a playmate by covering him completely with sand while playing at burying dead soldiers. He was spanked soundly by the child's aunt for this misdemeanor.

Stephen liked the Methodist military school he attended and made good marks there except in algebra. It was at the Hudson River Institute that he lost a tooth in a fight because he called Tennyson's writings "swill." He was at his best conducting battalion drill, leading his company in a blue silk sash, shouting "Ho, Hell!" He was an excellent baseball player and was "giftedly profane." However, he had no real intimacy with other boys and had a certain coldness and a distinct lack of respect for human beings in the mass. No teacher ever liked him.

His father was a gentle minister who wrote little tracts mildly reproving intemperance, card playing, and theater going. He loved animals and never drove his horses over two miles an hour even if a member of his congregation was dying. He turned Methodist when he could no longer abide the Presbyterian doctrine of predestination. Stephen, his fourteenth child, was eight when his father died.

Smothering Fathers

Among the Four Hundred families, there are eight fathers who might be designated as smothering, as seeking to withdraw the child unnecessarily from the mainstream of life, as being overly anxious about the child's health or diet, or as commanding an inappropriate share of the child's affection.

Whole families may be smothering also. It is the youngest child, particularly the youngest girl, who is most vulnerable to inappropriate overprotectiveness. If she is tiny and precocious, delicate and beautiful, and if she is much younger than her siblings, the whole family sometimes develops an overprotective attitude during her "baby-girl" years. The older Crane children had displayed some of this feeling toward Stephen, although it was his older brothers who insisted that his curls be cut.

In other families, there is more "family smothering" of the youngest. Clara Barton was family-smothered, but especially by her father. He could not forget the days when he was an Indian fighter with Mad Anthony Wayne, and he taught her to plot battles and to understand military strategy. She would have liked more than anything else to be a boy and to go to war, but her father explained that she was living in days of peace and that war would never come again. He held her on his knee for hours, delighting in her responsiveness.

Clara had her schooling at home with her five teachers—her father, two brothers, and two sisters. Both sisters and her oldest brother were employed as teachers in the community. Dorothy Barton taught Clara to read when the child was three, and Sally Barton taught her geography and spelling. From the age of six, Clara wrote reams of doggerel. Stephen Barton taught her arithmetic and how to drive nails. The quick-tempered mother taught Clara household skills.

At age eight, Clara was sent away to boarding school where the curriculum was on a secondary level. The principal, Richard Stone, an old friend of the family, tried to help the child adjust to the older children in his classes, but they laughed at the eight-year-old girl who cried when she missed an answer but who knew more than most of them would ever know. A conference with the parents, doctor, and school authorities resulted in Clara's being sent home to her parents' farm.

From her eighth to her eleventh year, Clara Barton had her "time-out" period. Very little was expected of her since she was already far advanced and no school could be found to meet her academic needs. She moved with her parents to the farm of a widowed relative who needed help, and for the first time she had young playmates, five of them, who ranged in age from three to thirteen. She became physically active, rode logs down the river, and helped wallpaper the house. There was no repetition of the kind of hysteria she had displayed at four when she believed that thunderclouds were angry rams descending to harm her. She remained, however, a father's girl. Her principal pride during this period was her muscular development, which she believed was more masculine than feminine.

An older brother and sister found their interests in their own homes and spouses, but Dorothy, the spinster schoolteacher, became an invalid. Their mother, always quick-tempered, had little time for Clara. David suffered a fall during a housewarming, and from the ages of eleven to thirteen, Clara, the tiny girl who grew up so quickly in some respects, assumed adult responsibilities. She nursed David assiduously for two years, applied leeches frequently, and made him completely dependent upon her. She responded to his neurotic weakness and permitted him to make selfish demands upon her. It was a doctor who broke up this relationship, got the boy out of the house and up on his feet, and dismissed the small nurse, who had not grown physically during the period and who had become extremely shy and introverted.

In early adolescence, Clara decided never to have a romance but concluded that animals could be loved without reservation or shyness. There was Buttons, her dog. Later there was her Arabian horse, Baba, and her Maltese cat, Tommy. She wrote of army mules as if they were human beings and of the Czars' black horses as if they were kings. Like D'Annunzio, she was sentimental about animals and about war. Dawn on the battlefield could set her to writing poetry. The little woman, never more than sixty inches tall, had an indomitable, unquenchable drive. This father's girl had many of the neurotic qualities of the mother's boys, and her life became complicated by emotional disturbances.

Clara Barton first lost her voice in 1854 when she was denied the superintendency of a free public school whose enrollment she had built up from four pupils to six hundred. The school board chose a man to replace her in authority, and she was literally speechless with rage. She had constant conflicts with her contemporaries, both male and female, and her many later nervous collapses were heralded by a lack of speech.

In 1875, she was treated in a sanatorium in Dansville, New York. By 1878, she was much improved and set out to persuade the American government to mitigate the cruelties of war by signing the Geneva Treaty and joining the International Red Cross. In 1881, she succeeded in this goal, but she continued to have conflicts with various persons, including President Theodore Roosevelt. Susan B. Anthony and Carrie Chapman Catt defended her and probably kept her from a second breakdown. At one time, she had her trunks packed, ready to go to Mexico or China—anyplace where there was no Red Cross.

She maintained her energy in her old age, studied Esperanto at eighty-eight, and learned to use the typewriter at ninety. Like some of the mother's boys—Mackenzie King, Harry Houdini, Conan Doyle, Hamlin Garland—she became engrossed in spiritualism in her old age.

Another sickly, family-smothered girl was Mary Baker Eddy, founder of the Christian Science religion, who was given to a strange sickness marked by physical debilitation, attacks of temper and hysteria, and acute pains in the spinal area. When the child had these attacks, the family physician, Dr. Nathaniel G. Ladd, could always be depended upon to bring her out of them, although the distracted family expected the child to die during each seizure. In these episodes Mary would fling herself upon the floor, pound with her heels, and pass into a state of unconsciousness. It was found easier to let her stay at home and amuse herself than to send her to school. She frequently heard voices calling her, which were interpreted by mother and child as "divine" voices.

This especially attractive child was like a pretty doll to her older sisters, who used to take her to school with them during her preschool years, set her on a table, and invite her to tell their playmates what she was going to do when she was grown. She always replied, "I'm going to write a book." Her maternal grandmother had aroused these ambitions in Mary by showing her a scrapbook in the attic filled with the poetic productions of some bygone ancestor. Mary often wrote sentimental doggerel when she was home from school alone. Within her neighborhood she became known as the young girl poetess; pretty, affected, arrogant, and vain.

There were three older brothers, Samuel, Albert, and George, and two sisters, Abigail and Martha. The father, Mark Baker, was a harsh and quick-tempered man, a hard-working farmer who was easily embroiled in factional disputes in the Congregational Church at Tilton where he belabored backsliders.

The older brothers, especially gifted Albert, taught their little sister at home from their own schoolbooks. There was a period in late adolescence when Mary was content to forget her own drives for eminence and looked forward to acting as the mistress of Albert's home. Albert was a talented boy who had gone to Dartmouth, who read law in the office of Franklin Pierce, and who was admitted to the bar, but died just after he had been nominated to Congress in a district where nomination was tantamount to election. Albert's death was a great blow to the nineteen-year-old girl, since she had identified herself completely with him and expected to share the bachelor brother's home and eminence.

Her quick-tempered father, rather than her compliant and defeated mother, assumed much of the burden of Mary's care when she became more ill as she grew older. When her attacks of hysteria grew increasingly terrible, he had the local road authorities cover the highway before the house with tanbark to stop the convulsive shudders the girl suffered when she heard horses' hoofs passing by. He rocked her in his arms like a baby when everything else failed. A cradle was built from an old sofa with a rail, and a boy was hired to rock Mary.

Abigail Tilton, her married sister, also provided a home and a haven for Mary in her times of trouble. When Mary was unable to care for a child born of her first marriage, he was cared for by his grandmother until the old woman died. At four, he was given by the family to a nurse who was fond of him. It was only in the later years, when the family repudiated Mary's religious beliefs, that the family's overprotectiveness of their "baby-girl" stopped.

Mary was vexed with recurring episodes of muscular spasm and rigidity all through her life. Neighbors persuaded Mary's father that it would be best to ignore her symptoms. He did so, and the experiment was successful, according to the description of her biographer, Edwin Franden Dakin.[14] When his daughter threw herself violently to the floor after he had challenged her in an argument, he walked away and left her lying alone. An hour later when he returned, Mary had retired to her room, and when supper was called, she came down in the calmest of moods.

In her old age, Mary's faithful followers assumed the role of the protective family, and they kept a twenty-four-hour watch about her to ward off the "animal magnetism" of the enemies who were seeking to destroy her. Her son instituted an unsuccessful suit against her to have her declared mentally ill.

Poet laureate C. Day Lewis was the son of a clergyman whose wife died when their only child was four. He worried about the boy's weak chest and coaxed him to eat by encouraging the lad to crawl around the table pretending to be a hungry bear. The poet says in his autobiography, "Relying solely on my father for that spiritual infusion which a child can accept only from a parent, and receiving from him the full force of a love which had nowhere else now to turn [since his wife's death] created between us a bond of abnormal tension."

Life in the home of the poet Stephen Spender was played against a background of calamity; there was always a sense of catastrophe in the house. Of his father, an overpossessive, anxious widower, Spender says, "The feeling that the death of my father was arranged at a time when his life had become intolerable to us [the children] did not leave me. I went home at once, prepared to live a newer and freer life." When Stephen recovered from the illness that was the "epilogue to my relationship with him," the adolescent boy began to enjoy perfect health. Unfortunately, his grandmother, previously jolly and sensible, took over the anxious role that the deceased father had played; on a holiday trip, she never let Stephen and his brothers and sisters out of her sight for a minute.

A soldier and amateur poet, George S. Patton, was spared the tedium of the classroom, the competition with his peers, and the usual tasks of childhood until he was twelve. The only other child resident of the eighteen hundred-acre ranch was his small sister, Nita. He was given no frustrating learning tasks to do, and when his father, a semi-retired lawyer, became tired of reading aloud to his son, an aunt took over the task. George's mother, an athletic, active woman, seems to have left the planning of the reading sessions to the opinionated father. At age twelve, George could not read for himself.

The boy experienced extreme peer rejection in preparatory school. At West Point he was dubbed a "quilloid"—a boy ready to curry favor by tattling on other cadets. He gained favor with his instructors by a punctilious keeping to the rules. He was stiff-necked, arrogant, and boastful. He never learned to read well, although his memory was extraordinary. He got through West Point by memorizing whole lectures and texts and parroting them verbatim.

When George was fifteen, he met a pretty little girl of his own age who had been as sheltered and overprotected as he. Beatrice Banning Ayer was the daughter of well-to-do friends of the Patton family. Her interests were literary and artistic. At fifteen, she still played with dolls and wore her hair in Alice in Wonderland fashion. Neither ever had another sweetheart, and their families were delighted with the romance. They married soon after George's graduation, had a happy marriage, and introduced their children to the Patton family habit of reciting poetry. Kipling was the General's favorite, according to his wife.

James Weiland, Patton's biographer, says that his slapping a sick soldier and soon after weeping at the bedside of another is evidence of a dichotomy in his nature. He feels that there was a "soft side" of Patton's nature that the General went to great lengths to conceal.

Weiland quotes from a poem entitled "God of Battles" published in *Woman's Home Companion* in which Patton speaks of a great God, who through the ages has "braced the blood stained hand." (Other generals besides Patton have used prayer on the battlefield.)

The military hero, whose nickname was "Blood and Guts" and whose speech to his soldiers going into battle was a montage of obscenity and profanity, could also coin such phrases as: "He who has heard all day the battle hymn, sung on all sides by a thousand throats of fire."

Patton was another of the overprotected boys who enjoyed battle. "War," he said, "is the supreme test of a man." He had a zest for killing and felt lost and useless when there was no battle to fight. His biographer says of him, "So he gained the generalship, the medals and the glory, but he was never to make many friends."

When the mother-dominated and mother-smothered are considered as one unit, they include 64 percent of the military men, adventurers, and dictators. The smothering mothers (or smothering fathers) and the dominating mothers also reared 54 percent of the poets, as well as the eight persons who found battle exhilarating and who also liked to read or recite martial poetry. The smothering parents and dominating parents can be considered as one unit because both devote unusually concentrated attention to their children. These children described their parents variously as adamant, bossy, strong-willed, overanxious, overprotective, overpossessive, interfering, and especially as dominating.

When the sixty-four smothering mothers are considered apart from the dominating mothers, we find that it is the smothering mothers who rear most of the dictators. It may also be significant that the sixty-four smothering mothers reared twenty-four of the fifty-seven bachelors among the Four Hundred. If the mother is kindly, if she admires her husband, or if there is a family opinionatedness that favors a humanitarian point of view, the mother-smothered boy may love freedom and equality as well as beauty. Some of the most able of the eminent are "mothers' boys." However, there is considerable evidence to indicate that the least desirable home in which potentially eminent sons were reared was the home in which a smothering mother disliked her husband.

Chapter 6
Troubled Homes

I must make it known that I do not believe it is required of art, science, religion, philosophy or family to assure every man born into this life a secure childhood, in which a child knows only love and harmony. If such a childhood happens to come to pass for a child, excellent. If the child, as a result of such a childhood, becomes a truly pleasant or excellent adult who functions in a satisfying manner... again excellent. The supplying of such a childhood to a child, however, appears to be impossible. It may not even be desirable. It may just create a nonentity.... I think it is inevitable and in order for the human creature to be unhappy in childhood. I think it is impossible, at the same time, for almost any new human being to be entirely unhappy at any time.... I was bitterly unhappy as a small child.

—William Saroyan, *The Bicycle Rider in Beverly Hills*

In the homes that cradle eminence, creativity and contentment are not congenial. Both parents and children are often irritable, explosive, changeable, and experimental. They are prone to depression and exaltation. They make terrible mistakes and win wonderful victories.

The "normal man," as measured by personality inventory tests, is not a likely candidate for the Hall of Fame. Dr. Jules Golden, of the department of psychiatry at Albany Medical College; Dr. Nathan Mandel, research sociologist in the Minnesota State Department of Correction; and Dr. Bernard C. Glueck, Jr., director of research at the Hartford Institute of Living, conducted surveys of seventy-three men, twenty-six years of age, who had been problem-free at age fourteen, and then compared them on the *Minnesota Multiphasic Personality Inventory*, a self-descriptive questionnaire which had been given to a group of 1,953 schoolboys. These seventy-three represented the most problem-free among them.[1]

The efficiency of the test was proved by the follow-up on these boys. They had remained stable and untroubled, and there was consistency and conformity in the life patterns of that group. Follow-up was not too expensive or difficult, since most of them had stayed in the same metropolitan area in which they had been tested—fifty of them were still there for the follow-up study. They had all completed high school; most of them held average, white-collar jobs.

These men were found to be living comfortable, well-adjusted lives and were untroubled by traumatic marital discords—no separations, no divorces. They had few job dissatisfactions, few particularly high aspirations. They led contented, home-centered lives, showed little imagination, and had limited interests in social activities. They had low aspirations for themselves and for their children. They rated highest in "contentment and compatibility with spouse" and lowest in "richness of personality and breadth of interest."

These data led the researchers to conclude that "normality," as evidenced by a lack of internal tension; adequate social, economic, and familial adaptation; and harmonious integration with other individuals at all levels, implies a lack of creativity, imagination, and spontaneity. The comfortable and contented do not ordinarily become creative.

This conclusion is adequately borne out by the survey of the family backgrounds of the Four Hundred, of whom only fifty-eight (less than 15 percent) can be said to have experienced the stereotyped picture of the supportive, warm, relatively untroubled home. Even these fifty-eight persons fit that picture awkwardly in significant respects, or they are so inadequately described that there is reason to suspect omission of pertinent facts that might change the picture if additional evidence were forthcoming.

Within the framework of turbulence and contention, there are group differences. Children who later make contributions to the theater or to literature have the most internal tension to report. The dramas enacted in the family theater are often more complex and fantastic than those that the child in the home grows up to invent. Actors and actresses come from stormy homes. The homes of the reformers and humanitarians are the most explosive with ideas and argument. The illegitimate children have their special problems, as do the very poor and the very rich. Poor parents are sometimes exploitive; rich parents, eccentric or neglectful.

Children in these turbulent and explosive homes do not always enjoy life. They suffer intensely at times, and they are deeply capable of suffering, since they are sensitive and aware individuals. The Four Hundred had problems, and yet they achieved eminence. There is no way of estimating how many equally capable and imaginative children lived in similar homes and became neurotic or psychotic, delinquent, or indifferent to such a degree that they were unproductive. A few of the Four Hundred came from warm, supportive, cohesive homes, and these will be described in the next chapter. But our immediate task is to report that contentment and creativity do not ordinarily go hand in hand in the homes that cradle eminence.

In the prime of his life, Pavel Chekhov, father of the novelist and playwright Anton Chekhov, was a vain and selfish man. His wife, in a letter to her son Michael (who became his brother Anton's biographer), described Pavel as a man possessed of "an inborn and inveterate spite." His pleasure was in ritual, uniforms, music, painting, and self-display. He held strong opinions, taking an active part in local elections and missing no public dinners or civic or church celebrations in his home town of Taganrog, Russia.

Pavel bought a small shop with money given to him by his father—a serf who had freed himself and his whole family by his hard work and ingenuity—and there he sold alcoholic drinks, patent medicines, and groceries. Anton was left to do much of the work in the shop because he was the quickest of the children at making change and keeping inventory. Pavel was seldom in his store because of his preoccupation with music, painting, and public affairs.

Anton's father had also been given enough money to buy a plot of land upon which to build a home for his wife and five children. He told the builder that he would pay him a certain sum of money for each thousand bricks used—he would not pay a lump sum for the whole job and be cheated. The builder responded to Pavel's lack of faith in him by building the walls twice the usual thickness. The distracted Pavel borrowed from moneylenders to pay for the piles of bricks, only to find he could pay neither principal nor interest on the loan. In order to escape debtor's prison, he left town and took the train to Moscow where his oldest sons, Alexander and Nicholas, were supporting and educating themselves—Alexander at the University of Moscow, Nicholas at art school. They were not happy to see him.

Pavel left his nagging wife, Eugenie Chekhov, to salvage what she could from the estate. The genuinely put-upon woman was cheated as badly as her husband had been, and she soon followed him to Moscow with the younger children, Mary and Michael. Anton and Ivan, then adolescents, were left behind to complete their secondary education. They would have to earn their own board and keep however they could.

Anton was happy to be left in Taganrog without any family except his brother. His father had beaten him often, overworked him in the store, and forced him to become a member of the children's choir, which Pavel directed. He had been dragged out of bed at two or three in the morning for special rehearsals and performances. He found it easy to earn his living by acting as a tutor to a wealthy boy, and he enjoyed his freedom.

Despite his cleverness, Anton was a poor student. He could not bring himself to study either Latin or Greek. Ivan, who was younger than he, finished his work and went to Moscow to rejoin the family. Anton failed his examinations twice. Not all of his time was spent in study. He had his first experiences in sex at thirteen and found that girls were responsive to his love-making. He loved parties, trips to the estates of his friends, dancing, and singing.

His failures at school bothered him so much that he had nightmares in which he tried unsuccessfully to cross a deep river bordered by huge, slippery boulders. In the river were tiny tugs hauling enormous barges. When he tried to run away from the river, he stumbled upon crumbling cemetery gates, funeral processions, and schoolteachers. All his life, he was haunted by dreams of teachers trying to catch him making a mistake.

After the third try on his examinations, he graduated, but he did not want to go to Moscow to join his family. He had responded to his mother's whining letters by capturing goldfinches to sell as pets and sending her a little money. His older brothers, his mother said, had taken to drink, women, and other follies. The family was sleeping on the floor with coats as covers, and there was inadequate food. Ivan was too timid to work, and Pavel had beaten him until the neighbors intervened and the landlord threatened to evict them. The father had pinned a schedule of duties on the dingy wall of the slum room and had driven his family to do his will. They had already moved eleven times. The mother feared that when Anton came to the wicked big city, he too would turn to drink and desert his family as his older brothers had done. But Aunt Feodossia, who was sick and alone and had moved in with them, was sure that Anton would be able to become the savior of the family if he would only come to Moscow.

Anton thought of striking out on his own, of abandoning his family and going to medical school, but when the time came, he was unable to cut his familial ties. He wrote to his well-to-do cousin Michael in Moscow and asked him to give Pavel a job in a warehouse so far from the apartment that Pavel could not come home except for infrequent weekends. He had no intention of going home if his father was to be there. The cousin was cooperative. Anton then coaxed two of his school friends to come with him to Moscow to board with the family. This would mean extra money for groceries. He would enroll in medical school and find work to support himself, his mother, and his young brother and sister. He would help Ivan find a job.

The prostitutes in the neighborhood hung out of the windows to see the three fresh-faced country boys arrive in Moscow. Anton and his two schoolfellows were welcomed with enthusiasm by the desperate family. Young Michael, outside on the street, did not recognize his brother, who had grown from adolescence to manhood since the family had fled from Taganrog.

When Anton came home, his two older brothers returned to the family home. Alexander had been doing some writing for humor magazines and found similar work for Anton, who wrote clever quips and long pot-boilers for inconsequential magazines—all in the midst of confusion and squalor. Nicholas drew cartoons for the humor magazines. Michael found work copying lectures for other students at a fee. Ivan was employed as an elementary-school teacher. His mother, his sister Mary, and his Aunt Feodossia kept house, and Mary trained as a teacher. Anton managed his classes and his writings and attended a great many parties among the intellectuals of Moscow. Pavel came home for an occasional weekend and added to the confusion in the three crowded rooms by reading aloud to his wife.

Still, Anton's nights were plagued by nightmares. After a hard day's work at the university, he fell into a deep sleep, from which he was suddenly awakened by a real terror. A strange force seemed to throw him out of bed, to tear him up by the roots, and he found it difficult to fall asleep again.

Alexander, the oldest son, though talented and creative, was a severe alcoholic. Nicholas became rather well known as a painter. Ivan, who passed his secondary examinations easily and was not as driving as his brothers, was a steady, uninspired (possibly very happy) schoolteacher. Mary, the only girl in the family, was a schoolmistress and artist. The youngest, Michael, who escaped the full force of his father's hostilities, was a writer of children's stories and his brother's biographer. Anton had a great zest for life, was most adequate to become the head of the family, and used his potential most effectively. Within the family, the person who is to achieve eminence is usually recognized as being exceptionally capable and original.

The Chekhov family, which produced a great writer, did so despite the cruelty and poor judgment of the father. It also produced four other children who had the same drive for learning which distinguished their father. During his middle age, Pavel was hated and despised by his family because of his temper and financial failures, but in old age, he became docile and kindly and was proud of his son, who had long since died of tuberculosis. Pavel died (appropriately enough as a father of a literary genius) on the operating table after having suffered a rupture from lifting a box of books.

It sometimes happens that a schoolteacher or a librarian discovers a child who is eager for intellectual companionship that the home does not provide. Novelist Theodore Dreiser had this experience, but he was unable to fit himself into the rigidity of the curriculum at Indiana University, to which his elderly female teacher would have sent him for more than one year had he desired to continue attending. While at college, he read widely and talked with people who interested him, but the classroom irked and bored him. It was from the hot, murky context of the family emotional climate that he drew the material for his best writing.

There seems to have been no love for learning in the Dreiser family, although Theodore became a writer and Paul became a composer of popular songs. It is possible that Theodore, even in his lengthy autobiography, did not give a fair picture of his father, possibly because he did not know the man in the days of his father's success—only as old and a failure. He does not explain the impetus that led his father to leave Germany and come to the United States. Nothing is known of the father's education or of his family. The extremely mother-centered writer may have owed more to his father in the way of intellectual endowment than he conveys in his writing about his family.

When Theodore Dreiser wrote *Sister Carrie* and *An American Tragedy*, he was writing of a world he had known in childhood. His mother, at sixteen, had run away from her Mennonite farm home to marry a strange young German immigrant who was a Roman Catholic. Her family disowned her. She was an illiterate, warm, amoral woman with a great faith in her children that survived many tests. Her son Theodore was a "mother's boy." His first memories were of stroking her feet, of weeping over her torn shoes, of crying because of her poverty, and of being comforted on her warm breasts. In his autobiography, he writes pages in praise of his "happy, hopeful, animal mother with the desire to live, and not much constructive ability to make real her dreams." She was the only person who ever wanted him enough.

His father was a thin, dour, bitter man who was out of work for the first seven years of Theodore's life. He had once been successful, even affluent, but his mill had burned and he felt cheated. He brooded and blamed his wife for his children's delinquencies.

As Theodore grew, he read hungrily and hated the parochial school to which his father made him go. There was anger, shame, and destitution in the home. The oldest son, Paul, had been arrested three times—once for forgery—and was living in a fine house in Evansville, Indiana, where he was "kept" by Anna Brace, madam of a house of prostitution. When Theodore visited there as a boy, he was impressed by the luxury of the establishment and by the glimpses of the lovely girls in appealing disarray. It was only the bounty of Anna Brace that kept the Dreiser family above the level of subsistence for two years. When Anna quarreled with Paul, the Dreisers became destitute again and began moving from place to place, each home more squalid than the last. It was Paul who composed the music for the popular song "On the Banks of the Wabash," for which Theodore wrote the lyrics. Their brother "Rome," next to Paul in age among the boys, was a gambler, drunkard, and wanderer.

Theodore's older sisters, Mame, Emma, Teresa, and Sylvia, came home with presents from men who had taken them out previously. Sarah Dreiser admired the pretty gifts the girls received from their gentlemen friends. If their father could not buy them nice things, she said, he should not complain if other men did. The father stormed, and no one heard him; he sulked, and nobody noticed.

There is no boy among the Four Hundred whose life was so complicated with sordid complications as was the life of Alexei Peshkov, also known as the writer Maxim Gorky. Through 616 pages of autobiography, the recital of tension and terror never stops. Yet his heavy-handed grandfather, who beat him insensible, taught Alexei at home so well that the school inspector noticed him, praised him, and chided him for wasting his talents by being disruptive in the classroom—a result of his boredom. In this patriarchal home, it was the quarreling grandparents who created the tumultuous family emotional climate in which the boy was reared.

Alexei Peshkov, when he was four, crouched behind a trunk in his parents' bedroom staring at the white-robed, stiff, twisted figure of his father who had just died of cholera. In another corner, his hunchbacked little grandmother was hopping about the figure of his mother, who was rolling about in agony while giving birth to her second son, Sascha. The dead father, Maxim Peshkov, as a boy had been hunted with dogs and flogged when he tried to run away from his father, an army officer who was finally exiled to Siberia for cruelty to his men. Alexei's mother, Varya Kashirin, daughter of a brutal dyemaker, had loved her dead husband dearly because he was kind, affectionate, and educated. Her bestial brothers, Mike and Jake, disliked their gentle brother-in-law, and they broke a hole in the ice and tossed him into the water as a welcome to the establishment of his in-laws.

The Kashirin household was shunned by its neighbors. The very house shook with the angers of the big men. Mike and Jake Kashirin beat their wives and their children. Servants were teased and tortured. Alexei made a flower garden, and his relatives turned the pigs into it to destroy it.

The patriarch of the household, old Vassili Kashirin, beat his wife from noon until dark on Easter Sunday and gave her no food while she lay half-dying. He beat his grandson unconscious when the boy dyed a white tablecloth blue.

Alexei's mother, Varya, was a tall and magnificent woman, but she could not protect her son from her father or her brothers. When she married again and her second husband beat her, Alexei nearly killed the fellow by knifing him. When he took a ruble from his stepfather's purse to buy sausages for his classmates and a copy of

Robinson Crusoe for himself, he quit school rather than be shamed about his theft by his classmates.

When he was forced to leave home at the age of ten by his grandfather, who had lost his business, to find work, there was only his beloved grandmother to miss him. Alexei loved her fully and uncritically, and she gave him the same complete devotion. She was illiterate, but she had an endless store of folklore and folk wisdom and an unshakable faith in humanity's essential goodness. He became an errand boy in a shoe store, a dishwasher, a draftsman's apprentice, an icon-painter's apprentice, and a bird catcher. In the homes of his successive masters, family life was not much better than in his own. He went to the country but found the people there even less sensitive than the people in the city. He thought the habit that the country boys had of capturing young girls, tying their skirts above their heads, and leaving them to run themselves exhausted, bare-bottomed and in screaming confusion, was both crude and cruel. He found the peasants antagonistic to learning and to the learned, and unconcerned about their own destinies.

He made no close friends, so that when he received a letter saying his grandmother had died, the world became cold and empty. He had no one to speak to about his sorrow, not even a horse or dog that was his own to share his grief. At nineteen, he was so weary with the world and the people in it that he decided to kill himself, and he shot himself in the left side. After a long convalescence, he recovered. He later gave himself a new name and became Maxim Gorky—"Man of Bitterness."

Sam Clemens, unlike Gorky, was not one to write of psychological conflicts of the kind he saw at home. When Sam's older brother, Orion Clemens, was approached by an editor who wanted to describe the Clemens family as Orion saw it, Sam was furious and forbade him to give any information. This is unfortunate, since Sam Clemens was also a "mother's boy" whose accounts of his mother omit some of the interesting details given by word of mouth to later descendants.

It is Samuel Charles Webster, son of Anne Moffett Webster and grandson of Pamela Clemens Moffett—who was Sam Clemens' sister, eight years older than he—who is our principal informant about Sam Clemens and his family. Samuel Charles Webster painstakingly collected the family legends while his own mother was still alive.

Jane Lampion Clemens, an unrepentant Southerner, put stepmothers in the same category as Yankees. It was her eagerness to get away from home that hurried her into a marriage with John Marshall Clemens, which was not a love-match; the man and woman, so different in personality, were never congenial.

Pamela, the second-born, was her father's child; Sam, the fifth-born, was his mother's boy. The only time Sam ever saw one member of the family kiss another was when his father called Pamela to his deathbed to bid her good-by. John Marshall Clemens was especially fond of his daughter and cautioned her to learn to be a good housekeeper, to see that her husband was comfortable, and advised her, "Don't have too many cats in the house." His wife, Jane, was never able to resist a stray cat; she sometimes kept as many as thirty-eight about the untidy place.

In her own old age, Anne Moffett Webster, Pamela's daughter, recalled the feelings of her mother about John Marshall Clemens:

> *My grandfather died long before I was born. Uncle Sam thought his father was very strict, but my mother was fond of him. From my mother I gained a picture of a man of great dignity, a keen sense of humor, and the highest degree of neatness and fastidiousness. He was always called "Squire" by his neighbors. Once on the street someone slapped him on the back, and the family was horrified. He was a scholarly type and had studied to be a lawyer. It must have been hard for a man of this character to have such a haphazard, happy-go-lucky wife.*[2]

It was natural that Samuel Clemens should have been his mother's favorite. Her son Orion was born in 1827, her daughter Pamela in 1827. She lost her next three children—Pleasants Hannibal, Margaret, and Benjamin—at young ages. It was Samuel, a seven-month-old baby who stayed sickly until he was six years old, who had to replace these lost children for her. To make Sam strong, Jane Clemens treating his frequent colds by dousing him in cold water.

Jane was as outgoing and dramatic as her husband was dignified and retiring. Like her son Sam, the truth never stopped her when she had a good story to tell. She once told a comparative stranger about her dear little daughter Pamela who had been taken away by the Indians and never returned. At fourteen, Sam Clemens was left in charge, for a week, of the paper where he worked. He tells a delightful, detailed, apologetic story in his autobiography about driving a rival editor out of town by publishing an account of how the lovesick man had pretended to commit suicide by drowning. The truth, as attested by old copies of the newspaper of that date, is that he published a drawing of the editor with a dog's head, pretending to drown himself because he was overly fearful of dogs during a rabies scare in the community.

Jane Clemens showed indifference to disaster and calamity. She showed no anxiety during a cholera epidemic, even when people to whom she had talked in the morning were dead by evening. A neighbor was killed because a calf ran in front of the horse on which he rode. Jane's first reaction was, "What happened to the calf?" When accused of liking cats better than babies, she replied blithely, "When you're tired of a cat, you can put it down."

She was never drawn to religion except for the drama of the ceremony. She went to various churches and to a Jewish synagogue—to see the sights and rituals, not out of interest in theology. Her granddaughter writes:

> *My grandmother has been represented in recent years as a Puritan, but nothing could be further from the truth. She loved any kind of excitement. She seemed to be always going to a parade, a circus or a funeral.... She was a great beauty, a fine dancer, and very witty. She kept her beauty to the last, as well as her love of color and dancing.... Grandma's room was always a perfect riot of red—the carpets, chairs, ornaments, were all red. She would have worn red, too, if she had not been restrained. She was modern in her ideas and*

> *insisted on wearing her skirts shorter than was conventional. Once when she was having an especially nice dress made, the family gave secret orders to the dressmaker to make it longer than she had said. When Grandma tried it on, she said nothing, but promptly sat down and ran a tuck in it.*[3]

Jane used to complain of Orion's pious ways. She saw no reason why he should let his love for various religions interfere with his success in life. She said that Orion had a "jugful of religion," but that she could make do with a "dipperful."

Biographers who confuse her with the more conventional and pious character "Aunt Polly," from *The Adventures of Tom Sawyer,* would seem to be at fault. Nor did she seem to have worried about Sam's quitting school when he was eleven. It was Sam's father, not his mother, who had a regard for disciplined learning. Jane had a fine disregard for spelling and exactness of expression. She once wrote to her son Samuel, "Kill Susy" (her granddaughter), instead of "Kiss Susy," and did not bother to change the wording. "He'll know what I mean," she said. Her son wrote back an amusing and gory letter in which he pretended to have carried out her whim, and she chortled with glee. He knew how to please her. She always had a great love for the dramatic and macabre and sensational, for mesmerism, spiritualism, strange creeds, and exciting events. She lived for the excitement the day brought.

Jane Lampton Clemens was another of the mothers of eminent men who was energetic and outgoing in personality until her death. At eighty-one, she danced for her sons Samuel and Orion as lightly as a girl. Although Samuel was her favorite, it was Orion, for whom neither his mother nor Samuel ever had a word of praise, who took over the care of his difficult mother in her extreme old age.

Sam was eleven when his father, Judge Clemens (Justice of the Peace), died, leaving the family in serious economic difficulties. Financial reverses had already caused them to give up their home and move into rooms above the father's office. Before the Judge died, he was hopeful that he might be appointed to the clerkship of the

Surrogate Court, a position that would have paid better than that of Justice of the Peace, which he held for many years. All that he left his family was seventy-five thousand acres of virgin Tennessee timber which he had bought for four hundred dollars a decade before as an investment. He figured the land would be worth a fortune to his descendants.

The Judge wrote a fine Spencerian hand, was fussy and hard-working, and once wrote thirteen hundred words on a case that paid him only thirteen dollars because he thought a matter of civil liberties was involved.

Orion, the oldest boy, was too temperamental to be reliable. Every day, Orion awakened with a new idea which absorbed him all day but died with the night. One day he was practicing to be an orator; the next he was studying French. He joined first one church, then another.

Sam Clemens was always very critical of Orion, but Sam was unable to handle money as well as his brother and father. The family lands were frittered away after much quarreling between Orion and Sam. Investment in a typesetting machine that never worked bankrupted the writer. Any romantic views of Sam Clemen's early days on the river are dispelled by a description by biographer DeLancey Ferguson of a recurrent nightmare that plagued Sam as an adult. There are also traces of what may have been boyhood anxieties over money in his dream.

> *There is never a month passes that I do not dream of being in reduced circumstances, and obliged to go back to the river to earn a living. It is never a pleasant dream either. I love to think about those days; but there is always something sickening about the thought that I have been obliged to go back to them; and usually in my dream I am just about to start into a black shadow without being able to tell whether it is Selma Bluff, or Hat Island, or only a black wall of night.*[4]

The Virginia novelist Ellen Glasgow, night after night, lay awake listening to her mother's voice as the unhappy woman walked the floor in anguish, "to and fro, back and forth, driven by a thought or vision from which she tried in vain to escape." When her mother was happy and played games with her children, the whole house was merry. When she plummeted suddenly into recurrent deep depressions, the younger children in the household of ten ate the "bread of helplessness with the mother."

"My father," Ellen Glasgow says in her autobiography, " was one of the last men on earth she [Mother] should have married." The wife could not bear her husband's callousness about animals, for which she had a quivering tenderness. During the week, the wealthy ironmonger was away on business. When Saturday came, the beds of Ellen and her sister Rebe were moved from their mother's room to an adjacent room. The family dogs, sensing it was Saturday, looked apprehensively at the whip in the hall.

Ellen describes her father as an entirely unselfish man who respected learning, whose word was as good as gold—a man of "complete integrity." He enjoyed weeping over sentimental stories about the return of prodigal daughters. He was a patient, tireless, efficient nurse in the sickroom when his children were ill, as they often were during childhood. But he never understood his wife—"not for a single minute," says her daughter. He had no sense of beauty, and he never knowingly "committed an act of pleasure." He tried to censor his daughter's reading when she was an adolescent.

Ellen herself was so sensitive that she was said to have been born "without a skin"; she screamed frequently during her first three weeks for no known reason and was carried about on a pillow. No one expected her to live.

When she was seven, she was sent to a school that was intolerable to her. Another girl ate Ellen's lunch when she could not bring herself to eat in strange surroundings. The teachers were kind but did not protect her from the other children, who called her a "White Rabbit" when she vomited and became ill with nervous headaches. Her mother was always waiting at the door for her return and greeted her with embraces and expressions of sympathy, and she convinced their family doctor that the frail child might slip out of their hands if they sent her back to school. So Ellen was permitted to stay home with her mother, who was the "sun of her universe" and an "innocent soul suffering an undeserved tragedy." The release from the classroom was accepted gratefully by Ellen, who found school so distasteful that "death from exposure would have been a simple escape."

Ellen's brother, Frank, who tried to be loyal to both parents, drowned himself. In divided homes, the sibling relationship is poor between children who do not agree as to which parent is the aggrieved party in the conflict. The children who empathize with their mother are more creative but less happy than the "father's children," who marry, rear families, and withdraw from the household drama. Ellen herself was twice engaged but never married.

Unfaithful Wives and Husbands

Extramarital love affairs are not common among the parents of the Four Hundred. Ellen Terry, actress mother of the stage designer Gordon Craig, had many lovers. The father of Lafcadio Hearn renewed his love affair with an ex-sweetheart after he brought a wife home from the Ionian Islands. Several fathers are said to have been physically unfaithful to their wives but not emotionally involved with the woman concerned.

Among the truly philandering husbands was Count Nicholas Tolstoi, to whom his son Leo Tolstoi credits two passions—cards and women. In his *Memoirs*, Tolstoi says of his father, "God knows if he had any moral convictions." The tall, stately man with a bald spot and a lisp grieved to realize that the companions of his youth had risen to high official positions, while he was only a retired lieutenant of the guards.

The complications of Nicholas Tolstoi's life are not surpassed by the plots and subplots in the novels his son wrote. When he was sixteen, a liaison was arranged for Nicholas (to encourage good health) with a young servant who bore him a son named Mishenka. It later embarrassed his legal sons to be asked for charity by this man, who looked more like their father than they did.

The old countess, Leo's grandmother, was a foolish, vain, rather stupid woman who had been spoiled by her husband and father and expected to be spoiled the rest of her life by her son. Nicholas fell in love with the orphan girl that she reared to be her companion and handmaiden, the pretty Tatyana Yergolski with the sturdy brown body, coarse black braids, agate eyes, and strong will.

Tatyana and Nicholas wanted to marry, but by the time they were twenty-seven years of age, they still had not. His mother did not approve of them getting married; Tatyana was an orphan, a distant relative, and poor—not a suitable bride for her only son. So Tatyana waited and made herself indispensable. Tatyana could take punishment without flinching. When she was a girl, she proved her courage by putting a white-hot piece of iron on her bare arm. She did not flinch, not even when her skin ripped and stuck to the bar. Her masochism found plenty of outlets during her lifetime. When Nicholas had to sell the country estate that was his inheritance, she moved with him and his demanding mother into a five-room apartment in Moscow.

Tatyana and his mother were not Leo's only dependents in this apartment; he also had a sister and a niece to care for in the small apartment. His sister Alexandra had made a very bad marriage. When she was pregnant, her husband had gone mad and beaten her. Her daughter was stillborn, but Nicholas and Tatyana tricked Alexandra by substituting the cook's newest daughter, Pashenka, for the dead child. The husband was institutionalized, and Alexandra and her daughter moved into the Tolstoi home.

Nicholas took a regular job in the government office for war orphans. He sat by his mother's bedside and held her hand while she sympathized with him for having to work. He walked the floor; he refused to see his friends. Tatyana agreed with Nicholas that he must marry a woman with money. Marya Volkonskaya, the woman he chose, was the heiress to an estate of twenty-five hundred acres and eight hundred serfs. She was five years older than Nicholas and Tatyana and was both ugly and shy. Romance had passed her by long before.

Marya's father, a scholar as well as a very rich man, had spent years educating his only daughter and had taught her French, German, English, and Italian. He took her sightseeing through Europe; made her study mathematics, physics, geometry, and geography; employed a piano teacher for her; and trained her to administer the estate. He was a stern teacher. Marya could never verbally express anger or distaste; instead, her face grew scarlet and she cried.

Nicholas brought her home with him to the apartment where his mother and his childhood sweetheart Tatyana waited for her. The old countess was never much more than polite, but Tatyana was honest and soon admitted that Marya was a good wife. When she also became a mother, the whole household moved to the wife's estate, the beautiful Yasnaya Polyana (Plain Field), where things had not gone well without the mistress.

"I think my mother was not in love with my father," Tolstoi wrote, "but loved him as a husband and chiefly as the father of her children." There were to be five of them.

Count Nicholas resumed his life as a gay and genial young man with no specific interests or talents. He was not interested in politics; his reading from his large library was desultory. Yet he never whipped one of the eight hundred serfs, among whom was his natural son Mishenka. The old countess had her own quarters and her luxuries. She kept a blind minstrel to amuse her, and she insisted that a grandchild sleep with her in her big bed each night. Aunt Alexandra had her own quarters and collected a motley group of hangers-on, eccentrics, pilgrims, monks, and nuns. Her favorite among them was a half-witted pilgrim named Marie who went about in male dress.

Marya occupied herself with her five children. The oldest boy, also named Nicholas, was especially brilliant and receptive. She used Rousseau's *Emile* as her nineteenth-century equivalent of Dr. Spock. It was Nicholas who told the other children that he had a secret that could make all men happy if it became generally known, the secret of brotherly love. Turgenev used to say, "Nicholas lacked only a few essential faults to be as great a writer as was his brother." Leo Tolstoi agreed, but Nicholas had no vanity and was unable to criticize others.

Marya was happy with her brilliant children. Her father had only had one child to teach; she had five. But the happy days ended abruptly when she had been married nine years. Marya, the only daughter, was then five months old. Leo, the ugly littlest boy who looked like his mother's father, was almost two. Her granddaughter, Alexandra Tolstoi, says of Marya's sudden demise:

> *The cause of her death was not exactly known. It occurred some months after the birth of her only daughter. Some said that it was caused by fever and others claimed that it was inflammation of the brain. Her aged maid said that it was the result of a blow.*

Marya had loved to swing, and the servant girls pushed her as high as they could. A swingboard somehow struck her sharply on the head. For a time, she was unable to speak. When she could talk, she reassured the maids and promised them that they would not be punished for what had happened.

Tolstoi, in his *Memoirs,* does not mention the swingboard incident. His mother, he says, had a sudden chill, then fever. She heard a noise in her ears and found herself suddenly unable to count consecutively. During a recovery period, she wrote a long letter to her husband, who was away. He was not to apologize for having taken money from the estate to pay his gambling debts, but: "Your unhappy passion for gambling deprives me of a portion of your tender attachment." She could not permit him to spend so much money that the children's inheritance would be threatened. The estate must be kept intact. Nor would she consent to send the children away to school. She wrote him that she expected to die soon, that something dreadful was wrong and she could not get well. "Mama," Tolstoi says, "died in terrible agony."

When Leo was nine, his father died on the streets of a distant city where he had gone on business with two serfs to accompany him. When he was found, his money and papers were gone. The papers were returned later by a beggar woman who said she found them on the steps of a church. The servants were suspected, but there was no proof—or investigation. The assassination of masters was not uncommon in those times.

Although Leo's grandmother became the guardian of Nicholas and Marya's five sons and daughters, it was Tatyana who continued to care for the children. But the old countess died of grief and old age soon after her son's death, and eccentric Aunt Alexandra took over their care.

Leo was growing up. His educational problems began. A French tutor locked Leo in a dark closet, commanded the boy to kneel before him, and twisted his back when he would not. The happy days in the nursery with his mother or Tatyana had ended.

Leo was very fond of Aunt Alexandra, with whom he associated the acrid smell of the unbathed. She had been dirty as a matter of principle. She had waited on her servants and would not permit them to wait on her. When Leo was thirteen and Aunt Alexandra died, another aunt came from Kazan and took the children home with her. Tatyana could not go with them because she had once had a proposal from that aunt's husband, and he still spoke of her with affection and respect. Tatyana stayed on the estate with the eight hundred serfs. As a result, Leo temporarily lost Tatyana, who had never given him anything but complete and uncritical love.

Adolescence was hard for Leo. A university teacher who was hired to tutor the three younger boys said, "Sergei can and will study; Dmitri will and cannot; Lev [Leo] neither will nor can." His lessons never went well; he was sexually precocious; his social life was involved. He was failed unjustly in history and German in his second year at college because the professor had quarreled with the family. Leo then dropped his major in Oriental languages and transferred to the law school at the University of Moscow. It was there that a certain Professor Meyer took such an interest in the gifted non-achiever that he resolved to stimulate him to love learning. He succeeded so well that Leo quit school to pursue his interest in philosophy without being bothered by adherence to the school's curriculum.

Leo became the nineteenth-century equivalent of a beatnik or a hippy, and his sister Marya was amused. "He probably considers himself a Diogenes, or else is under the influence of Rousseau." Obsessed by the idea of leading a simple, primitive life, he startled guests by appearing barefoot in a sailcloth costume he had devised for himself. He took to the deep woods where he lay staring at the sky with his head pillowed on volumes of Voltaire, Rousseau, and Hegel.

Back in Yasnaya Polyana, Tatyana helped to keep the estate in good order for Leo. It is quite difficult to convey briefly the complexity of the emotional and intellectual climate in which Leo Tolstoi was reared. Many individuals acted out the drama of their lives before the eyes of this small and ugly boy who was so self-conscious about his appearance. There were many servants he knew as well as he knew his relatives.

The dramas continued to play themselves out before him. His older brothers acted out the simple life he wrote about. Sergei gave up both wealth and social status to marry his gypsy mistress. Nicholas and Dmitri both lived in intentional poverty.

In the homes of the children who are to become eminent in the arts and literature, there continue to be especially intricate social and interpersonal relationships. There are plots, subplots, and counterplots in the homes of the playwrights and novelists. It may be that we are establishing the fact that children who are to be writers are especially sensitive to the relationships between the adults in their families. This is, however, somewhat belied by the greater number of divorces and separations in these families.[5]

Two eminent humanitarians, John La Farge and Eleanor Roosevelt, came from broken homes where the parents were drawn to creative expression. The elder John La Farge was a famous artist, and the mother of Eleanor Roosevelt was absorbed in her amateur theater group. Charles Lindbergh, who came from a divided home, had a father who wanted to be a poet but instead turned to law.

The elder John La Farge was such a sensitive artist that he could not endure the confusion of home life and lived apart from his family. His youngest son, John, born when his mother was forty-five and his father fifty-six, seldom saw his eminent father, the muralist and noted creator of stained-glass windows. When the elder La Farge did come home, he was completely indifferent to the feelings of the proper Newport neighbors and went to the beach in a Japanese kimono—in which he felt quite comfortable, but which embarrassed his children. It was only natural that his wife, whom he neglected, should turn to her youngest son for comfort and companionship.

Gifted children dislike broken homes and quarreling parents—as do other children. Although they are made miserable by the conflict or deprivation in their homes, unpleasantness does not destroy their capacity for achievement and, in some instances, obviously motivates it. The child in the broken family is often eager to give happiness to a mother who has had few satisfactions. Anger and frustration make contentment impossible and seem to whet constructive activity in some of these families.

Many of the children who came from troubled homes would probably have scored poorly on tests such as the *Minnesota Multiphasic Personality Inventory*, which is a good diagnostic tool of social and emotional problems. However, the interpretation and use of such a test can be harmful. It should not be used, for example, to keep a gifted child out of an enrichment program or a special class. In a recent national educational meeting, the principal of a public school for gifted children said that she did not accept students who have personality problems. A girl who cried easily, for example, would not be accepted. The rationale behind such statements is that the school community cannot afford to give special attention to children who may not make a good vocational adjustment because of personality problems. This may be true in the areas of competency where conformity is needed to cherish and maintain our inheritance and to pass it on, but not in other areas of competency.

Invaluable contributions are likely to be made by the creative child who is not problem-free and who is not a "good all-around student." He or she may very well come from a home where the parents are problems both to themselves and to the child whom they frequently frustrate and annoy. This is not the way life should be, but this is the way it has been in the past. There is no reason to suspect that the pattern does not still persist.

How to change procedures in order to enable the creative to be comfortable and serene is the contemporary challenge. To be creative is good. To be serene is good. To rear a child who is both serene and creative is presumably an admirable goal. The parents of the Four Hundred did not often achieve serenity for themselves or for their children, although they were frequently creative and intelligent.[6] To make the assumption that creativity plus serenity is the more or less automatic consequence of a parental display of endless patience, the providing of economic security, and a bottomless outpouring of affection is naive. It also puts a burden of guilt on the parents, who are bound to fail in the task they set themselves of being the child's constant bulwark against frustration and pain.

To swing to the other extreme and plan frustrations or purposely incite feelings of insecurity or "let oneself go" in interesting displays of emotion in order to release latent talents in a child is not only naive but dangerous. The end result may be an incapacitating emotional disturbance for the child or the parent or both. Most parents manage to make their children unhappy often enough without any intention of doing so; they do not need to fear that the child is being sated with contentment.

Facing the hard fact that serenity and creativity have not been compatible in the homes that have cradled eminence is in itself a frustrating experience, but frustration is a necessary prelude to insight.

Chapter 7
Not-So-Troubled Homes

He had a happy and orderly family background, and an orderly family life is something in the importance of which he has always believed.

—Alexander Werth, Mendes France

There are at most fifty-eight homes among the Four Hundred that were relatively trouble-free. These families, and a few others, will be measured against the yardstick of a mythical mid-twentieth-century family that represents the cultural norm for an ideal family.

John and Mary Smith have a comfortable, well-kept, attractive home. After several years of marriage, they are still devoted to each other. They enjoy their children, who are attractive, affectionate, and cooperative. The family is free of serious illness. The children consistently bring home good report cards. The teachers assure the parents that their children are well liked at school. There is adherence to the family code of right and wrong by all of its members. John and Mary are active participants in community affairs and enjoy the respect of their neighbors.

To what extent this mythical family exists outside the pages of women's magazines we do not know. It is possible that a survey of the emotional and intellectual climate in the homes of four hundred PTA presidents might find them far from problem-free. This we do not know, but it is possible to observe that even these fifty-eight families are not completely free of tension or trouble. Contemporary homes have one tremendous advantage over those that existed several decades ago. Medical science has removed many of the terrible anxieties which used to beset parents. There is no longer as much tuberculosis or diphtheria, and no longer as much chronic undiagnosed invalidism.

The pre- and post-Freudian subjects who report family happiness sometimes differ in the examples they offer as proof of felicity. Fitting these obstreperous, imaginative families into a conventional pattern is often a futile or frustrating experience.

"My parents loved each other when they were young and when they were old," says Constantine Stanislavski Alexeev, the Russian actor and director who originated the Stanislavski Method of acting. His wealthy parents cared little for society and spent their days enjoying their children. They were all fond of practical joking and once made a hairy monster with which to scare guests. Stanislavski, as proof of the family tradition of devotion, says that his father slept with his own father until the day of his marriage! Another deviation from the norm in this particular family was the unattractiveness of the small Constantine. He was chagrined when he heard guests talking of his ugliness.

This is what is meant by saying that it is difficult to make these cradles of eminence fit the conventional Mary and John Smith picture.

Another boy who fits into the pattern of the trouble-free family somewhat awkwardly is Charles de Gaulle. His father, Henri de Gaulle, married his cousin, Jeanne Maillott, and together they reared five children in a big, high-ceilinged apartment in the old Paris of the Left Bank. The father was both tender and stern with his children. He was a professor of philosophy, mathematics, and literature at a Jesuit college, and his children were thus brought up in an intellectual atmosphere. They had family arguments about Jules Verne and talked about the philosophy of Nietzsche. They read the English and German classics in French translations. Madame de Gaulle was a pious and patriotic woman. She and her husband lived peacefully in a home that was both pleasant and stimulating.

Although Charles' father could be very stern, he was always eager to encourage any imaginative leader the children devised for themselves. The summer Charles was thirteen, his father made it possible for him to organize a group of farm boys who lived near the family summer home into a mock army. They spent the summer on a camping trip, which took the form of an imaginary military campaign.

There were three ways in which Charles de Gaulle was something less than the ideal son. He was physically unattractive, his secondary school grades were mediocre, and he was not particularly popular. In his teens, he loved to play practical jokes and laughed uproariously when someone fell into his booby traps. His nickname at school was "the Long Asparagus." At military school, he was cold and withdrawn. He always had, however, a few close and special friends. His photographic memory helped to keep him in the upper third of his class there. He met his appearance problem head-on by memorizing and reciting Cyrano de Bergerac's famous speech about his oversized nose.

One boy among the Four Hundred who comes very close to being the ideal boy from the ideal home is Thomas Edmund Dewey, onetime governor of the state of New York and Republican candidate for the Presidency. His father, George Martin Dewey, Jr., was the editor of the *Owosso Times* in Michigan. George Dewey was a genial man for whom his son had both admiration and respect. He always left the job of spanking his two sons to his wife, a woman of wit and good nature. They were congenial parents. Tom himself says he never once heard his parents quarrel.

His family had prestige in the town. His paternal grandfather had been a Republican Party leader. His mother was also descended from a family of good repute. Her father, a merchant, had been a pillar of the community of Owosso. He belonged to the Episcopal church, and he had the best garden in town.

Thomas had the run of his father's newspaper office and knew almost everyone in the small town. At age eleven, he was selling the *Saturday Evening Post* and the *Detroit News*. By the time he was thirteen, he had ten other boys working as his assistants. When he was ready to enter college, he had already saved eight hundred dollars.

Work did not interfere with his school or recreational activities. He took part in school plays and debate, was director of the school yearbook, and became a lieutenant in the cadet corps. He sang and played chess and bridge. Summer vacations meant healthful farm work for pay. His grades were good; he was very handsome. He was popular with his peers, and he related well to his brother and his parents.

Young Tom Dewey continued his success as a student and as an adult at the University of Michigan. Although no one doubted his sincerity and strong sense of justice, fellow Republicans closest to him did not deny that he often merited the criticism of being stand-offish and cold in manner. He lost the national election on two occasions to a rival candidate, Franklin D. Roosevelt, who had been dubbed a mama's boy at Choate, had been a mediocre student at Harvard, and had suffered a severe case of polio in his early manhood. Being trouble-free obviously does not always correlate with the greatest success as a politician.

Another small-town boy with the same family name, John Dewey, the American philosopher and educator, was the son of a Burlington, Vermont storekeeper who joked with his customers and stammered when he had to ask people to pay their bills. He labeled his wheelbarrow: "Stolen from A. S. Dewey." He liked to tell how he had married the young daughter of Squire Rich of Richville, and how Squire Rich was not rich, although his neighbors had sent him to Congress.

A. S. Dewey and his wife had no serious problems with their son. Their daily lives were relatively uneventful. They permitted John to read dime novels and play marbles for keeps, but to not dance or play cards. Mrs. Dewey had been brought up a Universalist, but the family attended the White Street Congregational Church. John's report cards were rather ordinary until his junior year at the University of Vermont, but that did not bother his parents, who had no notion that their only son was to become a remarkable man. In his junior year in college, he read a book by Thomas H. Huxley and was swept off his feet by the rapture of scientific knowledge. From that time on, he read far into the night; he soon led his class and had the highest mark on record in philosophy.

Placing emphasis on the childhoods of eminent men does not give sufficient recognition to the later influence of their wives. John Dewey is one of those persons who might never have been able to reach a wide audience had he not been helped by his wife. Alice Chapman Dewey, a highly opinionated woman, "strong minded, descended from a family of radicals, and free-thinkers," was the woman who made a success of the late-blooming student. He was content just to think; it was she who grabbed his ideas, appreciated them, and insisted that something be done about them.

John Dewey would have been content with fewer honors. He was always at his best with a child climbing up his pant-leg or fishing in his inkwell. The boys and girls who come from the trouble-free families are almost certain to be good heads of families. Unlike the mother-dominated or the mother-smothered, they marry at appropriate ages and remain happily married. In this instance, the dominating wife supplied the "push" that John Dewey lacked.

Martin Luther King, African-American Baptist minister who adapted the Gandhian technique of nonviolence to the problem of racial prejudice in the United States, came from a family whose emotional and intellectual climate fits almost perfectly the current concept of the ideal home. His parents were devoted to each other and shared a common philosophy and interests. They had status in the community; they were both scholarly. They provided a warm, cohesive home for their three children.

Martin Luther King is the only individual among the Four Hundred who mentions having been sent to nursery school. From the very beginning, he had good peer relationships. He was a gifted child, skipped three grades, and was ready for college at fifteen. At the same time, he belonged to a close group of boys and girls who represented the "best" families in the black community and with them he swam, double-dated (often with his sister and her boyfriend), and played games. He belonged to the debate club and was popular with his teachers. He attended Morehouse, the college that his grandfather and father had attended before him. Martin was a handsome, healthy boy who was a joy and pride to his parents.

Martin started earning money very early. At four, he was given pennies by family friends who coaxed him to sing for them. At age seven, he and his sister put up a cold drink stand on the sidewalk outside the house and went into business, but they drank too freely from their stock to make a profit. At eight, he began selling weekly newspapers to earn pocket money. At thirteen, he had his own paper route, and a few years later, he had worked himself up to be an assistant manager in charge of thirty other boys.

He was not overprotected. He was knocked from his bicycle by automobiles on two occasions. He was hit in the head by a baseball bat, but "bounced up" and went on playing. He made kites and flew model airplanes and played with "anybody and everybody" who came along. His parents made no restrictions upon him other than to ask him to avoid boys with bad reputations.

The father of the family, Martin King, Sr., pastor of the Ebenezer Baptist church and a man of power and prominence in the large black community, was not one to take racial prejudice lightly. He gave his children the best life he could and sheltered them from being cast in racially subservient roles during childhood. He did not permit them to work for white families, nor did he buy goods that required that collections be made by white agents.

When he shopped in stores, he paid cash and insisted on being treated with courtesy. When a shoe clerk asked him to move to the rear of the store to sit in segregated seats, he did not buy shoes for the six-year-old Martin in that store. The family was sometimes fearful that the father's independence would get him into trouble. When a policeman called the elder King "Uncle" or "Boy," he refused to accept the condescending appellation. When a white policeman was rude to the young people at the church, Martin's father arranged for that man to be moved to another beat. Once in court, he talked back to the judge in defense of a member of the black community. A considerable part of his time was spent in "straightening out the white folks," and no harm was ever done to him. The family did not use the segregated buses in Atlanta because of the constant cursing and arguing over proper seating that went on in them.

During his childhood, young Martin Luther King moved with assurance within the black community and was seldom touched by the fringe of prejudice that surrounded him. At the Laboratory High School of the University of Atlanta, the contacts he had with white teachers were likely to be friendly. Miss Beatrice Boley, his biology teacher, a strict disciplinarian, was thorough in her counseling of the brilliant boy. She made a detailed study of his scholastic strengths and weaknesses and recommended certain remedial practices aimed at improving his study habits.

It was to his mother and his maternal grandmother that the boy looked for a depth of warmth and affection. His grandparents were very much a part of the children's lives. The children called their mother "Mother, Dear." Grandmother, a woman of good health and fine spirits, was "Mamma." "Granddaddy" was the person they looked to as the patriarch, although he was gentle and permissive in his role as a grandfather. He was a powerful man in the black community and was involved in business as well as religious affairs.

Alberta Williams King, Martin's mother, was a strong and amiable woman, tall, dark, and deliberate. She had roomed with her husband's sister when she was in high school at Spelman Seminary, and it was through this sister, Woodie Clara King, that she met her future husband. Her parents encouraged the romance with the young man and welcomed their only daughter and her husband into the twelve-room house, which was the church parsonage. The temporary arrangement was so satisfactory that it was never changed. Christine and Martin Luther were born and Alfred Daniel was on the way before their father completed divinity school. The children were congenial companions. When their father graduated, he became his father-in-law's assistant.

When Martin and his sister and brother were all in school, his strong and vital mother went back to college and finished her degree, which had been postponed by an early marriage to a young theological student. She later did some substitute teaching after her children were old enough not to need her constant care.

It was out of this secure, warm, exceptionally cohesive home that the dynamic social leader, Martin Luther King, Jr., came. His father's opinionatedness seems to be an important factor in the boy's subsequent development.

Martin's Luther's father, son of a sharecropper who beat his wife, felt strongly about the family's need to rise in social and intellectual status. He required academic accomplishment and drive for success from his sons. It is Martin Luther, the son who extended the parental occupation and his father's independent attitude toward segregation, who became eminent. The rebel in the family, Alfred Daniel, who resented his father, quit school and married very young, and he did not have an opportunity to use his talents so well.

A particular immigrant husband and wife in the United States, one of forty-six immigrant families among the Four Hundred, retained their sense of a world culture and also had an intense pleasure in their children

When Louis Brandeis graduated from his grade school in St. Louis, he won a gold medal for scholarship. His Jewish immigrant family was well accepted in that frontier town. They had had dreams of being farmers in the new country, but when that idea proved impractical, they had sought the hinterlands and avoided the cities where there were established Jewish communities. Their home was an impromptu intellectual center, a Mecca for scholarly residents and visitors to the growing city. The whole family was remarkable for its learning and culture. Both of the parents spoke three languages.

When a business depression struck the United States, Mr. Brandeis sold his business and the whole family went for a pleasure trip to Europe until times were better. Louis was to remember that period as the golden time of his life, although his sister Amy became ill with typhoid in Milan, Italy, and his mother and his other sister, Fanny, stayed in a hotel to nurse her. His father and the two boys, Alfred and Louis, went mountain climbing in Switzerland together. They made a point of searching for the sources of rivers until Louis exploded, "I don't see why I should have to find the source of every damned river in Europe." He was then, and continued to be, rather easily tired by physical activity.

When the mountain climbing was done, Louis tried to enter the Gymnasium in Vienna but was not accepted by the school authorities, so he traveled to Dresden and searched out the Annen-Realschule. For a time, he walked about it like a moth around a lantern. The rector dismissed his request for admission, saying that Louis had come without a birth certificate and without proof of his vaccination; he also had not passed the entrance examination. The implication was that no boy brought up in the wilds of the Western United States could ever accomplish such a feat.

Louis rolled up his sleeve and showed the rector his vaccination. "Now look at me," he said, "and observe that I am born." The amused rector accepted him without the formality of an examination. His parents were delighted with his initiative and were not surprised that he placed in the top section of his class in his studies. Brandeis grew up to be an attorney and Supreme Court Justice.

Louis Koren, Detroit psychiatrist, once observed that the chief need of children is to be enjoyed. Fredericka Brandeis was a woman whose principal joy was her children. She marveled at the comradeship between her sons and noted their tenderness to their sick sister. Both parents had faith and admiration for Louis. When his eyesight was poor during his Harvard years, they were sympathetic and supportive but not overprotective, and their attitude helped him to overcome the handicap.

When the children questioned their parents as to their reasons for not belonging to a synagogue or church even though they admired the ethical qualities of all religions, Fredericka wrote for them the following statement, which they treasured and saved:

> *I do not believe that sins can be expiated by going to divine services and observing this or that formula. Love, truth, and virtue are the foundation upon which the education of the child must be based.... I wanted to give them something*

> *that neither can be argued away, or given up as untenable, namely, a pure spirit and the highest ideals as to morals and love. God has blessed my endeavors.*[1]

A wealthy family that also took time to enjoy its children were the Kennedys. This family also gave the children physical and intellectual freedom. The two oldest Kennedy sons, Joe and Jack, used to go sailing alone when they were so small that the sailboats looked empty from the shore because the tops of the boys' heads did not show. All nine of the children were given both freedom and responsibility and were pitted against each other by their father in sports and in scholastic achievement. There were high expectations for each of them.

Among the statesmen of the Four Hundred, there are no instances of divorce or separation among the parents. A number of the men elected to office were orphans or half-orphans but were reared in warm, supportive homes. It is among the statesmen, the men and women whose special interests are peace or international good will, and the lawyers and scientists that the most excellent examples of the warm and cohesive homes are found.

Adlai Stevenson, Governor of Illinois and Democratic presidential candidate, was brought up in an explosive but essentially affectionate family. Both his father, Lewis Stevenson, and his mother, Helen Davis Stevenson, were given to repartee and to storytelling and were dynamic and vigorous individuals. His mother believed in spending money on education, travel, and furnishing a home; his father was extravagantly generous and often outraged at his wife's Quaker sense of thrift. Since the family was well-to-do and never suffered want because of these differences, this divergence in temperament was not crucial.

Both parents, and also the grandparents, enjoyed the two children—quiet, peacemaking Adlai and his bouncing, aggressive older sister Elizabeth, known as "Buffie." The family traveled so much with the children that Adlai had little formal schooling until he was nine. Adlai's sister, now Mrs. Ernest L. Ives, says that the classics never had for them the "bitter medicinal taste of compulsory education." Their mother read to them from Hawthorne's *Wonder Book*, from Hugo's *Les Miserables*, from Scott's *Waverley Novels*, and from Cooper's *Last of the Mohicans*. She read well and had a flair for drama.

Within the family, Adlai Stevenson was jokingly nicknamed "The Brute" because he was so gentle, well-behaved, and excessively conscientious. When his hands were slapped for pulling glasses and silver off of the table accidentally, he crept off to sleep in the dog kennel and was found there hours afterwards by contrite and frantic parents.

Although his parents were argumentative and extremely outspoken, Adlai was quiet and amiable. At school, he was marked "excellent" in behavior. His grades were low, partly because he was absent so often. In second grade, he attended school for only ten days during the first semester, and the teacher graded him poor in reading and spelling and fair in writing.

Among Adlai's peers, he was neither submissive nor overly aggressive. He had the usual number of fights, overturned outhouses on Halloween, hoisted wagon wheels to the roof, and put a black kitten into his sister's bed, which frightened her into hysterics.

The children went on long nature walks with their mother and were taught to observe specimens and to draw pictures of their findings. They improvised stories at the dinner table. One parent would start a story; the other would embroider it. They tossed the narrative back and forth until everyone was shouting with laughter. Adlai says of his father, "He was one of the funniest men I've ever known."

Since Adlai's father was the manager of forty-nine farms owned by a widowed aunt, he was the first man to be listed as a farmer in *Who's Who*, and his children knew the price of corn per bushel before they could spell. The adults shared their own interests with the children.

The classroom had little attraction for children whose home life was so rewarding. Adlai limited his formal studies to the barely acceptable minimum. His teachers complained that his interests were too wide, too varied. They interpreted his boredom as lack of concentration. It was not until he was at Princeton that he became an adequate student.

His grandfather, W. O. Davis, was one of the individuals with whom he often spoke. It was from this man that he heard long, detailed accounts of his ancestor Jesse Fell, a Quaker who was a peace-loving man, a man of large vision and great capability. Jesse Fell became Adlai's hero, the man he wished most to emulate. Biographer Kenneth Davis says, "Of all the boy's ancestral influences Jesse Fell's was the most important. Fell's influence might even be said to have become a central strand of meaning around which was woven the fabric of the boy's education."

Grandfather Adlai Ewing Stevenson, once Vice-President, was also important to Adlai. He learned history from the stories of his ancestors. History on this side of the family started with "Little Gabriel," a pious and loud-voiced great-great-great-grandfather who once prayed the devil out of a melancholy preacher sunk into silent gloom. Grandfather Stevenson used to coax his grandchildren into the library with milk and cookies, then read to them there while they enjoyed their refreshments. When Adlai was six, his grandfather read to him from *Hamlet* and from Robert Ingersoll's funeral oration for his brother. And this same grandfather so aroused Adlai's interest in history that he read all thirteen volumes of Markham's *The Real American Romance* before he was thirteen. Their Grandfather Davis read to them from Robert Burns with a fine Scotch accent.

P. M. Sheldon,[2] who has studied families of highly gifted children, has suggested that more attention be given to the influence of grandparents as it is transmitted to the grandchildren through the parents. He has suggested studying the transmission of pressures from grandparents, and he implies that the internalization of these pressures by the parents may produce a blooming of abilities in the next generation.

Adlai's mother tended to be overprotective, but he resisted this attitude stoutly and would not permit himself to be made a hypochondriac. He was active and had good peer relationships. He broke his nose twice. In adolescence, he was tragically involved in the accidental shooting of a young girl cousin. Though he was in no way to blame for the "gun that wasn't loaded," the tragic interruption of a holiday dinner nevertheless affected the boy deeply. His feelings of guilt always burdened him. His sister said of the home, "Underneath and all the time there was so much love."

Thirty American high school students who were Westinghouse Award winners were interviewed and studied by P. F. Brandwein in 1954-55. They were quiet, reflective, and inward-looking. They liked to hike, read serious books and magazines, and listen to classical rather than popular music. They often chose to do social work or read to the blind and were involved in religious work. A vast majority bought books for their own use. They did not smoke until their senior year in high school, or they did not smoke at all. They almost never found themselves in difficulties in school, although they often disagreed with teachers over the interpretation of schoolwork. They were conservative in dress and spent considerable time in self-initiated projects such as stamp collecting and ham radios. They were seldom elected to school offices; they were not the popular type. They came from homes with substantial libraries, and most of the parents had ambitions for a professional life for the children. Twenty-four of the thirty were first-born children; sixteen were only children.

Like the Westinghouse Award winners, neither parents nor children in homes that produced scientists in this sample were disposed to get involved in traumatic interpersonal relationships. There were no homes broken by divorce or desertion or separation among the parents of scientists, unless the long absence of Selman Waksman's father in the Army is interpreted as such.

Observation of homes that produced scientists and physicians uncovers some differences among them that correlate with the emotional atmosphere in the home. Doctors who were also writers of fiction or plays often came from turbulent, unhappy homes and must be omitted from this chapter. Examples are: Dr. Somerset Maugham, an unhappy orphan; Dr. A. J. Cronin, who described the tension in his family over his father's death and the differences in religion within his family in his semi-autobiographical novels; Dr. Anton Chekhov, who came from a very disturbed home; and Dr.

Conan Doyle, whose father was the unsuccessful member of an achieving family, and whose mother resented that fact.

Making collections was a favored hobby among the physicians, and their parents were encouraging and tolerant of this activity. They were especially fond of physical freedom, of roaming far and wide over the countryside.

Hans Zinsser, the physician-bacteriologist, took a great pleasure in his popular book, *Rats, Lice and History.* His autobiography, *As I Remember Him*, tells of his warm and cohesive home and the mother who lived only two weeks after his father died. "She seemed to die of his death," the son said. Zinsser was a much-overprotected youngest son who was kept home with his mother until he was eleven.

He had the love of mischief that characterizes so many of the pre-physicians. He dawdled through a preparatory school carefully chosen by his liberal and opinionated father and made a fair adjustment at Columbia, where he studied comparative literature. He intended to be a writer but became a scientist because of a prank. An impulse moved him to throw a snowball at a professor emerging from the Natural Science building. His aim was good, and the professor's hat flew off. In order to show the offended man that he had no personal animosity toward him, he enrolled in his class the next semester. Suddenly, Zinsser was cut loose from the department of comparative literature. The science department became to him a world of wonders and revelations.

Becoming engrossed in science did not cure his urge for practical jokes, however. He pretended to have a fit of hydrophobia in order to frighten a pedantic classmate. In the fracas, laboratory equipment was knocked over. A professor doused Zinsser with a bucketful of sea urchins to make him quit biting his classmate's leg.

William Osler, renowned Canadian surgeon, had extremely permissive parents. He ran home shouting with glee when he got himself expelled for shouting insults at his master through a keyhole. The clergyman and his wife obligingly found another school for their ingenious son, where he distinguished himself by fumigating a matron with sulphur. Since Osler had involved many other students in the practical joke, no one was expelled, but the matron sued the boys and was awarded costs and a dollar paid by each offender. The eight other children of this clergyman's family were not so difficult.

When the boy came under the influence of a teacher who stimulated him, he abandoned some of his mischief. This teacher's conception of knowledge did not lie in the greatest number of facts that could be drilled into boys, but in the ideas that radiated from them under given stimuli. The students were taken on all-day fossil hunts. William learned to make slides for the teacher's microscope to show to the other boys.

Osler's biographer is the cantankerous and eminent physician Harvey Cushing, whose explosive manners in the operating room have been the subject for comment by yet another medical writer, Dr. William Sharpe.

Sir Wilfred Grenfell, doctor, humanitarian, writer, and adventurer, had a mother who looked like Queen Victoria and a daydreaming clergyman-teacher father. His dominating mother ran the boarding school, which was the source of the family income; his father was the beloved teacher who seemed as childlike as his students.

Wilfred's parents gave their children almost complete freedom. When school closed for the summer, the boys were left unchaperoned. As soon as their parents left, the brothers invited adolescent guests to make merry with them. They sent their cousins a telegram advising them to come quickly—the coast was clear; the parents were gone. The parents thought it a great joke when the telegram came while they were visiting in the home to which the telegram was sent.

Dr. William Carlos Williams, the poet and uninhibited writer of autobiography from Rutherford, New Jersey, came from a home that was warm but explosive and turbulent. His engineer father was away much of the time. His parents were congenial, but there were erratic guests who came and stayed for months, an uncle who went mad and tried to murder them, and a grandmother who fought physically with his mother. He and his brother Ed, however, grew up as one person, were constantly together for twenty years, and loved each other completely. Their escapades caused their devoted mother real distress.

> *Poor mother, sometimes she'd whale hell out of us with anything she could lay her hands on. It was a piece of cordwood once. She laid it on good, too, and later took me upstairs to bathe the place with witch hazel.*[3]

Physicians tell more about their parents and childhood experiences than do scientists. Dr. Charles Mayo once said, "The biggest thing Will [his brother] and I ever did was to pick the father and mother we had." Dr. William Mayo said of their mother, "She accepted what good there was in folks and did not criticize the bad. I never knew her to say a hateful word about anyone."[4]

From the very beginning, brothers Charles and William were always together. "We were known as 'The Mayo Boys.' Anyone that picked on one of us had to contend with the other." Willie was the older; Charlie was the rather sickly, small brother. They had the freedom of the countryside, shot marbles, went fishing, bagged wild pigeons, and rode horseback. Will was the reader; Charles the mechanic. Charlie was always fixing something—a churn, a pump, a stove. He contrived a steam engine to do the family wash, cut wood, and pump water. At fourteen, he studied articles about the telephone, and he constructed one that led from his father's office to the house. The telephone company claimed an infringement of its patent, and the device had to be replaced by a conventional instrument.

Charles and William's father was a country physician, and the whole family assisted him as a matter of course. Mrs. Mayo helped to set limbs and coaxed medicine into sick babies. The boys dressed wounds, prepared microscope slides, went with their father on trips to the country, and talked with him about diagnosis and prognosis as they rode behind the horses their father drove at top speed. Will attended autopsies when he was so young that he could not see the body on the table. His father plunked him on the table near the corpse's head, and the child clutched the corpse's hair to steady himself as he watched the proceedings. Charlie took over the anesthetist's job when the man fainted during an especially gory operation, and he continued to help his father in this fashion, even though some of the patients were fearful to see a boy in this role. Both boys went to medical meetings with their father and read the books and papers he published.

Dr. Mayo was an original and imaginative researcher as well as a country doctor, and he never waited for a patient to pay before he treated him. He believed that any man with unusual abilities owed his services to the public in proportion to his own strength. There were always plenty of patients, and the countryside was plagued with drought, debt, bad crops, low prices, and homes lost because of mortgage foreclosures. Sometimes, however, tensions between the husband and wife kept them from speaking freely to each other for long periods of time.

There was no time or inclination for writing in the Mayo family, where there was more actual working together at the family business than occurs in most families. There was the freedom, the direct contact with earth and sweat and blood that was to stand the boys in good stead when they grew to be men.

In a home in Topeka, Kansas, another physician, Dr. Charles Menninger, brought up two sons who were to become eminent for the establishment of a diagnostic private hospital for mental patients. Flora Knisely Menninger is one of four mothers of the Four Hundred who wrote her own book about how she brought up her children. (The others are the mothers of Franklin D. Roosevelt and Robert A. Taft, and the stepmother of Gertrude Bell.) Flora says in her book, *Story of My Days*:

> *Daddy has always been a devoted husband and a loving father to his boys. I could ask no greater gift than that they might be like him in spirit and purpose toward those they love. My dream was for a husband who was tall and slender and intelligent and interesting. I hoped we would like the same things. My dreams have been fulfilled beyond anything I could have desired.*

Dr. Charles Menninger and his wife enjoyed their children. There was no thought of taking a vacation apart from them. Charles was also fond of his garden in the back yard. When the boys grew older and needed the space for their Boy Scout activities, he rented three lots close by and fenced the peony garden, which became a community attraction. He was also a member of the National Council of Boy Scouts during the formative years of that organization.

Flora Knisely Menninger began teaching a Bible class in her Presbyterian Sunday School when the youngest of her children was three weeks old. In 1919, she was supervising a total enrollment of four hundred persons. By 1923, the classes were incorporated with the YWCA, and five hundred men and women participated. The classes were interracial, and fourteen teachers were needed to teach the groups. To a lesser extent, Flora occupied herself with art classes. The children did not receive her undivided, smothering attention.

Walker Winslow, author of *The Menninger Story*, is of the opinion that Flora Menninger was overextended in her community activities and that her early experiences as a poor orphan girl on the farm kept her from filling her function as the wife of a well-to-do doctor with grace and aplomb—but he also indicates that her husband never showed the slightest awareness of this shortcoming in his wife.

Karl Menninger had difficulties as a child. His first-grade teacher thought him dull, and it was not until he was "double-promoted" that his real abilities evidenced themselves. It was he who became a popular writer as well as an eminent psychiatrist and founder of the famed Menninger Clinic in Topeka, Kansas.

A survey of four hundred families can indicate trends and discover the major likenesses and major differences between families. For instance, there is a relationship between the severity of the problems that the pre-medical man has in his childhood home and the probability of his also becoming a writer as an adult.

The famous people who are public servants come from comparatively serene homes, but writers of imaginative literature frequently come from troubled, fragmented, turbulent homes. A reexamination of the eighty-seven writers finds a scant handful of homes that have warmth and cohesion. Some of these homes are described here to demonstrate that a writer of prose or poetry can sometimes be reared in a home that fits the idealized John-Mary Smith pattern comfortably.

Of his schoolmaster father, A. A. Milne says, "He was the best man I have ever known." His mother, whom he felt he never really knew, was "simple, unemotional and common-sensible." The three Milne brothers never ceased to quarrel but never ceased to feel the need of each other. "We were," A. A. Milne said, "given much more freedom than most children." They spent whole days wandering about London together when they were quite small. They were always well behaved. They collected everything, including minerals and caterpillars, were read aloud to, went visiting, and had pets. There was laughter in the house. They were poor, and yet never knew they were poor. The father made learning fun. "In Papa's house it was natural to be interested; it was easy to be clever."

A poet from an immigrant family describes his mother thus: "The mother however couldn't help saying nice things when we did well at anything. Whether it was schoolwork, or learning the catechism or hanging out sheets and shirts on a cold winter day, she would speak thanks or say I was a good boy." So says Carl Sandburg in his autobiography, a documentary of a happy family. Of his parents' marriage he says, "Mama's wedding ring was never lost—it was a sign and seal of something that ran deep and held fast between the two of them." His father was a strong man who could hold up his end on a piece of work, who could come home after a ten-hour day with his shirt soaked with sweat and make no complaints, although he looked fatigued and worn.

Another country boy with poor parents, author and educator Jesse Stuart, makes his affection for his parents and his appreciation of his childhood home in Kentucky repeatedly known in his autobiographical volumes. Psychologist Havelock Ellis was the son of a sea captain who was absent each year for nine months, so the captain and his wife enjoyed a three-month honeymoon each year. Their son enjoyed both parents. The "Prince of Storytellers," author E. Phillips Oppenheim, was the son of a leather merchant who loved his wife and only son. The father raised funds to pay for the publication of the young man's first book, which a publisher had rejected. And there is no home more exciting or more admirable for easy affection, understanding, and warmth than the home of Lincoln Steffens, the well-known journalist who plunged into the problems of the corruption of cities.

Within a given family, there is not always agreement as to the merits of the family life experienced by the siblings. Mary Ellen Chase, the educator and author who writes with warming felicity about her childhood, says in her autobiography, *White Gate*: "I have never felt a trace of resentment toward my early upbringing, which still seems to me just, if stern and unyielding."

She is quick to add that two of her sisters, who have families of their own, contend that their parents needlessly controlled and repressed their children and have, in consequence, used different methods with their own children. She continues:

> *Unmarried myself and, therefore, with no urgent personal stake in this matter, I have, nevertheless, been interested through the years in trying to discover what improvements either in methods or in off-spring they have been able to achieve, given their own time and place.*

Her parents were always ready to use a slipper or a whittled shingle as a paddle when a child was disobedient or rude, neglected her chores, or lied. When the children became too difficult, their mother deftly attached them with rolled-up towels to the doorknobs and left them swinging with their toes barely touching the floor. As a less stringent discipline, a child might be fastened by a rolled-up towel to the top shelf of the large desk in the corner of the kitchen to read and watch while the mother made apple pies rich with cinnamon or baked ginger snaps in the oven.

Each child was taught to read at home before age five, and every evening after the dishes were done, the children gathered about the table for homework. Even the littlest child had to sit fifteen minutes with the others at the homework table. Their lawyer father set them to work measuring the woodpile to determine its volume in cubic feet. "Your father," their mother might say, "is planning to question you soon on the Roman Emperors."

When the fifty-eight homes chosen as most nearly trouble-free were studied, certain common behaviors were observed: the parents and children often enjoyed each other; they worked together and played together. When the parents liked each other, so did the children. The children had considerable intellectual and physical freedom. There was an absence of anxiety about their safety and health. There was more fun and humor in these families, more tolerance for minor misdemeanors. There was no absence of firm control, and usually there was a definite family code of ethics. Expectations were high, but not as high as in other homes where a parent was dominating.

There are three most impressive differences to be observed among the families of the Four Hundred: (1) the dearth of trouble-free homes among the actors, (2) the few trouble-free homes among the writers, artists, and musicians, and (3) the higher incidence of family solidarity in the homes of scientists, physicians, and some statesmen.

Chapter 8
Children With Handicaps

Or are these highly productive people more like the oyster that requires a grain of sand to make the pearl?
— Kenneth E. Andersen, Ed., *Research on the Academically Talented Student*

Children classified today as "gifted" are ordinarily superior in all areas—physically and emotionally, as well as intellectually—according to studies by Lewis Terman. They have a high tolerance for frustration, are commonly free from nervous disorders, are attractive and healthy, and are taller and stronger than most children.

This is by no means true of all of the Four Hundred, who may show intellectual and creative ability of the highest order yet be blind, crippled, small of stature, homely, overweight, or physically debilitated. A need to compensate for a handicap in physique is described by many of these persons as the reason for their urgent need to achieve.

In many biographies, and especially in autobiographies, there is frequent direct and strong reference to the spur to achievement that adverse circumstances in childhood gives to these individuals who achieve distinction.

Blindness and Poor Sight

Authors Helen Keller and Ved Mehta are the totally blind among the persons surveyed. Seriously handicapping eye disorders were suffered by Rudyard Kipling, Aldous Huxley, Sean O'Casey, and Syngman Rhee. Children less drastically affected by their poor eyesight were Harry Truman, Lafcadio Hearn, Reginald Fessenden, Louis Brandeis, Emile Zola, James Joyce, Carl Sandburg, and William James.

At age five, Helen Keller was a willful, wild animal with no way of communicating her thoughts. Her teacher, Anne Sullivan, a poor orphan who was also handicapped by limited vision, was responsible for Helen's graduation from Radcliffe, summa cum laude. Helen was quite capable of comparing the philosophies of Kant and Emerson and speculated about war and peace. She read French, German, Latin, Greek, and English. She rode, swam, and bicycled. Had her mother permitted, she would have married.

Meningitis took Ved Mehta's sight when he was so young an infant that he had no memory of being able to see. His well-to-do father, an Indian public health officer, realized that his first son would remain blind and would have to learn to live with his blindness. Blindness in India is often considered a curse—a punishment for a sin committed by one's parents—and the blind are shunned. Ved's mother turned frantically to native miracle workers, who put bitter drops in the boy's eyes which hurt and frightened him. His parents were not compatible.

At the age of five, Ved was sent away to a school for blind children. "You are now a man," his father told him as he left home. By the time he was fifteen, Ved Mehta was hitchhiking alone across the Western United States on his way from Arkansas to Los Angeles, and as an adult, he became a writer for the *New Yorker.*

A man from Dublin who became a playwright also had eye problems. When Sean O'Casey was five years old, small, shiny, pearly specks appeared on his eyeballs. He began to dread the light, to keep his eyes closed, and to sit and moan restlessly in the darkest places he could find.

Sean was his mother's last child, born after two other sons of the same name had died in infancy. One died while his mother sat pleading for help from callous nurses and doctors who said she must be quiet and wait her turn. They lingered over other patients who were not seriously ill while the child strangled to death from a respiratory infection.

If Sean O'Casey's father had not been so opinionated, the family would have had more financial security. Michael O'Casey's strong convictions about Protestantism led him to accept a poorly paid job as a clerk in an Irish church mission. When he died suddenly at forty-nine, he left his wife and six children with no inheritance except his library and his love for learning. The family was thrown into extreme poverty. The O'Caseys are the only family in this sample of the eminent who experienced both cold and hunger repeatedly.

Mrs. O'Casey was a fierce and partisan mother when her children were threatened, but she was warm and encouraging at home. Sean's eye problems meant endless trips to the hospital for drops, ointments, bandages, and hot and cold water soakings.

At the Protestant school Sean attended, the rector was not sympathetic. "Doctors differ and patients die.... If we all carried out the doctor's strict injunctions, none of us would ever move from the fire. What will the doctor do for him in after years when he has to make his way in life, unable to read or write?"[1] His mother withdrew Sean from the school after his sadistic master beat him unmercifully, then required him to kneel and beg forgiveness for having kicked the master's shins during the beating episode. Sean's three years of intermittent schooling were over.

Sean learned most from his older brother, Archie, who was active in amateur theatricals. The ten-year-old Sean, who could not read or write, learned scenes from Shakespeare and Boucicault. At fifteen, he made his own debut as an actor.

When Sean was thirteen and his eyes had somewhat improved, he set himself an ambitious program of self-education, holding the page close to his nose in order to read. He read Shakespeare, Dickens, Scott, Balzac, Byron, Shelley, Keats, and Goldsmith. Once, when his scanty wages were docked by two shillings in an office where he worked, he was so upset that he stole a copy of Milton from a neighboring bookstall. His older sister Isabella tried to teach him grammar, but he resisted. His escape from formal schooling, he felt, was fortuitous, and he believed that it was his bad eyes that made him a playwright.

John Lockwood Kipling, a professor of sculpture in a school in Bombay, India, and his wife, Alice MacDonald Kipling, lost their third baby soon after it was born. This experience sent them to England to search for a boarding home where they might leave their son Rudyard, who was then five and a half, and daughter Beatrice (Trix), who was not yet two. Through a newspaper advertisement, they found a couple who made a business of boarding English children whose parents were Indian civil servants. Once the children were placed, John and Alice Kipling slipped away to avoid tearful farewells. Rudyard was eleven years old when his mother finally returned to take him away, but there is nothing to indicate that she was ever an accepting mother who enjoyed her children.

In this tidy and proper-appearing household where the children spent six of their youngest years, things were not as they seemed. Rudyard was driven to near-blindness and near-madness. From the beginning, the boy from India annoyed his "Aunt Rosa," as he was told to call her, and her rather stupid and sadistic son, who was a few years older than Rudyard. The Old Sea Captain, who was the head of the family, treated the boarded-out boy well enough, but he soon died. "Aunt Rosa" did not like the table manners that Rudyard had learned from Indian servants. He sprawled over the furniture as he had sprawled over the studio furnishings in Bombay where no one had minded his careless ways. His continual conversation, his searching questions, and his lack of response to any demonstration of sentiment repelled his foster aunt. She introduced Rudyard to hell and its terrors for the good of his soul. An unexplained smile (which she probably correctly viewed as a smirk) could be cause for punishment. Trix, on the other hand, the charming and obedient infant, she always liked.

> *Myself, I was regularly beaten. The Woman had an only son of twelve or thirteen as religious as she. I was a real joy to him,*

> *for when his mother finished with me for the day he (we slept in the same room) took me on and roasted the other side.*[2]

The Kipling children had two grandmothers and a great number of young, celebrated, well-to-do uncles and aunts with young children of their own who all lived in England. The Burne-Joneses, the Poynters, and Baldwins all took a very casual attitude toward Mary MacDonald Kipling's children. The MacDonald grandmother and two aunts made one duty call. They noted that the children were well fed, clean, and adequately clothed, and they left satisfied. "Aunt Rosa" was a pious and proper woman.

Aunt Georgiana Burne-Jones was the most considerate of Rudyard and Trix's biological aunts. Each year in December, he was invited to visit at the Burne-Jones home for a whole month. The guests represented the most imaginative of the new intellectuals. The furniture was of the latest design. William Morris himself was one of the courtesy "uncles" he knew well there. The Rossettis and Ford Madox Ford and Swinburne had attended the wedding of Rudyard's parents. The only crotchety visitor was an old man they all called "Browning," who was annoyed by the swarm of children in the entry hall.

Rudyard liked best to lean over the banisters on the top landing to listen to the rise and fall of the deep voices of men talking at the table about politics and art and literature. There was nothing like this at the dull house in Southsea.

"Aunt Rosa," when she discovered that Rudyard liked to read, restricted the pastime. He learned to read secretly in semi-darkness, but his eyes began to bother him. His schoolwork suffered, and when he pretended not to have received a poor report card, he was sent to school with "Liar" placarded on his back.

This episode precipitated an emotional disturbance. He saw shadows that were not there and objects that did not exist. "Aunt Rosa" isolated him as if he were a leper. Trix, who defended him faithfully during those miserable six years, was not permitted to be near him. His Aunt Georgiana appeared suddenly, then a strange doctor, and finally his mother, from whom he shrank, expecting a blow when she bent over to kiss him.

When he had been fitted with thick-lensed new glasses, which were unusual for a boy to be wearing at that time, Alice Kipling took Trix and Rudyard and Stanley Baldwin, her nephew, to a little farm near the edge of Epping Forest for a few months. She let the children run free; the only requirement was that they wash before meals. Stanley and Rudyard annoyed their farmer host, who questioned whether they were good for each other.

Rudyard's mother did not know what to do with her stranger-son. In the fall, she moved into lodgings in London. She bought Rudyard and Trix season tickets to the old South Kensington Museum, which was across the road. This gave their "sorely tired" mother a rest. The children invaded the museum, went into the places marked "Private," and divided among themselves small treasures they found there.

At night, Rudyard roamed the house because he could not sleep. It was the beginning of his recurrent insomnia. Soon his mother went back to India, and Rudyard was left with three "dear old ladies" who were cultured and kind and vague. From there he went to the United Services College, whose head was one of the courtesy "uncles" he had known during his holidays at the Burne-Jones home.

The precocious, youthfully mature, "cheeky" boy with a mustache and new thick-lensed glasses was not popular at school. He looked, Beresford says, something like a small cave man. It was not until he was fourteen and could defend himself against any other boy in school that he had some relief from bullying. During that first year and a half, he had made friends with two other boys who were, like himself, "different."

At the end of his first horrible term at school, Rudyard had to spend the holiday on the school premises. He went back to "Aunt Rosa's" rather frequently because his sister Trix was still there, despite the ill treatment that he had experienced in this home. A pale, dark-haired girl two years older than he had taken his place as a boarding child, and he fell madly in love with her. They became engaged when he was fourteen and were still engaged when he went to India after he graduated at seventeen. Time and distance later broke the tie.

Rudyard Kipling is typical of the gifted child with problems. Teachers of children selected for special intellectual ability often find them well behaved except for an inability to wait their turn to talk. They are prone to annoy adults with their verbosity, hair-splitting opinionatedness, and persistence in pursuing their own goals. If they become impudent, they are efficiently so. To a person of limited capacities, such a child can be especially infuriating, and the tension between the adult and the child can mushroom to alarming proportions. The emotionally disturbed bright boy may seem less like a child than like a needling, hateful adult who happens to be inhabiting a child's body. He or she has none of the appeal of the innocent and unaware.

Kipling's seemingly neglectful English aunts and uncles can be absolved to some extent. He was not always a good houseguest. On one occasion, he arrived at the MacDonald household in a rage because he had been slapped by a railroad porter for his impudence. He rolled with rage on the nursery floor, then jumped up and announced his intention of going straight back to the station to "cheek that porter again." He was a little older than most of his cousins and experienced pubescence early. Having him as a guest may have worried and wearied his aunts, since his cousins are said to have found him exciting.

Even so, his eye problems, thick glasses, and odd appearance made his social adjustments difficult. When he graduated, he spent his last few days with the Burne-Joneses at their cottage in Rottingdean—the only place he could remember feeling happy. (When Kipling was grown, he asked for the bell rope from that house and transferred it to his own so that other children might have the pleasure of feeling happy when they rang it.) His Aunt Georgiana asked him why he had not told how he was mistreated by "Aunt Rosa." "Children," Kipling says in his autobiography, "tell little more than animals, for what comes to them they accept as eternally established. Also, badly treated children have a clear notion of what they are likely to get if they betray the secrets of a prison-house before they are clear of it."

He later attributed certain traits that stood him in good stead to his sorry experiences between the ages of five and eleven. He learned to notice discrepancies between speech and action; he was always suspicious of sudden favors, was wary and observant, and noticed moods and tempers in others.

Syngman Rhee's smothering mother sobbed as she took her blind son to the Protestant doctor-missionary, who cured him. To her, it was like taking him to the devil. The cure was successful, but she lost her Buddhist son to the new faith, and subsequently to politics. He became South Korea's first President.

British novelist Aldous Huxley contracted a painful eye disease while at Eton and was thereby saved from becoming just another "public school gentleman." He had intended to be a doctor. His eye infection turned him to journalism as an occupation. He came to believe that the harshness of Providence is sometimes actually kindness.

When Louis Brandeis was advised by the first eye specialist he consulted to quit law school because of repeated attacks of severe eyestrain, he went to another physician, who told him to "read less, and think more." Brandeis took this advice and soon had a reputation for erudition. He also asked his classmates to read to him. One of his readers, son of a wealthy paper manufacturer, asked Brandeis to join him in his own law office after they graduated. This relationship accelerated his career. He was known as the "people's attorney" and later became the first Jewish Supreme Court Justice.

Reginald Fessenden, the Canadian-born scientist-inventor, had a serious eye operation when he was seventeen. Not until he was middle-aged did he find complete relief. When doing close work, he removed his glasses and focused his eyes on the object under scrutiny.

"The other boy made it to Annapolis. I failed it because of poor eyesight," says Harry Truman,[3] who had been coached for the examination by his history teacher. He was disappointed, since he had always been a good student. When he was in the second grade, he had diphtheria and was so paralyzed for a time that his mother pushed him about in a baby carriage. He went to summer school to make up for lost time and then skipped the third grade, which he had missed because of illness. In high school, he was a good student and helped establish the school paper. His slight frame and glasses predisposed him to business rather than farming. He became a senator, and in 1945, he won election as President of the United States.

Journalist and Japanese professor Lafcadio Hearn felt like a gargoyle because a playground injury to one of his eyes made it appear small, and his other eye looked correspondingly large. A rejecting father, rejecting aunts, and a mentally ill mother were other burdens. Irish writer James Joyce had lifetime problems with sore and painful eyes. French novelist Emile Zola was a sickly boy with deformed features, myopic eyes, and a lisp.

To Be Small or Slight Is a Handicap

To be smaller than other children, particularly if one is a boy, can often make adjustment difficult. Some slight youths become belligerent; others withdraw. Fiorello LaGuardia, the dynamic and controversial mayor of New York City, stood barely five feet tall. He was not only short, he was also not very handsome. LaGuardia was a member of two minority groups as the son of an Italian father and a Jewish mother. In Prescott, Arizona, the family was accepted as being Italian, although the agnostic ex-Catholic father and the only nominally Jewish mother sent the boy to Episcopal Sunday school. When an organ grinder came to town with a monkey, the other boys turned to Fiorello with: "A Dago with a monkey! Hey, Fiorello, you're a Dago, too! Where's your monkey?"[4]

As a boy, Fiorello was exceedingly small and fought his way through grade school. Once, when he could not reach an opponent's face with his fists, he ran sobbing to the schoolhouse and lugged out a chair. One of his classmates, Joe Bauer, boasted that he licked Fiorello every day. Fiorello, however, according to biographer Arthur Mann, was pugnacious, loquacious, competitive, and blunt.

Arthur Koestler, the Hungarian-born novelist and journalist, at age sixteen was changing his clothes in a bathing cabin at the beach when he heard two women talking. One had made a fondly apologetic remark about her own child's rapid growth. The other had responded, "That's no reason for worry. The terrible thing would be if he were as short as that Koestler boy."[5] A few years later, a Comintern (Communist International) agent referred to Koestler's inferiority complex not as a complex but as a cathedral.

Koestler turned to the classroom for real satisfactions. He liked the Realschule, where he studied modern languages and science. In his early teens, he spoke four languages—Hungarian, German, French, and English. He read Darwin, Spencer, Kepler, Newton, Edison, Herz, and Marconi. He made mechanical toys. At fourteen, he felt that aside from the paradox of infinity and eternity, he had solved all of the riddles of the universe.

By sixteen, Koestler's knowledge did not shield him from fear of embarrassment. He refused to go to dancing parties for fear he might be shorter than his partners. If he was asked to a party and was told that a "tall, beautiful blonde would be included among the guests," he pleaded illness and stayed home.

"I cursed my littleness," said T. E. Lawrence, who called himself "a pocket Hercules." Thomas Hardy, J. M. Barrie, Henry Ford, Hamlin Garland, Joseph Goebbels, Maurice Ravel, Adolf Hitler, and Mohandas Gandhi were other small boys.

In twenty-three of the Four Hundred, being small was seen as a deeply significant factor in their development. This does not mean that there were not other slight or short youths who were also self-conscious in this respect.

In the Gandhi household, the undersized, ailing youngest child, Mohandas, was left to the care of his mother, Putlibai. He was a slight, timid, homely boy who preferred his books to any companions. When he was first sent to school, he ran home quickly so that no one could poke fun at him en route. His mother, conservative as to food, was not particularly concerned about his slightness. The tradition of patient fasting was in the climate of the Gandhi home. It was largely due to Putlibai's piety, which impressed all of her children deeply. For four months of the year (during a kind of Hindu Lent), she ate only a single meal a day. Although her fasts were always begun during the rainy season, she once vowed not to eat until she saw sunshine.

Gandhi's father, Karamchand Gandhi, a fiery, impatient, emotional man of strong principles, was once arrested and held for a few hours because he defended a native ruler against the unjust criticism of a British political agent. He believed in laying up vast sums of money for his children to inherit, and his son Mohandas, in his autobiography, described him as "a lover of his clan, truthful, brave and generous, but short-tempered."

The insignificant Mohandas was the fourth and last child of his father's fourth marriage. His brothers, Laxmidas and Karsandas, more handsome, more aggressive, and much better students than their droll, ugly little brother, paid him little attention. No one expected much of this last child. He was fearful of serpents, ghosts, and darkness, and he clung to his mother for support and affection. His mother loved him, but she did not exclude others from her affection, nor did she dislike his father.

Despite his shyness, Mohandas refused to cheat when he was urged to do so by a teacher who wanted the students to perform well before a visiting inspector. He was inconsolable when a teacher accused him wrongly of having given a false excuse for a school absence. As he grew older, he began to play on the street with the boys, became involved in various delinquencies with a friend, ate forbidden meat, smoked, and visited a brothel where he was cursed and chased away by an indignant woman whom he insulted by merely sitting shyly on the edge of her bed.

At thirteen, he was a sexually aggressive husband, but he developed feelings of guilt about enjoying his marital relationship because his father had died while Mohandas was making love. At eighteen, twice a father, he was obstinate about his decision to go to London to study law. When he promised never to touch wine or women or meat, his mother reluctantly consented. He broke the mother-son circle gradually but definitely during his adolescent years. Boys who admire their fathers usually escape their overly possessive mothers when they become adult.

As a family man, Mohandas Gandhi had the self-centeredness characteristic of small, sickly, mother-smothered boys. His wife and children were given no choice as to behavior, even when it was based upon his convictions and not their own. He denied his sons schooling and refused to receive his son's bride when Harilal married without his consent. In his battle for the political freedom of one-fifth of the human race, the tiny little man in a loincloth was indomitable. In gaining that freedom, he was often heavily dependent upon women followers: Annie Besant, Olive Schreiner, Millie Polak, Spnya Schlesin, Sarojini Naidu, and Madeleine Slade, and upon the love and loyalty of his wife, Kasturbai Gandhi, which grew and deepened with the years.

His smallness and his being a mother's boy may have been factors in his lifelong attention to diet and his preoccupation with health foods and unorthodox methods of healing. At one time, he became prejudiced against milk and forbade his children and followers to drink it because he thought it excited the lower passions of man's nature.

Crippled Children

If there is any common trait among the crippled children of this study, it is the extremely close relationship that most of them have with one or both of their parents. When a child cannot move freely, that child is of necessity often about the house. It is difficult to foresee a day when the child is not going to be an extension of the parents; it is easy to make a puppet of the child who is dependent. Compassion for the child's handicap makes for a tenderness and leniency, which, if carried to extremes, can in itself become a handicap.

The most handicapping situation is a maternal inability to accept the reality of the situation. Since the child becomes very close to the parent, it seems especially important that the parent be sound of character, firm, and forward-looking, as well as sympathetic. To give in to apathy or inactivity is especially easy for the parents of the crippled. Feelings of guilt, which divide the parents of the abnormally formed child, also do inexorable damage to the child's chance for happiness, although the division in the home may not interfere with creativeness.

Charles Proteus Steinmetz suffered from a spinal deformity. His widowed grandmother and his father were so compassionate toward the extremely malformed, motherless child that they gave him complete freedom of the house, let him burn the rug and damage the furniture—but always in the cause of his scientific curiosity, not in wanton destructiveness. This was the critical difference. When he rebelled against school, they helped him and his teachers work out the problems that their overpermissiveness had caused, and they did not defend the boy for his tantrums and early defiance against an authority that was just and kind.

Charles Steinmetz was not only a great electrical engineer, he also worked as a member of the Board of Education in Rochester to set up special programs for retarded children. He was eager to be helpful to all young people—to the bright and eager as well as the retarded. The warmth and compassion of his childhood home reached many individuals, including Dave Garroway, television personality, who once lived in Steinmetz's home. Despite cruel discrimination against Charles because of his grotesque body, he was never bitter or socially isolated.

Some boys are more forcible than others in breaking through the overprotective smothering of a mother whose judgment is overridden by her anxieties. The mother of William O. Douglas, Justice of the Supreme Court who was also a writer and nature lover, had two catastrophic blows. Her husband, whom she loved deeply, died suddenly while still a young and active man. One day he was present, and the next day he was gone forever. His small son missed him also. In *Of Men and Mountains*, William Douglas says, "The step in the hallway, the laugh, the jingle of coins in the pocket—these were gone as silently as the water of the great Columbia." It was years before the young wife and mother could keep from showing how crushed and alone she felt.

Infantile paralysis (polio) then struck William, her only son. Once the crisis was past, his doctor explained that William could not be expected to live past forty. He advised bathing the helpless limbs of the boy in salt water and massaging him for fifteen minutes every two hours until there was evidence of recovery.

Day after day, night after night, the impoverished widow carried out the doctor's instructions. William learned to walk, and the frailty that the disease had left seemed to pass. The widow believed that everything the doctor had said was true—and therefore that William was doomed to die before he was forty. She coddled him, tried to restrict his activities, and asked his teachers and friends not to overtire him. William finally became rebellious. "But I believe my rebellion was not so much against her as against the kind of person I thought I was going to be." His love for her did not make him her puppet. Stung by the ridicule of schoolmates who made fun of his thin legs, he began to search for ways to improve his physical stature. Another boy advised hikes in the mountains to strengthen muscles debilitated by illness, so William used the foothills near his home as his gymnasium.

In the meantime, he defeated the boys who had made fun of his black-stockinged, pipe-stem legs by being an almost perfect student. At the end of a year of hiking, his legs began to fill out. He became a young man of the mountains as well as a scholar.

A boy who was not so fortunate was Joseph Goebbels, who, like William O. Douglas, was born healthy and normal. But an operation for osteomyelitis, contracted when he was four, seriously foreshortened one of Joseph's legs and left him limping for life. Neither his mother nor the boy could accept the deformity. His father turned, halfheartedly, to his normal boys. There was no strong love for learning or warm cohesiveness in this lower-middle-class home.

Even when he grew older and had repudiated religion, Joseph Goebbels was fond of telling how his mother, an extremely pious woman, had once asked her children to join in a prayer circle to beg for the life of their father, who lay dying. Their father subsequently miraculously improved. In Joseph's youth, he went often with his mother to pray on his own behalf for his deformity to be corrected. For many years, both mother and son hoped for—and expected—a miraculous cure.

Joseph could not accept his permanent disability. He withdrew from other children. He spent much time in his own room reading and rereading an old edition of an encyclopedia in the family's library. He was not liked by his classmates or his teachers. His nickname was "the Sly One"; he was known as a boy who sought occasion to be a tattletale.

His bitterness against everyone except his mother, whom he always idolized and idealized, grew with the years. In his diary, which he started at the age of twelve, he described his rejection of mankind. "The more I get to know about the human species, the more I care for my Benno [dog].... As soon as I am with a person for three days, I don't like him any longer, and if I am with him for a whole week I hate him like the plague.... I have learned to despise the human being from the bottom of my soul. He makes me sick in my stomach. Phoooooey!"

He also recorded in his diary his clashes with his father, as well as family quarrels and arguments, especially about his later espousal of the cause of Hitler. He tried to enlist in the army in 1914 and was refused, as he must have known he would be. He wept all night and spoke to no one for two days.

Like Hitler, Goebbels failed in his early efforts to express himself artistically. His two plays were never published. A novel he wrote in his youth was embarrassingly emotional and ineptly written. Like Hitler, he continued to receive the unqualified admiration and love of his mother, who could see no fault in him. Like Hitler, he turned to music for comfort and distraction. Like Hitler, he hated his peers and had ambitions impossible for him to fulfill. Unlike Hitler, he was attractive and had many affairs with women, whom he treated badly. His mother was the one woman he loved.

When he decided to commit suicide, however, he did not ask his mother to die with him. This he required of his wife, Magda, whom he had also treated badly, and of their six beautiful young children. He could have sent his children to live with his mother, who fled the city as the Allied forces moved in. But Magda and Joseph Goebbels were both of the thought that their suicides would perpetuate their memories, that dying for their cause would make them historical figures. Magda asked to have her oldest son, a half-brother to the young children, informed that she died honorably. She then asked one of the Nazi doctors to poison her children hypodermically when the time came for all of them to die. In the meantime, she and her husband played games with the children and told them stories. As the invading army approached, the children were told that they were to be inoculated, and they submitted their arms willingly. Then Magda poisoned herself and Joseph shot himself. He died wrapped up in the dream world of Nazi superiority. His mother outlived him by many years.

The mother of Toulouse-Lautrec, when her second child died suddenly and her first was crippled, devoted her whole life to trying to seize upon the immediate pleasure of helping Henri to be happy. Her marriage of expedience dissolved in the face of family calamity, and Henri's father was excluded from companionship with his son.

W. H. Hudson had a crablike gait that set him apart. Gustav Mahler did not limp because he was physically malformed. He reportedly limped because his mother was crippled and he wanted to share her pain with her.

In the James family, which produced both a novelist and a psychologist of great eminence, there were "family backaches" and various other disorders which William finally decided were psychosomatic. Yet there was no other family so determinedly cohesive and so given to warm expressions about each other as the wealthy James family.

At the age of thirteen, Henry James, Sr. lost a leg when he tried to stamp out a fire that he and other schoolboys set inadvertently while playing with a gas-filled balloon. He was an introspective and anxious man. One evening during young manhood, Henry, Sr. had a sudden hallucination as he sat alone at the supper table where his wife had left him while she cared for their two young sons. He was relaxed, comfortable, completely untroubled, when he had a sudden awareness of a mysterious shape in the corner, a fetid moving thing capable of sending rays that could kill. It was a ten-second hallucination, and he regarded it as such. However, the memory of it unnerved him. For months, no doctor could give him relief, but an elderly woman at a spa cured him of his depression by introducing him to the religion of Swedenborgianism.

For a long period, Henry James, Sr. had a great lack of faith in mankind and truly believed that the man who wished to perfect his character must first regard himself as "mere rubbish." At the same time, he had a bottomless, if somewhat ambivalent, love for his family. He once told Emerson that he sometimes wished that lightning would strike his wife and children out of existence so that he would suffer no more from loving them. He deplored anxiety, thinking it a sin, yet he was overanxious.

He played the maternal role in his family, staying home and keeping his children close to him. His wife, a simple but patient woman, played the paternal role. Even the children were likely to scold their father in a paternal fashion. Henry James, Jr. says of his mother, "She was our life, she was the house, the keystone of the arch." The children were not inclined to move out of the shelter of the family. "Henry," his brother William once said, referring to their travels and internationalism, "was really a native of the James family."

Alice, the brilliant, stoic, affectionate only daughter, fainted at parties when she was overstimulated. She took to her bed and suffered from an obscure ailment diagnosed variously as "rheumatic gout" or "spinal neurosis" or "nervous hyperaesthesia." Her own insight and that of her brother William as to the probable psychosomatic derivation of her pains did not help her to conquer them.

William James' late youth was clouded by insomnia, digestive disorders, eye troubles, weakness of the back, and frequent deep depressions. His discovery that neurotic oppression could have a mental rather than necessarily a physical basis was crucial to his own development and his choice of psychology as a career.

All of his life, Henry James was miserable with spinal and digestive problems. His crippled back—during a long lifetime in which he rode horseback, hiked, and traveled—caused him excruciating agony; but it did not actually incapacitate him or keep him from doing things he really wanted to do. He, too, was injured while lighting a fire. Robert James, the youngest boy, became a minor employee of the Milwaukee Railroad. He had a certain frail, poetic talent; he died alcoholic. Another brother, who died in his thirties, had an open, friendly manner, but made little use of his real abilities, which all of the James children shared.

Within this tight, cohesive, affectionate family there were wide spaces of noncommunication. Henry James, Sr. did not think that men of science filled any real function. William James once wrote to his father, "You live in such mental isolation that I cannot help often feeling bitterly at the thought that you must see in even your own children strangers to what you consider the best part of yourself."[6] William, the scientist, medical doctor, and later psychologist, had little respect for his brother's novels. Henry, Jr. had no respect for the social group of which he was a member. This son, who best pleased his father and best expressed his father's ambitions, did not choose to marry because he did not respect mankind enough to want to perpetuate it.

When Diana Manners, who later became the socially prominent Lady Diana Manners, was almost four, her twelve-year-old brother, Haddon, died. His death threw her mother into such an agony of grief that she withdrew into a studio in London "where in her terrible pain she was able to sculpture a recumbent figure of her dead son," the plaster case of which is now in the Tate Gallery. "All her artistic soul," says her daughter, "went into this tomb."[7]

There was no comparable release in creativity for Diana. Already a ridiculously anxious child, she developed a fear and certainty of death at five. Soon she could not raise her arms higher than her shoulders. She could not turn the music page on the piano rack. She tumbled and fell and banged her knees. Visiting doctors (in a day when little girls were trained to be very modest) required her to disrobe, then sat in a headshaking, solemn ring while she paraded before them like a naked worm. The diagnosis was progressive paralysis. She would surely die before she was twenty. A doctor came each day to give the invalid her galvanic (mild electrical stimulation) treatments. In the meantime, her life was to be made as pleasant as possible: "I was never to be gainsaid [contradicted] and spoiling was the order."

The expected death did not come. Instead, she grew into a chubby, healthy girl with a passionate desire to be loved and to be clever. Still, she continued to have an obsession about death. She was always anxious about her mother and fancied her dead or murdered if she was late coming home from a social affair. Her prayers were a nightly insurance policy. She prayed that death might not destroy the Indians and Chinese who were famine stricken, that no member of the family would be ill or have an operation, that the house would not burn, and that neither her father nor her mother would die before she was eighty or ninety. For years, she prayed that a dead neighbor whom she had known slightly might be accepted in heaven.

At age eleven, Diana fell in love with Fridtjof Nansen, who called her his "Viking." She loved him obsessively and read the two-volume work on his expedition to the North Pole. Adolescence changed the direction of her anxieties. She found a pleasurable excitement in hand-holding and in hidden letters; at fifteen, she could run downstairs. But her ugliness discontented her. She disliked the unbecoming clothes that her mother insisted she wear—peasant shirts, ill-fitting skirts, and black stockings. Her schooling, since she was not expected to live, had been pleasant, and she had spasmodic instruction from tutors. Her mother was not concerned for the conventional disciplines, had no respect for timetables, regularity of bedtime, for going out, or for lessons—she thought them all unnecessary. In late adolescence, Diana became beautiful, popular, and gregarious, and she married biographer Duff Cooper and became a friend of Winston and Clemmie Churchill.

Ring Lardner wore braces on one misshapen foot, and consequently, he read and studied often with his mother and played less frequently with other children. Eleanor Roosevelt and Bela Bartok all had spinal problems. Jane Addams, who had a spinal deformity, was exceptionally close to her Hicksite Quaker father, who was honest and uncompromising in his idealism. Like him, she accepted the burden of troubled mankind as her own.

Joseph Stalin had a withered arm and webbed toes. Orozco, after he lost his left hand, resigned himself to becoming an artist. "Stanislavski" became an actor to overcome his clumsiness. Although Norbert Wiener and David Lloyd George were certainly not crippled, they both lacked manual dexterity to a marked degree. Wiener never outgrew the clumsiness that made his childhood days intolerable at times. Lloyd George had difficulty tying his shoes and closing doors properly. Only four of Four Hundred, however, were obviously crippled as youths and as adults.

Children Who Were Overweight

One overweight child was thought stupid and dull. Another in adolescence was suddenly left out of new social groups based on boy-girl relationships. The most seriously overweight children, who were said to suffer from glandular difficulties, continued to be overweight as adults. Other overprotected and inactive children, children who ate mostly because they were neglected and lonely, usually had normal figures by the time they were grown.

One of G. K. Chesterton's first teachers is reported to have said that if anyone were to open Gilbert Chesterton's head, all he would find would be a lump of fat. Gilbert, grossly overweight and as tall as a man at age twelve, went around wearing sailor suits as if he were a little boy. He annoyed his teacher by forgetting to do his homework. He perpetually lost his dog-eared books, which had pictures drawn on the text as well as in the margins. He bit his nails; his hands were always dirty. He had colds, but no handkerchief.

When his mother took him to the doctor to find out why her son was so overweight and so absent-minded, the doctor told her that the boy would surely be either a genius or an idiot, and that she must not be too hard on him. This was an easy assignment for her, since she was by nature a kindly, permissive woman who kept a haphazard house.

Gilbert's father, who looked like the Dickens character Mr. Pickwick with a full head of hair, was a jolly fellow who was always engrossed in some new artistic project. He sold real estate and made a good living, but his real pleasure was in watercolors, painting, modeling, photography, stained glass, ornamental work, and magic lantern shows. He wrote and directed historical plays, knew English literature backward and forward, and was an argumentative liberal. His sons, Gilbert and Cecil, were the only boys among their acquaintances who had their own toy theater with inch-high actors and actresses.

In the midst of all of this activity, Mrs. Chesterton wandered amiably about, keeping the food warm for their irregular meals by setting the dishes in the ashes in the fireplace. When visiting boys got used to her clothes, which were thrown on haphazardly, and to her protruding black teeth, they were enchanted with the whole house and its occupants. They loved being asked to visit the Chesterton home, and they often were.

Gilbert was friendly, and the boys at school all liked him. If bullied, he didn't seem to notice. Although he never remembered to do his school lessons, he read straight through *Chambers' Encyclopedia* like a cow eating grass—and, his teachers thought, with as little comprehension. One of Gilbert's teachers confessed that the boy was too much for him, and this was not a statement about his weight. He found he boy unable to originate anything. But Chesterton later wrote poetry, literary criticism, and biography.

No one enjoyed the school debate club more than did Gilbert. As an adult, he still counted as his best friends the members of the junior debating society. Gilbert helped to start a chess club, a naturalist club, and a sketching club. He was also chairman of a committee to produce a magazine called *The Debater*.

Scenic designer Gordon ("Ted") Craig, the illegitimate son of Edward William Gordon, a London architect, and the actress Ellen Terry, was a fat, small boy. When Ellen Terry separated from her lover, she had two children, the dynamic, bossy daughter Edy and the white-haired, fat, lethargic Ted, who was a glutton. He liked food, lots of it, with plenty of gravy. Vegetables he disliked. He had an extreme distaste for walking, especially with his long-legged, rejecting nurse and his sister, who pulled and pushed him about.

Ted's mother thought men too aggressive and cruel to women and believed that women were too sedentary. Therefore, she deliberately trained her daughter to be bold and bossy and her son to be yielding. Ted had the additional burden of not understanding his biological origin. He knew from loud whispers among the servants that he was a creature born without a father. As far as he knew, he was the only such creature who existed. As an aged man, Ted Craig still lamented his role as a neglected child. He writes in his autobiography:

> *Even a mother can fail to understand [her child] if she has any other occupation that takes more than half her attention from her home and its occupants. Read in her Memoirs what she has to say about the "struggle" to get me to do a simple thing. Why struggle? A smile, a laugh about sheep's tails and lamb's tails, and all would have ended happily.*

Another rejected boy was American actor Douglas Fairbanks, Jr., whose parents were divorced.[8] He was plump and unattractive and often heard himself compared unfavorably with his father, the romantic movie actor, and also with his grandfather, Dan Sully, who prior to his spectacular business failure had been the cotton king of the South. Nothing young Douglas ever did was quite right or quite good enough. He was brought up in hotels and was always underfoot and in the way. He roller-skated through the lobby of the Algonquin Hotel in New York City and once was petrified with fear when he bumped into aged actor John Drew.

Katherine Mansfield, a writer born in New Zealand and brought up in a well-to-do home, had nightmares in the dark of butchers with long knives. She also had daytime nightmares when the Nathan children next door kept calling her "Fatty! Fatty!" She described her mother as "Linda Burnell" in a story called "We Are at the Bay" as "a woman whose courage was gone through too much child-bearing. And what made it doubly hard to bear was that she did not even love her children. It was useless pretending. Even if she had the strength she would never have nursed and played with the little girls."

Amy Lowell wrote in her diary as a young girl, "I am ugly, fat, conspicuous and dull; to say nothing of a very bad temper. Oh Lord, please let it be all right and let Paul love me, and don't let me be a fool,"[9] The poetess was not ugly, but she was fat. She would have been pretty if she had not been so heavy. She had delicate fingers, small feet, blue-gray eyes, and regular features.

Amy was apt at learning, opinionated, bookish, and critical. She was the baby girl in a cultured family that doted on her early intellectual promise. Yet she was not always a satisfactory student, despite her ability. She jumped to conclusions. She was a terrible speller and had her own idea of what French words should mean. She disliked grammar.

While she was in a girls' school, Amy dominated the other students, talked down to them, corrected them, and told them more than they wanted to know about her writer brother, who was an authority on Japan and sent her fabulous presents. When she became an adolescent and lacked the attention of boys, she was miserable. The girls she had antagonized did not help her to make friends with boys, and boys avoided her because of her appearance. She took to having accidents, broken bones, and sprained ankles.

Amy pretended to be reserved and to need solitude, and she spent hours in her room with her books and daydreams. The only real happiness she had was at the theater, where she could sit in the dark and identify herself with a slim, beloved heroine on the stage.

Other children who were overweight were Maria Callas, Henry Morton Stanley, and Oscar Wilde. Maria Callas, born in New York, had disappointed her mother by not being born a boy who could replace a dead brother. The rejecting mother stuffed the child with starches and would not let her play in the street with other girls who talked of sweethearts or played with dolls. Maria was kept in the house, where she read or played the piano until eleven o'clock at night. She later studied in Athens and became a world famous operatic soprano.

Sickly Children

The thirty-eight very sickly children among the Four Hundred actually had a tendency to live long and energetic lives. Among them are such hardy and indefatigable specimens as Joseph Stalin, Clara Barton, William O. Douglas, Thomas Edison, Arturo Toscanini, and Vilhjalmur Stefansson, the explorer who shared the life of the most primitive of Eskimos.

In almost every home where there is a sickly child, there is an overconcerned or driving parent, or parental antagonisms. Attitudes are not casual or optimistic in these homes. The child's illness often seems to fill some kind of a need in the child or the parent or both. Sickness and isolation can protect the child against bad, big boys who the parent fears will hurt the child. It can also serve to keep the child close to a parent who is unhappy because of a failure in the marital relationship.

The luckiest children are those who rebel, as did William O. Douglas, usually in adolescence, against being cast forever in the role of invalid child. Theodore Roosevelt, who was sickly as a boy, also became robust in late adolescence. He was asthmatic, as were French writer Marcel Proust and African-born writer Olive Schreiner, who became a dynamic and dominating woman.

"I have written this at night, being the only time unoccupied with the dear, troublesome little children deserted by their Papa,"[10] wrote a young wife, Martha Bullock Roosevelt, to her husband, Theodore, who was working during the Civil War for the Northern cause. Those dear and troublesome children were the crippled Anna, age seven; Theodore, age four; Elliott, who was two; and Corinne, who was one. But Martha also worried about her sixteen-year-old brother, Irvine, who was a blockade runner for the South. Martha Bullock, her mother, and her spinster sister Anna lived in perpetual anxiety about their relatives in the South. Grandmother Bullock used to say that she hoped she would die before she heard that her son had been killed or before Richmond was taken by the Yankees. She also had a stepson who was an admiral in the Southern navy.

Theodore Roosevelt, Sr., a very wealthy man, paid a substitute to fight for him in the actual battles of the war. His peculiar family circumstances did not make him feel free to carry a gun that might kill his wife's closest relatives. He volunteered to do propaganda work, to organize and equip African-American soldiers, and to do extensive social service work for the widows and children of men in service.

Theodore, Sr. was always described as the ideal father by his children and as an ideal man by his friends. "My father was the best man I ever knew. He combined strength and courage with gentleness, tenderness and a great unselfishness. He would not tolerate in us children selfishness, or cruelty, idleness, cowardice or untruthfulness,"[11] said his son, Theodore (Teddy) Roosevelt, Jr.

Six-year-old Theodore, Jr., the oldest boy, felt his responsibilities keenly as the son of a Northern patriot, but he was not able to live up to the difficult code of his father. There is no doubt that he was sometimes cruel to his mother, his aunt, and his grandmother, whose Southern cause he rejected in favor of his father's espousal of the Lincoln Republicans. He used prayers both as a safe propaganda medium and as an expression of hostility to the Southern women. He knelt at his young aunt's knee and prayed that the Southern troops might be ground to powder. He punished his mother, when she scolded him, by threatening to pray for the North.

Theodore, Jr.'s health problems coincided with his father's absence and his own determination to champion his father's cause. Until his father went away, Theodore seemed to be in good health. His mother had found him hideous at birth, said he looked like a terrapin, but there is no indication that he was then regarded as a sickly boy. However, Grandmother Bullock wrote to her Yankee son-in-law, telling him about his children, those "pitiful sick things," and advising him that his wife "had her hands full." The letters described Theodore, Jr.'s "milk crust" (probably an allergy), but his father in 1860 indicated that the "milk crust" was gone and that Theodore was "almost a beauty."

Carleton Putnam says in his Roosevelt biography: "Starting with the fall of 1861 the [family] account of colds, fevers, coughs and stomach upsets is continuous." This is also, significantly, the date of the beginning of the Civil War. It would seem that the very deep emotional tension in the house may have contributed inadvertently to Theodore's asthma.

Martha ("Mittie") Bullock Roosevelt was a sweet and charming but extremely immature individual. It was her beauty that made her memorable. Her magnolia complexion and coral cheeks, her dark hair and blue eyes made her one of New York's most beautiful society women. Life was never easy for her, for she had no sense of money or time. "Please don't be hard on me," she once wrote to her husband, who was exceedingly capable. She had such distaste for dirt that a sheet had to be spread beside her bed before she could say her prayers, for she wanted no consciousness of dirt to destroy her communication with her Deity.

Along with her husband's absence during the early days of the Civil War, she must have been deeply hurt by Theodore's militant espousal of the North; all of her life she was an "unreconstructed rebel." The Bullock women were sweet, gushing, and sentimental. Forthright anger and caustic criticism were inconsistent with their upbringing and beliefs. Martha's letters are of the "dear-but-troublesome" variety. Each negative comment was matched by an equally positive statement. Real feelings were lost in the nebulous mists of propriety and sentiment. She wrote to her absent husband to tell him that their oldest son was brimful of mischief and had to be watched all the time. She then assured him that the boy was an affectionate and endearing little fellow.

While she was stroking baby Elliott's ears to put him back to sleep early one morning, Theodore, Jr. invaded the room and was "jealous." He was later described as "hysterical" with glee whenever he succeeded in getting his younger brother (who was always handsome) to obey him. Martha felt that he needed discipline, but there was always ambivalence and a suggestion of recurrent nagging in the mother's attitude toward her homely first boy. Like Eleanor Roosevelt, who was an unattractive child, Theodore, Jr. could never quite please his mother. But his father's code permitted no expression of hostility or rebellion toward her.

After his father's return, Theodore's asthmatic attacks grew more and more serious. During an ill-fated first trip to Europe, taken when Theodore was eleven, the family letters still recorded his mother's impatience with him. Theodore, she advised her correspondents, "took nothing in" of the sights of Europe. Instead, he looked about with an aristocratic air, then turned to his father with inappropriate questions such as, "Father, why did Texas wish to annex itself to the United States?" Elliott, on the other hand, declared everything to be lovely, "only having taken a hasty glance but taking it all in." His mother resolved to "make" Theodore see the worthwhile sights of Europe. It was she who insisted on the trip. His father had not wanted to go. But Theodore frustrated his parents by having a severe asthmatic attack every four or five days. In Venice, he was sick and could not sleep until after two in the morning. In Trieste, he sat up for four hours during the night while his father made him smoke a cigar to stop his wheezing. Black coffee poured into him by his mother and older sister seemed to do the most good. Between attacks, he was taken relentlessly to see the sights. They missed nothing. The young children raced through hotels, irritated other guests, and dragged their feet through museums and cathedrals.

Theodore was annoyingly homesick and begged to go home. He wanted his solitude, his nature collections, his books, and his next-door neighbor, whom he designated "Eidieth." Edith Carow, the neighbor, later became his second wife and the woman who helped more than any other person to make him a great man.

Theodore never openly disobeyed his mother. When she asked him to do something, he said, "Oh, yes, you pretty sweet thing," and exasperated her by immediately going off to skin a bird or perform some other such task—which must have been nauseating to a person of her temperament and ideas about cleanliness. The children called their mother "Motherling" and never accorded her the status of a mature woman. The crippled Anna, at fourteen, took over the role of housekeeper of the elaborate establishment. (Anna fared better than did most overly responsible older sisters. She grew up to be a wonderful, dynamic woman, married at forty, and became a mother at forty-three.)

It was Theodore's father who helped him when the boy finally grew rebellious about his own constant illness and weakness. He responded to his father's idea that he should "make his body." Thus, Theodore began gymnastics at Wood's gymnasium on a "ride porch" where he could exercise his chest on horizontal bars. He went on camping trips, slept on damp ground, forced himself to take hardship. When he was thirteen, he was so shamed by an encounter with some boys who bullied him that he took up boxing. His whole energy and his driving will were centered on this task of "making his own body."

At no time had he been coddled, and between attacks, he had always been active. Theodore praised his father in his autobiography for not centering his whole attention on his own sick son. Theodore was never made to feel that his sickness excused him or his family from a sympathetic interest in other children who were worse off than he. His father was so absorbed in the problems of all sick children that his friends, of whom he had so many, reached for their pocketbooks when they saw him coming. Theodore Roosevelt, Sr. took newsboys off the street and sent them out west to farms. He took his own children with him to visit his Newsboy's Lodging House and the Night School for Little Italians.

His wife, who seemingly took no interest in his projects, was once entertaining some of New York's wealthiest matrons when her husband, who had been currently unsuccessful in getting aid for a proposed hospital for crippled children, invaded her social gathering with several of these helpless children from the slums, whom he laid on tables cleared for the purpose. Beside the children, he placed steel appliances that he wanted these underprivileged children to have. His daughter Corinne was pressed into service to explain the devices to the startled guests, who were quickly sympathetic. When Mrs. John Jacob Astor responded by offering money, other women followed suit. The result was the New York Orthopedic Hospital, to which the adult Corinne was to take her little niece, Eleanor Roosevelt, on a memorable visit many years later.

As Theodore grew close to pubescence, his mother found him increasingly rude and crude, yet she noted that he was protective as he walked with her and Corinne on the streets, and that he purposely placed himself in a protecting position between the women and some street rowdies. At puberty, his asthma disappeared.

As a college junior, Theodore had mastered the art of maintaining the effusiveness demanded by the feminine family code, but he also betrayed his awareness of his widowed mother's continued immaturity. He began a letter to her: "Darling, beloved, little Motherling, I have just loved your dear, funny, pathetic little letter...."[12]

Theodore Roosevelt ultimately became Governor of New York, Vice-President, and later the twenty-sixth President of the United States.

Eczema covered nearly the whole body of Hungarian composer Béla Bartók when he was three months old, and he had no relief from the condition until he was five or six. He developed a fear of being near strangers, seldom left the house, and regarded children his own age as his worst enemies. At the age of five, he was misdiagnosed as having curvature of the spine and was not permitted to sit; he took his meals standing, and he rested by lying flat on the floor. His mother neglected the rest of the family and gave him her almost complete attention. At three, he played the drums while she played the piano. At four, he could play forty melodies on the piano. At nine, he was composing. The precocious, mother-tutored boy went to school when he was seven years old and completed four grades in one year with top grades in everything. Dependence upon his mother, or a mother-figure, and a painful inability to relate to other people characterized him throughout his life. During WWII, he was driven to exile in the United States and died in New York City.

Stella Cabrini was fifty-two when her thirteenth child, the premature, delicate Francesca Maria Cabrini, was born near Lodi, Italy. Since the child was not expected to live, she was christened at once with the names of two children who also had not lived. Francesca retained her delicacy throughout childhood and was denied entrance into the Daughters of the Sacred Heart and the Canossian Sisters. No religious order wanted the young girl, who coughed drops of blood during her frequent illnesses. After a grueling apprenticeship in an orphan's home, she formed her own religious order, Missionary Sisters of the Sacred Heart. The world was not big enough for the tireless Sister Cabrini, who founded schools, orphanages, and hospitals in far corners of the globe. During the first twenty-five years of her order, one hundred thousand persons were treated in her hospitals. Like Theodore Roosevelt, she was careless of her physical strength and enjoyed testing her endurance. She was canonized in 1946, the first American saint.

Thomas Edison, who was a sickly child, slept only five or so hours a day as an adult. Harry Truman, also sickly as a child, later walked the legs off his Secret Service men and had a brusque vigor. Jan C. Smuts, Charles Evans Hughes, and most of the other thirty-eight sickly children were indefatigable workers and lived a normal life span.

Homely Children and Attractive Parents

Various investigators, particularly psychologist Leta Hollingworth, make much of the attractive appearance of groups of gifted children selected by tests. Among the Four Hundred, however, there are a good number of boys and girls who considered themselves homely. Biographers attest to the lack of attractiveness in others.

Women, especially, tend to find themselves unattractive as children. Sheila Kaye-Smith describes herself as a girl whose forehead was half of a hideous, gray face. Edith Sitwell, very tall, had a rejecting father who tried to alter her looks by putting a painful clamp device on her nose. Sarah Bernhardt was a sharp-featured, scrawny girl. Diana Cooper, who later became a celebrated beauty, said no one considered her a pretty child except her mother. Jane Addams was afraid to shame her handsome father by letting people know he had such a homely daughter. Ernestine Schumann-Heink described herself as short, sallow, and plain, and she feared that her plainness would keep her from fame as a singer. Eleanor Roosevelt was a gawky girl in braces. Marian Anderson was tall, thin, and plain. Santha Rama Rau did not fit her grandmother's idea of a delicate, petite Indian maiden. English novelist Mary Louise de la Ramee (known as "Ouida" and author of *A Dog of Flanders*) was an especially ugly girl. Gertrude Stein and Clara Barton were square chunks of girls, and masculine in appearance.

William Henry Hudson, novelist, had a hook nose and a strange walk. Laurence Housman was an unattractive boy. Houdini, the magician, was small and bowlegged. Maurice Chevalier was teased because of his big head and small body. Enrico Fermi, Joseph McCarthy, Ivar Kreuger, and Charles de Gaulle all felt the handicap of an unprepossessing appearance. Tolstoy thought no one would ever be able to love him because of his sunken eyes, low forehead, heavy lips, large bulbous nose, and enormous ears. Adolescent Franz Kafka lamented his "inescapable ugliness," which prompted him to wear badly cut clothes and to walk with his back bent, his shoulders crooked, and his hands all over the place. A. E. Housman was called "The Mouse" by other boys who trod on him and pretended they could not see him. Henry Ford, John D. Rockefeller, Bertrand Russell, and Paul Gauguin were all scrawny, irregular-featured boys.

There were also "pretty" boys who were too effeminate to be well accepted by their peers. Scott Fitzgerald had this handicap and was cast as the leading lady in his college shows. Arthur Balfour, delicate of feature, was considered effeminate. The boys who did not experience pubescence were severely handicapped; Alexander Woollcott and Edward Marsh had mumps, which made them impotent. Cecil Rhodes always spoke with an unchanged voice and was not known to have an interest in women.

Statesmen were more likely to be handsome as children. Franklin D. Roosevelt (but not Theodore), Dwight D. Eisenhower, Nehru, and Thomas E. Dewey were all said to be strikingly handsome as youths and as men. Rupert Brooke was a rarely beautiful young man, as was Hart Crane. Theodore Herzl was an unusually beautiful child. Marie Curie was a delicate, graceful girl with a mop of curls.

Fathers are not often described as being especially handsome, and the mothers who are described as beauties were almost always neglectful or rejecting. Lady Randolph Churchill was a brunette American beauty who was a lovely but "distant star" to her son, Winston. She seldom saw him until he was old enough to be her escort at social functions. Gertrude Atherton describes her rejecting but beautiful mother as a woman whose major interest was her own appearance and who had a tremendous ineptness for choosing lovers. Theodore Roosevelt's lovely little mother was, as we have noted, an extremely immature woman.

Arthur Quiller-Couch, a British man of letters who later edited the *Oxford Book of English Verse*, describes his mother's wonderful wealth of red-auburn hair and her Devon complexion of cream and roses, which she kept to the end of her days. "I thought her the most beautiful woman in the world and adored her," Arthur says in his memoirs. She was a wildly generous woman and compassionate, given to nursing her doctor-husband's indigent patients. Her difficulty was her willful extravagance, which was a terrible burden to her devoted husband. She loved entertaining and fine clothes to such an extent that the family experienced financial insecurity. Her son spent six of his adult years paying off his deceased father's debts.

In the Robinson home, in the village of Head Tide in southern Maine, there were three brilliant sons who all came to personal grief: Dean, the brilliant physician who became a drug addict; Herman, the handsome, outgoing boy who went into business, failed, and became an alcoholic; and Edwin Arlington Robinson, the homely, odd bachelor who was always being disappointed when his male friends matured and married, and who was driven to nervous collapse when the whole burden of the disintegrating family fell upon his sickly shoulders.

The home seemingly had every virtue. Hermann Hagedom says of the Robinson house and parents:

> *The house had grace of line... a perfect frame for the idyll of married love which the storekeeper and his wife provided. A*

> *tender imaginative strain in her found its complement in his more solid philosophic bent. He treated her like a flower....*[13]

The father was always so much in love with his beautiful young wife that the children were seemingly left outside the circle of love that encompassed the parents and shut out the rest of the world. Their children often felt as if their parents did not know they were present when they were with them.

When her third child, Edwin, was born, Mrs. Robinson was very disappointed because she had wanted this child to be a girl. Since the birth was difficult, her husband sent her to a summer resort to regain her health and spirits. When the infant was six months old, he was still unnamed, and his mother was apathetic over the insistence of the other women at the resort that something be done. At last, the women resolved the matter by each writing a favorite name on a slip, which was put into a hat. A woman from Arlington, Massachusetts, who had submitted the name of Edwin, had the distinction of calling the child Edwin Arlington Robinson.

Edwin was burdened for years with the fragmentation of his distressed family. Women never meant anything to him—Isadora Duncan must have frightened him terribly when she asked him to father a child for her.

A vain and beautiful mother, it seems, can have a negative effect on a daughter with different values. Willa Cather's beautiful mother regarded herself as an authority on high fashion and never left her bedroom until she was perfectly groomed. She liked to carry a parasol to match her costume and to wear fresh violets whenever she could. She infringed very little on her children's activities unless they disobeyed her or threatened her comfort. Then she was likely to whip them with a rawhide whip. She had an immense energy and a corresponding devotion to doing things the right way. She and her daughter Willa organized their respective lives to avoid too frequent meetings. Willa and her two oldest brothers had a room of their own in the unfinished attic, where the snow sifted in and there was no heat except from the chimney, and where the rest of the large family left them alone.

Their father was a kindly Southern gentleman, refined and delicate, whose business interests were not remunerative enough to keep his large family solvent. His mother-in-law, patient, hard-working, and self-effacing, fed the boarders who came at noon, never removed her apron, and walked with a limp because her hip had been broken wrestling with a gate on a windy night. She did most of the housework and pampered her beautiful daughter. Her granddaughter, Willa, would later write about her with love and compassion.

Willa reacted against her mother by becoming "William." She cropped her hair and wore a boy's hat and jacket or loud and garish female garments that offended her mother's exquisite taste. Willa's heroes became the "Big Eight," her father's influential friends who were lampooned with him in the county paper when they investigated what they said was the misuse of funds by the county treasurer. She came to prefer the company of adult men. She made calls with the doctors and once gave chloroform to a boy patient whose leg was being amputated. She dissected frogs and rode horseback through the countryside. The teachers at the high school let her come and go as she pleased because she was so extremely accelerated that school was obviously a bore to her. She read Latin and Greek and did science experiments with Mr. Ducker, the town eccentric and scholar. She was glad she resembled her father, not her mother, in appearance.

In a child's memory book,[14] she described herself by filling in blanks. Her favorite amusement was vivisection; her favorite occupation, slicing toads. The trait she admired most in women was "flirting." In men she admired "an original mind." "Passion" was the trait for which she had the most toleration in another individual, and "lack of nerve" she could not tolerate in others. She desired a matrimonial partner who had a "lamb-like meekness." Her idea of perfect happiness was to "amputate limbs" and real misery was to do "fancy work." As a traveling companion, she would most desire a "cultured gentleman." If shipwrecked on a desolate island, she would most desire "pants and a coat." The greatest wonder of the world was a "good-looking woman." The memory book was signed Wm. Cather, M.D.—not simply Willa Cather.

When this girl decided to be a boy, she was consistent in her reactions. It was not until she was a junior in college that she gave up her cropped hair and male attire. It would seem to be more than sheer coincidence that mothers who are remembered as being particularly beautiful are not among those who influenced their children in the most constructive ways.

Only two mothers were spoken of as being especially homely: Jack London's mother, who was indifferent to her son, and Leo Tolstoi's devoted mother, who shared her interest in people and ideas with her children.

The physical appearance of fathers is not often mentioned, but horse-faced Woodrow Wilson once said bitterly that if he had his father's good looks, he could speak without regard to content.

It is wise to remember that the child who has one handicap is by no means necessarily free from other agonies. George Orwell once said, "I had no money, I was weak, I was ugly, I was unpopular, I had a chronic cough, I was cowardly, I smelt."[15] George did not trust his mother, he disliked his father, and he found his boarding school, described in his *Such Were the Joys*, intolerable.

Thirty-nine of the Four Hundred spoke of themselves as being made miserable because of their appearance. If we include appearance, approximately one-fourth of the Four Hundred had reason to try to compensate for one or more handicaps.

Chapter 9
Early Agonies

For the most part I do the thing which my own nature drives me to do. It is shameful to earn so much respect and love for it. Arrows of hate have been shot at me, too; but they never hit me; because somehow they belong to another world, with which I have no connection whatsoever.

I live in that solitude which is painful in youth, but delicious in the years of maturity.

—Albert Einstein,
Portraits and Self Portraits, edited by Georges Schreiber

There are almost no adverse circumstances of the kind commonly thought to induce mental illness, delinquency, or neurosis that some one of the Four Hundred did not experience during childhood. Some of the Four Hundred were illegitimate. Others were profoundly affected by the death of a brother or sister. Many were orphaned, half-orphaned, neglected, or rejected.

Despite these circumstances, there are few of the Four Hundred, their siblings, or their parents who withdrew from reality and were hospitalized as mentally ill. They may have been depressed, eccentric, or neurotic, but they held fast to a sense of reality. Motivated by a common love for learning and a drive for accomplishment, they were seen as preoccupied, as was Albert Einstein, with self-rewarding activities that offered deep satisfactions.

During the process of working out the very real problems in their home environments, many of these children developed easily recognized neurotic symptoms. They bit their nails, were hyperactive, withdrawn, rebellious, or resentful. Yet despite being handicapped by environmental circumstances, they were nonetheless persistent in developing their individual talents and skills.

The Intruder Complex

Ferenc Molnár, the Hungarian-born playwright, related many of the inhibitions that complicated his existence to what he called "that intruder complex of mine." Although his parents never said so, he was always quite certain that he was an exceedingly poor substitute for his blond, angelic brother who died before he was born. Molnár's father, who was a physician, kept only the placid, sunny Lacika's picture on his desk. Nothing that dark, active Ferenc ever accomplished seemed to erase his father's longing for his lost son.

At seventeen, Ferenc finished high school and brought home a record so outstanding that it opened the doors of every university in Europe to him, but Ferenc could see on his father's face the fleeting shadow of a thought, "Why not Lacika?" The identical look was manifest when Ferenc brought him clippings from the morning paper extolling the production of Ferenc's first play. Molnár attributed his lifelong shyness, his exaggerated modesty, and his uneasy feeling that he did not deserve the rights freely given to others to this intruder complex.

Emotional disturbance is a frequent aftermath of a death in the family. Children who are bereft of a brother or sister are suddenly aware of the transitory nature of life, and they may respond by a powerful urge to achieve quickly before death also strikes them down. The living child is sometimes jealous of the dead child, who is always spoken of as perfect, and consequently feels rejected and is determined to out-perform the lost child in a spectacular fashion. Children are also often faced with a bereaved parent whose whole personality is changed by the sudden tragedy in the family. Gloom and despair displace serenity, and the living child feels that he or she must now "live for two" in order to compensate stricken parents for the loss they have sustained. If the family becomes fragmented and noncohesive as a result of the tragedy, the child who is to become eminent may mature quickly, leave home, and seek satisfaction and rewards outside the family or within him- or herself.

Mary Austin, novelist, had no champion in the family after her father died. It was her understanding lawyer father who had insisted that she have a library card. Her mother, whose affections were centered on her favored first-born son, tried to keep Mary from reading books if her brother could not also enjoy them. Mary's principal joy was in the affection of her little sister Jennie, who tried to comfort her big sister when Mary had a high fever and a sore throat. The doctor was not called until Jennie became ill as well and was near death with diphtheria. Mary recovered from her own diphtheria attack without medical attention, but Jennie died. Mary overheard heard her mother ask, "Why couldn't it have been Mary?"

The precocious oldest daughter in this household invented an imaginary "I-Mary" to be her companion and punished her rejecting mother by blurting out unpleasant truths when company came; she also became agnostic in defiance of her mother's piety. Not even when Mary was an adult and a successful novelist did she develop the ability to experience satisfying personal relationships, and most persons who knew her well found her to be caustic and unpleasant.

The eccentric artist Salvador Dalí was a "reborn Salvador." The name, "Salvador," had first been given to an angelic, perfect Salvador Dalí who died at the age of seven.[1] To his parents, the second son, born three years after his brother's death from meningitis, was an exact replica of the dead Salvador. To them, he was the deceased child come back to their arms. But the second Salvador was grossly unable to compete with their selective memories and soon became hyperactive and even sadistic. He kicked his sister's head as if it were a football. At five, he threw another child over a railing and nearly killed him. He bit into a dead, putrid bat; he broke the doctor's glasses; he trod upon a classmate's violin. By the time he was an adolescent, he was so eccentric in his manner and dress that he was stoned when he went to the movies. He had no satisfying relationships with the boys and girls in his immediate neighborhood.

Brooks Adams, the political-biographer historian grandson of John Quincy Adams, born soon after his most promising and beloved five-year-old brother Arthur died, was also defiant and incomprehensible to his erudite family. By the time that he was old enough to join the nightly family reading circle, he was a puzzle to his father and mother, who isolated him on a hassock in the middle of the room, where he wore out his clothes and the rug with his pulling and twisting. He laughed, ranted, twisted, and jumped about while his father, Charles Francis Adams, read to the children. At school, he performed wretchedly and could neither read nor spell tolerably. His parents took him to the family physician to ask whether a blow on the head by a cricket ball could possibly account for the boy's stupidity, but the doctor assured them that the boy was perfectly normal physically and had suffered no brain damage. Neither parent expected that this problem child would ever be able to go to college. He retained his childhood awareness of rejection as an adult.

Biographer Daniel Aaron, who describes Adams in *Men of Good Hope: Latter-Day Progressives*, pictures the eighty-year-old Brooks as an arrogant, blunt, audacious man who conducted a "one-man mutiny against the whole world." He so exasperated his relatives that his niece called him an "unusable man." His prejudices colored and distorted his very genuine scholarship. He disliked Jews, whom he called "gold bugs," and thought them a secret force behind the League of Nations, which he also mistrusted. To the last, he was defensive, mistrustful of himself, apologetic. Aaron quotes him as once moved to protest: "I am not a man with a maggot in my brain—and in all the years when I have been wandering from New York to Jerusalem speculating on the causes which seem to be crushing the world, I have not been morbid, crazy or ill."

In an upper-middle-class family in Guanajuato, Mexico, painter Diego Rivera became an "intruder" to his mother when he was a year and a half old. The home into which the Portuguese-Jewish-African-Spanish-Indian twins, Carlos and Diego, were born was a small marble palace in the heart of the city in which their father, Diego Rivera, Sr., was a councilor and man of considerable status and importance. Four previous pregnancies had resulted in miscarriages or stillborn babies, and the full-term twins were the first living children born to the twenty-two-year-old mother.

Carlos died when he was a year and a half old, and Maria, his mother, would not be consoled. She spent each night weeping by the side of the grave of the deceased child. Her husband rented a room from the caretaker of the cemetery in order to be near her. Diego, the living twin, was so rickety and debilitated that his ability to survive was questioned.

The family doctor said that the young mother would lose her sanity unless she could be distracted by becoming a career woman. Maria consented enthusiastically to being enrolled in a course in obstetrics, at which she was so adept that she finished it in half the usual time. Diego, meanwhile, was sent away to the country to be reared by a nurse in a primitive shack in the middle of a wooded area. When he was brought home at the age of four, he was fat and healthy, but neither he nor his mother could ever feel an affection for each other. It was the nurse, Antonia, to whom Diego gave his complete devotion. Later, as an adult, Diego always felt the need to hurt his wives and mistresses, even when he loved them.

Not long after his return from the mountains, Diego's mother told him that he must go to the railway station and wait there until the stationmaster gave him a box in which he would find a new brother or sister. The disgruntled boy went home after several hours of fruitless waiting and was greeted with news of the arrival of a new baby sister, who was in his mother's bedroom. The angry five-year-old found a pregnant mouse, cut it open to show the embryonic mice inside, and made his mother look at them in an effort to convince her that she had lied to him. She retaliated by crying out that she had whelped a monster when she had given birth to Diego. His father comforted the boy, who was beside himself with anger at having been tricked. He soon learned to read so that he might spell out the words in his mother's obstetrics books and prove again that she had lied to him about the birth of his sister.

When he was six, Diego shamed his mother again by his behavior in church. His father was an agnostic and freethinker who had forbidden Diego's aunts or mother to take the boy to church, but a great-aunt disobeyed and took him with her so that he might pray for his mother, who was taking her final examinations that day. The priest fled and the congregation was appalled and frightened when the six-year-old boy mounted the pulpit and gave an impassioned anti-clerical speech. He spoke so fluently that the parishioners were convinced that the devil had taken possession of the boy's body to speak through his childish mouth.

Although Diego had many difficulties, he demonstrated his ability in art and his precocity in language very early and was called "The Boy Wonder of Guanajuato." Despite this, however, the community reaction to Diego's behavior was negative, and it irked his mother so deeply that she sold the family's possessions while her husband was away on a business trip and took the children with her to Mexico City. Diego Rivera, Sr. gave up his remunerative position in Guanajuato and followed her. Since he had lost money in mining ventures, they set up housekeeping again in a small apartment in a poor section of town. During a period when the family diet was limited, Diego had scarlet fever and typhoid, and a new baby born into the family lived less than a week. Again, Diego was the "intruder."

The fifty-seven individuals in our study who were profoundly affected by the death of one or more brothers and sisters were not all as rejected as were Mary Austin or Brooks Adams. There was, however, an immediacy in all their drives that often cut their childhoods short. Some, like Eleanor Roosevelt, were overanxious to please and were insecure adolescents. Sigmund Freud, who resented the birth of a brother born when Sigmund was nineteen months old, was filled with guilt eight months later when the "intruder" to whom he had relinquished his mother's breast died. In opposite but related fashion, psychiatrist Alfred Adler could never forgive his mother for smiling too soon after his baby brother died.

Sean O'Casey replaced two brothers of his own name and could never forget his mother's grief. He felt a need to comfort her by his own accomplishments. Adolf Hitler failed miserably to compensate his mother for the three children before him who had not lived. Joseph Stalin was another of the sickly children who had to make up for his mother's lost babies. Oscar Wilde, Ranier Rilke, and Vachel Lindsay all suffered by having to replace dead sisters. There is no evidence that the death of a child in the family brings a divided family together in storybook fashion.

Medicine and psychology have lessened but not eliminated the threat of the "intruder complex" in contemporary homes. Because of the severity of the reactions of these fifty-seven bereaved families, more research is needed on the relationship between bereavement and rejection.

The Orphaned and the Half-Orphaned

When a parent dies, the child is ordinarily able to take the loss without undue emotional upset, and the natural grief is eased with the passing of time. The child seems to think of the parental death as a part of the historical process of being born, of living, aging, and dying. No personal threat is involved as happens when a brother or sister dies. Among those who lost parents or a parent, a few individuals, such as novelist Somerset Maugham and Italian actress Eleonora Duse, felt that this loss created circumstances that made the rest of their childhood intolerable. In many instances, the sudden new responsibility hastened the maturity of the child or enriched the child's life by making new experiences possible.

For generations, children's books about orphans or half-orphans have been popular. Characters like David Copperfield, Cosette, Anne of Green Gables, Rebecca of Sunnybrook Farm, Cinderella, Freckles, and whole families of half-orphans like the Careys and the Wiggses and the Mortars have won the hearts of youthful readers. There are doubtless many children who have secretly dreamed of being suddenly orphaned and catapulted into a new and challenging environment.

The orphaned among the Four Hundred are not disappointing to those who hold the storybook concept of the orphan. Among them are several whose lives became more exciting and challenging after they were orphaned. The orphaned Herbert Hoover was later nostalgic about the days when he was boarded around with various welcoming aunts and uncles who vied for the pleasure of having him in their homes. They would not let him be adopted by a spinster schoolteacher because they believed that the boy needed to be reared in a home where there was both a father- and a mother-figure. His first home away from home (when half-orphaned) was on an Indian reservation where his uncle was employed as an agent. He and his cousins were the only white children in the Indian school. His last childhood home was with another uncle who was a doctor and who helped him prepare for his college entrance exams at Stanford.

Each of the three children in the Hoover family went to live with a different relative, but their feelings of responsibility for each other were not lessened. When the grandmother who had taken his young sister died, brothers Herbert and Theodore set up a household and took care of her. Theodore gave up his schooling and worked as a typesetting machine operator. Herbert, out of a job at the time, moved into the household and brought with him a cousin who he had lived with on the Indian reservation. She was a sterling young woman who was a good cook and had a knack for entertaining with Indian dialect stories. The four young people had a jolly time together.

The half-orphaned also have challenges and adventures that give them an opportunity for early maturity and resourcefulness.

When Wanda Gag, who became a successful illustrator and author of popular children's books, was fifteen, her father, a lovable but unsuccessful artist, told her shortly before he died, "What Papa couldn't do, Wanda will have to finish." This meant becoming a famous artist and also helping to rear and support her six younger brothers and sisters.

The friendly neighbors in New Ulm, Minnesota who gave the Gag family food and money, as well as good advice, were inclined to believe that Wanda should give up any idea of education beyond the eighth grade and take a job as a clerk in a store. They believed that art was unreliable as a source of income. In the Gag family, there had always been parental pleasure in the children's absorption in every kind of creative activity, in painting, modeling, and writing. Wanda would not give up her plans for schooling, even though the family was on welfare. She found it easy to get a full scholarship at an art school in Minneapolis.

Like the Hoover children, Wanda and her sisters and brothers maintained a warm cohesiveness, were cooperative, and were zealous for each other's welfare. This was also notably true of the Curie, Chamberlain, and Flexner children.

Widows in this study, of whom there were fifty-eight, seldom remarried. Four of the five who sought new mates separated from their husbands or divorced them. One reason for the predominance of widows is the rather high incidence of fathers who were much older than their wives. There were twenty-six widowers among the parents in this survey, fourteen of whom are known to have remarried. Eleven of the fourteen stepmothers were praised by the later-to-be-eminent child in the family.

The fourteen fully orphaned children of the Four Hundred were commonly reared by grandmothers, uncles, or aunts. Sibling relationships were close in these families. The orphaned and half-orphaned were frequently given sympathetic assistance by adults in the community.

Illegitimate Children

Men or women of the Four Hundred who were born out of wedlock do not seek to advertise their illegitimacy and may try to keep the details about their parentage from the press and curious public. The famous men tell of their boyhood delinquencies, and the famous women tell of how they were homely, unpopular girls. They may speak with good grace of being thought dull, and they may describe their adjustments to poverty, physical handicaps, or severe or neglectful parents. But they do not dwell upon their illegitimacy. The writer born out of wedlock also seems to avoid that topic as a subject in his writings. Nevertheless, there seems to be no evidence that being illegitimate is an insurmountable barrier to either success or fame.

Some of the illegitimate children were brought up with brothers and sisters in homes that were established in open unconventionality. Examples of these were the Argentinian dictator's wife Eva Peron, Welsh archeologist and soldier T. E. Lawrence, Japanese social reformer Toyohiko Kagawa, and French painter Paul Cézanne. Each of these eminent persons knew his or her father intimately because their father was the head of their household, despite his unmarried status to their mother.

On the other hand, Jack London, Booker T. Washington, Ramsay MacDonald, and Sir Henry Stanley were not acknowledged by their fathers or supported by them. And Gordon Craig and Sarah Bernhardt were brought up in homes that were broken before the children were old enough to remember their fathers.

Eva Peron, at the height of her popularity as the wife of the Argentinian dictator Juan Peron (who was also illegitimate), destroyed as many records as she could find which related to her birth. Her father, Juan Duarte, a man of modest means, maintained two establishments. Eva was the youngest of the five children in her father's second family. When he died, Eva was two years old, and only the children were invited to the funeral. Her mother, left unprovided for, soon found herself another protector. At fifteen, Eva ran away from her turbulent home with an itinerant musician who abandoned her. She became a third-rate actress, but she had a talent for manipulating people and influencing events. She set up an extramarital relationship with a "mother's boy" whose father had deserted his mother, and she used her talent for intrigue to help him set up a dictatorship that lasted for many years.

In his late teens, T. E. Lawrence, soldier, writer, and adventurer known widely as "Lawrence of Arabia," ran away from his upper-middle-class home and enlisted as a private in the Royal Artillery. His discovery that he and his four brothers were the illegitimate offspring of their parents is thought to have been the reason for his flight from home. His gentleman father, who preferred to live on a very limited income rather than work, had left his wife and four daughters and run away with a governess who bore him five sons.

Despite her irregular status, Lawrence's ex-governess was exceedingly pious and prim. She developed a distaste for women, who, she said, wasted time chattering, and she seldom permitted women visitors in the home. Her son was correspondingly unable to relate to women, but was also rejecting of his parents, declaring them both unfit to be parents and his home intolerable. His oldest brother, a physician, described their as home quite happy, and this was the appearance it gave to the community, which did not know of its legal status.

Toyohiko Kagawa, social reformer and evangelist, was another child in a "second" household. His father, Denjiro Kagawa, a wealthy man with driving energy, was secretary to the Privy Council in Japan, a cabinet member, and the owner of a shipping company. Like many other men of his class, he took a mistress. He left his wife, Michi, on his farm with his scolding mother-in-law and set up a second household for gentle and kindly Kame, a Geisha girl from Kobe whom he had purchased. His first wife had been chosen for him by his parents when he was fifteen and she was eight; he chose his mistress for himself and lived with her for twenty-five years. Five children were born to them, of whom Toyohiko was the youngest son.

When both of his parents died, four-year-old Toyohiko and his emotionally disturbed sister Ei were sent to be reared by his father's legal wife and his mother-in-law. Since he had been legally adopted, the women were obliged to give him a home and an education. But both women, especially the older, hated the two children and treated them badly.

Toyohiko was sent to school, where his sympathies for all indigent and rejected persons led him to bring a dirty and diseased beggar into his room to live with him. When he graduated, he moved into the slums and deliberately lived as the very poorest people lived. His book recounting his adventures made him a wealthy man, but he reserved only forty dollars a month for the use of himself, his wife, and his five children, and he used the rest to set up schools, hospitals, and restaurants. Although he was affected by an eye disease contracted from the sick people among whom he lived, he retained a childlike gaiety and spontaneity. His wife, who was as interested as he in his work, carried on his institutions while he went to the United States to take a graduate degree at Princeton. He concerned himself with world peace and was an internationalist.

Paul Cézanne, the painter, was born to parents who did not get around to making their relationship legal until their third child was born, when Paul was six. Since this was not an unusual circumstance in their community, Paul's illegitimacy does not seem to have affected him. The conflict in this home was between the business interests of the father and the great indifference of the son to the practical aspects of life.

Gordon Craig, son of actress Ellen Terry, resented the devotion of his mother to her career, which impelled her to separate from his father. He married at twenty and had a family, which Ellen grumbled about to George Bernard Shaw. Gordon was also the father of Deirdre, dancer Isadora Duncan's daughter, who tragically drowned along with her brother. Professionally, Gordon extended his architect father (whom he never knew) through his stage designs—not his mother. Although he was given a chance to act when he was very young, he was never good at it.

Actress Sarah Bernhardt saw her father only twice and remembered him as a kindly, handsome man. He was Edouard Bernhardt, a well-to-do French law student who picked up the abandoned Dutch mistress of a French consular agent, Julie, and set up housekeeping with her. When the affair was over, their child, Sarah, was sent to the country to be reared by the father's old nurse. He also settled a small income on his daughter in his will. Since he died while she was still very young, Edouard did not live to protect Sarah from the neglect and abuse of the nurse.

Julie Bernhardt, Sarah's mother, soon became a famous courtesan of Paris, as did Julie's sister, Rosine. The two women, who were well known in fashionable circles, were kept in luxury by a series of influential and wealthy men. Two other daughters were born to Julie, who had an affection for only one of them. Sarah she disliked.

Kindly Aunt Rosine visited Sarah and was appalled by the child's unhappiness. Sarah was taken from her father's old nurse and sent to a convent school where she kicked and hit any nun or child who touched her—even inadvertently. When she was expelled for the third time from her school, the wealthy Duc de Morny, her mother's patron, sent her to be trained as an actress.

Jack London, American novelist, was never acknowledged by his father (but biographer Irving Stone is convinced that the father was astrologer W. H. Cheney). It was not Cheney, however, who assumed the responsibility of being a father to the eight-month-old infant; rather, it was a San Francisco working-man with a kindly disposition, John London, who reared the young child and gave him his name. After Jack's mother died, John London was forlorn and visited a medium in an attempt to communicate with his late wife. His two young daughters had been temporarily placed in a home, and he was distraught and lonely. He soon found himself married to the medium, Flora Wellman, a homely, wiry woman, a rejecting mother, and a problem wife. It was her new stepdaughter, eight-year-old Eliza London, who shooed the flies from the sleeping baby and became a mother to him. A friendly African-American woman in the neighborhood was also a mother figure to Jack. John London, however, was a patient and kindly foster father.

Jack London resembled W. H. Cheney in appearance—and both were distinctive-looking men. In a letter to Jack in which he denied paternity, Cheney's writing of the name "Jack London" could not be distinguished from Jack's own signature. Jack London's style of writing was also much like that of Cheney, according to Stone, who has examined the documents.

Both Flora Wellman and W. H. Cheney were well educated. Flora left her proper, well-to-do home when she was twenty-five to become a medium and a wanderer. The family she deserted always blamed a fever, which took her hair and forced her to wear a wig, for the personality change that made her repudiate her home and parents. Although she paid little attention to her stepson, it was she who started him writing by suggesting that he enter a writing contest held by a local newspaper.

Ramsay MacDonald, who became a Prime Minister of England, was reared by his grandmother, a woman of rare beauty with a habit of falling into trances during which she experienced heavenly visitations. The boy lived with her in a simple cottage. His mother was a servant girl, his father unknown. MacDonald wrote a moving essay praising his village schoolmaster, who was as close as a father to him and whose teaching methods were truly commendable.

Booker T. Washington, born to a loving and ambitious slave mother, had no special feelings about not knowing who his father was, because the other boys he knew were also likely not to have fathers. There was a rumor that his father was a white man on an adjoining plantation, but he did not know it there was any merit in it. His last name he chose for himself when he found that his teacher expected him to be called more than just "Booker."

Sir Henry M. Stanley, when he found the explorer Dr. David Livingstone in Central Africa, may have been searching for a father-figure. The newspapers were extremely critical and unfair to him when they discovered that he had tried to conceal his illegitimacy and workhouse origins. They also professed to disbelieve his African accounts of the slave trade, and he was accused of having been cruel to the natives.

Illegitimacy, while it may not enhance success, does not seem to inhibit its expression.[2] What does seem to be inhibited is eminence among the abandoned or adopted children who are kept unaware of their natural parentage. Because of the higher death rate in the years in which the Four Hundred lived, there were more orphaned children. Many children, unnamed, must have been left on institutional doorsteps. The lack of abandoned or adopted babies among the Four Hundred raises the question as to the reason for the absence of unusual achievement among children who never knew who their parents were.

It seems reasonable to assume that both the parent and child in the foster home would find it safer to stay within conventional boundaries and to keep goals and aspirations sensible and fairly simple. A tendency to be creative or experimental in the home where the child's genetic background is unknown could be threatening and confusing. A deliberate toning down of aspirations may result and would account for the lack of eminence among abandoned and adopted or foster children. In 1960, approximately 5 percent of the children in the United States were born out of wedlock; by 1995, that number had increased to 32 percent. We may be wasting a tremendous potential in many of these children by lowering our expectations of them. Guidance for adoptive parents who are given a child with ability seems especially necessary. The modern attitude, which does not stigmatize illegitimate children and leaves them with their mother, may make for a better development of talent.

Adoptive parents chosen by professional agencies are likely to be people who are stable economically and emotionally. On this basis, many of the eccentric and failure-prone parents that we have studied would not have been eligible to adopt. However, as previously described, even eccentricity and failure-proneness may be factors that contribute to later eminence. A survey of the reactions of adults who have been adopted might be illuminating.

The Fearful Boys and the Risk-Takers

Charles A. Lindbergh was subject to terrific nightmares about falling off a roof or precipice, but he met his fears head-on in daylight. He frightened a playmate by announcing that he intended to jump from a high tree, and only his mother's command deterred him. While he was in high school, he raced his motorcycle along the bank of a stream until the local police, hesitating to bring legal pressure on the son of an eminent politician, plowed up the area so that he could not endanger himself in this particular way.

Charles had few interests that were not either mechanical or in some way connected with proving his lack of fear. He sat through his classes without speaking unless he was called upon and earned mediocre grades. He never wore a white shirt, and he never dressed up to please the girls. He took no part in sports and never went hunting or fishing or skating with the boys.

His mother, a silent, dour woman, estranged from her husband, never encouraged him to play with other children. To her husband, Senator C. A. Lindbergh, being stoic under danger or pain was the true test of manhood. Senator Lindbergh was proud of his son when he was able to withstand the physical rigors of a thirty-day camping trip in an undeveloped country where the mosquitoes and black flies tested their endurance. He told his son about an exhausting thirty-mile walk he had taken with his own father, who was too proud to admit that he did not have train fare home from the city after he paid his taxes and debts in full.

When Senator Lindbergh underwent abdominal surgery, he refused an anesthetic, and although the ordeal lasted more than an hour, he never gritted his teeth and only once gripped the hand of a friend who sat beside him—during the few seconds when the surgeon's knife pierced his abdominal cavity. During the operation, he talked with the friend, a fellow senator, about international banking.

The boy who had nightmares about falling and whose father valued the ability to face danger and death so highly was the same Charles A. Lindbergh, Jr. who flew the ocean alone in a flimsy plane. His preparation had been a sleepless, roistering night; his food, a few sandwiches.

There are other boys who also had a need to face their fears. The Spanish bullfighter Manolete, a widow's only son, was a timid, fearful boy who was teased because he clung to his mother. Although he was famous for facing death so calmly, he was always frightened in the ring and did not enjoy his skirmishes with death. Robert Peary, the North Pole explorer, also the only son of a widow, clung to her and stayed in his yard to evade the boys who called him "Skinny" and teased him about his fearfulness.

During his childhood, Artic explorer Vilhjalmur Stefansson was not robust and was called "Softy" by his classmates. He spent hours by himself, sailing a toy boat in a tub of water. Greenland explorer and Nobel Peace Prize-winner Fridtjof Nansen was not a fearful boy, but he was incurably absent-minded and accident-prone. He set himself on fire at three, cut his forehead on the ice at four, and once caught a fishhook in his lower lip and had to have it cut out with a razor. He peppered his face with gunpowder by setting off a home-made cannon, and he daydreamed and nearly broke his neck on his first ski-jump. He broke both of his skis in a contest in which his brother took first prize. Antarctic explorer Admiral Richard E. Byrd was also accident-prone, injured his right leg three times, and was given a medical discharge from the Navy.

Gandhi was fearful of snakes and of the dark, and also that his child-wife, Kasturbai, would discover this weakness. James Joyce was terrified by thunderstorms; he was also afraid of dogs and was bitten twice by them. Ernest Hemingway was among the most accident-prone; he had a shattered nose and damaged eyesight at fourteen, and he later got 227 steel splinters in his right leg; gunshot wounds in both feet, both hands, and both knees; six severe head injuries; six broken ribs; and ten brain concussions.

Speech Problems

Emile Zola, Winston Churchill, Marcel Proust, and Robert Peary lisped. Somerset Maugham, Arnold Bennett, Aneurin Bevan, Thomas Wolfe, and Marc Chagall were stammerers.

Marc Chagall began to stammer in a secondary school after he was discriminated against by a rejecting teacher. Psychiatrists have recently noted that an injury to a limb or other body part can also precede stammering. Arnold Bennett began stammering after he caught his hand in a mangle.

When Arshile Gorki's father deserted his family, the five-year-old son stopped talking. Later, a tutor pretended to leap from a cliff, and the boy called out in dismay. The emotional shock had restored his speech.

Both Churchill and Bevan conquered their speech problems through practice and patience. Churchill planned his talks so that the terminal "s" was eliminated, memorized his speeches, and spoke from notes, taking infinite pains with every detail. A specialist whom he visited while he was in Sandhurst told him that only his own determination could help him.

The Delinquents and the Rebels

Studies of gifted children indicate that the likelihood of their becoming delinquent to the point of being apprehended is very slight. They are commonly law-abiding and have an early sensitivity for the rights and privileges of others. Although this is also true of the Four Hundred, they cannot be categorized as a sedentary, inactive group of boys and girls. A few ran away from home, several were school truants or were expelled for being rude to the teacher. Seven found themselves in jail during their adolescence.

Jazz trumpeter Louis Armstrong is the only member of the Four Hundred who was committed to an institution for delinquent boys. This neglected boy, whose father had deserted the family and whose mother was "out on the town," was picked up for firing blank cartridges into the air from his stepfather's revolver. He found life rewarding at the school to which he was sentenced in New Orleans, though. In his autobiography, he says, "The place was more like a health center or a boarding school than a boys' jail. All in all I am very proud of the days I spent at the Colored Waifs Home for Boys." It was there that he learned to play an instrument and became a bandleader.

Another boy sent to jail was neither fortunate nor contented. George Robert Gissing, the English novelist, served a short prison term for stealing money from the lockers of his well-to-do classmates to buy a sewing machine for a young prostitute who had convinced him that she wished to change her occupation. This tenderness for the underprivileged or oppressed is common among exceptionally intelligent children, as Leta Hollingworth noted in *Children Above 180 IQ*. Gissing was discovered and disgraced; he served his term and never went back to school—which was unfortunate, because he was always a scholar without enough companionship from other scholars. His entire career was stormy and tragic.

Labor leader David Dubinsky was made assistant secretary of his baker's union at age fifteen, despite the fact that he was the boss's son. He was a scholar who could read and write and keep books, while most of the other workers were illiterate. David was arrested for his part in a labor strike and spent two weeks in jail; but his father, pleased with his son's aggressiveness and his loyalty to his cause, bribed the jailer and got him out. Israeli Prime Minister David Ben Gurion was arrested when he, too, was an adolescent, and his father was also pleased to come to the rescue of his son, who had spoken at a Zionist street meeting in Warsaw.

Brendan Behan, Irish playwright, at age sixteen was discovered in Liverpool near the shipyards carrying a suitcase full of high explosives. He was jailed as an Irish terrorist and sent to an English reform school, which he described in his riotous and memorable *Borstal Boy.* Although his mother worked in the house of Irish revolutionary Maude Gonne, and his uncle was an intimate of the poet Yeats, Brendan came from a family of opinionated housepainters. He had been expelled from the Christian Brothers School earlier in his career.

William Osler, the famous physician, spent three days in jail after he harassed the matron at his school. Manuel Quezon, first President of the Commonwealth of the Philippines, was locked in his school building for fifteen days because he clubbed and injured a corporal of the civil guard who had been molesting young girls but had escaped punishment because his official position gave him immunity. His parents were supportive, and Manuel became a local hero.

If William Randolph Hearst, American newspaper editor, had not come from a fabulously wealthy family, he might have been sentenced for a much longer period to a school for delinquent boys than was the ebullient Louis Armstrong. When Hearst shot toy darts into the ceiling of a Paris hotel and tried to pull them out again, the whole ceiling fell, sculptured cupids and all. "My father," he says casually in his autobiography, "had to buy them a new hotel." Hearst also had a penchant for playing with fire and water in hotels.

During the panic of 1874, William's father, George Hearst, suffered financial reverses that forced the family to sell its chalet, its horses, carriages, and other valuables. The parents were reduced to boarding out with old friends, and the eleven-year-old "Billy Buster" was farmed out to his grandfather's ranch. This period did not last long, however, and within the year, George was a millionaire again.

No boy was more extravagantly indulged than William Randolph Hearst. Once, before the lad was taken to Europe for a holiday, he had a farewell party that lasted for ten days. But money did not bring William friends. When he was painfully rejected at school, he begged his parents not to be sent to back again overdressed and chauffeur-driven, and he asked for patches to be sewn on his clothes. His parents, however, were unmoved by his distress and continued to shower him with gold coins and extravagant toys. The elderly husband and his young wife disliked each other but vied in indulging their only son.

William's luxurious quarters at Harvard were the nightly site of beer parties, oyster suppers, and bull sessions. He was suspended for six months when he celebrated the Democratic victory of 1884 by hiring several bands to parade through the yard, having fireworks set off in all directions, and buying wagonloads of beer for all the student body. He was expelled permanently in the middle of his senior year for sending his professors chamber pots decorated with their names and photographs

William Randolph Hearst was not the only member of the Four Hundred who was expelled from school for defiance of his teachers. Salvador Dalí was expelled when he refused to allow teachers whom he considered less skilled than he to judge his art work. Musical conductor Erich Kleiber was dismissed for impudence and for showing lack of respect for his school. Writer Negley Farson was expelled when he helped to throw a tattling teacher into an Andover duck pond.

The world might have lost a great physicist if Enrico Fermi had been expelled when he led a stink-bomb attack on the faculty of his secondary school, the Reale Nonnale of Pisa. Enrico was a member of the Anti-Neighbor Society, whose purpose was to play pranks on the other students. As a symbol of their membership, they carried red or yellow painted padlocks in their pockets. While one member of the society engaged a victim in conversation, the other slipped the shackle through the victim's clothes and locked him in his suit or topcoat. They set pails of water on the tops of doors left ajar. They engaged in make-believe duels defending the honor of girls who were not in the slightest danger of losing it. They had water fights on the roof. They dubbed a homely girl May Queen, much to her embarrassment. Most of their pranks went unheeded, but the stink-bomb attack on the faculty almost brought dismissal. It was only because of the recommendation of a teacher who recognized Fermi's rare ability that he was not expelled. Both he and his best friend, Rasetti, who were the ringleaders in this mischief, were bored and restive because of the inadequate challenge to their ability in the classroom.

Ignace Jan Paderewski, pianist and composer, was a runaway and a school rebel and was expelled. Joseph Stalin was expelled for his political activities; William Osler, for rudeness and rebellion. Leon Trotsky was suspended for a time from his secondary school when he was falsely accused of being the instigator of a class "concert" for the teacher. A "concert" was a howling noise, made with the lips closed, which marked the teacher's footsteps as he walked. Jealousy of Trotsky's status as top boy in the class made another boy name him as a ringleader when he was merely a participant.

Louisiana politician "Kingfish" Huey Long was not suspended when he organized a group of boys into a gang and demanded obedience from the other students. Instead, he succeeded in having a principal who tried to curb him fired. Swedish business speculator and manipulator Ivar Kreuger, known as the "Match King" because of his near monopoly of the match business, was a solitary, elfish boy, odd in appearance, who crawled through the school windows, read the teacher's records, and sold the information gained to other students. His hobby, at which he was unsurpassed, was cheating. Mussolini's parents had to send him away from his home town to find a school that could manage him.

Buffalo Bill Cody left school and joined a wagon train because he fought and seriously injured another student who tore up the playhouse Bill was making in the schoolyard with a girl. Young Cody feared the boy's retaliation. Orphaned Ernest Bevin ran away from the farm where he worked after forcing the farmer to hide in a closet to escape the tool Ernest was brandishing. Jack London was an oyster pirate. Sun Yat-Sen overturned religious shrines in his community after he became a Christian. Chiang Kai-Shek was cuffed about by his male relatives for his mischievous ways, and at age eighteen, he became abusive to local dignitaries in a restaurant. He cut off his pigtail to show his defiance of the old-fashioned ways when he believed he had gained entrance to a school in Japan. When he was not admitted, he was left short-haired and vulnerable to ridicule.

Noel Coward was a school truant. The Barrymore brothers, Lionel and John, were incorrigible in their behavior at school and were exceedingly poor students. When John was admitted to preparatory school at Seton Hall, New Jersey, a priest asked him to demonstrate his ability as an athlete on bars in the gymnasium. Liquor, playing cards, and a pair of "brass knuckels" fell from the boy's pocket.

Ramon Magsaysay, of the Philippines, was often a truant in elementary school and once took his father's gun and went hunting for a week. John R. Mott, founder of the YMCA, was spanked for running down the tracks in front of railroad trains. He and his friends took bolts off of freight cars and hubs off of farm wagons and buggies. Explorer Richard Byrd once went spelunking and found the source of a lost river that was said to run under a cave. He went to sleep there and was discovered hours later after friends and neighbors had searched the countryside for him. He and his brothers once dug a five-foot trench across a beautiful lawn as part of war games they were playing.

Grover Cleveland, who heard his father preach twice every Sunday, was annoyed when his Latin teacher opened class with a long prayer. While the other students sat with devoutly bowed heads, he and his friend threw their books out the window and stealthily followed them.

Will Rogers was incorrigible at school and ran away from home. Eddie Cantor called himself a liar, truant, pilferer from pushcarts, and a street fighter. He once had his head cracked open in a gang fight, and although an obliging druggist sewed it up, the wound became infected and an operation was performed to save his life. Irvin S. Cobb was known as the naughtiest small boy in Paducah, Kentucky, and in his autobiography, he professed an inability to pass a pile of shingles without backing up to something—since he had been spanked so often with shingles. Orville Wright was suspended from his sixth-grade class in Richmond, Indiana because he was mischievous, but his tolerant parents did not force him to return to school, since they were planning to move in a few months.

Girls were no less troublesome than the boys. Sarah Bernhardt was expelled three times—for imitating a bishop, for throwing stones at the Royal Dragoons, and finally for climbing over a wall to stay with a young soldier until long after dark. Gertrude Atherton was an incorrigible child. Ernestine Schumann-Heink was a school truant. Eleonora Duse, Katherine Mansfield, Isadora Duncan, and Sarah Bernhardt all experienced extramarital pregnancies when they were in their twenties. One boy, Artur Schnabel, is recorded as having fathered an illegitimate daughter who was born when Artur was seventeen.

As seen in the above, the concept of the gifted and promising child as a bookworm cloistered in the library is not upheld by the Four Hundred. Although they almost all read omnivorously, they clearly had other strong interests. Among equally talented and promising boys and girls today, there are no doubt many who are shunted into unproductive and unchallenging careers because they have been involved in similar escapades. It is the mother-smothered and mother-dominated who are the least likely to be involved in serious childhood mischief. Perhaps a project to visit schools for the delinquent to pick out the hungry readers and children with special talents—and then to develop a constructive program for such boys and girls—would interest some adventurous, inquisitive foundation executive.

Psychosis Is Rare in Homes Which Rear Eminent Children

There are very few men and women reared in the homes that cradle eminence who were institutionalized as a result of mental illness. Nor were they treated at home or secluded in isolated settings. Since being psychotic is both time-consuming and incapacitating, perhaps this is not surprising. However, what seems to be a low incidence of mental illness among the parents, brothers, and sisters— and possibly even among the offspring—of the Four Hundred is an unexpected finding that bears examination.

More than one in ten persons living in the United States today can expect to be a patient at a mental hospital at some time during his or her life, according to United States Public Health Service estimates. Half of all hospital beds in the United States are occupied by the mentally ill, most of the younger of whom are diagnosed as schizophrenic. These are patients whose behavior makes it impossible for them to participate in the community or whose communities lack tolerance for their bizarre or withdrawn behavior. The cause of this condition is not understood, but most authorities believe that genetic, biochemical, and social factors may all play a significant role and that schizophrenia is an international phenomenon.

Since the families cradling eminence appear to produce few individuals with incapacitating psychotic disorders, it is worthwhile to speculate as to the reasons for this immunity. The limitations of this biographical method, however, make it inadvisable to do more than sort out those who suffered psychosis from this larger group.

Four men among the Four Hundred were institutionalized, and one eminent woman was under professional treatment in an institution for several years. Among the parents, there were two fathers and two mothers who were institutionalized for disorders not connected with injury or terminal illness. Two brothers and two sisters of the eminent were said to be mentally ill.

Maurice Barrymore, the popular and successful actor who was the father of three of the Four Hundred, was discovered sitting on the cast iron steps of the West Thirtieth Street Station in New York City staring into space. A friend saw him there, coaxed him into a taxi and took him to Bellevue. Maurice went docilely, talking all the while about his favorite song, "The Garden of Sleep." He was soon transferred to a private hospital, where he spent several years writing an endless novel, which consisted of only one line repeated over and over, "It was a lovely day in June."

Charlie Chaplin's mother was out of touch with reality for many years and was first hospitalized when her son was eight, but she retained her beauty, her charming manner, and a youthful appearance for many years. Max Eastman tells in *Great Companions* of a visit with her at the time when her eminent son brought her from England to an apartment in Hollywood. She had been warned about behaving properly when she went through customs and was repentant when she forgot and hailed the customs officer as "Jesus Christ." She tried to conceal her error by saying quickly, "I mean by that, sir, that when I looked into your eyes, I realized that notwithstanding the blue cap, that you have a gentle and spiritual nature." When she was brought to the apartment, she put on a phonograph record and danced for Max Eastman, pausing between dips and twirls to sympathize with a caged bird in the room.

Lafcadio Hearn's mother died in a mental institution in Malta. Her first breakdown came after the birth of her second son in England. She was grimly silent, then wildly violent. Sent back to her native country of Greece by her rejecting husband, she did not recover.

Elliott Paul was in his teens before his mother felt she could tell him that his father had died in an insane asylum before Elliott was four years old. Elliott was twenty-eight when he wrote his first novel. The opening scene describes his father, who is on his knees with other men trying to quiet him. The mother in the story is in tears as a cold, black wagon drives up to the house and strange men in white coats take the sick man away. Strips of torn sheeting are used to bind the father's hands and feet. When Elliott's mother, who had never described the scene to her son, read this description, she was shocked and dismayed by its brutal accuracy. She had not thought that a three-year-old could remember so much, not even such a precocious child as Elliott.

When Elliott's father was taken away, his mother turned to her son for comfort and companionship. Before he was six, she had taught him most of what children were supposed to learn in grammar school. No fear of overtaxing his young mind deterred her, and Elliott was always grateful for her teachings because he was permitted to skip grades. He hated school; he found it an "unjust imprisonment for offenses he had not yet committed." Since his father died soon after being admitted to the hospital, it is possible that his insanity was a result of medical rather than psychological causes.

There are other parents whose breakdown was connected with a terminal illness. The father of Friedrich Nietzsche is said by his daughter to have fallen down a flight of stairs and injured his head several months before his suddenly disturbed and painful days were cut short by death. Since Friedrich always feared inheriting his father's illness, his sister's blow-on-the-head theory can be questioned. The highly opinionated Nietzsche family was not always in agreement.

Lord Randolph Churchill had his first paralytic attack when he was thirty-two. His speech and gait were affected, and he had periods of depression and elation. His son, Winston Churchill, told of the small brain hemorrhages that preceded his father's death, of the periods of coma, and of the added impairment after each attack. The man's illness did not bring him closer to his oldest son, who was icily repulsed when he volunteered to be his father's secretary. During his lifetime, Lord Randolph spoke at length with Winston only four times. During the fourth conversation, Lord Randolph cautioned Winston against believing all that he heard about his father, and he spoke pathetically of his "enemies."

After his father died, Winston resolved to repeat the man's life and to do him honor by succeeding where the elder Churchill had failed because of his illness and early death. He wrote a two-volume biography of Lord Randolph, adopted his father's views, sought out his father's friends, rejected his father's opponents, memorized his father's speeches, and told his friends that he expected to die at forty-six as his father had done. When he abandoned some of his father's political beliefs, he was not able to work on the biography for a considerable period of time and resorted to various rationalizations to justify himself in his own eyes. As he matured, he was finally able to think of himself as a separate and whole individual apart from his father. To his own children, he was a willing and delightful companion.

There are many parents who are eccentric, neurotic, or are incapacitated by psychosomatic disorders. The mothers of Fritz Kreisler and Arthur Koestler had painful illnesses that were observed but not treated by Freud. Sir Thomas Beecham's wealthy mother used to periodically leave home for lengths of time because of her "nerves." As young adults, Sir Thomas and his sister Emily successfully championed their mother's cause when her unfaithful husband tried to have her hospitalized for mental illness. Hart Crane's mother suffered a nervous collapse during a period of conflict with her husband. David Daiches' mother had a postpartum breakdown but recovered.

Some of the fathers also display neurosis or eccentricity. There are fathers who are too engrossed in self-initiated, unprofitable learning projects to make a living for their families and who have been regarded as exceptionally "odd" by their contemporaries. There are fathers who cannot keep their waistcoats buttoned straight, fathers who are perpetually on a soapbox, fathers who walk at night to avoid having to speak to their neighbors. Among the Four Hundred, the fathers tend to be ebullient, grandiose, imaginative, and failure-prone, but they are not often sent to mental institutions.

The children in the homes under survey can perhaps be emotionally comfortable among their own misadventures because nothing they do will be worse than something their fathers have already done. Or if the father is stable and a pillar in the community, then it may be the mother who provides the neighbors with cause to speak of her inexplicable behavior. One very real characteristic of many of the families who were surveyed is that they are remarkably unconcerned about their public image.

Vaslav Nijinsky, the dancer, was rejected so severely by classmates who were also training for the Russian Imperial Ballet that the student he displaced as the top boy, Ronzai, felt free to play a trick on Vaslav that nearly killed him. The boys were prone to play sadistic pranks on each other after hours at the boarding school. They lashed at each other with whips and tried to tear off each other's clothes with buttonhooks. Ronzai was angry at Vaslav because when he dared the Polish boy to hit him with a big India rubber ball at thirty paces,

Vaslav did so, knocking out four of Ronzai's teeth and giving him a bloody nose. Ronzai retaliated by raising the standard on a heavy music stand over which the boys were jumping several inches above Vaslav's known limit and then spreading soap flakes on the floor. Vaslav fell heavily; his head was terribly injured, and his chest was crushed. He was not expected to live. The incident shocked the adult ballet dancers of Moscow, who filled the young student's room with flowers. Vaslav's mother wept by his bedside alone. Vaslav's father was an unreliable fellow who appeared infrequently with fine presents and little money for food.

After months of convalescence, Vaslav had to learn to walk again as if he were an infant. During this period, one of the boys in his class, a wealthy boy from an aristocratic family, felt impelled to make friends with the persecuted Polish boy whom the other boys had not been willing to sit next to in class and whom they had excluded from all their games. It was he who helped Vaslav prepare a party, a real feast with sausages and sweets, upon which the affectionate mother spent her last coin. Although every boy in the class had accepted the invitation—even the offending Ronzai—no one came. Vaslav and his mother both wept bitterly. Vaslav, according to his wife, was always a mother's boy, her most tender, affectionate, faithful child.

But Vaslav did not receive the whole attention of his mother because she was preoccupied with his oldest brother, who was mentally ill, and she had given up her own dancing career to look after him. Vaslav had little companionship from his father, himself a ballet dancer who had not succeeded in accordance with his ability on account of his Polish origin. At the height of his own career, Vaslav Nijinsky became schizophrenic and was hospitalized for many years.

Rudolph Hess, a Nazi leader who fled to England, puzzled the psychiatrists who examined him because they had reason to suspect that his loss of memory and fear of being poisoned might be feigned. His life-pattern, regardless of diagnosis, resembled that of other mother-smothered, father-hating boys. The Hess children dared not play in the house when their irascible father was at home. As an adult, Hess continued to identify with his mother, and he adopted her unusual ideas about food, the occult, and the efficacy of nature cures. Brutal men frightened him, controversy dismayed him; he was kind to insects, animals, and older women. The didactic, punctilious man was called the "Brown Mouse" by his associates and is said to have married in order to quell rumors concerning his tendencies to homosexuality.

The exception among those who were hospitalized is Van Wyck Brooks, whose home life as a child is described as relatively untroubled and whose parents were not seen by him as over- possessive. Brooks describes himself as an artistically-oriented, accelerated boy who was closer to adults than to his peers. He said little about his classroom experiences until he reached Harvard, which met many of his needs. He said much more about a year spent abroad when he was thirteen with a tutor whom he liked. As Van Wyck matured, he became deeply concerned with what he considered the failure of the United States to provide a background for genius. Later, he was hospitalized for his incapacitating depression, during which time he wrote articles for magazines and a weekly newspaper. Like Clara Barton, who was also hospitalized, the work that brought him the widest fame was done after his hospitalization. In 1931, after four years passed in mental hospitals, he came out into a new era dazed, with a feeling of youth, and with a hard ball of panic in his stomach that was never entirely to disappear.

The lack of psychologically-based illness among the Four Hundred cannot be attributed to the absence of early symptoms thought to indicate the onset of mental illness. Albert Schweitzer used to laugh aloud in the classroom with no apparent cause. Albert Einstein went about chanting hymns to himself which he dedicated to his self-created deity. Thomas Edison set fire to a barn and smashed eggs by sitting on them to hatch them. Eleanor Roosevelt lived in a fantasy world where she was the mistress of her dead father's household. Stanley Baldwin nursed a grudge against his headmaster to such an extent that he spoiled his secondary-school and college years for himself. He resented being flogged before the student body for being caught with ordinary schoolboy pornography in his possession. Salvador Dalí waited until his classmates, with whom he had no satisfying contacts, were watching, then leaped from the top of the stairs to attract their attention. Nasser tried to kill himself when he was six; Maxim Gorky almost did so at nineteen. Among the Four Hundred are dozens of withdrawn, hyperactive, overaggressive, moody, or easily depressed children.

Nor do the Four Hundred escape being erratic or neurotic as adults. They seem to be subject to depression, especially in middle life. Many have periods of prolonged depression and "nervous exhaustion" which take them from their work at times. Paderewski turned to farming at one period in his life because he could not bear to play the piano. Actor Chevalier, another boy who was extremely close to his mother and could not relate to women with any depth of affection, suddenly found himself unable to memorize his lines and required a prolonged rest cure and treatment. He married the girl who helped him recover, but found her overpossessive when he was well again. Pianist and composer Rachmaninoff required hypnotic treatment periodically to pull him out of his depressions.

Author Gustav Regler, while a young soldier in the German army, was overcome by carbon monoxide poisoning while recuperating in a field hospital. Thought to be incurably ill, he was sent back to Germany to a mental hospital, where for a time he was unable to speak. During periods of acute disturbance, however, he spoke freely, and he recovered with the help of a Dr. Schomberg, who had similar attitudes to those held by Gustav's pacifist father. During his hospitalization Gustav, still in late adolescence, spent his recuperative period reorganizing his beliefs about religion and society. The doctor let him go reluctantly, saying, "Only one part of you despises war. I have read your diary [Regler had read Rilke on the battlefield]. You will volunteer for other wars as senseless as this one."[3] Once the effects of being gassed had passed, Regler did not break down again, despite repeated involvements in various traumatic situations.

Composer Maurice Ravel died in surgery during a brain operation calculated to cure the aphasia that had made him unable to work. There were also those who died mentally ill as a result of having contracted syphilis—Toulouse-Lautrec and Nietzsche. While institutionalized, Nietzsche had continued his writing.

The small number of psychotically ill among these families cannot be easily attributed to willful concealment. When an individual becomes interesting enough to the public to be the subject of a book-length biography, such concealment is improbable. Mental retardation is also an undesirable condition, and there are several references to mental retardation among the family members. Since individuals considered to be retarded are frequently found to be mentally ill rather than mentally retarded, there may be family members who should have been regarded as psychotic instead of retarded. The references to them as retarded, however, indicate a certain honesty in reporting and suggests that psychotic behavior is also honestly reported.

Pearl Buck has contributed a valuable account of her adjustment to her mentally retarded daughter. Mary Austin, another novelist, also had a mentally retarded daughter. William Beveridge, Wilfred Grenfell, and William Dean Howells had small brothers who were mentally retarded and became uncontrollable following illnesses. Sigmund Freud had a cousin who was diagnosed a "hydrocephalic imbecile," two other cousins who became insane, and another who suffered epilepsy. Gertrude Stein had two mentally retarded siblings.

It is the whole family, rather than the one child who becomes eminent, that seems to share a freedom from psychosis. Only five of the brothers and sisters in these prolific families are described as mentally ill—the brother of Vaslav Nijinsky, the sisters of Toyohiko Kagawa and of Olive Schreiner, and Dr. Dean Robinson, brilliant brother of the poet Edwin Arlington Robinson. In the latter instance, drug addiction was a contributing factor to the mental illness. And finally, the spinster schoolteacher sister of Robert Frost, Jean, became mentally ill, according to her brother, as a reaction to the outbreak of war.

The primary function of this survey is not to interpret behavior but to catalog types of behavior. The families in which eminent persons of the twentieth century were reared, as we have said, had a great love for learning, strong physical and achievement drives, and were highly opinionated—and this persisted even when they became mentally ill. But these families were also observed to have few psychotics among them. It can therefore be suggested—but by no means proved—that these factors may have had some role in producing a climate that helped to keep the family members from losing touch with reality and from a withdrawal from society that took them to the mental hospital. Perhaps they simply did not have time to be mentally ill. The intensity of the drive toward a goal may have been too compelling to leave time for the individual to nurse his or her anxieties to the breaking point.

There are some similarities in persons suffering mental disorders. For example, there are comparatively few mental breakdowns in a country that is being invaded. Persons withdrawn in a catatonic stupor who are on a hospital ship have been known to come into quick touch with reality and try to save themselves in an intelligent fashion when the ship is bombed. Milton H. Erikson, psychiatrist, tells of a fire in a hospital where a patient who had been catatonic for years took the keys from a frightened attendant and efficiently engineered the evacuation of the ward. After the fire, he returned the keys to the attendant and went back into his stupor. Can it be possible that becoming famous or eminent is comparable to being in a perpetual crisis?

There are many references to periods of acute depression in the biographies and autobiographies of eminent men and women. Depression and suicide seem to be more of a threat to the eminent than psychosis. That this is not irrelevant or accidental is evidenced by the findings of the Terman study, in which the fifteen suicides among the one thousand intellectually gifted men and women, when they reached mid-life, is a slightly higher suicide rate than that of the general population.

Among the Four Hundred, there have been eight suicides: Jack London, Virginia Woolf, Stefan Zweig, Paul Goebbels, Vachel Lindsay, Arshile Gorki, Ivar Kreuger, and Robert La Follette, Jr. The manner of the violent deaths of Jan Masaryk, Hart Crane, Ernest Hemingway, and Adolf Hitler are not fully agreed upon. This means that there are more suicides than instances of psychosis among the Four Hundred, which is the reverse of the relationship of suicide to psychosis in populations generally.

There is no way of determining whether the Four Hundred had fewer or more environmental handicaps than did most persons in their times and communities. It is fairly evident, however, that almost any conceivable handicap has been successfully overcome by some eminent person somewhere. In many instances, the handicaps are considered by those who experience them as having been motivating factors in their achievements. This does not mean that other individuals may not "break" under similar stress. Both parents and children in the families of the Four Hundred are seemingly protected from incapacitating mental illness. This protection may possibly be associated with their physical resilience and an all-consuming concentration on a chosen task.

Chapter 10

Dislike of School and Schoolteachers

> *. . . his back*
> *Slumped to the old half-cringe, his hands fell slack,*
> *A big boy's arm went around him—and a twist,*
> *Sent shattering pain along his tortured wrist.*
> *As a voice cried, a bloated voice and fat,*
> *"Why it's Miss Nancy. Come along you rat!"*
>
> —Stephen Vincent Benét, *Going Back to School*

Three out of every five of the Four Hundred had serious school problems. In order of importance, their dissatisfactions were: with the curriculum; with dull, irrational, or cruel teachers; with other students who bullied, ignored, or bored them; and with school failure. In general, it is the totality of the school situation with which they are concerned, and they seldom have one clear-cut, isolated complaint.

Tutors are accepted with better grace than is the classroom teacher, for the tutor has good personal communication with the student and can adapt to his or her varying levels of attainment in a more realistic fashion. Boys and girls who are tutored by parents are usually grateful and responsive. Grandparents, friends of the family, and literate men and women of the community who develop a special interest in an inquiring youngster are also well accepted.

Librarians often fill a useful function. The school paper, the debating society, the peer group of intellectuals with whom the late adolescent frequently consorts, the theater, books which are self-discovered, the parental dinner table with its highly articulate guests, the parental library or studio are all given precedence over the classroom as sources of learning and insight. Rejection or dislike of the classroom is an international phenomenon and has little to do with whether the schools are public or private, secular or clerical, or with the philosophy of teaching employed in the various schools.

Rabindranath Tagore, of India, whose parents were wealthy and literate and highly opinionated, says that it was fortunate that he ended his school life at thirteen, because he could not have endured the unbearable torture of school for a longer period. In an autobiographical sketch, he declares:

> *According to the school, life is perfect when it allows itself to be treated as dead, to be cut into symmetrical conveniences. And this was the cause of my suffering in school.... I was fortunate enough to extricate myself before insensibility set in.*[1]

Thomas Mann, who also came from a well-to-do and literate home, describes in his memoirs a school experience that was "stagnating and unsatisfactory." Ernest Jones, a beloved only son reared in a supportive, comfortable, upper-class English home, found his secondary school a preparation for helping him to understand the abuses in Nazi concentration camps. Victims in his school were lowered headfirst into latrines. Another favorite sport was to lay a boy on his back, lie across him face downward, and get six or seven others to add to the weight by doing the same. The only way the victim could escape was to hurt one of his tormentors badly.

The Russia Leon Trotsky says in his autobiography, "The percentage of freaks among people in general is high, but it is especially high among teachers." He proceeds to prove the point by describing in minute detail several of his instructors.

A teacher shook thirteen-year-old Edward Grieg and shouted at him when he found him completing his *Opus 1, Variation of a*

German Melody for the Piano in class. Grieg was so resistant to school that he used to stand under the rainspout in order to get so wet that the teacher would send him home to change clothes. When the teacher discovered this stratagem, Grieg had to invent others. Henry T. Finck quotes him as saying:

> *The only excuse I will make for myself is that school was in the last degree unsympathetic to me; its materialism, its coarseness, its coldness were so abhorrent to my nature that I thought of the most incredible ways of escaping from it, if only for a short time.... I have not the least doubt that school developed in me nothing but what was evil and left the good untouched.*[2]

Pope John XXIII, when an Italian schoolboy, was once sent home from school with a note to his village priest "begging him to reprove the boy for not being conscientious about his studies and always coming to class unprepared." The boy, however, suspecting the contents of the note, failed to deliver it.

An American schoolboy of Armenian ancestry, a poor widow's son who had spent some time in an orphanage, was less than grateful for his schooling. In his autobiography, William Saroyan says:

> *I must remember also the peculiar smell of the school, and of every classroom; warm oil on the wood floor, chalk dust, desks, old books, paper, pencils, pencil shavings, ink, the teacher herself. The wretched smell of school. Every school has it. Emerson school had it bad.... I resented school, but I never resented learning.*[3]

At the same time that he was being problematic in school, he read nearly every book in the Fresno, California public library.

In England, Vera Brittain was bullied by two unpleasant schoolgirls, older than she, who twisted her arm to make her listen to sexual information described in revolting terms.

Although girls in general are overall less resistant to school than are boys, American girls among the Four Hundred—Susan B. Anthony,

Pearl Buck, Mary Austin, Gertrude Atherton, Isadora Duncan, and Willa Gather—did not like school. A Norwegian girl, Sigrid Undset, shared their feelings:

> *I hated school so intensely. It interfered with my freedom. I avoided the discipline by an elaborate technique of being absent-minded during classes. But my schoolmates found me out from the very beginning...and they set about to make me see how unpleasant life ought to be made for anyone who is different from other people.*[4]

These burgeoning, exploding, highly verbal boys and girls were undoubtedly problems in their classrooms. They were too eager to get at the truth of things to be satisfied with what they were told. A voracity for new ideas and a relish for reading irked students who were indifferent to learning or who failed to rival them in the classroom. So they were sometimes suspended over fires or over sword points, doused with water until they were half drowned, mimicked, snickered at, or nicknamed derisively. They were often isolated and ignored and were frequently asked to keep still. Sometimes they were even feared as children who were supernaturally endowed.

Three out of five of the Four Hundred disliked school, yet four out of five of them showed evidences of being unusually intelligent and/or exceptionally talented.

Prokofiev, at the age of five, composed a galloping horse song and at seven composed an opera titled "The Giant" (in which he ignored the black piano keys). Yehudi Menuhin was studying the violin seriously at the age of three and a half and was admitted to the Vienna Conservatory at age seven. At three, Paderewski picked out melodies with one finger, and at four, he used all of his fingers. (This did not prevent a teacher from telling him that he could never expect to be a good pianist because his third fingers were too short.) Sousa organized his first band when he was eleven. Schweitzer played the organ for church services when he was nine. Norman Angell was editor of a newspaper at fifteen.

Steinmetz could do multiplication and division with fractions when he was only five years old. Inventor Marconi began working on his idea for a radio when he was fourteen, and he sent his first wireless message when he was twenty-one. Reginald Fessenden was ready for college at fourteen. Norbert Wiener, founder of cybernetics, received his doctorate from Harvard at eighteen. Sigmund Freud was top boy in his class for six years and was seldom called upon because he knew all of the answers. After finishing a book on mathematical physics, schoolboy (and later nuclear physicist) Enrico Fermi remarked to his sister that he had not noticed it was written in Latin. When Fermi was in elementary school, he also designed electric motors that worked.

At four, Marie Curie was memorizing the names of the intricate objects that her father, a physics teacher, used, and in elementary school, she was at least two years ahead of her classmates in every subject. As a child, she spoke German, French, and Russian with equal ease. At eleven, Albert Einstein was reading philosophy and textbooks on science and mathematics. For recreation, he played the music of the great composers on his violin. Although he usually took seven courses instead of the required four, J. Robert Oppenheimer, nuclear physicist and developer of the atom bomb, gave a scientific lecture before a learned society at age eleven, and he graduated from Harvard summa cum laude with the highest honors ever given an undergraduate.

At ten, novelist George Gissing was reading Shakespeare and Dickens. Vera Brittain wrote novels on scrap paper from her father's pottery factory while she was in elementary school. At ten, author and journalist Arthur Koestler had a passion for mathematics, physics, and the construction of mechanical toys, and he had a facility for learning languages.

Politicians from disadvantaged homes must have exceptional drive and ability to get to positions of power. Joseph McCarthy and Huey Long were the sons of poor farmers. McCarthy, a homely, mother-smothered boy who disliked his father, skipped a grade in grammar school and, when he was nineteen, completed four years of high school work in a single year. Huey Long completed a three-year law course in eight months. David Lloyd George, a widow's son, prepared for the Preliminary Law Examination at the age of fifteen with only his fifty-year-old uncle, a shoemaker by trade, to help him. They worked in secret to avoid ridicule.

At the age of twelve, Jan Christiaan Smuts, who later became a South African statesman, was a skilled ranch hand but could neither read nor write. After his brother, who was being prepared for the pulpit of the Dutch Reformed Church, died, Jan was sent to school. On the open prairie of the veld, he had run from approaching strangers. At school, he behaved "like a wild bird." However, he was soon memorizing books after a single reading. In one week, he learned enough Greek to make the highest mark in a class that had been in session for many months.

Among the Four Hundred, the children who seemed to show the most extreme intellectual precocity were Jan Christiaan Smuts, Norbert Wiener, J. Robert Oppenheimer, Arthur Koestler, Norman Angell, J. Middleton Murry, and Bertrand Russell. Mary Ellen Chase was assigned a fifth-grade text on the first day of school. Unfortunately, she had to continue reading from this same textbook for seven more years. Isadora Duncan started teaching her unique form of modern dancing professionally at the age of seven, and at ten, with her mother's permission, she gave up school to teach full time. Helen Keller, who dictated a letter in colloquial French at the age of ten, was perhaps the most brilliant girl of the Four Hundred.

The least recognized and often the most unhappy children are those who have an early empathy that other children do not have. Their sensitivity to injustice and inequalities and their easily aroused feelings of guilt frequently bring them into disfavor with adults and cause them to be ridiculed by other children. Adults praised Albert Schweitzer when he could substitute for the church organist at age nine, yet he was punished or ridiculed when he refused to wear the proper clothes that his parents so painfully provided for him, when he insisted on being as poorly clad as the village boys, and when he would not join in robbing birds' nests. Early evidences of altruism are often not well received from children, especially from boys.

Lord Robert Cecil, despite the encouragement of his father and the help of his brother, tried in vain to reform the conditions at Eton that made the study of the great classical authors a farce. He later became a statesman and Prime Minister. Father Dominique Pire, who won the Nobel Peace Prize in 1958 for his work with displaced persons, was deeply affected by being a displaced person himself at four and a half years of age. Gandhi ate forbidden meat because he believed that the Hindu practice of vegetarianism might account for India's subservience to England. Jane Addams observed the shabby homes of working people and asked pointed questions. Pearl Buck identified with the Chinese children she knew. Altruism and sympathy are qualities that are often undervalued or unnoticed when displayed by gifted children.

Children Who Were Thought to Be Dull or Who Were Academic Failures

Intellectually capable children who fail to achieve often do so because they limit their interests to a particular academic subject and neglect their other lessons. Or sometimes the originality of their presentations antagonizes the teacher. Students who feel very strongly about their work may be embarrassed when other students laugh or fail to understand their attempts to be creative or their unusual response to stimuli, and so these students may seek safety in withdrawal and non-participation. Some students fail because they are not neat or punctual. Others bore age peers because they want to talk about matters that interest no one but themselves. Children who have odd mannerisms or are unusual in appearance, such as G. K. Chesterton, may also be wrongly classified as dull because they look stupid. Still others are emotionally disturbed—like Adolf Hitler—whose hostile, hyperactive, or withdrawn behavior causes them to be thought dull. A total of twenty-six of the Four Hundred were thought dull.

Future novelist Marcel Proust wrote on and on, and his teachers thought his compositions disorganized. British novelist Hugh Walpole wrote long historical novels when he was a schoolboy, but no one wanted to read them.

A student often fails in a school where form rather than content is stressed, but will do well in another kind of school where the teachers have different standards. French novelist Emile Zola got a "0" in literature at the Lycée St. Louis in France and also failed German and rhetoric. He passed, however, in algebra, mathematics, physics, and chemistry. Sent to another lycée in Marseilles, he failed again. He then proceeded to place second in written examinations at the Sorbonne, although these tests were supposed to be much more difficult.

American writers Stephen Crane, Eugene O'Neill, William Faulkner, and F. Scott Fitzgerald all experienced failure in college because they did not enjoy the content of the courses they took. British poet and novelist D. H. Lawrence stood thirteenth in a class of twenty-one pupils enrolled in composition in the Nottingham High School. The Beaux Arts rejected the French painter Cézanne when he applied for entrance.

Among military men and politicians in the Four Hundred are those who were always slow students and evidenced little interest in cultural matters as adults. Egyptian statesman and Prime Minister Gamal Abdel Nasser spent two years in grade two, failed to pass grade three, and was twelve years old before he finally passed his primary-school examinations. He was finally admitted to a secondary school where the principal, aware of Nasser's role as a student agitator and of his popularity, passed him. When he failed law school, he went into the army.

Special skills in oratory, a dogged persistence, a high tolerance for frustration, and social adaptation are the most frequently observed characteristics of the slow and average students who succeed in making themselves well known. A drive for power and attention can sometimes substitute for ability.

The stubborn boys who fail because they will not scatter their energies seem especially important because it is often they who make the giant steps forward which change life significantly for the total population. These include Edison, the Wright brothers, Henry Ford, and Einstein.

Thomas Edison said of school, "I remember that I was never able to get along at school. I was always at the foot of the class. I used to feel that the teachers did not sympathize with me, and that my father thought I was stupid."[5]

Albert Einstein was considered dull by his teachers and by his parents. His son, Albert, Jr., while a professor of agriculture at the University of California in Berkeley, told Bela Komitzer, who interviewed him while gathering data for his book *American Fathers and Sons*:

> *Actually, I understand my father was a very well-behaved child. He was shy, lonely and withdrawn from the world even then. He was even considered backward by his teachers. He told me that his teachers reported to his father that he was mentally slow, unsociable and adrift forever in his foolish dreams.*

It was for this reason that Albert's father, when Albert was sixteen, urged him to forget his "philosophical nonsense" and apply himself to the "sensible trade" of electrical engineering. A slowness of speech had unfortunately predisposed his parents to think him dull.

Among the students who show strong evidence of ability and still fail, there is usually more than one inhibiting factor. Having a broken home and an unsatisfactory teacher, however, do not necessarily mean that there is no chance of fulfillment for the child.

When pianist Sergei Rachmaninoff made poor grades at the Conservatory of St. Petersburg, he turned his "1's" into "4's" on his report card and thus forestalled his mother's discovery that he was an unsatisfactory student. After one of his teachers dropped in to commiserate with her about her son's failures, his mother withdrew him from school and sent him to Moscow to live in the household of an exceptionally famous teacher, several of whose pupils had become widely known. No one doubted the lazy, hyperactive boy's talents, but his mother could not manage him.

Sergei was not close to his mother, whom he found stern and depressing. He missed his kind and expansive father, who had once sat at the piano for hours improvising and who told the children fantastic tales to entertain them. This same father, Vasily Rachmaninoff, lost the fifth and last estate that his wife purchased for him. When the family was bankrupt, the parents separated, and the mother and six children moved into an uncomfortable, crowded flat. Sergei became distressed by the death of his favorite sister, Yelena, who died at a time when she had been selected to be coached for an operatic role. He neglected practicing, played truant, and wept bitterly when he had to leave home at age eleven for Moscow to live under strict discipline.

Although the musical instruction he received there was superior, the four years he spent in his teacher's turbulent and demanding household changed him from a heedless boy to a youth who had the appearance and mannerisms of an old man. One biography reports that Sergei had a look of perpetual disappointment, his face was lined, and his manners were shy and awkward. After four years, he had a violent quarrel with his teacher, who shouted at him and threw objects at him, presumably because Sergei had asked for a room of his own with a piano in it. The enraged music master called Sergei's Moscow relatives to a conference from which the boy was excluded, and he let them know that he could no longer have the boy as a student-resident. Victor I. Seroff, Rachmaninoff's biographer, quotes Yury Sakhnovsky, a Moscow critic and old friend of the composer, saying it was the teacher's known homosexuality which caused the quarrel and Sergei's leaving the house.

If this was in fact the real reason, Sergei did not advance it to shield himself from the wrath of his relatives. Only one person among them, an aunt, his father's sister, who was personally aware of his teacher's autocratic and unpleasant ways, defended the boy. This aunt welcomed him into her own home and gave him a room of his own with a piano in it. He delighted in the companionship of her four young children and was warmly received by the three servants who accepted him as someone for whom they expected to have lifelong responsibility. It was in this understanding household that he entered into a period of rich, independent composition.

There were several possible causes for Rachmaninoff's failure in school. For Pablo Picasso, however, there was only the excuse of his devotion to a single form of expression. He stubbornly refused to do anything but paint. Since he did learn to read and write and count, he may have learned more in school than he pretended.

When Pablo was ten, his father, Don José Ruiz Blasco, a fun-loving young artist previously subsidized by his family, had to admit his inadequacy in providing for his wife and three children and accept a mediocre post as an art master at the Institutio de Guardia, a school for secondary education in Corunna. Don José, the ninth professional painter in his family, proudly accepted the talent of his son Pablo as a matter of course, as did his patient wife, whose maiden name, Picasso, the artist used professionally because he thought it more distinctive.

Don José's inability to make his talent profitable prompted him to want Pablo to have an education other than the one the boy could receive by simply setting his easel beside his father's and painting all day long, but Pablo resisted school stubbornly and seemed completely unable to learn to read or write. The other students grew used to seeing him come late with his pet pigeon—and with the paintbrush he always carried as if it were a part of his own body. His father used pigeons as models, and Pablo, who was so much his father's boy, needed his own pigeon for companionship and tried to make school an extension of his father's studio. His worst days were those when his father failed to come for him at one o'clock as he had promised because he became so engrossed in his own painting that he forgot to fetch his lonesome son.

The teacher of the little private school, an old friend of the family, did not harass the gentle, affectionate child who was given to getting up and leaving the classroom without permission. Pablo followed the wife of his teacher about like a small puppy and spent much of his time with her in her kitchen quarters. If he had to sit among the other boys, he watched the clock and recited in a singsong to himself, "One o'clock, one o'clock!" If asked to pay attention, he obediently tried so hard that all he could think of was paying attention; the words of the teacher flowed over and about him, and he understood nothing.

Picasso's biographer, Jaime Sabartes, tells how Don José, affectionate but concerned for the boy's future, took him out of school when he was ten (the year Don José, too, took a job against his will) and hired a tutor to prepare the reluctant Pablo for the entrance examinations for secondary school. The tutor gave up in despair when he simply could not teach Pablo arithmetic. During this time, Pablo's talent in art became increasingly obvious, and hopeful relatives helped Don José send his son to Madrid to the Academia de Bellas Artes. There was a flurry of excitement in the family when Pablo not only passed the entrance exams, but also passed them with ease, accomplishing in a day tests devised to last a month. Relatives and friends confidently expected the talented youth to win scholarships and prizes and to bring them honor, if not wealth, from the little shares they had bought in him by donating money for his tuition.

Pablo was completely happy in Madrid but saw no reason to study with teachers who obviously had nothing to teach him. So he wandered about the city, enjoying the street scenes, sketching, painting as he pleased. His relatives were disappointed, but the sympathetic Don José kept sending him as much money as he could. Pablo soon had to come back home to set up his own little studio in the entranceway of an umbrella shop. He gave his first one-man show before he began to shave.

When Albert Einstein was fifteen, his father, Hermann Einstein, who operated a small electrochemical factory in Munich, Germany, failed in business and left for Milan, where he thought that business might be better. Hermann was a jovial, hopeful man, fond of beer and good food, and of the written works of Schiller and Heine. Albert's mother was an amateur musician, and the engineers from the factory often dropped in to hear her play Beethoven.

Hermann's brother, another engineer who lived with them, was an intellectual who was interested in politics.

In this home, which did not lack love for learning and books and music, the boy that they thought was so dull was playing for hours on his own violin. He was reading Kant and other philosophers at eleven or twelve and books such as *Buchner's Force and Matter*. His speech was always hesitant, and learning languages was difficult for him.

The family went to Milan when Einstein was fifteen, and he was left behind in Munich to complete his work at the Gymnasium, but he found school so intolerable that he asked the school doctor to give him a certificate saying he had a nervous breakdown and must spend at least six months with his parents in Italy. It was at the formative age of sixteen, then, that Einstein had a "time-out," a period of freedom from the classroom and scheduled activities. The warmth and beauty of Italy gave him complete satisfaction. He wandered through churches and hiked through the Apennines. It was at this time that he began to ponder what would happen if a ray of light were to be imprisoned—a query important to his later intellectual development.

In his upper-middle-class Jewish family, there could be no tolerance for an idle boy who did not do well in school. Other relatives did better than Hermann Einstein, whose business in Milan was also unsuccessful, and it was they who gave a hundred Swiss francs a month to subsidize Albert—not out of faith, but out of family charity so that he might attend the Polytechnic Institute in Zurich, which took expatriate students. Albert had by now given up his German citizenship. When he failed to pass his entrance exams in zoology, botany, and languages, there was nothing to do but go back to the secondary school and remedy his deficiencies. Einstein enrolled in an ordinary canton school in Arau, Switzerland and after a year was finally admitted to Zurich's Polytechnic Institute.

He once replied to a girl who wrote him a personal letter complaining about her teacher's not appreciating her: "I, too, was once treated so by my professors who did not like my spirit of independence, and although they needed an assistant, refused to appoint me as one."[6]

None of Einstein's schoolmates boasted of his friendship, and his teachers, when approached in later years, did not remember having had him in class. When he graduated, he had difficulty in finding a position. He wanted to be a secondary-school teacher but could not find a post. He answered newspaper advertisements to no avail. He was a temporary assistant in a technical school for a few months; then he took a job tutoring slow students in a boarding school and was discharged because he insisted on teaching in his own way. He took a job in the patent office but kept on studying and publishing. As early as 1907, he presented material that was the main support for his theory of relativity, but it made not the slightest impression on the learned world.

In his autobiographical notes, written at the age of sixty-seven, Einstein said:

> *It is, in fact, nothing short of a miracle that the modern methods of instruction have not yet entirely strangled the holy curiosity of inquiry; for this delicate little plant, aside from stimulation, stands mostly in need of freedom; without this it goes to wreck and ruin without fail. It is a very grave mistake to think that the enjoyment of seeing and searching can be promoted by means of coercion and a sense of duty.*[7]

Einstein disliked any artificial show of knowledge or learning of facts that cluttered up the mind. When asked about the speed of sound, he said that he did not know the answer to that question, but he knew where to find the fact in a reference book if and when he needed it. The important thing was to react delicately and to have a perpetual sense of wonder.

The examination was the part of traditional schooling that he most disliked. Its elimination, he believed, would do away with painful dulling of the memory, and it would no longer be necessary to take years to hammer facts into students' heads which they would be certain to forget in a few months.

Einstein never forgot the strain of preparation for the exam that he had to take before he could enter the school at Zurich. "The constraint was so terrifying that after I passed the final examination I found myself unable to think of a scientific problem for almost a year," his friend and biographer Antonina Vallentin quotes him as saying.

Other students could not, or would not, take exams with ease or competence. Gertrude Stein refused to take her final exam in William James' class. He admired her for her spirit, said he understood—and gave her the highest mark in his class. French writer and Nobel Prize-winner Anatole France, during an oral examination, was tricked into agreeing with a didactic professor who ironically stated that the River Rhone flowed into Lake Michigan. Great operatic composer Puccini consistently failed exams.

Bacteriologist Paul Ehrlich hated exams of any kind, and all his life, he profoundly pitied anybody who had to pass one. His complete ineptness at composition led his teachers to excuse him from this requirement. His speech, copied from that of his father, was hasty, full of interjections and frequent gesticulations. In college, he barely passed his assigned work. Someone once pointed him out to Robert Koch saying, "That is little Ehrlich. He is very good at staining [microscopic slides], but he will never pass his examinations."[8]

The Importance of Time-Out

There are frequent references among the Four Hundred to a "time-out," a period, when the normal activities of life are suspended and the boy or girl has a free period in which to think, to plan, to read unrestrainedly, or to meet an entirely new group of people under novel circumstances. Ten percent of the Four Hundred describe a time-out period that significantly influenced their later development.

Winston Churchill had two such periods. John Kennedy, in late adolescence, contracted jaundice while in school in England which resulted in a free period traveling about Europe with a friend. H. G. Wells had such a period when he broke his leg at the age of eight. The habit of reading he formed then kept him from becoming a draper's assistant. An illness in young manhood also set him writing. Matisse started painting during a convalescence. Einstein formulated important scientific questions during his time-out in Italy.

As a youth of nineteen, British physician Havelock Ellis took a job teaching school in the Australian bush. His duties were light, and he had evenings entirely to himself in a small, isolated hut where he read stacks of books in English, French, German, and Latin. It was to this year that he attributed his later exceptional development.

Charles Evans Hughes graduated from high school twice before he was twelve but could not enter college because of his youth. At Newark High School, he had lost two front teeth when larger boys flung him against the wall while playing a crack-the-whip game. While getting used to his changed appearance, he wandered the streets of New York for six months, benefiting from the enrichment the city offered, enjoying his freedom. He felt better prepared to enter college after this interval. William Randolph Hearst and John La Farge also had profitable time-out periods during which they wandered in New York City. Richard Byrd went around the world alone at thirteen. Norman Angell, at seventeen, went off to America to be a cowboy. Louis Brandeis never forgot the free summer when he tramped about Europe with his father and brother. Marie Curie had a free year in the country at fifteen.

Poet Edna St. Vincent Millay was given a grade of "C" by her eighth-grade English teacher for whom she had consistently done "A" work. The teacher resented Edna's criticism of the book report assignment on *The Last of the Mohicans* and would not accept a report on any of the six other books that Edna had recently read as a substitute. Her mother, an independent woman who had sent her husband away because he gambled, quarreled with the principal over the incident and took her daughter out of school. Edna, who had been a popular straight-A student, was chagrined, unhappy, and lonely at home by herself. Her sisters were properly in school, and her mother was away all day and often at night, working as a nurse. The ensuing period of isolation, during which she prepared herself most adequately for high school and improvised at the piano which one of her mother's patients provided for her, was formative—if unhappy.

A Minority Do Not Complain

Two in five of the Four Hundred either say they did not have school problems or failed to describe any. To a few of them, public education came as a tremendous advantage because the child had no other place in which to read and learn and to meet adults who also read books. George Washington Carver was uncomplaining about the intellectual poverty of the early schools he attended, but at no time was he ever so happy as when he was a graduate student at Iowa State College, where young Henry Wallace was privileged to know and learn from him.

The other students who do not complain about school were those who, recognized by teachers as having unusual abilities, were given special guidance and encouragement and were accelerated. Ernest Rutherford, later a world-renowned physicist, was born on a flax farm near Brightwater, New Zealand. His father, James Rutherford, a wheelwright who had to change his occupation after a severe accident handicapped him, harnessed water power to drive his new flax mill, experimented with different methods of soaking the flax, and developed a special labor-saving device for scraping flax fiber. Ernest's mother, who liked to sing and read, had been a teacher. Although his father made a good living, the seven sons (two of whom drowned while sailing) and five daughters had no reason to expect that their parents could give them much except an education.

In Rutherford's primary school at Havelock, New Zealand, a teacher named Mr. Reynolds, who had more than the usual interest in ability, taught the brighter children for an hour each morning before regular classes began. In the community-sponsored secondary school, Nelson College, science was optional, and Ernest was often the only boy in his class. He had won his scholarship by answering 580 out of 600 test items correctly. The science teacher, Dr. W. S. Littlejohn, and his enthusiastic student were often seen walking and talking together, stopping to draw diagrams in the dust, completely oblivious of passers-by. When Ernest was absorbed in a book, he could be hit on the head and not be disturbed, his classmates found. Ernest was not only a good science student but also won prizes in history, English literature, French, and Latin.

When the news came that he had been awarded a scholarship to the University of New Zealand, he tossed his spade aside with the remark, "That's the last potato I'll ever dig," and left his father's farm. Although the university had less science equipment than many an ordinary high school, he became deeply interested in experiments with magnetization of iron, which led to his later invention of a magnetic detector of radio waves. He spent hours doing ingenious experiments in a miserable, cold, drafty, concrete-floored cellar ordinarily used for a storeroom. He became engaged to his landlady's daughter, Mary Newton, who waited several years before he could support her as his wife. Another scholarship sent him to Cambridge. When he chose his first job, it was a research chair at McGill University in Canada that attracted him, although he could have earned much more in his native New Zealand. The laboratory at McGill, financed by a tobacco millionaire, was one of the best equipped in the world. Thus, school for this well-rounded scholar was not described as an unpleasant experience.

Carlos Romulo was another all-around good student who was not described as a boy who disliked school. He won a medal for oratory in high school, was editor of his high-school yearbook, and a was an apprentice reporter for the *Manila Times* in the Philippines. It was his gift for public speaking that resulted in his being sent to Columbia University, where he majored in English literature.

Tutors Are Well Liked

There is an acute need in the Four Hundred for direct and frequent communication with intelligent adults. When this need is met to a reasonable degree in school, school rebellion is much lessened. The tutor, who is after all a teacher, does not draw upon him- or herself the venom that the classroom teacher often elicits from the Four Hundred. Although the tutor often lacks the proper qualifications for teaching in a well-accredited school, he or she is valued by the pupil with whom he or she can work in a one-to-one relationship.

Benjamin Cardozo was prepared for Columbia by Horatio Alger, a funny, roly-poly little man who had a deep desire to be a great poet. Alger had written a book-length satirical poem in criticism of the government which did not win acclaim. At the same time, his children's books, which he pretty obviously wrote tongue in cheek, made him renowned as the author of books about poor boys who became rich through hard work, frugality, and good character. Horatio Alger had been recommended to the Cardozos by Joseph Seligman, the banker whose children he taught for twelve years. Under Alger's direction, Benjamin Cardozo was able to pass his entrance exams for Columbia when he was thirteen.

Lincoln Steffens, who was acutely unhappy in his military school and was awarded twenty days in solitary confinement for drunkenness, was transferred by his sympathetic father to the care of a tutor, an English expatriate in San Francisco, who introduced the boy to conversation the like of which he had never heard before. The tutor's room was a center for several Oxford men who gathered there to talk endlessly and well of cultural matters. To the boy, it was an exhilarating experience. During his solitary confinement, he had profited by doing vast amounts of reading so that he was prepared for the baptism of ideas that he received from his tutor and his tutor's friends.

There is no parent-tutored boy or girl among the Four Hundred who was not grateful for the experience. Elizabeth Kenny, the Australian nurse who developed her own way of treating infantile paralysis, in her autobiography says of her mother's teaching:

> *The memory of those quiet evenings with my mother has lived with me down through the years, and I have always found it hard to understand why teaching should be thought so irksome to him who imparts the knowledge, as well as to the young mind that balks at receiving it.*[9]

During the day, Elizabeth was left to her own devices. By the age of six, she was practically living on horseback, riding to the village for the mail, helping to round up stock, and racing her cousin Douglas to the home of her grandparents ten miles away. When her younger brother seemed frail, she improvised a gymnasium for him and exercised him until he was as strong and sturdy as the other children. When her father needed assistance marketing his agricultural products, she helped him and the entire community by undertaking to find new markets—and was overwhelmingly successful. But her foray into business brought upon her the condemnation of many of the men and most of the women in the community, who thought that business was not a young girl's concern—not even when it saved the community from bankruptcy. Her mother was Elizabeth's only teacher until the young girl entered nurse's training.

Problems in home tutoring occur when the parent cannot relinquish the role of teacher and constant companion when the child becomes adult. Dmitri Shostakovitch was one of the three musically talented children of a Russian widow, Sonya Shostakovitch. Sonya worked as a typist after the Revolution in the office of Weights and Measures, where her husband had worked before his death. When Dmitri, whose inability in arithmetic made his schoolwork a nightmare to both himself and his teachers, wanted to stay home and study only music, his mother consented. He also read omnivorously, as did his two sisters. Although they were poor, they managed to have two grand pianos in the house. Marusia, two years older than her brother, graduated from high school and planned to continue her music studies at the conservatory. When she and Dmitri made their first appearance at a concert, Marusia wore a dress made of an old bedspread. There was never enough money for all of their needs, and the youngest daughter, Zoya, who had to give up her dancing lessons, became bitter and alienated from her mother because she felt that all of the special advantages went to the two older children.

The scanty meals, hours of practice, and constant pressure took their toll, and Dmitri developed a glandular infection in his throat. When twenty-year-old Marusia and seventeen-year-old Dmitri went away for a rest cure to the Crimea, they both wept bitterly, for they had not been away from their mother before.

The children's maturity, their marriages, and their later engrossment in their own families and careers hurt their mother terribly. She resented her son's marriage to a lovely young wife whom he loved and with whom she could find no fault. On New Year's Eve in 1932, she sat alone and wrote a most unhappy letter to her sister in the United States begging her to come live with her in her son's home and be a companion to her. Dmitri and Nina had gone to see their friends. Marusia and her husband were celebrating at the University. Zoya, still unreconciled and alienated, was far away in Moscow. Their mother hated staying with Zoya and her husband. She felt that she now played the role of a useless servant in Dmitri's apartment. She slept on the couch in the living room and resented their going out, their parties, their automobiles, and the expensive restaurants they frequented.

"We are modest people," she wrote to her sister, "we love work.... How will I live...not waiting for his [Dmitri's] wakening in the morning...not opening the door for him when he comes home. If they move to a new apartment they may not want me.... The nest is destroyed."[10]

Although it was doubtless his mother's decision to let Dmitri stay home from school—together with her early tutoring that made the round-faced, bespectacled, immature boy an early success in his musical career—the cost to both of them was terrific when his mother was not able to let him grow away from her and live the life of a normal adult. Although she tried to destroy his marriage and refused to be pacified even by the birth of her grandchildren, Dmitri fortunately had the strength to resist her influence.

William Cooper Howells and his wife Mary shared a common philosophy throughout their thirty-seven years of marriage and were happy despite periods of tension and misfortune. William was a printer and, in the early days of their marriage, wandered from job to job. Husband and wife took long walks in the country together, talking and enjoying the landscape. William Dean Howells, the second of their eight children, was embarrassingly small for his age, but his big brother Joe, four years older and aggressive, was on hand to protect him. None of the children attended school with any regularity, since they found their father's newspaper office, the family library, and their father's teaching better suited to their learning needs. A total of sixteen or eighteen months, in random periods, was all the formal schooling that the future novelist, William Dean, ever received. He could set type at the age of six, began to write verse at seven or eight, and at eleven could do a man's work in the print shop.

Howells was profoundly influenced by his father. All his life, he believed, like his father, that work and good works saved and that self-concern damned. Other boys found that they could tease him by working on his early-developed sense of justice. Their insensitivity pained him. He found it hard to be apart from his father as he began to grow up.

During one period, when there were seven young children in the family, their father lost his printing business as a result of customers who were alienated by his idealism about slavery. He had previously gone bankrupt when he published an opinionated book on the nature of aristocracy. The family moved into a tiny, dilapidated cabin in a remote area. Here, the father, encouraged by his brothers, was determined to start a Utopia, a community in which he and the settlers he hoped to attract could live apart from the world. The community's economic basis was an existing gristmill, which was to be turned into a paper mill. The venture was not successful, and William's mother, Mary Dean Howells, was unhappy and frightened. She drew apart from her husband with her oldest son, Joe, as her champion. But William was close to his father, with whom he read and walked and talked during the crisp autumn days. This was his time-out period—a waiting time and a thinking time. He was deeply sensitive to the family tension, which, however, did not go deep enough to disturb the love that the family members felt for each other.

His close family ties made it hard for William to leave home; his own creativity seemed to depend upon knowing that his family was happy and secure. When he was asked to go to Xenia, Ohio to work for a week, he was so emotionally upset at being away from home that he begged to return on the same night of his arrival. He went on to Dayton to a similar job and lived there with his favorite uncle Isaac.

The fifteen-year-old boy was so homesick for his parents that he sobbed at the table while he ate. His mother, when he returned home, let him know that she felt satisfaction in his inability to stay away, although she knew she was wrong and the family needed his wages.

When William Cooper Howells's brothers withdrew their financial support for the Utopia that did not materialize, the entire family moved to Columbus, Ohio, where abolitionists were better tolerated. There the father took a job with the *Ohio State Journal* and was eventually made clerk of the Ohio House of Representatives. It was then that William Dean Howells had his creative spurt, began to write, had his first poem published, and found remunerative employment.

In the family of Winston Churchill, about which so much has been written, there are multiple examples of the qualities in parents and other relatives that seem to be related to the production of an eminent man. There was respect for learning, an experimental attitude, failure-proneness, a plentitude of opinionated relatives, a lack of dependence upon the opinions of others, and turbulence in the family life as a result of the erratic behavior of Winston's irrepressible uncle and father.

During the time that Winston was thought dull, he was, like other such boys, showing qualities that presaged his abilities. Rejected by his father and neglected by his mother, he experienced a smothering relationship with his mother-figure Mrs. Everest, and he developed a love for martial poetry, an enthusiasm for battle, and a disregard for personal safety which other such boys evidence. He was hyperactive, prone to constant colds, and had poor peer relationships. He also had the handicap of a speech defect.

On both sides of the family, American and British, there was strong drive, both physical and intellectual. Aurora Murray Jerome, Winston's maternal great-grandmother, who lived with her husband Isaac and nine children in Massachusetts, was a woman of such energy and resourcefulness that there are still legends about her in her native Berkshire Hills. Her son, Leonard Jerome, Winston's American grandfather, was a diplomat, a newspaper man, a financier, and a Wall Street stock-market gambler whose spectacular failure came at the time of the marriage of his daughter, Jennie Jerome, to Lord Randolph Churchill, who would become Winston's father. Aurora Murray Jerome produced more than one energetic, erratic, experimental son. The oldest of her sons, Aaron, while still a theology student at Princeton, made forty thousand dollars on a mulberry tree speculation and used his gains to house needy fellow students. Addison Jerome, another son, was known as a wit and the leader of an international social set. Lawrence Jerome was, with his brother Leonard, one of the founders of the Rochester *Daily American.*

Clarissa Jerome, Winston's American grandmother, was a strong and positive woman with ideas about diet, good hygiene, and fashionable attire. She reintroduced the fichu, a small lace shawl, as an item of flattering neckwear, and she turned her daughter over to Ward McAllister, the self-styled "snob of snobs," to teach her the secrets of fashion, perfect manners, and good eating.

Lord Randolph Churchill, Winston's father, was an idler and a playboy until he became an enthusiastic and tireless politician. He failed his Oxford examinations on the first try and was a problem student at Eton. His brother, the Marquess of Blandford, established a chemical laboratory on the ground floor of Blenheim Palace. Their mother, Winston's paternal grandmother, the Duchess of Marlborough, was an overmasterful, high-handed, but fundamentally kind woman who kept the erratic Churchills together during a period when the failing family fortunes were being mended by marriages to rich American women.

There is failure-proneness among the family members. Lord Randolph, Winston's father, was out of politics by the time he was thirty-seven. His wife, after his death, bankrupted herself by the publication of eleven issues of the *Anglo-Saxon Review,* which did not sell well enough at the price of five dollars per issue to warrant further publication. "Jeanette had lost her last penny on the glorious enterprise. She laughed. It had, indeed, been a wonderful time while it lasted."[11]

This dynamic mother of Winston Churchill had tremendous physical stamina. She was an enthusiastic horsewoman and a tireless traveler. One of her favorite sports was fishing for huge eel in the stagnant waters of a bog near Blenheim Palace. "No one," says Kraus, "understood this strange proclivity. She actually laughed at the eel's ferocious fight to the end.... Dying, and even after skinning, the eel still wriggles in a horrible fashion."

In 1912, shortly before her divorce from George Cornwallis-West, Winston's mother was described in the *Literary Digest* as the organizer of the great spectacle "Shakespeare's Day," which she staged almost single-handedly at Earls Court. She is described as a strong-chinned woman with the manners of a born organizer. Great crowds came to see the tournaments, the plays—presented in a replica of the Globe Theatre—the authentic dances, and the queen of the beauty contest.

During a period of family turbulence, while his parents were not being accepted in British society because of a quarrel with the Prince of Wales, and were deeply involved in controversial political issues as well, Winston was in the nursery or elementary school. He had the undivided, uncritical attention of his nurse, Mrs. Everest, during this time. In his autobiography, he says, "My nurse was my confidante.... At her death she was my dearest and most intimate friend during the twenty years I had lived...innocent and loving...of simple faith."[12]

It was this nurse who taught him to read and count and do simple arithmetic and who introduced him to his hobby of playing with toy soldiers. She was quite helpless in controlling his hyperactivity, and she worried over his constant colds and his double pneumonia. He won his way with her sometimes by threatening to worship idols, which frightened the woman, for she feared for the soul of the obstreperous boy to whom she was so devoted. He once displayed great moral courage by inviting this fat, commonplace nurse to Harrow to visit him and by kissing her unashamedly before the other boys.

As we have seen, his mother was a star whom he worshipped—but at a distance—and his father, with whom he had only three or four long conversations, was hostile and indifferent. Any approach by the son to the father was met with icy withdrawal.

Winston's first school was chosen by his mother for its good reputation and social prestige, but Winston resisted the sadistic headmaster's behavior, stoutly kicked the man's hat to pieces, and was withdrawn by his mother and sent to a school in Brighton that was run by two kindly old ladies. In this benign atmosphere, Winston was called the naughtiest small boy in England by his dancing teacher. He was frequently permitted to leave the classroom and run about in the schoolyard to release his exuberant energies. He did not want to study Latin or Greek or mathematics, and he was not coerced.

Eton, his father's school, was in a swamp; Harrow was on a hill. The latter was selected because the family thought Winston might be healthier there. Since his father was at that time Chancellor of the Exchequer, Winston's malingering and other obvious deficiencies as a student were ignored. But once he was admitted, the school felt no obligation to give him any honors he did not win. He remained in the lowest group in his class all during his days in Harrow, a period he described in manhood as a wasted time and a miserable interlude.

While still a young man, Churchill discussed with Frank Harris his poor relationship with his father. Harris asked him if he had liked Lord Randolph, and Churchill replied, "How could I?... I was ready enough to as a boy, but he wouldn't let me. He treated me as if I was a fool; barked at me whenever I questioned him. I owe everything to my mother, to my father nothing."[13]

Winston had some bitter memories of Harrow. He tried to talk of politics on his first day at school, but the teacher was not responsive. His only prizes were for fencing and for reciting martial poetry. He refused to study mathematics, Greek, or Latin and was placed in the lowest group in his class—in what would today be termed the remedial reading class, where slow boys were taught English. His English, however, was not poor; his knowledge of Shakespeare was unusual and self-motivated. He had no intimate friends and was "cheeky" at school at the time that his father, who was much in the press, was being verbally abusive and controversial in Parliament. The boy who did not know his rejecting father well nonetheless kept a scrapbook of the man's exploits as they were described in the press and was unfriendly to boys whose fathers disagreed with Lord Randolph on political issues. In a very determined way, he was imitating his father while at public school, but this devotion went unrewarded.

Lord Randolph, ashamed of his son's seeming dullness, was sure that Winston would never be able to earn a living in England and contemplated sending him to one of the colonies, possibly to Africa, when he was a young adult. Winston was taken from Harrow and put in the care of a tutor who was well known for his success at getting boys into Sandhurst. The exasperated tutor concluded that Winston had not gone through Harrow, but over it or under it.

It was during this period that Lord Randolph, perturbed by his increasing illness and lack of funds, sold twenty letters (in advance of writing) to a sensational newspaper, the *Daily Graphic*, and went off to Africa to hunt and send news of his exploits to the paper. The two thousand pounds he earned he invested well in African mines. He lived outdoors, went unshaven, enjoyed his exploits, and came back in better health. In the meantime, his wife had fled to the Continent to escape the ribbing that other papers were giving her husband, and Winston failed his examinations for Sandhurst a second time.

Lord Randolph came home less tense, and his wife thought they might enjoy an interlude of quiet, close family life during the Christmas holidays. Lady Wimbourne, Jennie's sister, loaned them the use of a house in Bournemouth, but Randolph went away to attend one of the famous parties of the wild Lord Fitzgibbon of Ireland.

During these years, Winston lacked close friends of his own age, but he enjoyed playing with his younger brother and his younger cousins. His mother's sisters had reason to fear for the physical welfare of their children when Winston was about; and his cousins found him fascinatingly dangerous. He organized them into battle with the village children during holidays, built forts, and initiated intricate strategies. Each morning, the servants held an agitated counsel to determine what to do with Winston that day. His own nurse was helpless to check him. However, it was not the younger children but Winston himself who was injured in an accident that ended his childhood. He was eighteen, his brother was twelve, and his cousin was fourteen years old when a game of fox and hare brought Winston to a bridge with the other boys in hot pursuit. Behind him was certain capture; below was the top of a welcoming fir tree. He leaped for the tree, missed, and fell thirty feet to hard ground. He did not regain consciousness for three days and was bedridden for three months.

During his convalescence from an operation on a kidney that was ruptured in the fall, Winston found himself intellectually. He spent much time in London and at Parliament, where various relatives were politically influential. He met Balfour, Chamberlain, Rosebery, Asquith, and other men of consequence who would become important to him in the future. He listened to sessions of Parliament. He was also able to do the work that finally enabled him to pass the Sandhurst examinations, although barely, on the third try.

While enumerating their complaints about the classroom, Churchill and the others among the Four Hundred also indicated classroom preferences and appreciations. They best liked teachers who let them go ahead at their own pace and who gave them permission to work unimpeded in the area of their special interest. They remember affectionately all adults and classmates who challenged their thinking, introduced them to exciting books, or supplied them with materials for work. They especially liked the time-out periods, which gave them time for self-evaluation. They sought out places where ideas were being bandied about, such as the debate club, the school newspaper, and the discussion groups. They liked to be needed and to be used and to have early responsibility. They responded warmly to people who took time to listen to them and to those who had faith in them. Intelligent appreciation of their special interests was most highly valued. These preferences ought to have something to say to current educators of bright and promising children.

Any attempt to equate their degree of education with eminence only serves to indicate that the public demands certification for professional workers. It is the lawyers, teachers, doctors, and engineers who have the most formal training. The writers, artists, actors, and inventors have the least academic training and also are those prone to dislike the classroom most intensely. Politicians run the gamut in amount of schooling.

But who can say that the informally educated Wright brothers, Edison, Marconi, Noel Coward, Pablo Picasso, Pablo Casals, and Sam Clemens gave less or more to society than the more formally schooled Schweitzer, Einstein, Gandhi, Freud, Fessenden, Fermi, Cushing, and Brandeis? Discovering what is happening to children who are the contemporary counterparts of those who were informally educated—in these days of compulsory education—is more to the point.

In the past, it has been the family itself which has supplied the motivation for formal training in specialized services, and often, it has also been the family who has given much-needed encouragement to those young people who do more individual and self-initiated tasks or who seek their training in the theater, pressroom, political or labor organization, or studio. Three hundred fifty-eight of the Four Hundred came from business or professional homes, and nearly all of these homes had a love for learning and achievement. Horace Mann Bond, dean of the school of education at Atlanta University, says:

> *If we could give to every child in the land the same opportunities for intellectual stimulation now enjoyed by the children of the professional, technical and kindred workers, we would increase our "talent pool" five fold.*[14]

His conclusion is supported by extensive studies which have indicated that it is still largely the sons and daughters of professional workers or business executives who are encouraged by their parents to train for white-collar occupations.

There is, however, an increasing awareness that something has gone wrong in the homes that were once the source of high achievers and the highly creative. Students coming from such homes are too frequently uninterested and unimaginative. These children from professional or learning-centered homes can pass tests, do competent papers, make the grades of "C" or "B" required of them, and yet remain totally uninvolved in the learning process during or outside of class hours. The college diploma is valued for the social and economic benefits that it brings. The young graduates plan to make a good living, enjoy leisure hours, and be financially secure in their old age.

This attitude is prevalent among students who come from schools which are expensively staffed and where the competition to gain admittance to top colleges is high. The parents have long since been discouraged by these schools from participating in the learning process as it involves the child. They are told that it is the duty of the teacher to teach; the duty of the parent is to provide financial and emotional security.

Intellectually able children are not often taught by their parents to read now as they were in many homes among the Four Hundred, for parents who do so nowadays are subject to sharp criticism and are accused of trying to "push" their child in order to bolster their own presumably weak egos. The school does not want children in the first grade who can already read, because such children do not fit into the organized activities. At all levels of learning throughout the early years, this lock step is maintained.

Peer pressures are used to make children feel that deviating from this pattern makes them socially undesirable. In what anthropologists tell us is the most peer-oriented culture in the world, children become almost afraid to think until they learn what their classmates are thinking. Creative thinking is at its peak in about the second grade. Children are still eager to learn, excited by the wonders of the world, perceptive to a degree that they may never attain again. The high school is a particularly barren period for any expression of intellectual vigor or originality. Often, it is not until they are in college, and sometimes not even then, that students regain the drive for self-initiated learning, originality and intuitiveness, the seeking of truth and beauty. Highly achieving adults—Einstein is a good example—often have a great joy in their work and retain a childish pleasure in learning which may make them seem naive to the public.

Famed and intellectually sophisticated adults can withstand the pressures against them for conformity; third-grade children cannot. E. Paul Torrance of the Bureau of Educational Research at the

University of Minnesota says, "Unusual or original ideas are common targets of peer pressures to conformity."

The phenomenon of indifference in students who come to college well prepared and with good scores on tests has led to various experiments and to deliberation about the lack of a love for learning in the students. Harvard University has been offering a dozen scholarships a year to students with culturally and socially disadvantaged backgrounds. Most of these students were valedictorians of high schools that do not ordinarily send students to prestigious colleges. Students accepted in this program come to Harvard because some high-school teacher recognized in them an insatiable desire for knowledge. In their high school, they were self-motivated and set the pace for other students. These are sometimes students from "risky" backgrounds, and their performance has been about what might be expected. Some are doing well; some are failing. But both Harvard and the foundation that supplies the scholarship funds are pleased with the results. Some students who had the most glaring deficiencies in their backgrounds have been sent to preparatory schools, such as Andover, for remedial work.

The Harvard program is one of several on various levels which recognizes the compelling need to make good use of all students, anywhere and everywhere, who have marked ability. The school rebellions of so many of the Four Hundred highlight the need to do something more for eager and inquiring students than the sheer physical expansion of school buildings, in which children of the same chronological age but with widely varying abilities and interests are required to perform essentially identical tasks.

Chapter 11
"Out of the Cradle Endlessly Rocking"

What is needed is... a readiness for boldness or even extravagance—a capacity for informed and serious guessing as to the potentialities utterly different from those that a different epoch can directly suggest. We can often be wrong. In all such efforts, to be wrong fifty times is far more forgivable than to be timid once.

—Gardner Murphy, Human Potentialities

There is a danger in trying too hard to be conclusive and of being drawn into tidying data to give easy answers to difficult problems. Such efforts too often lead to putting the right saddle on the wrong horse.

An uncritical adoption of new ideas has already caused many abrupt reversals in methods of child rearing. Parents raised on strict schedules are convinced of a need for demand-feeding for their own infants. Fathers and mothers reared permissively are attracted to the idea that setting limits makes for emotional security in their own children.

There are no easy answers as to how to rear capable, creative children who will happily make effective use of their talents and skills. However, an overall view of the experiences of the Four Hundred may stimulate us to some informed and serious guessing as to the best way to initiate a new level of creativeness and a new flowering of excellence.

Summarizing the Findings

Most of the eminent are not born in the great metropolitan centers but drift in to the larger centers from farms, villages, and smaller cities. Stage celebrities more often come from the cities than do persons of other occupations.

In almost all of the homes, there was a love for learning in one or both parents, often accompanied by a physical exuberance and a persistent drive toward goals. Fewer than 10 percent of the parents failed to show a strong love for learning.

Three-fourths of the children were troubled—by poverty; by a broken home; by rejecting, overpossessive, estranged, or dominating parents; by financial ups and downs; by physical handicaps; or by parental dissatisfaction over the children's school failures or vocational choices.

One-half of the parents were opinionated about a controversial subject, which set them apart in their own time but is accepted with little or no animosity today. Opinionated parents reared nearly all of the statesmen, the humanitarians, and the reformers.

None of the twenty poets among the Four Hundred is the son or daughter of a poet.

Seventy-four of eighty-five writers of fiction or drama and sixteen of twenty poets came from homes where, as children, they saw tense psychological dramas played out by their parents.

Twenty-one of thirty-two physicians, lawyers, and scientists came from family backgrounds which gave them opportunities for outdoor explorations, considerable personal freedom, and early responsibility. They were often physically active, made collections, and were mischievous.

Nearly half of the fathers were subject to traumatic hardships in their business or professional careers.

One-fourth of the mothers were described as dominating, but only one-twentieth of the fathers earned this description.

Wealth is much more frequent than is abject poverty. One family had public assistance; one subject was reared in a workhouse;

two were in orphanages. Five others experienced extreme deprivation. There were twenty-one families that lived on inherited income or were known to be very wealthy. Three hundred and fifty-eight families (some wealthy) could be classified as representing the business or professional classes.

Handicaps such as blindness; deafness; being crippled, sickly, homely, undersized, or overweight; or having a speech defect occurred in the childhoods of over one-fourth of the sample. In many of these individuals, the need to compensate for such handicaps was seen by them as a determining factor in their drive for achievement.

Among explorers and adventurers, there was almost always a history of accident-proneness.

Dictators, military men, and poets had the highest percentage of dominating or overpossessive (smothering) mothers. An over-possessive parent of a peer-rejected child (especially a mother who disliked her husband) was the most likely to rear a dictator or a military hero who enjoyed the carnage of battle.

The loss by death of a brother or sister was described as extremely traumatic by fifty-seven persons.

Stepmothers, of whom there were fourteen, played a helpful role to eleven stepsons or stepdaughters, and were not appreciated by three stepsons.

Among the children of twenty-three alcoholic fathers, there were fourteen who became humorous writers, actors or actresses, or singers.

The homes of the Four Hundred were exceptionally free of mental illnesses requiring hospitalization.

The children enjoyed being tutored, whether by professional tutors or by their parents.

The secondary school was the most frequently disliked, and the prestigious college was the best accepted.

Three-fifths of the Four Hundred expressed dissatisfaction with schools and schoolteachers, although four-fifths showed exceptional talent.

Comparison with Other Studies

While sifting raw data from our notes and making observations derived from scanning or reading in their entirety some five thousand volumes, we have been uneasily aware that we may inadvertently have reflected some personal bias. We are reassured, however, by studies made by psychological and social scientists that tend to corroborate the observations that we have made on the Four Hundred and which raise similar questions.

The troubled home has been the subject of inquiry by others, some of whom share our anxieties as to the interpretation of findings concerning this relationship between troubled homes and creativity. In the July 1961 *Quarterly*, published by the Carnegie Corporation, which has given financial support to various studies of creativity, the editor says:

> *It must be reported that creative people claim more than others do that their childhoods were not entirely happy. (They may be telling the objective truth, or it may be that this is simply another sign of their often-noted ability to see accurately and accept what others may repress.) At any rate, the finding should not be interpreted by parents as meaning that they should make their children miserable in the hope of making them creative.*

This article advocates less emphasis on "togetherness" and on producing "well-rounded children," and it encourages the provision of maximum opportunities for the able student to work out his or her own interests under the supervision of creative teachers.

Dislike of school, the troubled home, the dominating mother, and the ability to risk failure are all found again in a study of highly successful architects done at the University of California Institute of Personality Assessment and Research, the director of which, Dr. Donald W. MacKinnon, says:

> *...not all of them [the highly successful architects] had the kind of happy homes...generally thought to be conducive to sound psychological development.*[1]

Almost without exception, one or both of the parents of these architects showed considerable skill in drawing or painting. Often, it was the mother who, in the architect's early years, fostered his artistic potentialities by her own example and by teaching him herself. There were a few among these architects who had experienced the most brutal treatment from sadistic fathers with no impairment of their architectural ability; however, they were less successful businessmen than the architects who had more kindly fathers.

The outstanding architects tended to be superior in intellect, but not necessarily "highly gifted." In a test of concept mastery, they were slightly superior to undergraduate students but slightly below research scientists also studied at the Institute. In college, they did as little work as possible in courses that did not interest them, and made "A's" in courses that pleased them. One of the most creative of them was once advised by the dean of his college to quit because he had no talent. Another failed his design dissertation when he attacked the stylism of the faculty, and he was obliged to take his degree in art. Similar circumstances were observed among research scientists who made good grades in high school (and were unhappy both at home and at school), but who dropped to the minimum passing level when they were in college and their self-initiated interests began deflecting their attention.

The quality most often noted by MacKinnon among the architects was perceptiveness. He says in the same study:

> *[They] were characterized by an unusual openness to experience, a wide perceptiveness of what exists within as well as what goes on outside. They had the capacity to admit complexity and disorder into their perceptions without being made anxious by the chaos, and the ability to form a new order out of the richness thus permitted.*
>
> *They were found to have persistent intensity, relative independence and a high level of energy effectively channeled; and were able to risk failure and override periods of depression, from which they were found not to be immune. They were not "easy to take" in the classroom.*

Gender Identification

Biographers, sometimes openly, sometimes hesitantly, indicate that certain gifted men are regarded as being somewhat effeminate and certain gifted women overly masculine. Among the parents, the dominating mother is the woman with the long, firm stride and independent ways, and the father is often the dreamer.

E. Paul Torrance, director of the Bureau of Educational Research of the University of Minnesota and a perceptive observer of the creative, finds that creative girls often seem masculine and creative boys often seem effeminate. He believes that this merely reflects the nature of creativity itself, which demands both sensitivity and independence in the same person. Indifferent observers do not notice that the effeminate boys are also independent and that the independent girls are also sensitive. Their contemporaries and the biographers of the Four Hundred may have been equally unobservant on this score.

MacKinnon strengthens this observation by citing the fact that the architects he studied were masculine in appearance and in overt behavior, and he reported no problems with sex identification in interviews, yet these young men were made to appear effeminate by tests which equate a breadth of interests, a sensitive intellect, self-awareness, and openness to one's own inner feelings as being effeminate. It would seem advisable to try to change the cultural stereotypes of "male" and "female" traits. The result might well be a flowering of excellence in a climate where both independence and sensitivity are valued in any one human being.

An unusual degree of intelligence is in itself a social handicap in a society geared to conformity. Terman and Oden found that, although most of their subjects married, the spinsters and bachelors were those who scored highest on the Concept Mastery Test—the best "brains" in the group.

Creative Children as School Problems

Highly creative elementary-school children observed by Torrance[2] are younger editions of some of the more teacher-harassing of the Four Hundred. They seem to be playing around when they should be working at assigned tasks. They engage in manipulative and/or exploratory activities, many of which are discouraged or even forbidden. They enjoy learning, and this looks to the teacher like play rather than work. They are intuitive and imaginative; enjoy fantasy; see unusual uses in ordinary objects; are flexible, inventive, original, perceptive, and sensitive to problems. They respond readily to such questions as "What could be done to make this toy more fun to play with?" They have vital energy.

Torrance found that 70 percent of the children who rated high in creativity would not be selected to be members of a special class for intellectually gifted children. Some children who are intellectually gifted are highly creative as well. Other children of average or superior intelligence are also highly creative. Still other children with extremely high intelligence quotients are not at all creative.

Teachers, Torrance discovered, are partial to the child of high intelligence and low creativity. This child is not a rebel and does school assignments with dispatch and perfection. The creative child is often thought to have wild or silly ideas or to be naughty. He or she is not regarded as being serious or dependable or even promising—although this child is likely to do as well on a standardized achievement test as does the highly intelligent child who is not creative. This annoys the teacher, who deduces from this that the child could "do classroom work better if he would only try." This kind of child makes discipline hard for the teacher, as for instance when he or she gives a unique answer to a prosaic question and starts the class laughing.

In a number of studies of highly creative children, Torrance says, "It is evident that many of them bring upon themselves many of their woes. Obviously, one task of education is to aid such children to become less obnoxious without sacrificing their creativity."

Throughout the generations, such children have been distracting influences in the classroom. Harold L. Lakes graduated from the eighth grade one year late because a peppery teacher set him back a year for laughing uproariously in class at the wrong time. Claude Monet was turbulent and irreverent in school, especially in drawing class, and played truant at will; yet he did his schoolwork as well as the other children when he chose to. He set his classmates laughing with his caricatures, for which their parents soon insisted on paying him very well. While still a schoolboy, he was earning a substantial income as a caricaturist. However, neither his parents nor his teacher could manage him.

The mothers of highly creative children are different from mothers of the highly intelligent children who are not creative, according to Jacob W. Getzels and Philip W. Jackson of the University of Chicago.[3] It is the mothers of the highly creative children who most nearly resemble the mothers of the Four Hundred. The "high creativity" mothers want their children to have friends who are interested in ideas, who are not easily bored, who have an openness and a fine sense of values. They are relatively indifferent to monetary values and are themselves liberal in their political views.

The mothers of adolescents who are intellectually gifted but lack creative ability are much more concerned with financial problems, although their husbands are better educated and better employed than are the husbands of the less materialistic mothers of the highly creative students. The high-IQ mothers are more bent on having companions for their children who are clean-mouthed, well-behaved, and from good families. These mothers are conservative when compared to the mothers of highly creative children.

From the total group of the highly intelligent and the highly creative children, Getzels and Jackson isolated two sub-groups: one composed of highly intelligent children without marked creative ability whose median IQ is about 150, and another consisting of highly creative children whose median IQ—about 127—places them in the category of superior but not highly gifted children. Of the two extreme groups, one not intellectually gifted, and the other not creatively gifted, Getzels and Jackson say:

> *The essence of the performance of our creative adolescents lay in their ability to produce new forms, to risk conjoining elements that are customarily thought of as independent and dissimilar, to go off in new directions.... The high-I.Q.*

> *adolescent seemed to possess to a high degree the ability and the need to focus on the usual, to be channeled and controlled in the direction of the right answer.*

The high-IQ students were likely to choose the conventional occupations: doctor, lawyer, or engineer. More than half of the "high creatives" planned unconventional careers: adventurer, writer, inventor.

We have seen that both the Chicago and the Minnesota researchers found that the teacher is likely to prefer the child who has a high intelligence and low creative ability. Such children are regarded as being serious, ambitious, and promising.

The life histories of the largely teacher-nominated Terman group of gifted children gives further support to the contention that teachers prefer the highly intelligent child who is not particularly creative. The teachers were asked for the names of the three brightest children and that of the youngest child in their room. The teachers were also asked for the name of the brightest child they had taught the year before. As Terman expected, it was the youngest child who most often proved to be the most intellectually superior. Since the 1920s, when these children were selected for the Terman study, the lock step curriculum in education has made acceleration less popular, and selecting the youngest child is not now likely to uncover the brightest child in the room. The teacher's ability to choose the child in his or her class who subsequently scored highest on the Stanford-Binet intelligence test was poorer than if one simply guessed by chance.

If a potential Edison or Einstein or Picasso or Churchill or Clemens had been in school in California in those days, that child would surely not have been chosen to be screened for inclusion in the Stanford study of genius.

Teachers, then as now, value conformity and clerical skills. Careful and definitive studies on these gifted individuals, which have continued at intervals during their adult lives, show that the largest single group (9.53%) of the men in the Terman study who were still residing in California in 1940 were lawyers. The second largest group (8.97%) was classified as "higher clerical workers"—junior accountants, statistical clerks, bookkeepers, and the like. However, as a total group, they did well from the standpoint of "professional and business accomplishment as measured by responsibility, and importance, prestige and income." Four percent are in Who's Who.

The childhood backgrounds of these competent and conforming men and women included in the Stanford study resemble that of the children of high IQ and low creativity studied by Getzels and Jackson. Only a few came from "inferior or very inferior families." Most of the fathers were professional or business men, and there were books in the homes. In marked contrast to the Four Hundred, only one child in one hundred showed a sharp dislike for the classroom, and only 7 percent showed even a mild dislike. The childhood traits of conformity and competence continue into adult life.

Politically, those in the Terman study are near center; more than half are Republican. They are good community members, Scout leaders, school trustees, leaders in religious groups; and they belong to sports clubs and community organizations. They volunteer for responsibilities in civic, political, and professional organizations.

The Terman group has a mental hospitalization rate approaching that of the general population. Their suicide rate is at the norm for men and slightly above the norm for women. Two women killed themselves shortly before they were to obtain their Ph.D.'s. Most of the mentally ill were not schizophrenic but were alcoholic or manic-depressive (bipolar).

Although they were, as a total group, extremely successful and valuable citizens, there is little evidence of the quality that advances rather than enhances the status quo. Terman and Oden say of them:

> *There are, however, a few fields, all dependent on special talent in which there has been a lack of outstanding accomplishment. These are the fine arts, music, and to a lesser extent, literature. The group has produced no great musical composer and no great creative artist.*[4]

Today's Counterparts of the Four Hundred

The following excerpts from life histories of children in elementary school are given to emphasize the continuity of problems peculiar to the creative child. Although these are children from comfortable suburbs in the United States, there is no reason, from the professional literature, to assume that they are isolated cases or that they do not have thousands of counterparts in other nations.

The eleven-year-old boy whom we shall call "Boy A" has a Stanford-Binet IQ of 151. In examination, he shows even performance in all areas, except that he is not as good in routine clerical work. His highest achievements are in vocabulary and mathematics. His appearance is attractive; he has no unusual mannerisms, shows no signs of immaturity or emotional disturbance, is friendly and cooperative, and has an assured manner and a droll sense of humor. His mother is employed in research, is a member of Phi Beta Kappa, holds a graduate degree, and attended a prestigious college. His father, although an engineer, has a hobby of learning languages—can read a newspaper in twenty languages and can speak several of them well enough to communicate. The home is learning-centered, opinionated, non-rejecting. There are other children, also capable. Boy A is descended from an important figure in American history, a man of daring and imagination.

The parents play conventional roles in suburbia. The home is well kept and attractive; the parents make themselves useful in the church and in Boy Scouts, and they are warm and friendly neighbors. They read with their children, take them on trips, and supply them with educational toys. They subscribe to children's book clubs.

An early interest in electricity has absorbed the attention of Boy A. The family basement is a tangle of old TV sets, radios, lamps, irons, and the like which he assembles and reassembles. At eight, he was able to search for needed information in the encyclopedia rapidly and efficiency. Now, at eleven, he has drawn—for fun—a diagram of the workings of a transistor radio with delicately shaded drawings and written commentary. He sings in the church choir and has composed a *Boy's Hymn* that is pleasing and melodious. His interest in music may eclipse his enthusiasm for electricity and science. His wide reading is mostly in the areas of biography, science, and music. He has a record collection.

His talent in organization was demonstrated when he secured his friends' cooperation in his "Inventor's Fair," which was actually a rummage sale to raise money to pay for things he needs for his inventions. He seeks children who share his interests among both boys and girls. He is independent and seems happy outside of school, but he has the quality which made Schweitzer's life complicated at school—a sensitivity and deep empathy that make him the champion of right and justice. When other children engage in their habitual pastime of bullying a child in the neighborhood who is handicapped, he flies to the rescue with shouts and imprecations and flailing fists. (Schweitzer also was prone to sudden rages when his feelings were touched.) Boy A is habitually concerned with anyone in trouble—a child, an old person, an animal. This may be an extension of his mother's warmth, for she is the person on her block who is most responsive to the needs of others.

His teacher in kindergarten found him unlike other children and "held him back" on the basis of "emotional immaturity." He was no doubt more interested in the electrical outlets than in making paper chains. Over the years, his resistance to school has not lessened. Although his achievement and high IQ are known, the school feels that he must be made to conform, and that he must go through the curriculum as it is planned. In a primary school class, he once tore an arithmetic workbook to shreds and was sent home with a new one and a warning that if he did not fill in all the blanks properly, he could not be promoted to the next grade. Motivated by a desire to please a friend of the family who convinced him that the teacher really had no choice but to try to make him conform, he finished the semester's work in three or four after-school sessions, pausing frequently for conversation, consolation—and cookies. The assigned task obviously had no relevance to his learning needs.

The school principal, when interviewed at that time, thought it wise to try to take Boy A's interest away from electricity and focus it on baseball in order to make him more like other children. There was no thought of putting him ahead instead of retaining him academically. The school has demanded that the routine set-up for all children be followed—otherwise, the authority of the school is challenged. This school has a class for academically talented children, but apparently no one has thought of putting Boy A into this group.

The resiliency of creative, intelligent Boy A has kept him emotionally stable despite his reputation for eccentricity and instability at school. He is teased and derided in the school atmosphere, but not among children who do not know him from there. Those teachers who are aware of his real needs are not able to make things right for him in a situation that is basically wrong. He has maintained an achievement score commensurate with his ability, but his grades in school are low—they will not be good enough for college entrance unless they improve.

In Boy A, and also as we will see in Boy B, who is described below, there are qualities which appear frequently among the Four Hundred that are ordinarily judged as harbingers of excellence. These boys are sensitive to the feelings and emotions of others and also seem more responsive to touch, sight, sound, and smell than most other children.

In several of the Four Hundred, we found an exceptionally keen response to sensory stimuli which set them apart from others. First memories, for example, are of jewels, landscapes, or the varicolored stripes on a nurse's dress. Albert Schweitzer nearly fainted when he first heard brass instruments played in harmony. Jean Sibelius, fearing ridicule, tried to conceal from his classmates the mysterious connection that sound and color had for him. His acute perceptiveness always made him appear as if he were someone dropped from a distant planet. Salvador Dalí painstakingly described himself as a person reacting to sensations rather than ideas or words. Frank Lloyd Wright was grateful for the colored papers and cubes of wood his mother gave him as first playthings. Shouts and blows and rejections that other children can take in their stride are often devastating and traumatic to such sensitive children. These children are also often acutely aware of the unhappiness and the miseries of other children and of adults, and they evidence an empathy that is never experienced in such depth by some adults.

Boy B is another creative child whose scores place him among the gifted group in intelligence. His parents also are bookish, have a love for learning, and are opinionated. This boy is also self-assured, attractive, and perpetually engaged in his own ingenious inventions and self-initiated studies. The following life history, written by his mother, is reprinted with her permission:

> *The year is 1954. Our son Jimmie was born on an eventful day. Even at that time, the nurses told me he didn't act like a newborn baby. They thought because he wasn't hungry immediately that he was in some way different. Of course, he changed when we took him home from the hospital; he demanded formula every two hours around the clock. He continued this pattern of eating and growing rapidly all throughout infancy. Other than this, I had no indication that he was different. Since he was a non-aggressive, shy, dreamy-eyed baby, I thought he was average in intelligence. What was even more confusing was the fact that he did not even say words when the books said he was supposed to. When he finally did, at the age of two and one half, he spoke in sentences, both clearly and accurately. He taught himself to walk one week before his first birthday, and then he walked like a two-year-old child. This pattern stayed with him in everything he undertook later on. Whenever Jimmie decided to do anything, he never gave up until the task was completed to his satisfaction....*
>
> *When we bought Jimmie his first Christmas toys, we were confused when we found out he showed no interest in playing with them. They were made specifically for his age, which was one year at the time. He had even tried them out*

briefly in the store and seemed to like them. Little did we know that toys were never going to interest Jimmie very much, and once he played with a game and mastered it, he was through with it. At fourteen months, he pointed to the little pictures on the back of a hard cover story book and asked me (in pantomime) the name of each picture.

He "drilled" me for a few weeks, and then when I asked him to point to the fireman, taxi, bear, etc., he could do it perfectly. He was fifteen months old. When I realized how advanced he was, I was both joyous and panic-stricken. Even at that time, I could foresee the eventual problems he would have with children and school. I had heard of all the dangers of pushing and I was actually afraid to answer his questions, knowing this would certainly put him that much more ahead of his age group. But I soon realized that with a truly gifted child, he is the one who does all the pushing of those around him in his search for answers. It was interesting for me to observe how differently the gifted child learns. All Jimmie needed was somebody to answer his questions; learning was always his choice as to subject and method. For instance, when he was two, I took him to the children's section of our town library. In one corner, there was a huge globe of the world. He ran over to it, and instead of just spinning the globe in typical two-year-old fashion, he asked what the names of several of the countries were. We then bought him a map of the world, and for some time he would repeat his original pattern of learning, by asking the names of countries and islands, until he had mastered it himself.

The first time Jimmie got excited about any toys was when my husband brought home some advanced wooden puzzles. He was two at the time, and when he saw the puzzles and started to do them, we noticed how quickly he moved and how stimulated he appeared. Needless to say, puzzles were the order of the day from that time on.

Around the age of two and one half, I began to worry about playmates for him. Being an only child, his first experience with another child was almost disastrous. This child was aggressive to the point that Jimmie never knew when he was going to get socked in the head or pushed. Jimmie was peace-loving and not aggressive and could not understand why the other child even wanted to strike him. Here again, as new parents, we were determined to follow the trend and see to it that Jimmie learned "how to get along with all kinds of children"; so we let him associate with this other child frequently, hoping Jimmie would adjust. The reverse happened, and Jimmie withdrew into his little shell so that when any strange child approached him, he would cringe. We were terribly worried. After all, we were trying to do the right thing, weren't we? Hadn't we written to a psychiatrist who had done extensive work with gifted children and explained our dilemma with Jimmie? We had told her of Jimmie's preoccupation with maps, puzzles, encyclopedias, etc., at the age of two and one half. She in turn was very concerned about his social and emotional adjustment and felt Jimmie didn't really need all this enrichment, that perhaps it was confusing to him. We also realized that the average two-year-old could be expected to at least play side by side with other two-year-olds, and that they did resort to hitting, biting, scratching, etc. But Jimmie wasn't average, and how was he ever going to have any pleasant play experiences with other children? I thought surely there must be other bright preschool children in our area; so out of desperation, I called our local newspaper and inserted some publicity to the effect that I was anxious to meet mothers who had children with similar problems. I was able to find five children who appeared to be bright. They met once a week at our home for a preschool workshop session. After consultations with the mothers, we agreed on a program which I originated. It included simple science experiments, games and puzzles, story telling and outdoor activities. It was here that Jimmie found himself and other children, who because of their brightness were also more mature socially and better able to participate in group play.

Jimmie was very happy those days, and we noticed he was beginning to show rather an intense interest in the world around him. At two years and nine months, he asked the names of letters, and by three, was picking out small words. When he was three, he started on a range of interests far beyond his years. I can remember how he used to cry for flower and vegetable seeds every time he saw them in a store. When we finally gave in and bought them for him, he would proceed to plant them on his "farm." By summer, we were eating Jimmie's corn, string beans, water melons, tomatoes, radishes, and potatoes. He wasn't nearly so excited about planting these seeds as he was about watching the plants grow. It is interesting to note that neither my husband nor I have green thumbs and never exhibited any interest in growing things before Jimmie did. In fact, our lawn probably had the most crabgrass in the neighborhood.

Around the age of three and one half, Jimmie became interested in rocks. He noticed their difference and wanted us to tell him their names. After exhausting his search in our yard, we took him for a walk near a mountain. We could see how motivated and happy he was collecting rocks of all shapes and colors. It was difficult for his father and me to identify these for him, but with the aid of some rock manuals, we survived. Of course, Jimmie never forgot those names.

At four, his planetarium projector was his favorite toy, and a secondary interest in stamp collecting started at this time and has continued. At his present age of six years and eight months, he has five completed albums of stamps.

The philosophical aspects of science often absorb him and result in such statements as: "The moon is the machine of the ocean because it controls the tides," or "If we shoot rockets into space and they all bounce back from the same place, that would be the end of space." He likes to talk about ideas and to speculate about the unknown.

All went well with Jimmie until his first day in kindergarten. One might say he was ready for school, but school was not ready for him. His first teacher didn't know what to do with him during those beginning weeks. Jimmie showed a reluctance to attending and finally became ill. Upon questioning him, he said that all he did those early weeks was just sit by himself and stare at the teacher. The toys held no interest for him. Needless to say, the time came for our first parent-teacher conference, which took place on the sidewalk outside the school. She said she was worried about him. Her biggest complaint was that he didn't act like other children; he was too good, not aggressive enough, and too serious. She would like to experiment with him so that she could prevent him from becoming a recluse. This teacher made it quite clear that she had had experience with one other gifted child and it was not pleasant.

It was in this class that Jimmie was exposed to intolerance by both the teacher and the children. When she made it plain to Jimmie that she wanted him to act silly like the other children, he obeyed. In fact, he soon discovered that the sillier he acted, the more approval he got from his teacher and the children. Her experiment was a success. He became the class clown, not only in school, but also in our home. I complained to the principal, who recommended that he be tested by their own school psychologist. However, she wanted to know if we would like to withdraw him from school. Of course, we were horrified at such a thought. Wasn't he entitled to an education; did it have to be the same education every child had? We decided to let him be tested and, perhaps on the basis of this evaluation, they would place him in first grade in January. At the age of five, he was tested for two and one half hours. The results showed that he was a highly gifted child, but they felt he was socially maladjusted and should be placed in a next-to-slow kindergarten, so he could "catch up"! They were afraid if they put him in first grade, he would become bored, and second grade would be too much for him physically. Obviously, they hadn't read Terman's studies of how a gifted child is also advanced socially and that there is a correlation between mental age and social age.

Rather than expose him to any more of this intolerance which had already manifested itself in psychosomatic disturbances during his sleeping and eating behavior, we did finally withdraw him from public school.

This was the darkest hour. We had hit rock bottom. What is just as sad as a man without a country is a child without a school. Naturally we felt bitter; was this the equal opportunity in education we had heard so much about? We soon discovered that "equality" meant "sameness" to some educators.

For the remaining part of the year, we enrolled Jimmie in a private school we could hardly afford. The school was overly permissive and allowed the children to wrestle and fight in the classroom. Academically, it offered little for Jimmie, and coupled with the chaotic atmosphere of the classroom, he found the whole thing distasteful. By this time, he had developed a neurosis about having children hit him, even accidentally. He felt this showed that they disliked him. He would strike back, but he soon discovered this still did not stop them. Being children, they did not understand Jimmie, so being fearful of what they did not comprehend, they would hit him. Today, in dealing with parents of other gifted children, I find most of the children to not like fighting and preferring to rather avoid physical contact. Perhaps it's because they have other, more adult methods of settling arguments. Whatever it is, I should think society would be more concerned with children who enjoy hurting other human beings. We certainly need more peace-loving individuals in this war-tense world we live in today.

By the end of his first school year, Jimmie was very upset, and it took all summer to get him in condition for school again the next year. This time we enrolled him in another private school, which taught the children love and tolerance and did not permit hitting in the classroom. In a few weeks, he was fine again, since it was here he finally felt accepted. Here again, the teacher was unaware of his giftedness, because he was interested in materials instead of just books. The gifted children she has known have done nothing but read. Since he was always the first one through with his work, he found enough time on his hands to become a behavior problem. We then decided to have him tested again. The results this time made more sense to us since they were closely correlated with his performance at home. The Director of Education at his new school took his I.Q. evaluation into account and has agreed to accelerate him to the third grade next year and to enrich him in subject matter. Only the next chapter can tell us how Jimmie will prosper.

Jimmie is six years and eight months old as of this writing, and this year, he has shown a deep interest in paleontology, meteorology (he has his own weather station), and electronics. He builds his own radio and transmitter sets with hardly any assistance. He has forged ahead with his inventions, too. Jimmie has always had the ability to use ordinary materials in new and unusual ways with a definite purpose in mind. This year, when he heard about the airplane disasters at Idlewild and La Guardia airfields, he felt quite dismayed and decided to do something about it. Using a cardboard shoebox, two strips of paper, and two magnets, he invented a device that the pilot could use in the cockpit of his plane, which would tell him when a plane was "off course" or "approaching." Needless to say, Thomas Edison is his idol.

> *Jimmie knows he is a gifted child, and he knows why some people resent him. But he also knows that this is a God-given gift and... that one day Jimmie could use his gifts to better the world and serve humanity. In this way, he can be helping all the people.*
>
> *No one can accuse Jimmie of not trying to adjust to the average or slow child. When he has invited them to our house, it was always Jimmie who would play their way, no matter how uncomfortable for him. Is it too much to ask to have other children try to learn to adjust to gifted children? To use a shopworn phrase, they too "have to learn how to get along with all kinds of people," even gifted people.*
>
> *As parents of a gifted child, we have felt so alone in trying to find the solution to the best way of nurturing our child to his fullest potential. I can remember saying to my husband a few years ago: God sent us a gifted one, but He forgot to enclose a book of instructions.*

Teachers are sometimes parents of creative and intelligent children, and as such, they are made all the more uncomfortable by the plights of the children who cannot fit into the classroom. Gifted teachers, like gifted students, often have difficulties in the lock-step classroom. Sometimes their rebellions, as parents or as teachers, make them newsworthy. A New Jersey scientist and his wife were brought into court by their suburban school system when they kept their three musically and academically advanced children at home and taught them themselves. Another teacher went to court to try to establish his right not to turn in lesson plans, since he wanted to be free to follow the lead of his pupil's curiosities. Yet another teacher in a well-to-do suburb made the headlines for a whole summer because the parents of his pupils resented the dismissal of this man who had communicated his own love for learning to their children but had not been loyal to the curriculum. A volume could be written on the creative and intelligent approaches that are currently being made by classroom teachers here and there to the problem of how to deal with gifted and talented children—approaches that reach, however, only a small minority of such children.

The following description by a high-school teacher of the experiences of his five-year-old daughter in kindergarten during 1960-1961 is reprinted with the permission of E. Paul Torrance of the Bureau of Educational Research, University of Minnesota:

> *As I watched my oldest child develop, I was impressed by her interest in the world about her. She was so different from the high school students I was accustomed to working with. She seemed so eager to learn and to explore. Then when she started talking in sentences at fourteen months, I was surprised how quickly she learned nursery rhymes we had been reading to her....*
>
> *As she grew older, her curiosity and interest in the world around her seemed to grow rapidly. She asked endless questions—everything from where babies come from to what makes the leaves turn color in the fall. I determined to answer all of these questions as they came up, never putting her off with "I don't know" or "I'll tell you later." I gave fairly complete explanations to her questions and showed her how we could look up answers in books to questions I didn't know. All the time, I felt she was just nodding her head and accepting what I said without understanding. Soon, however, I was startled to find her asking more questions based on these first answers I had given.*
>
> *Before long, we began to accumulate such things as a telescope, microscope, plastic skeleton, butterfly and insect collection, baby mice, bird eggs, and a number of fossil trilobites and crinoids which she found in the rock driveway. All of these areas we pursued as long as she showed interest in them, with the whole procedure treated as a game and no attempt made to consciously learn anything.*
>
> *After seeing her first ballet at age three, she decided to become a ballerina and took great pleasure in spending*

hours creating new dance steps to the music of Tchaikovsky and others. This interest in ballet was dulled for a period by an authoritarian teacher who insisted that she conform to the forward rolls the rest of the class was learning. However, the interest was renewed with a change in teachers and a more advanced class....

Then this year, she started kindergarten. She had been anxious all summer, even though I kept reminding her that she would not be allowed to read until a year later in the first grade.... The first few weeks of kindergarten, she was delirious with excitement. Every day she was eager for school. Show-and-Tell time was her favorite. She collected leaves from twenty-two different varieties of trees. Then she pasted them in a book, printed their names underneath, and took them to Show-and-Tell with an explanation of what makes leaves change color. Next she took her pet turtle with her book illustrating the life cycles of fishes, reptiles, and amphibians.

About November, she began to complain that all the other kids were bringing their toys and dolls for Show-and-Tell or telling what they saw on TV. Her interest dropped further as she found that the teacher did all of the reading instead of letting the kids read. The end came when the teacher refused to let her use the "Teach-a-Time" clock to show the other kids how to tell time and made her paste paper instead.

Her interests then began to move in the direction of what she wore that was different from the other children. She began to quote more and more what the teacher said and accepted it as law over anything else.

Interest was revived briefly when the teacher said she could bring her telescope and book on astronomy during the week they were to talk about outer space. However, the teacher didn't understand her explanation of how the reflecting-type telescope works and pointed the wrong end at the sun during an observation attempt. By this time, she accepted the teacher's word to the point where she was afraid to correct the teacher and turn the telescope around. From that day on, she has refused to bring another thing for Show-and-Tell and began talking only of when the next school vacation would begin.

These three gifted children are reminiscent of many of the intellectually gifted among the Four Hundred, but they are also from a segment that is better accepted because of the current respect for talent in science. They are children from homes where there is a love for learning; they are enrolled in schools generally considered to be superior in quality. In the past, it has been the family that has been the prime influence in developing such children's potentials. The parents of the Four Hundred had strong intellectual and physical drives, were open to new experiences, and kept their own love for learning intact even into old age. Today's parents of gifted children are subject to stronger pressure to have the child conform to mediocrity than were the parents of the Four Hundred.

Now, as in the days of the Four Hundred, the children who are both intelligent and creative remains society's most valuable resource. When we learn to work with them instead of against them, their talents may reward us in ways beyond our ability to imagine.

Chapter 12
Cradles of Eminence Today

by Ted George Goertzel and Ariel M. W. Hansen

More than forty years have passed since *Cradles of Eminence* was first published, yet it remains one of very few studies of the childhoods of eminent people. There have been two sequels by members of the Goertzel family—*Three Hundred Eminent Personalities: A Psychosocial Analysis of the Famous*, published in 1978, which added a newer sample and more statistics, and in 1992, *Turncoats and True Believers: The Dynamics of Political Belief and Disillusionment,* which focused on the life histories of political activists.[1] In this chapter, we carry on the family tradition with another update.

After the publication of *Three Hundred Eminent Personalities,* the family was contacted by Dean Keith Simonton, professor of psychology at the University of California, Davis, who asked us for a copy of our IBM cards—in those days, statistical data was stored on punched cards. He did some elegant statistical analyses, supplementing our data with the best data he could find from other sources, and published the results in his 1999 book, *Genius, Creativity, and Leadership.*[2]

Jane Piirto's 1998 book, *Understanding Those Who Create, 2nd Edition,* includes childhood material in many of its cases, and she offers a fine analysis of the literature on creativity in different fields (a third edition is in the works for 2004).[3] Arnold Ludwig's 1995 book, *The Price of Greatness: Resolving the Creativity and Madness Controversy,* used a sample drawn from biographies published in the *New*

York Times Book Review to test many of the findings from *Cradles of Eminence.*[4] We were pleased that Ludwig's rigorous study confirmed the key findings in *Cradles of Eminence* with regard to parental characteristics, birth order, broken homes, family size, the death of parents, health problems, social behavior, school problems, and career choices, among other things. We particularly recommend Chapter Two of *The Price of Greatness* to anyone who likes to back up qualitative insights with hard data.

Despite the large size of the sample, *Cradles of Eminence* was not fundamentally a statistical work. It used a method described by Abraham Maslow in which the data consist "not so much in the usual gathering of specific and discrete facts as in the slow development of a global or holistic impression of the sort that we form of our friends and acquaintances."[5] This approach is typically used by biographers or ethnographers who immerse themselves in the lives of a single individual or a handful of individuals.

There are other works of comparative biography that look for common patterns in large numbers of biographies, such as Clive James' *Fame in the Twentieth Century*[6] and *Time's Great People of the Twentieth Century.*[7] These studies only occasionally mention childhood experiences. There simply has not been enough comparative biographical work about the childhoods and school experiences of the very important people who have made our world what it is.

In this chapter, we are updating *Cradles of Eminence* and *Three Hundred Eminent Personalities* without the statistical work that Arnold Ludwig and Dean Keith Simonton have done so well. Statistical patterns are of great interest sociologically, but are of limited practical usefulness because they cannot be applied to specific individuals. For example, one of the strongest statistical findings is that firstborn and only children are more likely to be eminent than later-born children. Fred Trump might have had this finding in mind when he named his firstborn son Fred, Jr., and groomed him to inherit his real estate business. But Fred, Jr. could not handle his father's expectations and went in a different direction, becoming an airline pilot, then suffering from depression and alcoholism. His younger brother, Donald, fought tooth and nail for his father's approval and went on to become America's most famous real estate baron.

Other statistics find that children often do better when their fathers are not too successful, perhaps explaining Fred Jr.'s difficulties. But firstborn son President George W. Bush overcame that handicap, perhaps because his parents gave him the slack he needed to work through his problems at his own pace. Statistical patterns may alert us to problems that children may face, but no parent or educator should assume that they apply directly to any specific child. We believe parents and educators can learn more from stories of how eminent people overcame challenges and how they built on opportunities they had as children.

For this update, we are especially interested in how people have dealt with the new challenges and opportunities that society has presented in the last few decades. This means drawing a new sample of names, which raises the same sampling issues Mildred and Victor faced in 1962. Who are the newly eminent people of today? There is no one correct answer to this question. Eminence is a subjective concept used interchangeably with words such as "fame," "greatness," or "genius," but each term has different connotations, and each is a matter of judgment.

When Clive James, of the *New York Review of Books*, prepared a public television program, "Fame in the 20th Century," he and a dozen colleagues spent almost the entire first week trying to agree on the 250 twentieth-century people who were "genuinely, undeniably world-famous."[8] They made many arbitrary choices, such as including Luciano Pavarotti but not Placido Domingo, because they thought the first was known to everyone but the second only to people who like good singing. They included Pablo Picasso but not Henri Matisse, and chose Margaret Mitchell but not T. S. Eliot. Stefan Edberg was excluded because only tennis fans knew his name, but John McEnroe was included because everyone was interested in bad behavior.

Mildred and Victor Goertzel had wanted a sampling method that was more objective, and they needed subjects for whom childhood information was available. So they let the librarians in the local public library choose their sample for them. This was convenient, and it eliminated personal biases on their part. It was not the most rigorous sampling method one might imagine, but it worked well enough, and the results were similar to those obtained with other methods.

For example, in *The Price of Greatness,* Ludwig compared the samples in *Cradles of Eminence* and *Three Hundred Eminent Personalities* to his own sample of biographies reviewed in *The New York Times Book Review.* He also compared his sample to listings in *Book Review Digest*, S. M. Stievater's *Biographies of Creative Artists*, and P. E. Shellinger's *St. James Guide to Biography.* He found that the percentages of people from these different sources that were included in his own sample ranged from 67-85 percent.[9]

For this 2003 update, we began by drawing a new sample from the Montclair Public Library, in order to make sure that any changes we found were not due to changing libraries. Neither of us lives in Montclair, but the library catalog is searchable over the Internet. We soon decided that replicating the exact procedure Mildred and Victor used was not the best approach. Victor had always told his three sons that one of his proudest accomplishments was not having been so successful that we could not surpass him. We knew that he and our mother would want us to improve on their work if we could. We noted that the electronic catalog contained youth and juvenile biographies as well as biographies written for adults, and we decided to include them although Mildred and Victor had not. We were interested in role models presented to young people, and we also thought that biographies written for young people might include more recent eminent figures because of young readers' limited interest in people who lived long before their time.

We decided to require two biographical books from foreign-born and native-born alike, although Mildred and Victor had only required one book from foreign-born individuals, because the number of biographies of foreign-born people is much larger than it was in 1962. Finally, we included only books published since 1995, in the hope of tapping into recent trends, and only examined books devoted to a single individual. Even with these limitations, our new sample included 794 names, about as many individuals as were researched in *Cradles of Eminence* and *Three Hundred Eminent Personalities* combined. This was far too many for us to read, of course, though we could look at statistical patterns and select a subset for in-depth reading.

One of the first things we did was to compare individuals with the most biographies in the new sample with those with those who led the previous samples. The results showed striking differences. Table One lists the individuals with the most biographies in each of the samples. The 1962 sample contained five superstars: Franklin Delano Roosevelt, Mahatma Gandhi, Winston Churchill, Albert Schweitzer, and Theodore Roosevelt. Among the 13 individuals with five or more biographies, Gandhi was the only non-white person, and there were no women.

The 1976 individuals with five or more biographies included three women, all of them writers. The top two new figures were Robert Kennedy and Lyndon Johnson, both contemporary political leaders, with 14 and 11 biographies respectively. Nine eminent persons from the 1962 sample also had one or more new biographies. For example, there were twelve new biographies of Sigmund Freud, eight of Franklin Delano Roosevelt, seven of Mark Twain, and six each of Tolstoy and Gandhi. Ché Guevara and César Chavez joined as representatives of movements for social change.

The 2003 sample is different in many ways. There are many more women among the leading figures, as one might expect, and most of them are social activists rather than writers. Sports figures appear much more frequently, in part because we included biographies written for young people. The top two biography subjects are Hillary Rodham Clinton, first lady and U.S. senator, and Tiger Woods, a golf prodigy of mixed ethnic background. Oprah Winfrey, African-American talk show hostess and magazine publisher, was tied with President George W. Bush in the number of biographies. Well-known social activists include: Nelson Mandela, South African freedom fighter; Thurgood Marshall, Supreme Court justice; Rosa Parks and Ida B. Wells, civil rights leaders; and Elizabeth Cady Stanton, suffragist.

Table One: Eminent Personalities in 1962, 1978, and 2003
(Name and Number of Biographies in Public Library Collections)

Montclair Public Library, 1995-2003 1962-1976	**Menlo Park Public Library, before 1962**	**Montclair Public Library**
Hillary Rodham Clinton (11)	Robert F. Kennedy (14, 11 in Montclair)	Franklin Delano Roosevelt (28)
Eldrick "Tiger" Woods (11)	Lyndon F. Johnson (11, 13)	Mahatma Gandhi (21)
Michael Jeffrey Jordan (9)	Simone de Beauvoir (5, 5)	Winston Churchill (20)
Oprah Winfrey (9)	Anaïs Nîn (9, 2)	Albert Schweitzer (17)
George W. Bush (9)	Sidonie Colette (8, 7)	Theodore Roosevelt (17)
Jane Goodall (6)	T. S. Eliot (7, 9)	Albert Einstein (5 or 6)
Nelson Mandela (6)	Ché Guevara (7, 7)	Sean O'Casey (5 or 6)
Thurgood Marshall (6)	Carl Jung (7, 6)	Nelson Rockefeller (5 or 6)
Mother Teresa of Calcutta (6)	Edgar Cayce (6, 7)	Leo Tolstoy (5 or 6)
Rosa Lee Parks (6)	César Chavez (6, 3)	Mark Twain (5 or 6)
Ida B. Wells (6)	Hermann Hesse (6, 10)	William James (5 or 6)*
Walt Disney (5)	Ezra Pound (6, 10)	Henry James (5 or 6)*
Derek Jeter (5)		Sigmund Freud (5 or 6)
Pope John Paul II (5)	*Repeats (1962 to 1976 biographies)*:	
Frida Kahlo (5)	Sigmund Freud (12)	* includes books on both
Mark McGwire (5)	Franklin Delano Roosevelt (8)	
Thomas Merton (5)	Mark Twain (7)	
Elizabeth Cady Stanton (5)	Leo Tolstoy (6)	
Laura Ingalls Wilder (5)	Mahatma Gandhi (6)	
	Albert Schweitzer (2)	
Repeats	Henry James (2)	
(1995 and later biographies):	William James (2)	
Mark Twain (7)	Sean O'Casey (1)	
Albert Einstein (6)		
Mahatma Gandhi (5)		
Winston Churchill (4)		
César Chavez (3)		
Robert Kennedy (2)		
Franklin Roosevelt (2)		
Sigmund Freud (2)		
Theodore Roosevelt (1)		
Henry James (1)		
Simone de Beauvoir (1)		
Anaïs Nîn (1)		
Ché Guevara (1)		
Carl Jung (1)		
Edgar Cayce (1)		
Nelson Rockefeller (1)		

At the top of the list, Hillary Rodham Clinton reflects a new tendency for wives of famous people to become famous in their own right.[10] Our new sample includes Nancy Reagan, Coretta Scott King, and Winnie Mandela. Of course, Hillary Rodham Clinton was active in her husband's administration and is now a U.S. senator, but her heavy weight on the biography shelves may reflect as much interest in the couple's marital problems as in her separate accomplishments. Nancy Reagan was a well-known actress before her marriage, and both Coretta Scott King and Winnie Mandela were important as social activists in their own right, yet the fame of all of these women was inextricably linked to their marriages.

Hillary Rodham Clinton came from a middle class, suburban home that her biographers describe as idyllic. Her mother was a classic child-centered homemaker, and while her father may have had ups and downs in his drapery business, he always provided well for the family. Hillary both enjoyed and did well in school and had a generally untroubled life until her marital problems, which were linked with the very public life of her charismatic, ambitious, and political husband. Hillary's mother, by contrast, was abandoned by divorced parents (neither of whom wanted her) and was sent to live with exploitative relatives. She succeeded admirably in her determination to break the chain of abuse and give her children all the advantages she had been denied. Hillary married Bill Clinton, an individual who had had a troubled childhood that contributed to his famous ability to empathize with the suffering of others but created other difficulties for him. Although Hillary's own childhood did not include the kinds of problems highlighted in *Cradles of Eminence,* she devoted her career to helping disadvantaged children, and she became famous for her support of a husband who needed help overcoming a troubled childhood. Supporting a troubled spouse is often an essential contribution of those who become eminent wives and family members.

In our new sample, we were pleased to find more women and minorities, but we were surprised and a bit disappointed that so many of the subjects (other than sports and music figures) were of the same generation as those in the previous studies. Elizabeth Cady

Stanton and Ida B. Wells are more properly categorized as nineteenth-century figures, but because each lived into the twentieth century, they qualified under our criteria.

Elizabeth Cady Stanton's major life crisis was the death of her older brother when she was eleven. She tried to take his place, proving that she could do everything as well as he did, including mastering Greek and horsemanship, but her father was inconsolable. No matter how much she achieved, he continued to say, "If only you were a boy." As an adult, she devoted her life to the struggle to gain women equal rights and respect.

Noted journalist and activist Ida B. Wells had a happy and supportive home, despite the difficulties of growing up black in small-town Mississippi. She was educated by Protestant missionaries who exposed her to a world of books that had been denied to her slave-born parents, although her mother encouraged her by learning to read along with her. When she was 16, both of her parents died of yellow fever during an epidemic. With help from neighbors, she took over the responsibility for five younger siblings (including a disabled sister who could not walk), earning a living as a rural schoolteacher, a job to which she commuted by mule. The strength of character she developed through these ordeals helped her to later earn an outstanding role as a crusading journalist and civil-rights activist.

Biographies of historical figures such as Elizabeth Cady Stanton and Ida B. Wells are now being published to correct racial and gender biases of the past, especially in editions for young readers. Teachers assign students to read these books, and public librarians stock them. The intention is to make these people famous in order to provide more diverse role models for young people. Of course, one traditional role of biographies has always been to provide role models for children, as with the classic Horatio Alger stories, but the emphasis on diversity has increased in recent decades. Making the selection of biographies more diverse on race and gender lines is, in our opinion, a good thing, and we were glad that our sampling reflects this.

Broadening the pool is not the only reason new biographies are published about historical figures. Each new generation of biographers reinterprets the lives of important people from the past, and many add newly discovered information. It is noteworthy that the Montclair library catalog lists seven books published since 1995 about Mark Twain, six about Einstein, five about Gandhi, and three about Churchill. These newer interpretations help to make the classic figures more relevant to today's readers.

However, especially for younger readers, heroines such as Elizabeth Cady Stanton and Ida B. Wells seem distant because their struggles were in a bygone era. Oprah Winfrey is a role model for today. Her life neatly illustrates the mix of natural ability, misfortune, and timely assistance that some theorists believe is most likely to produce creative adults.[11] Oprah's unmarried mother left her to be raised on a pig farm in rural Mississippi by a grandmother who was domineering and overbearing and beat her, but who also took her to Sunday school and taught her to read at a very young age. She was a voracious reader and was so bright that the local grade school skipped her from first to third grade.

When Oprah was six, she went to live with her mother in the slums of Milwaukee where, unfortunately, she was sexually abused by a relative. She also had the opportunity to attend an integrated school in an affluent suburb as part of a racial integration program. At fourteen, her life turned around when her father took her to live with him in Nashville and gave her the discipline and encouragement that she had not received from her mother. She got her first television job while still in college and proved to have the mix of brightness and personality essential for success as a talk show host.

Oprah attended a predominately black university during the height of the civil rights movement, but she chose not to put her energy into activism. She focused all her attention on her acting and TV career goals. Other students called her an "Oreo" (a derogatory term for an individual who has a dark skin color but who "acts" white) for taking advantage of opportunities within the system, but she persisted, encouraged by instructors who wisely advised her to make the most of the opportunities she was finding. Single-minded pursuit of their own goals and interests is a trait that eminent people have in common.

While Oprah's formal college education may not have contributed much to her career, at least her instructors encouraged her and did not try to stand in her way. This was not true for Woody Allen, (born Allen Stewart Konigsberg to Orthodox Jewish parents), whose teachers consistently discouraged him. He repeatedly got bad grades on his writing, mostly because he was irreverent and funny. On one paper, he wrote that a woman "had an hourglass figure and I'd like to play in the sand." He was sent to the principal, who advised his mother to take him to a psychiatrist. Woody scored high on intelligence tests and was placed in classes for the gifted, but the strictures of the classroom did not allow him to express himself in his own way or to use his imagination in his lessons. Instead, he expressed his creativity by becoming a troublemaker and was dropped from the gifted classes. As he grew older, he became more rebellious, failed to turn in homework, played hooky, and spent his time going to the movies and playing the clarinet, which he learned at age twelve.

Woody Allen's school behavior demonstrates a trait that some psychologists today call "overexcitability."[12] This is a tendency, common to many eminent persons, to be especially intense in response to stimuli of various kinds. Bright young people with this trait, for example, may have a great deal of nervous or intellectual energy and have a hard time waiting for slower students to catch up. A typical classroom, where everyone has to sit quietly and pay attention, can be oppressively difficult for young people who might flourish best, for instance, if given the opportunity to work at their own pace or on their own project. Some of these children may be diagnosed with Attention Deficit Disorder or other maladaptive conditions and recommended for psychological or psychiatric treatment.[13] Such diagnosis is often an unrecognized misdiagnosis, simply because the child is not like other children. This may have been the case with Woody Allen.

Fortunately, Woody's mother was supportive and had hopes that his creative gifts would enable him to have a more successful career than his father, who was continually changing jobs. Living in Brooklyn, he enjoyed the richness of life in New York City and soon found that he could make money by writing jokes for comedians. His parents encouraged him to try college, and he enrolled at New York University. He got a "D" in motion picture production, probably because he skipped classes to go to the movies. He also did poorly in English classes, where he "wrote funny essays for humorless teachers."[14] His teachers tried to discourage him, but he was already making a living from his writing, so he wisely ignored them.

Youthful rebelliousness also characterized Nelson Mandela. He was given many advantages, but he rejected them to follow his own path. His father was a village headman who had four wives and thirteen children, but who lost his position following a dispute with the local white magistrate. After his father's death when Nelson was nine, he was adopted by the tribal chief and given the best of opportunities available to blacks in South Africa, including an education at University College in Fort Hare. Nelson left in protest when the administration demanded an apology for a revolt he helped to lead against poor cafeteria food. Later, he rebelled against a marriage arranged for him by the chief and ran off to Johannesburg where he got involved in even more radical politics.

As we can see from the above examples, the Montclair library certainly pointed us to books about interesting and important people. The current sample was far more diverse than the sample Victor and Mildred found in 1962. But what did the various samples have in common? Did they still represent eminent people today? Or had Montclair and its library changed? Just to make sure that the Montclair library was still representative, we checked the top subjects in the Montclair sample against a number of other libraries. As Table Two shows, there were plenty of books about all of our top subjects in all of the libraries we checked, with the partial exception of Derek Jeter, who is a New York Yankee shortstop and thus of greater local interest. As another measure of eminence, we used the Google Internet search engine to count the number of hits for each of our top subjects. All of our subjects are on thousands of websites, with

President George W. Bush leading the group—as one might expect. The number of hits for Walt Disney is deceptive because most of them were for the Walt Disney Corporation, and it is difficult to control for this in a Web search. Results of this search are listed in Table Two.

As another measure of eminence, we tried checking the best-seller lists on both Amazon.com and BarnesandNoble.com, but these yielded only recently popular books. In our search for biographies, the top ranked was Hillary Clinton's autobiography, reflecting its recent publication, followed by a book about Seabiscuit, an underdog racehorse that became famous during the Depression.

Table Two: Biographical Books in Selected Public Libraries
and Websites in a Google Search

	C	H	A	MP	P	LA	M	Google
George W. Bush	19	34	18	35	32	42	20	2,120,000
Walt Disney	50	39	28	37	26	52	14	1,690,000
Tiger Woods	42	32	36	37	24	51	13	597,000
Michael Jordan	75	63	54	61	30	79	14	539,000
Hillary Clinton	20	40	20	39	30	62	14	395,000
Pope John Paul II	47	48	25	38	45	75	10	327,000
Nelson Mandela	43	49	31	43	31	53	19	277,000
Mother Teresa	60	59	37	50	39	78	17	197,000
Oprah Winfrey	35	40	33	31	20	38	16	151,000
Derek Jeter	7	11	6	6	6	14	5	103,000
Rosa Parks	35	44	35	39	30	44	18	95,000
Frida Kahlo	32	36	20	42	14	55	7	95,000
Jane Goodall	20	26	18	30	19	34	8	91,100
Mark McGwire	20	23	16	21	12	31	8	84,500
Thurgood Marshall	52	47	40	37	33	53	12	66,700
Thomas Merton	18	27	15	25	32	48	9	51,100
Laura Ingalls Wilder	17	23	20	24	19	32	9	50,100
Elizabeth Cady Stanton	32	30	24	35	26	41	11	34,300
Ida B. Wells	28	27	23	26	27	33	12	14,800

C = Chicago H = Houston A = Atlanta MP = Menlo Park P = Philadelphia
LA = Los Angeles M = Montclair, NJ

Note: Library searching was done by entering the name and the word "biography", e.g., "Hillary Clinton biography," in the keyword search or subject search, depending upon the library. "Menlo Park" refers to the Peninsula County, California library of which Menlo Park is a part. It was included because it was used for the book *Three Hundred Eminent Personalities.* These searches include books published in any year and books that discuss more than one individual, so the count for Montclair is different than the count in Table Two. The searches include juvenile as well as adult books. The websites were counted in a Google search on June 27, 2003. On the Google search, the name was put in quotation marks, e.g., "Hillary Clinton." The count for Ida B. Wells is an underestimate because there are various forms of her name. Including all of them would have meant double counting, although it would not have increased it by more than a few thousand. Walt Disney is the name of a corporation as well as an individual, but it is difficult to separate the two in Internet searches.

We are convinced that our sample from the Montclair Public Library has given us a reasonable list of people whose biographies have been published since 1995 and have been purchased by public libraries. But who are these individuals? How might they differ from the individuals listed in earlier samples? The first thing we noticed was that the percentage of women essentially doubled. In the original 1962 sample, only 14 percent of the subjects were women, a bias that reflected the sexist nature of society up to that time. By 1976, the percentage of women in the sample had risen to 24 percent, and in the 2003 sample, it was 27 percent.

The societal gender biases reflected in the sample are even stronger when one observes that in the 1962 sample, 44 percent of the women were writers, 14 percent were singers or musicians, and 10 percent were actresses (Table Three). These biases persist in the later samples, with very few women in the categories of political leader, an important category for men. Indeed, part of the increase of women in the sample is due to growth in the category "Wives, Family Members, and Socialites." There is also a significant increase in biographies of female athletes. This bias is not a defect in the sampling; it reflects current social reality. There simply are many more eminent women who are writers, singers, athletes, and actresses than eminent women in top political positions.

Table Three: Fields of Eminence by Gender in 2003, 1978, and 1962
(Number of Biographies of Individuals Living into the Twentieth Century Sampled in Public Library Collections)

Library and Years Sampled	**Montclair** 1995-2003		**Menlo Park** 1962-1976		**Montclair** before 1962	
	F	M	F	M	F	M
Percent of Sample by Gender:	26.8%	73.2%	23.8%	76.2%	14.0%	86.0%
Percent of Biographies by Field:						
Actors	20.6%	10.0%	17.3%	5.4%	10.3%	3.1%
Artists	3.3%	3.3%	2.7%	8.8%	1.7%	5.4%
Athletes and Sports Figures	8.4%	12.4%	0.0%	3.8%	0.0%	0.3%
Business Leaders	2.3%	3.4%	4.0%	1.7%	0.0%	2.0%
Criminals, Assassins, and Spies	0.5%	1.4%	1.3%	0.8%	0.0%	0.0%
Dancers and Choreographers	1.4%	0.9%	2.7%	1.3%	3.4%	0.3%
Diplomats	0.5%	0.2%	0.0%	2.5%	0.0%	0.8%
Editors and Publishers	0.0%	0.7%	1.3%	2.1%	0.0%	2.8%
Entertainers and TV Personalities	1.9%	3.6%	0.0%	0.0%	0.0%	1.1%
Explorers and Adventurers	0.0%	0.5%	0.0%	1.3%	1.7%	1.7%
Filmmakers	0.9%	2.6%	0.0%	1.3%	0.0%	0.6%
Inventors	0.0%	0.3%	0.0%	0.0%	0.0%	0.8%
Journalists	4.7%	3.6%	2.7%	0.8%	1.7%	1.1%
Judges and Lawyers	0.5%	2.2%	0.0%	0.8%	0.0%	2.8%
Labor Leaders	0.0%	0.2%	0.0%	0.4%	0.0%	2.0%
Military Leaders	0.0%	1.7%	0.0%	0.8%	0.0%	3.1%
Musicians, Singers, and Composers	9.8%	12.2%	4.0%	5.8%	13.8%	9.0%
Photographers	1.4%	1.4%	1.3%	0.8%	0.0%	0.0%
Physicians and Nurses	1.4%	1.2%	0.0%	0.4%	1.7%	1.4%
Pilots and Astronauts	1.9%	1.4%	0.0%	0.4%	1.7%	0.8%
Political Leaders	2.3%	10.1%	4.0%	17.1%	1.7%	19.7%
Psychiatrists and Psychologists	0.5%	0.2%	1.3%	1.7%	0.0%	0.3%
Psychics and Hypnotists	0.0%	0.0%	4.0%	2.5%	0.0%	0.0%
Religious and Spiritual Leaders	1.4%	2.4%	0.0%	1.3%	1.7%	2.0%
Scientists, Scholars, and Educators	3.3%	6.0%	2.7%	6.7%	6.9%	9.0%
Social Activists	5.1%	2.1%	9.3%	4.5%	8.6%	2.3%
Wives, Family Members, and Socialites	8.5%	0.0%	12.0%	1.7%	0.0%	0.0%
Writers, Poets, and Playwrights	17.3%	16.5%	29.3%	24.6%	44.8%	28.7%
TOTAL	**100%**	**100%**	**100%**	**100%**	**100%**	**100%**

One important gap in the sample should be emphasized, and it is a result of the biographical method itself. While scientists and business leaders play a key role in modern society and are important role models for young people, there are comparatively few biographies of either group, either intended for adults or for young readers. In the 1962 *Cradles of Eminence* sample, 31 percent of the subjects (men and women together) were writers, 17 percent political leaders, 9 percent scientists, scholars, or educators, and fewer than 2 percent business leaders. In our 2003 sample, 17 percent were writers, 11 percent athletes, 8 percent political leaders, 5 percent scientists, scholars, or educators, and 3 percent business leaders.

We hypothesize that writers are over-represented because they write interesting autobiographies and because biographers may enjoy writing about other writers, not because they are more important than the other groups. We suspect that athletes, actors, musicians, and other celebrities are well represented on the biographical shelves because they interest the current reading public, as much as because of historical importance. Educators may have done much to correct the racial biases of the past, but they have so far not done much to fill the gap in biographies of scientists or business leaders.

Mildred and Victor Goertzel were aware of this bias when they were first researching, and they did their best compensate for it in the interpretation of their data. They also tried to help fill the gap in biographies of eminent scientists by writing a biography of chemist Linus Pauling.[15] For this update, however, we decided to correct the problem of under-representation of scientists and businessmen by supplementing the public library sampling with three other lists—a list of "The 100 Most Influential Americans of the Twentieth Century" published in *Life* magazine in 1990, the *Time* book *Great People of the Twentieth Century*, and a list of "The Most Important People of the Twentieth Century," posted in 2000 by Time.com.[16] These lists were compiled by committees of journalists advised by panels of historians and reflect their judgment as to historical importance.

For our final update sample, we eliminated all of the people who were already covered in the original *Cradles of Eminence* or in

Three Hundred Eminent Personalities, and we limited the new Montclair Public Library sample to those individuals with four or five biographies (depending upon their field of eminence). This gave us a manageable and reasonably representative group of 199 eminent people with which to update the material in the earlier books.

Table Four lists the names of these individuals, arranged by field of eminence. It also tells which sample they came from: MPL (Montclair Public Library), *Life* or *Time* (either the book or the website). This is in no sense a comprehensive list of the most eminent people of the twentieth century, because most of those people are already covered in *Cradles of Eminence* and *Three Hundred Eminent Personalities* (whose names are listed in the appendices to this book). It is simply a list of people whose lives we selected to update and fill gaps in the earlier books. There are hundreds of additional people with two or more biographies in the Montclair and other libraries, but for reasons already mentioned, these are the names we chose for the update.

Table Four: *Cradles of Eminence* 2003 Update Sample

Name and Dates	Field of Eminence	Sample
Actors		
Ball, Lucille (1911-1989)	Actress, Comedienne	*Time*, MPL
Davis, Bette (1908-1989)	Actress	MPL
Grant, Cary (1904-1986)	Actor	MPL
Henson, Jim (1936-1990)	Puppeteer	*Time*, MPL
Hepburn, Audrey (1929-1993)	Actress	MPL
Kelly, Grace (1929-1982)	Actress, Princess of Monaco	MPL
Lee, Bruce (1940-1973)	Actor, Martial Arts Expert	*Time*, MPL
Streisand, Barbra (1942-)	Actress, Singer	MPL
Wayne, John (1907-1979)	Actor	MPL
Architects		
Le Corbusier (1867-1965)	Architect	*Time*
Mies van der Rohe, Ludwig (1886-1956)	Architect	*Life*
Olmsted, Frederick Law (1870-1947)	Landscape Architect	MPL
Sullivan, Louis (1856-1924)	Architect	MPL
Artists		
Degas, Edgar (1834-1917)	Artist	MPL
Kahlo, Frida (1907-1954)	Artist	MPL
Lawrence, Jacob (1917-2000)	Artist	MPL
Remington, Frederick (1861-1909)	Artist	MPL
Sargent, John Singer (1861-1909)	Artist	MPL
Vanderbilt, Gloria (1924-)	Artist	MPL
Warhol, Andy (1928-1987)	Artist, Filmmaker	*Life*
Athletes and Sports Figures		
Aaron, Hank (1934-)	Baseball Player	MPL
Ashe, Arthur (1943-1993)	Tennis Player	MPL
Berra, Yogi (1925-)	Baseball Player	MPL
Gooden, Dwight (1964-)	Baseball Player	MPL
Gretzky, Wayne (1961-)	Hockey Player	MPL
Jeter, Derek (1964-)	Baseball Player	MPL
Johnson, Magic (1959-)	Basketball Player	MPL
Jordan, Michael (1963-)	Basketball Player	MPL
Joyner-Kersee, Jacqueline (1962-)	Track and Field Athlete	MPL
King, Billie Jean (1943-)	Tennis Player	MPL
Louis, Joe (1914-1981)	Boxer	*Life*
McGwire, Mark (1963-)	Baseball Player	MPL
Owens, Jesse (1913-1980)	Track and Field Athlete	MPL
Rozelle, Pete (1926-1996)	Football Commissioner	*Time*
Simpson, O. J. (1947-)	Football Player	MPL
Woods, Tiger (1975-)	Golf Player	MPL
Zaharias, Babe (1914-1956)	Athlete, Olympic Champion	MPL

Name and Dates	Field of Eminence	Sample
Business Leaders		
Arledge, Roone (1931-2002)	Television Producer, Executive	*Life*
Bechtel, Stephen (1900-1989)	Builder	*Time*
Bernays, Edward (1891-1995)	Public Relations Executive	*Life*
Burnett, Leo (1891-1971)	Advertising Executive	*Time*
DeLorean, John (1925-)	Automobile Executive	MPL
Gates, Bill (1955-)	Entrepreneur, founded Microsoft	*Time*, MPL
Giannini, A. P. (1870-1949)	Banker, founded Bank of America	*Life*, *Time*
Hall, Joyce C. (1891-1982)	Greeting Card Manufacturer	*Life*
Iacocca, Lee (1924-)	Automobile Executive	MPL
Kroc, Ray (1902-1984)	Restaurant Entrepreneur, McDonald's	Life, *Time*
Lauder, Estée (1910-1982)	Cosmetics Executive	*Time*, MPL
Levitt, William (1907-1994)	Builder, Levittown	*Time*
Loewy, Raymond (1893-1986)	Industrial Designer	*Life*
McCardell, Claire (1905-1958)	Fashion Designer	*Life*
Merrill, Charles E. (1885-1956)	Stock Broker	*Life*, *Time*
Morita, Akio (1921-1999)	Entrepreneur, founded Sony	*Time*
Sloan, Jr., Alfred P. (1875-1966)	Industrialist, Philanthropist	*Life*
Trippe, Juan (1899-1981)	Airline Entrepreneur, Pan Am	*Time*
Trump, Donald (1946-)	Real Estate Developer	MPL
Turner, Ted (1938-)	Media Entrepreneur	*Time*
Walker, Sarah "Madame C. J." (1876-1919)	Marketer of hair care products for African-American women	MPL
Walton, Sam (1918-1992)	Entrepreneur, founded Walmart	*Time*
Watson, Jr., Thomas J. (1914-1993)	Entrepreneur, founded IBM	*Life*, *Time*
Criminals, Spies, and Assassins		
Hiss, Alger (1904-1996)	State Dept. official convicted of spying	MPL
Luciano, Lucky (1897-1962)	Organized Crime Leader	*Time*
Oswald, Lee Harvey (1939-1963)	Assassin of John F. Kennedy	MPL
Diplomats		
Dulles, Allen (1893-1969)	Diplomat and Public Official	*Life*
Wallenberg, Raoul (1912-)	Swedish Diplomat, Holocaust Hero	MPL
Editors and Publishers		
de Graff, Robert (1895?-1981)	Publisher, founded Pocket Books	*Life*
Forbes, Malcolm (1919-1990)	Magazine Publisher	MPL
Graham, Katharine (1917-2001)	Publisher of *Washington Post*	MPL
Entertainers and TV Personalities		
Baker, Josephine (1906-1975)	Entertainer, Singer	MPL
Burns, George (1896-1996)	Comedian, Actor	MPL
Cosby, Bill (1937-)	Comedian, Actor	MPL
Gleason, Jackie (1916-1987)	Comedian, Actor	MPL
Hope, Bob (1903-2003)	Comedian, Actor	MPL
Marx, Groucho (1890-1977)	Comedian, Television Personality	MPL

Name and Dates	Field of Eminence	Sample
Winfrey, Oprah (1954-)	Television Personality	*Time*, MPL
Explorers and Adventurers		
Hillary, Edmund (1919-)	Mountain Climber	*Time*
Norgay, Tenzing (1914-1986)	Mountain Climber	*Time*
Filmmakers		
Allen, Woody (1935-)	Filmmaker, Actor, Comedian	MPL
Disney, Walt (1901-1966)	Film Animator, Producer	*Life*, *Time*, MPL
Ford, John (1894-1973)	Film Director	MPL
Griffith, D. W. (1875-1948)	Film Director, Writer, Actor	*Life*
Hitchcock, Alfred (1899-1980)	Filmmaker, Actor	MPL
Lee, Spike (1957-)	Filmmaker	MPL
Mayer, Louis B. (1885-1957)	Motion Picture Entrepreneur	*Life*
Spielberg, Steven (1946-)	Filmmaker	*Time*, MPL
Inventors		
Farnsworth, Philo (1906-1971)	Inventor, Television	*Time*, MPL
Land, Edwin (1909-1991)	Inventor, Polaroid Cameras	*Life*
Journalists		
Barber, Red (1908-1992)	Baseball Broadcaster	MPL
Buckley, William F. (1925-)	Journalist and Publisher	MPL
Murrow, Edward R. (1908-1965)	Television Journalist	MPL, *Life*
Paley, William (1901-1990)	Broadcaster, founded CBS	*Life*
Rather, Dan (1931-)	Television News Anchorman	MPL
Wells-Barnett, Ida Bell (1862-1931)	Journalist, Civil Rights Activist	MPL
Winchell, Walter (1897-1972)	Journalist	*Life*
Judges		
Marshall, Thurgood (1908-1993)	Supreme Court Justice, Activist	MPL
O'Connor, Sandra Day (1930-)	Supreme Court Justice	MPL
Musicians, Singers, Composers, and Dancers		
Balanchine, George (1901-1983)	Ballet Dancer, Choreographer	MPL, *Life*
Berlin, Irving (1888-1989)	Composer, Lyricist	MPL, *Life*
Bowie, David (1947-)	Rock Singer	MPL
Crosby, Bing (1901-1977)	Singer. Actor	MPL, *Life*
Davis, Miles (1926-1991)	Jazz Musician	MPL
Fitzgerald, Ella (1917-1996)	Singer	MPL
Franklin, Aretha (1941-)	Singer	*Time*, MPL
Hammerstein II, Oscar (1895-1960)	Lyricist	*Time*, MPL
Hendrix, Jimi (1942-1970)	Guitarist, Singer, Songwriter	MPL
Lennon, John (1940-1980)	Singer	*Time*, MPL
Presley, Elvis (1935-1977)	Singer, Actor	MPL, *Life*
Rodgers, Richard (1902-1979)	Composer	*Life*, *Time*, MPL
Springsteen, Bruce (1949-)	Singer, Songwriter, Guitarist	MPL

Name and Dates	Field of Eminence	Sample
Photographers		
Bourke-White, Margaret (1904-1971)	Commercial Photographer	MPL
Stieglitz, Alfred (1864-1946)	Photographer	MPL, *Life*
Physicians and Nurses		
Kolff, Willem (1911-)	Surgeon, Inventor	*Life*
Nightingale, Florence (1820-1910)	Founder of Modern Nursing	MPL
Spock, Benjamin (1903-1998)	Pediatrician, Author, Activist	MPL, *Life*
Pilots and Astronauts		
Rickenbacker, Eddie (1980-1973)	Pilot, Military Aviator	*Time*
Political and Military Leaders		
Bush, George W. (1946-)	President of the U.S.	MPL
Gorbachev, Mikhail (1931-)	Soviet Reformer, Political Leader	*Time*, MPL
Khomeini, Ayatullah (1902-1989)	Iranian Revolutionary, Political Leader	*Time*, MPL
Mandela, Nelson (1918-)	Activist, Political Leader	*Time*, MPL
Milk, Harvey (1930-1978)	Political Leader, Activist	*Time*, MPL
Moses, Robert (1888-1981)	Public Administrator, Planner	*Life*
Powell, Colin (1937-)	General, Secretary of State	MPL
Stryker, Roy (1893-1975)	Farm Security Advocate	*Life*
Thatcher, Margaret (1925-)	British Prime Minister	*Time*
Religious Leaders		
Dalai Lama, The (1935-)	Tibetan Spiritual Leader	*Time*
Graham, Billy (1918-)	Religious Leader	*Life*, *Time*, MPL
John Paul II, Pope (1920-)	Catholic Pope	*Time*, MPL
Merton, Thomas (1915-1968)	Theologian, Catholic Monk, Writer	MPL
Mother Teresa (1910-1997)	Religious Leader, Activist	*Time*, MPL
Scientists, Scholars, and Educators		
Baekeland, Leo (1863-1944)	Chemist, Inventor	*Time*
Bardeen, John (1908-1991)	Physicist	*Life*
Berners-Lee, Tim (1955-)	Invented World Wide Web	*Time*
Carothers, Wallace (1896-1937)	Chemist, Inventor	*Life*
Carrier, Willis (1876-1950)	Engineer, Inventor	*Life*, *Time*
Cousteau, Jacques (1919-1997)	Oceanographer	*Time*
Crick, Francis (1916-)	Biophysicist	*Time*
Feynman, Richard (1918-1988)	Physicist	MPL
Fossey, Diane (1932-1985)	Primatologist	MPL
Friedman, Milton (1912-)	Economist	*Life*
Gallup, George (1901-1981)	Survey Researcher	*Life*
Goddard, Robert (1882-1945)	Rocket Scientist	*Time*
Goedel, Kurt (1906-1978)	Mathematician	*Time*
Goodall, Jane (1934-)	Ethologist, lived with apes	MPL

Name and Dates	Field of Eminence	Sample
Hawking, Stephen (1942-)	Cosmologist	MPL
Hubble, Edwin (1889-1953)	Astronomer	*Time*, MPL
Hutchins, Robert (1899-1977)	University President	MPL, *Life*
Keynes, John M. (1883-1946)	Economist	*Time*, MPL
Kinsey, Alfred (1891-1956)	Sexuality Researcher	*Life*
Muir, John (1838-1914)	Naturalist	MPL
Mulholland, William (1855-1935)	Civil Engineer	*Life*
Pauling, Linus (1901-1994)	Chemist, Social Activist	*Time*
Piaget, Jean (1896-1980)	Psychologist, Philosopher	*Time*
Salk, Jonas (1944-1955)	Virologist, first polio vaccine	*Life*, *Time*
Sartre, Jean-Paul (1905-1980)	Philosopher, Writer	*Time*
Shockley, William (1910-1989)	Physicist, Inventor of Transistor	*Time*
Turing, Alan (1912-1954)	Mathematician, Computer Scientist	*Time*, MPL
von Braun, Wernher 1912-1977)	Rocket Engineer	*Life*
von Neumann, John (1903-1957)	Mathematician, Computer Scientist	*Life*
Watson, James D. (1928-)	Geneticist	*Life*, *Time*
Wittgenstein, Ludwig (1889-1951)	Philosopher	*Time*
Social Activists		
Friedan, Betty (1924-)	Feminist Author and Activist	MPL, *Life*
Hamer, Fannie Lou (1917-1977)	Civil Rights Activist	MPL
Mankiller, Wilma (1945-)	Cherokee Activist, Chief	MPL
Pankhurst, Emmeline (1857-1928)	Women's Suffrage Activist	*Time*
Parks, Rosa (1913-)	Civil Rights Activist	*Time*, MPL
Stanton, Elizabeth Cady (1815-1902)	Suffragist, Editor, Writer	MPL
Steinem, Gloria (1934-)	Feminist Activist	MPL
Tubman, Harriet (1829-1913)	Abolitionist, Spy, Nurse	MPL
Walesa, Lech (1943-)	Labor Leader, Activist, Political Leader	*Time*, MPL
Wilson, Bill ("Bill W.") (1895-1971)	Founded Alcoholics Anonymous	*Life*, *Time*
Wives, Family Members, and Socialites		
Clinton, Hillary (1947-)	Wife of former President Bill Clinton, U.S. Senator	MPL
Diana, Princess of Wales (1961-1997)	Wife of Prince of Wales	*Time*, MPL
Duke, Doris (1912-1993)	Tobacco Heiress, Philanthropist	MPL
King, Coretta Scott (1927-)	Wife of Martin Luther King	MPL
Mandela, Winnie (1934-)	Wife of Nelson Mandela	MPL
Reagan, Nancy (1923-)	Wife of Ronald Reagan	MPL
Writers, Poets, and Playwrights		
Asimov, Isaac (1920-1922)	Science Fiction Writer	MPL
Borges, Jorge Luis (1899-1986)	Poet, Writer	MPL
Carnegie, Dale (1888-1955)	Author, Public Speaker	*Life*
Christie, Agatha (1890-1976)	Mystery Writer	MPL
Fisher, Mary Francis (1908-1992)	Food Writer	MPL
Hammett, Dashiell (1894-1961)	Novelist, Script Writer	MPL
Herriot, James (1916-1995)	Writer, Veterinary Surgeon	MPL

Name and Dates	**Field of Eminence**	**Sample**
Hughes, Ted (1930-1998)	Poet	MPL
Hurston, Zora Neale (1903-1960)	Writer, Folklorist	MPL
Kerouac, Jack (1922-1969)	Poet, Novelist	MPL, *Life*
King, Stephen (1947-)	Novelist	MPL
Lewis, Clive (1898-1963)	Novelist	MPL
Lowell, Robert (1917-1977)	Poet	MPL
Miller, Arthur (1915-)	Playwright	MPL
Post, Emily (1873-1960)	Authority on Etiquette	*Life*
Potter, Helen (1866-1943)	Writer of Children's Books	MPL
Roth, Philip (1933-)	Novelist	MPL
Sakharov, Andrei (1921-1989)	Writer, Activist	*Time*
Tolkien, J. R. R. (1892-1973)	Writer	MPL
Updike, John (1932-)	Writer, Poet, Critic	MPL
Vonnegut, Kurt (1922-)	Novelist	MPL
Wiesel, Elie (1928-)	Writer, Holocaust Survivor	MPL
Wilder, Laura Ingalls (1867-1957)	Novelist	MPL

A gifted observer of earlier generations of eminent people remarked that "some are born great, some achieve greatness, and some have greatness thrust upon them."[17] Newspaper magnate Katharine Graham is among the last group. She would never have become publisher of the *Washington Post* had her husband not committed suicide after receiving ineffective psychiatric care. Her father had left the controlling interest in the company to her husband on the theory that no man should have to work for his wife. Katharine had been raised with all the advantages great wealth could buy and seemed to have inherited her father's talent for leadership, but she willingly accepted a traditional woman's role as mother and socialite. The tragedy of her husband's death made her a feminist in spite of herself, as well as a brilliant leader of the *Post* through the infamous Watergate break-in, subsequent Nixon impeachment, and the critical struggles with organized labor.

The popularity that propelled President George W. Bush to the head of our sample is, we think, in some part due to his actions following the events of September 11, 2001. Even one of his most admiring biographers notes that on September 10, he "was not on his way to a very successful presidency," largely because he "lacked a big organizing idea." The same admiring writer conceded that Bush has many faults: "He is impatient and quick to anger; sometimes glib, even dogmatic; often uncurious and as a result ill informed; more conventional in his thinking than a leader probably should be. But outweighing the faults are his virtues: decency, honesty, rectitude, courage, and tenacity."[18]

George W. won the presidency, thanks in part to his family name and a highly disputed electoral result, but also thanks to his charisma and interpersonal skills, his phenomenal ability to remember names, and his unwavering commitment to his own values and goals. He attended Yale University at the height of the anti-war and anti-establishment movements, yet remained loyal to the establishment, including membership in Skull and Bones, a fraternity for well-connected men. His disgust with the political climate at Yale was shared by another of our subjects, William F. Buckley, Jr., who remained adamant in his conservative Catholic values and achieved considerable fame with his first book denouncing the anti-religious climate at the university.

The major emotional crisis of George W.'s life was the death of his younger sister when he was seven. His parents were so involved with her needs, and suffering from their own grief that they neglected to let him know what was happening or to share their mourning with him.

George W. dealt with the stress of being the scion of two long-distinguished families with some difficulty. He ran with a popular crowd in school and valued the social life over the academic. After graduating, he lived a classic bachelor life, chasing women, recklessly driving a sports car, and drinking to excess, instead of seriously pursuing a career. His mother, often thought of as a woman of high standards, must have gritted her teeth more than once over the years. But his parents had the forbearance to allow him to live his own life. He says, "I can't exaggerate to you what wonderful parents George and Barbara Bush were. They were liberating people. There was never that oppressiveness you see with other parents, never the idea that their way was the only way. My dad went out of his way to make sure that I felt accepted by him."[19]

George W. was an indifferent student, doing enough to get by but seldom if ever excelling. In an interview, he said, "I was never a great intellectual. I like books and pick them up and read them for the fun of it. I think all of us [in the family] are basically in the same vein. We're not real serious, studious readers. We are readers for fun."[20] In school, he stated, "I wasn't exactly an Ivy League scholar. What I was good at was getting to know people."[21] It may have been these interpersonal skills that led George W. to become the first U.S. president with an MBA, as he parlayed business contacts into a major political advantage.

Biographies of businesspeople tend to be of leaders who have a particular flair for publicity or who are in a flashy field. These would include people like real estate tycoon Donald Trump, whose name is prominent in casinos and skyscrapers, and businessman Lee Iacocca, who mobilized labor and community forces to lobby the government to save Daimler-Chrysler from bankruptcy. Those whose field of business is especially glamorous include people such as Estée Lauder, perfume and cosmetics magnate, or fashion designer Claire McCardell, who invented the wrap-and-tie "popover" housedress, the strapless swimsuit, and popularized the leotard, epitomizing the simple "American look." McCardell wanted to go to New York to study fashion design after high school, but her protective father insisted she live and home and go to a local college with a standard curriculum. She majored in home economics so she could take sewing, but did poorly in her other classes. Finally, after two unhappy and unsuccessful college years, her mother prevailed on her father to let her go to the Parsons School of Design in New York City.

Less glamorous, but perhaps even more influential in business, are the eminent individuals who created the tract homes, fast-food restaurants, and shopping centers of suburban America. William Levitt's father, Abraham, quit school at ten years of age, but was an avid reader of philosophy and went back to law school at age twenty. He became a real estate lawyer and developer. William attended New York public schools but dropped out of New York University at the age of nineteen because he couldn't wait to start making money in his father's home building business. By age twenty-two, he was president of the company, in charge of everything but design, which was handled by his then seventeen-year-old brother. They built expensive homes during the Depression but made their fortune building Levittowns—low cost suburban tract housing—after World War II.

Fast-food magnate Ray Kroc was even more impatient with school, dropping out of high school after his sophomore year. He said, "My sophomore year in high school passed like a funeral. I began to feel about school the way I had felt earlier about the Boy Scouts. It was simply too slow for me. School was...full of aggravations and little progress."[22] He was a textbook example of a child with intensity and "overexcitabilities" in certain areas; books bored him—he craved action. These were the days before World War I, when a college or even high school degree was not a *sine qua non* for business success. Ray started a music business while still in high school, later lying about his age to volunteer as an ambulance driver in the war.

Ray's great passion was sales, and he made a respectable living selling food service equipment for many years, despite the traditionalism of the industry. His big opportunity came when he was fifty-two and he noticed that two McDonald brothers were ordering a great many of his milkshake machines. The McDonalds had invented the fast food restaurant, but they failed at franchising their idea. Kroc had the right business model—maintain rigid standards and allow the franchisees to keep enough of the revenue to make a good profit—at a time when most franchise operators were profiteering off their investors.

Business mogul Sam Walton, who was reputed to be the richest American before Bill Gates surpassed him, has a biography worthy of Horatio Alger. He was born in Kingfisher, Oklahoma, where his father was a mortgage broker. His father went broke during the Depression and moved his family back to his hometown in Missouri. Sam made "A's" in school, was an Eagle Scout, held part-time jobs in high school, and worked his way through the University of Missouri. He couldn't afford graduate school, but retail chains were recruiting managers, so he took a job with J.C. Penney and learned the retail business. His success in building the Wal-Mart chain came by working hard and intelligently, exemplified by his use of state-of-the-art computer data mining to manage inventory.

There was no major crisis in Walton's childhood, although his parents divorced when he was in college and he had a problem with the lease on a five-and-dime store he opened early in his career. His wife's father was more successful than his own and helped him start his career. In terms of creativity theory, he could be considered a "dedicated" individual who built on his talents without suffering the misfortunes characteristic of the "challenged" type.[23] Theirs are the lives many people would like to live, but few care to read about.

During the Internet boom, the "computer nerd who became a billionaire" emerged as the latest incarnation of the pull-yourself-up-by-your-bootstraps American dream. Bill Gates actually fits the stereotype pretty well. He was a shy, awkward young man who wrote his first computer program at the age of thirteen at a time when no one had a personal computer and very few young people were interested. His father was a prominent Seattle attorney, his mother active in charitable activities. He was another "overexcited" child frustrated with the slow pace of public school, but he did better when his parents transferred him out of public school to an elite private school where gifted students were the norm. He went to Harvard because his parents thought he should have an undergraduate experience, but he found the classes boring. He seldom attended class, cramming for exams at the last minute, and spent as much time as he could in the computer center or playing poker. In his junior year, he dropped out to start a software business.

Gates was a textbook example of an overexcited gifted youngster who "was an unusually energetic child, even as a baby" and who "was impatient with those not as quick as he was, teachers included."[24] His childhood friends said they always knew he was brighter than they were, especially in math, while his mother said that he pretty much did what he wanted since the age of eight. He was fortunate to have parents and teachers who put up with his demands and helped him get access to computer time.

Gates' phenomenal success was due to intelligence and hard work, a strong competitive spirit, and a sense for business as well as technology. There was a good deal of luck involved as well— Microsoft won the contract to develop an operating system for the IBM personal computer only because the owners of the CP/M operating system (Control Program for Microcomputers, popular in the 1980s) were poorly advised by their lawyers and refused to meet with IBM, a company that believed the profits were in hardware. A big part of success in business comes from being in the right place at the right time and knowing how to take advantage of it.

Eminent scientists and scholars are also likely to have been raised in supportive families and to have enjoyed a life without the serious misfortunes that often contribute so much to the drive and creativity of writers, artists, actors, and religious, political, and social activists.

Tim Berners-Lee, the inventor of the World Wide Web, was raised by supportive parents who were mathematicians and computer science pioneers. Programming, imaginary numbers, and abstract mathematics were ordinary dinner table conversation, and as a child, Tim built toy computers from cardboard boxes. While a student at Oxford University in 1976, he built a real one with leftover parts, a soldering iron, and an old television set.

Physicist Richard Feynman's father, Melville, started teaching him to think scientifically when he was still in his high chair. He used a collection of colored bathroom tiles, encouraging Richard to set them up in patterns, such as two whites and a blue, two whites and a blue, and so on. When the two took walks in the woods, Melville encouraged Richard to make observations about what the birds were doing, instead of just memorizing their names. In school, Richard was always ahead of the class in science and math, finding a role as the star of his high school's team in the Interscholastic Algebra League. Although Richard had to work odd jobs to help with the family's finances during the Depression, there were no major crises in his father's career or in his family.

Economist Milton Friedman lived above his parents' store on Main Street in Rahway, New Jersey, a small town twenty miles from New York. His immigrant parents had to scrape to get by, often depending on post-dated checks to pay their bills. Milton went to the local public elementary school where he did so well that, in the middle of the sixth grade, the teachers transferred him to the seventh grade in another school, completing two years in one. Unlike many creative people who were unhappy in school, Friedman says his high school years were "pleasant and rewarding but mostly uneventful."

Unlike writers, religious leaders, musicians, or artists who may draw on events from their personal lives in their creative work, scientific, scholarly, athletic, and business careers require intense concentration on matters that are abstract or impersonal. For them, personal tragedies or conflicts may simply be distractions rather than grist for the creative mill. This is not to say that tragedies do not occur in the lives of budding scientists. Chemist Linus Pauling's father died when he was nine, oceanographer Jacque Cousteau's before he was two. As a child, physicist Stephen Hawking was "eccentric and awkward, skinny and puny" and was teased for a speech impediment in grade school (which may have contributed to his ability to professionally ignore his disability from ALS— Amyotrophic Lateral Sclerosis, better known as Lou Gehrig's disease—as an adult).[25]

Though personal tragedies do not stimulate creativity for scientists, nevertheless the attitudes and habits of mind that they develop in coping with personal problems may shape their ways of working and thinking. Linus Pauling took control of his own life after his father died because his mother was preoccupied by illnesses and family problems. He pursued doctoral studies in chemistry against the wishes of his mother, who thought an undergraduate degree was plenty for a young man whose wages were needed to support the family. The self-confidence he developed by making his own successful decisions against the advice of his family stuck with him throughout his life. Following his path-breaking work extending quantum theory to the chemical bond, his tremendous self-confidence allowed him to take on the military establishment in the crusade against nuclear testing that won him his second Nobel Prize and, again, at the age of sixty-five, to take on the medical community in a controversial crusade to show that vitamin C was the cure for cancer and the common cold.

Mathematician Kurt Gödel had rheumatic fever when he was eight and believed for the rest of his life that his heart had been damaged, although the physicians assured him it had not been. He suffered from hypochondria all his life, which developed into serious paranoia in old age. Kurt's biographer believed that his paranoia was the "culmination of a lifelong quest for a consistent world view" that began with childhood efforts to find order in a chaotic world.[26] His life centered around the belief that the universe was rational and orderly and that it could be understood through introspection. Tragically, his powers of logic were so powerful they inexorably led him to disprove his own fundamental principle; thus, his greatest accomplishment was to prove that all systems of logic must be incomplete.

Tragedy has played an important part in the lives of other individuals in our sample, sometimes leading them into their field of eminence, and sometimes providing the emotional fodder upon which their careers developed. Catholic monk Thomas Merton's mother died when he was five, his father when he was fifteen, and his younger brother when he was twenty-eight. His father was an artist who spent long months in different parts of the world, leaving him and his brother with a number of different relatives, godparents, and friends. His best-known work, *The Seven Storey Mountain*, is a spiritual autobiography chronicling his quest for what he called "beingness," or a sense of serenity and purpose in existence itself. He observed that "anything I create is only a symbol for some completely interior preoccupation of my own."[27] It is possible this interior quest became a preoccupation because he was unable to rely upon the permanence of his family.

Social activist and Catholic nun Mother Teresa's life reflected a similar interior quest, though she left her family voluntarily. Her father was killed in an apparent poisoning by political opponents when she was eight. But the young Agnes Bojaxhiu was well-loved by her mother, who was an example of charity and faith in their community, even though her father's business partners left the family with little after his death. Agnes first heard her call from God on a pilgrimage to a healing shrine, and though she rarely spoke of her childhood, her brother recalled, "[Our mother] sometimes said that we would not have long to enjoy Agnes' company, for two reasons: either because of her frail health, or because she would give herself to God."[28]

In the case of actress Barbra Streisand, the abuse she suffered as a child was what seemed to give her the determination to pursue acting as a career. Her father died when she was a year old, and her mother had to move in with her parents who were in ill health. Barbra's mother and grandparents were too exhausted and depressed to give her the affection she needed, but when she was five, she found warmth from a neighbor family who had a television. She "adored the flickery images dancing from that tiny set through the magnifying screen, loved the laughter and the emotion...." To a little girl who felt ugly and unwanted, "a few hours of respite were not enough."[29] From that day on, she knew she just had to become an actress.

She pursued that goal despite a stepfather who told her she was too ugly to deserve fifteen cents for the ice-cream truck and a mother who persistently tried to talk her out of acting because she, too, thought that Barbra was not pretty enough. The kids in grade school teased her for her large nose and her wandering left eye. Although she graduated from high school at sixteen with a 91 average, she could not be persuaded to go to college. Instead, she worked as a secretary and kept going to auditions and workshops until she got some acting and singing roles; in time, her career took off, much to everyone's surprise.

Difficult childhood experiences figure into the lives of many actors and artists. Actress Bette Davis' parents divorced when she was seven, but her mother was devoted to Bette's career and encouraged her to study acting. Actress Audrey Hepburn got stuck in the Netherlands during the Nazi occupation when her parents separated, but her wealthy and aristocratic family was able to indulge her in her career. Grace Kelly's mother was an athlete and a photographer's model and her father a construction entrepreneur; Grace was frail and unathletic in comparison to her siblings but managed to succeed. Actor Bruce Lee and his parents moved from San Francisco to their native Hong Kong just before the Japanese began the occupation in 1941. By 1946, he had appeared in twenty films and learned kung fu from his involvement in youth gangs in the treacherous city.

As a child, Mexican artist Frida Kahlo suffered first from polio and then from a terrible Mexico City trolley car accident that left her disabled and in terrible pain for life. Painting was one activity that she could engage in while bedridden for months at a time. It is impossible to say whether her artistic creativity might have taken a different direction without the suffering caused by these accidents.

Pain and suffering are not necessary for an eminent artistic career, though unusual family behaviors and patterns are fairly frequent in well-known artists. American painter Georgia O'Keeffe claimed to be one of the few people she knew who had no complaints about their childhood. She grew up on a farm in Wisconsin with a beautiful view of a red barn and six hundred acres of alfalfa looking out from her bedroom window. Despite her lack of complaints, she was "a homely, uningratiating child" and remembers being locked in a back room when company came because her mother "judged her too ugly to be seen by visitors."[30] Kahlo's father was a photographer who was quite devoted to his daughter, while O'Keeffe, the second of seven children, was largely left alone to find her own diversions. Both of these women artist's careers benefited from a romantic involvement with an older man who served as mentor—Mexican artist Diego Rivera in Kahlo's case, and American photographer Alfred Steiglitz in O'Keeffe's.

Guitarist Jimi Hendrix's mother was an alcoholic who would show up for a few days, then disappear for weeks or months at a time, finally dying of cirrhosis when he was fifteen. Actor Cary Grant's mother never recovered from the death of his older brother and was committed to a mental health sanitarium when Cary was ten. When he was fourteen, Cary forged his alcoholic father's signature on a permission form to join a troop of acrobats.

The forging of parental signatures or dissembling about birth dates appeared in the biographies of several eminent individuals, including Walt Disney, who, like the aforementioned Ray Kroc, lied about his age to get into the ambulance corps during World War I. Walt Disney's childhood was marked by the many places he lived as his father tried multiple careers to support the family. From the Missouri small town that closely resembled Disneyland's Main Street, U.S.A. to the factories of Kansas City, Walt learned to rely on his own hard work and ingenuity. As one biographer noted, "The precariousness of the family's livelihood undoubtedly shaped his own desire not merely to succeed but to do so in a particular way—namely, to avoid surrendering any part of his autonomy to outsiders and to hold his company's stock and its decision-making power as closely as he could."[31]

Sports figures are no different from other eminent people in their response to hardship. Like most sports superstars, golfer Tiger Woods was naturally gifted and excelled at a very early age. He suffered some harassment because of his mixed racial background, but nothing comparable to the experiences of Jackie Robinson or other minority athletes of previous generations. With an ancestry containing a mixture of African-American, Chinese, Thai, Native American, and Caucasian elements, Woods calls himself the 'United Nations,' reflecting, "I don't want to be the best black golfer ever, I want to be the best golfer ever."[32]

Outstanding success in athletics requires a single-minded devotion to practice, practice, practice. It usually requires an adult, in Tiger Woods' case, both parents, who coaches, takes care of travel and other practical problems, and devotes him- or herself to developing the young person's talent. Baseball player Derek Jeter's parents were equally devoted. When five-year-old Derek predicted he would be a shortstop for the Yankees, everyone except his parents told him to be more realistic. Derek recalls that they were just as emphatic about academics: "They treated parent-teacher meetings like sessions with the Internal Revenue Service, bringing evidence to support their opinions. They made me present oral reports to them the day before I was scheduled to read them in class.... They were relentless about their involvement in their children's lives and in what we dreamed of doing with ourselves."[33]

Famous for her success in many sports, Mildred "Babe" Zaharias had the same apparently wild childhood dreams, predicting that she would become the greatest athlete who ever lived. While the achievement of this goal may be disputed, the Associated Press elected her Woman Athlete of the Year six times and in 1950 named her Woman Athlete of the Half Century.

Basketball player Michael Jordan was cut from his high school basketball team, and as one coach recalled, "Michael never thought he was as good as he could be. Even now. I don't think he's ever had the attitude that, 'I don't need to work.' One thing he has always done is work extremely hard, whether it's at practices, in games or in the off-season. I think that is what has separated him from others who have a lot of talent."[34]

As a child, power hitter Mark McGwire was nicknamed "Tree" for his tall, stocky, redheaded resemblance to the redwoods that grew near his California hometown. Though he has extremely poor eyesight, Mark played baseball, golf, and football with his four brothers and their neighborhood friends, who delighted in playing practical jokes on the easily scared boy. His father, who had become athletic despite having polio as a child, was concerned about the negative influence that Little League coaches and meddling parents might have on the youngster and so kept him out of the league until Mark's talent became clear.

Physical handicaps can be as much an impetus toward athletic achievement as they can be a disability. Track and field star Jesse Owens was a sickly, thin boy, so frail he was unable to help his siblings and father in the cotton fields. However, when the family moved to Cleveland, Ohio, Jesse found time between his odd jobs to race his friends through the alleys and schoolyards, where a local coach discovered him. The rest is history. And the speech impediment that embarrassed boxer Joe Louis and landed him in a vocational school ended up encouraging him to develop a career where his level of education would not be an issue.

Conclusions

Most of the young people in our sample had exceptional talents or abilities that could have qualified them for programs for the gifted and talented, especially since today these programs often use multiple intelligence models that incorporate musical, artistic, interpersonal, spatial, and psychomotor abilities, as well as exceptional abilities in verbal and mathematical skills. But there are millions of people with similar abilities. Our subjects had something more, something that enabled them to stand out from the crowd, something that made them famous. It is risky to use our subjects as models precisely because they are exceptional. The percentage of aspiring actresses who become stars must be very small. The percentage of high school dropouts who become business tycoons may be even smaller. Even with hindsight, it is hard to fault Barbra Streisand's mother for thinking her daughter should keep other career options in mind, or Ray Kroc's parents for thinking he should finish high school. One can sympathize with Claire McCardell's father for thinking she should get a few years of college under her belt before striking on her own to study fashion design, or with Derek Jeter's parents for insisting that he should pursue a college degree along with a career in professional baseball. Certainly talented young people deserve a shot at fame and stardom, if that is what they want, but they should probably also have an alternate plan, that is, a "Plan B" in the event that their first plan doesn't work out. There is a risk, however, that having an alternative plan in mind may lessen their single-minded dedication to their primary goal.

Sometimes becoming famous is a matter of chance, of being in the right place at the right time (or the wrong place at the wrong time). If the Nazis had not occupied Poland and systematically exterminated Polish intellectuals, Karol Wojtyla might have stuck with his first career as an actor and might never have found the religious vocation that led to his later becoming Pope John Paul II. Presidential assassin Lee Harvey Oswald achieved infamy by getting off a few lucky shots with a cheap rifle (or, if you believe the conspiracy theorists, by being the fall guy for others more devious than he). Had the McDonald brothers not ordered their milk shake machines from Ray Kroc, he might have finished his working life as a restaurant equipment salesman. If Hillary Rodham had fallen in love with someone other than Bill Clinton, she might have been a successful lawyer and children's advocate, but probably would not have had a book reach the top of the bestseller list. Even in science, fame is sometimes due to the luck of being the first one to make an important discovery. If Linus Pauling had not been denied a passport to travel to London because of his politics, he would have seen X-Ray diffraction photographs that probably would have enabled him to discover the correct structure of the DNA molecule before Francis Crick and James Watson

So luck is important, but luck favors those who are well prepared and persistent, and these are useful traits even if one has no desire to appear on the biography shelves. If there is one trait that all of our subjects had in common, it is persistence in pursuing their own vision and goals. They followed their own inner voice and did what they wanted to do, or what they felt they had to do, regardless of what others were doing or what various authority figures told them. Psychologists call this trait having an "internal locus of control."[1] Poets may call it marching to the beat of a different drummer. Others may call it a strong streak of independent thought, of not caring if they are "different." Whatever we call it, it is this extra ingredient, vision-persistence, combined with talent, hard work, and luck (in that order), that leads to fame and fortune.

There are many examples, both in the original sample and in the update. Oprah Winfrey pursued her television career in defiance of fellow students who called her a sell-out. George W. Bush turned his back on the radical student culture at Yale and remained true to his own traditional values. Nelson Mandela defied a chief who promised him all the benefits a young black man of his generation in South Africa could reasonably hope for in order to pursue his revolutionary ideals. Woody Allen and Barbra Streisand doggedly pursued theatrical careers against the advice of family and experts in the field.

This is not to say that all of the subjects were rebels or that rebellion was an end in itself. Many of our subjects had no need to defy parents or teachers because these key figures supported their ambitions. Most successful young athletes, like Tiger Woods, had parents who devoted endless hours to coaching them, taking them to games and tournaments, and otherwise facilitating their lives. Bill Gates' parents switched him to a more progressive private school when he found public school too constraining. Sam Walton's father was delighted to see his son succeed in retailing. Richard Feynman's father could not have been more pleased with his son's scientific interest.

What parents and teachers can learn from this research study of eminent people is that it is important to encourage and support children to pursue their own interests, even if the likelihood of success may seem slim. This is not to say that parents of gifted children should not set limits, assign household chores, or encourage children to do reasonable homework. Barbra Streisand got excellent grades in her academic subjects in high school, even though she had no real interest in anything but her acting. Walt Disney's many hours of hard work on the family farms and in part-time jobs did not destroy his creativity. But parents and teachers should be aware that, in addition to the chores and structured activities, creative children need time and space to do their own thing. Sometimes they get this because their parents encourage it and plan for it, and sometimes the parents are just busy and leave them alone.

How do highly creative people develop the single-minded, persistent dedication to a cause or career that can lead to outstanding accomplishment? Psychologist Abraham Maslow argued that there is a hierarchy of needs and that people must satisfy their safety, physical, and emotional needs before turning to their creative or "self-actualizing" needs. According to this popular theory, creative people should be those whose physical and emotional needs have been met or satisfied. Maslow tested this theory by examining biographical information about a number of the world's most prominent achievers. He found that some of them fit the theory, including Abraham Lincoln, Thomas Jefferson, Albert Einstein, Eleanor Roosevelt, Jane Addams, William James, and Baruch Spinoza. But many more did not, including Walt Whitman, Henry Thoreau, Ludwig van Beethoven, Franklin D. Roosevelt, Sigmund Freud, George Washington Carver, Eugene Debs, Albert Schweitzer, Thomas Eakins, Fritz Kreisler, and Johann Goethe.[2]

This is quite an impressive list of people. If they do not fit Maslow's theory, then the problem is with his theory, not with their accomplishments. They might have been happier had their lives followed his theory, but there is no reason to believe that they would have accomplished more. Based on our own studies as well as Maslow's, we must strongly reject the hypothesis that self-actualization and creative accomplishment come only after other needs have been met. A great many highly creative people have unresolved emotional problems, and some of them suffer economic, health, or safety problems.

It may be that creative achievement can also be a way of expressing unhappiness or frustration in other areas of one's life—or a way of trying to resolve difficulties in an area of one's life. Certainly, this is true of those writers who write poetry, fiction, and non-fiction, which is semi-autobiographical. Painters often put their feelings and emotions on canvas. Likewise composers.

Intense emotional agony led Thomas Merton to the religious inspiration that he shared so movingly in his writing. Frida Kahlo was in physical pain most of her life after her trolley accident, and she struggled with social isolation as an invalid, yet she painted magnificently through it all. Elizabeth Cady Stanton never succeeded in replacing her brother in her father's eyes, but she did succeed in changing the world for women by helping them win the right to vote. Oprah Winfrey's sensitivity to the suffering of many of the guests on her television shows is rooted in having lived through similar experiences herself. Her television career took off while she was still working on her own personal problems, not after they had all been resolved.

Creative people need something beyond talent and encouragement to drive them to achieve. They need something to transform a hobby or casual interest into a consuming, passionate calling. The ancient Greeks called this a muse; Carl Jung called it an archetypal passion. Jane Piirto calls it simply a thorn in the side. In some cases, this may simply be getting "hooked" on solving a difficult problem. One sees this in the lives of scientists who become entranced with the challenge of solving puzzles, or in the lives of athletes who feel driven to win against competitors. But in some cases, especially in the lives of writers, artists, performers, and spiritual leaders, it is rooted in frustration or anger about misfortune or mistreatment.

If a child lacks this thorn in the side, this drive to triumph in some field, what should parents do? Probably count their blessings. There is no evidence that famous people are happier than people who take a more balanced approach to life. Nor do they necessarily contribute more to society. Our subjects include Adolph Hitler and Lee Harvey Oswald as well as Nelson Mandela and Mother Teresa. But if the desire and the drive are there, gifted children may need help in channeling their frustrations, disappointments, and even personal tragedies into creative and constructive outlets. No one should deliberately make a child suffer on the theory that their resulting pain may produce great art or science or leadership. But life brings disappointment and misfortune to everyone, and children do need help in making the best of it.

Barbara Bush expressed one regret—that she did not help her son George mourn for his sister's death. She said, "you have to remember that children grieve…he felt cheated."[3] Today, thankfully, most children do not have to deal with the death of a sibling or a parent. But lesser tragedies also loom large in the life of a child. Perhaps the best advice comes from Jane Piirto, who says, "If hardship comes into your life, use it positively to teach the child expression through metaphor."[4] Encourage the child to write, paint, listen to or compose music, spend time in reflection, walk in nature—to express feelings in whatever way seems to work.

What can we learn from our subjects about how schools can help bright, gifted, sensitive, and creative children? In our sample, the people who got most from the schools were those—like Nelson Mandela, Ida B. Wells, Thurgood Marshall, and Oprah Winfrey—whose parents simply did not have the educational background or resources to supply what their children needed themselves. For many of our subjects, schooling was something they had to get out of the way so they could work on what was really important for them. Many found school boring and tedious because the pace was too slow or because it took too much time away from other things they wanted to do.

More flexibility from the schools would help bright, talented children. Teachers who are sensitive to the learning and motivation needs of these bright students might negotiate with the child to do a "different" or "unusual" independent project, still giving some guidelines and timelines. Teachers and principals might allow a student to progress to an advanced math class, if math is the area of talent and interest. Thus, a second grader might actually work at a fourth- or fifth-grade level in his or her area of talent.

Advanced classes for the gifted may help, especially for those interested in mathematics and the sciences, where a great deal of formal knowledge must be assimilated. A few hours of enrichment per week is not enough. Bright children are bright all day every day, not just once or twice a week. Bill Gates had plenty of opportunities to work with computers in addition to his regular schooling, but he needed a more challenging environment all day long to hold his interest. Even at Harvard, he did not find the classroom situation stimulating. Fortunately, he went into a field—computer science—where demands for formal credentials were not yet a barrier to youthful talent. Oprah Winfrey benefited greatly from being bussed to a suburban school where the academic work was more challenging. In college, she also benefited from giving her own interests higher priority than the formal curriculum and from going into a field where academic credentials counted for little.

The people who achieved fame and fortune in the 1990s were in many ways similar to those who did so in the 1960s and before. For example, a great many came from families where there was a love of learning in their childhood homes, many disliked school, and a substantial number compensated for physical, environmental, or family handicaps.[5]

But in other ways, the more recently recognized eminent persons were different from their predecessors. Those whose lives will fill the biographies of the future will differ as well. Just as the statistical findings cannot be applied to individuals, neither will today's young people follow the exact paths taken by the subjects in this book. Today's society offers many more options for the education of gifted children: home schooling, charter schools, specialized high schools, alternative private schools, and so on. If young people delay going to college immediately after high school to pursue some other interest such as travel, an internship, or volunteer work, college will be available for them later on.

The freedom to follow paths that are non-traditional is important if one is to learn to be independent in thought and action. Parents and educators can perhaps help best by encouraging young people to explore their options and make the most of available resources as they follow their own muse wherever it leads them.

End Notes

End Notes: Introduction

1 J. Cox, N. Daniel, and B. O. Boston, *Educating Able Learners: Programs and Promising Practices* (Austin: University of Texas Press, 1985).

2 U.S. Department of Education, *National Excellence: A Case for Developing America's Talent* (Washington, D.C. USGPO, PIP 93-1201, 1993).

3 S. P. Marland, *Education of the Gifted and Talented, Volume 1. Report to the Congress of the United States by the U.S. Commissioner of Education.* (U.S. Commission on Education, 92nd Congress, 2nd Session. Washington, D.C. USGPO, 1972).

4 Council for Exceptional Children, *Educating Exceptional Children: A Statistical Profile* (ED-99-CO-0026. U.S. Department of Education, OERI, 1999).

5 U.S. Department of Education, *Op. cit.*

6 Council for Exceptional Children, *Op. cit.*

7 Karen B. Rogers, *Re-Forming Gifted Education: How Parents and Teachers Can Match the Program to the Child* (Scottsdale, Ariz.: Great Potential Press, 2002).

8 G. Betts and J. Kercher, *Autonomous Learner Model: Optimizing Ability* (Greeley, Colo.: Alps Publishing, 2000).

9 Lisa Rivero, *Creative Home Schooling for Gifted Children: A Resource Guide* (Scottsdale, Ariz.: Great Potential Press, 2002).

End Notes: Foreword for the Second Edition

1 Gene Currivan, "Learning Found the Key to Fame," *The New York Times* (April 21, 1961).

2 Terry Ferrer, "'Madness' Rare Mark of Genius," *New York Herald Tribune* (April 21, 1961).

3 Mildred G. and Victor Goertzel, "400 Famous People and How Their Childhood Affected Them," *McCall's* (April 1961): 84.

4 www.family.org/docstudy/solid/a0006697.html

5 www.family.org/welcome/bios/A0022947.cfm

6 www.2.sd43.bc.ca/gifted/MarNewsletter.pdf

7 http://suzyred.com/1note.html

8 www.eucom.mil/Directorates/ECCH/index.htm?, www.eucom.mil/Dictorates/ECCH/padre0402.htm&2

End Notes: Chapter 1

1 John F. Fulton, *Harvey Cushing, a Biography* (Oxford: Blackwell, 1947).

2 Anne Roe, *The Making of a Scientist* (New York: Dodd, Mead, 1953).

3 *One Hundred Gifted Children* (Lawrence, Kans.: Kansas University Publications, 1930).

4 *The Gifted Student* (New York: Harcourt, Brace, 1955).

5 *America's Resources of Specialized Talent* (New York: Harper, 1954).

6 Kari Flesch, *Memoirs* (London: Rockliff, 1957), 7.

7 *Dance to the Piper* (Boston: Little, Brown, 1951), 25.

8 Jose Maria Corredor, *Conversations with Casals* (London: Hutchinson, 1956) 21-22.

9 *Ibid.*, 40.

10 *Ibid.*, 46.

11 Brian Connell, *Knight Errant: A Biography of Douglas Fairbanks, Jr.* (London: Hodder & Stoughton, 1955).

12 *Ibid.*

13 César Saerchinger, *Artur Schnabel, a Biography* (London: Cassell, 1957).

14 Hesketh Pearson, *Gilbert: His Life and Strife* (London: Methuen 1957).

15 John Cowper Powys, *Autobiography* (London: Lane, 1934).

16 William Beveridge, *India Called Them* (London: Allen, 1947).

17 David C. McClelland et al., *Talent and Society* (Princeton, N.J.: Van Nostrand, 1958).

End Notes: Chapter 2

1 Jane Addams, *Twenty Years at Hull House, with Autobiographical Notes* (New York: Macmillan, 1910), 15.

2 *Days of Our Years* (New York: Hillman-Gurl, 1939), 5-6.

3 *The Autobiography of William Allen White* (New York: Macmillan, 1946).

4 Barnet Litvinoff, *Ben Gurion of Israel* (London: Vallentine Mitchell, 1960).

5 Patricia Strauss, *Cripps, Advocate Extraordinary* (New York: Duell, 1942), 27, 30.

6 Lawrence Hanson, *Noble Savage* (London; Chatto & Windus, 1954).

7 Families in which one or both parents were agnostic had the following eminent children: Konrad Bercovici, Bernard Berenson, William Beveridge, Lazaro Cardenas, George Washington Carver, Salvador Dalí, Clarence Darrow, Eugene Debs, Isadora Duncan, Thomas Alva Edison, Albert Einstein, Havelock Ellis, Ford Madox Ford, Anatole France, Paul Gauguin, Fiorello La Guardia, Charles Lindbergh, H. L. Mencken, Benito Mussolini, Sergei Prokofiev, Diego Rivera, Romain Rolland, Bertrand Russell, Margaret Sanger, George Santayana, George Bernard Shaw, Sigrid Undset, William Allen White, Alexander Woollcott, and Hans Zinsser.

8 Ministers' sons and daughters noted among the Four Hundred included: Phyllis Bottome, Pearl Buck, Grover Cleveland, Stephen Crane, Reginald Fessenden, Charles Evans Hughes, Henry and William James, Martin Luther King, C. Day Lewis, Field Marshal Montgomery, Reinhold Neibuhr, Martin Niemoller, Freidrich Nietzsche, William Osier, John Cowper Powys, Cecil Rhodes, William Saroyan, Olive Schreiner, Albert Schweitzer, Woodrow Wilson, and Orville and Wilbur Wright. Sean O'Casey was the son of a paid Protestant executive. Lloyd George was reared by a minister uncle. Grenfell's father left teaching to go into missionary work in a hospital. The fathers of Clarence Darrow, Cecil de Mille, and Frank Lloyd Wright left the ministry or other occupations.

9 *Who's Who in America* (Chicago: A. N. Marquis, 1921).

10 Sister Cabrini; the Roman Catholic fathers John LaFarge and Dominiqi Pire; and Rufus Jones, John R. Mott, Reinhold Neibuhr, and Martin Niemoller.

11 Robert H. Knapp and H. B. Goodrich, *Origins of American Scientists* (Middletown, Conn.: Wesleyan University Press, 1952).

12 *The Making of a Scientist* (New York: Dodd, Mead, 1953).

End Notes: Chapter 3

1 Harold H. Anderson, ed., *Creativity and Its Cultivation* (London: Hamish Hamilton, 1959).

2 *Arrow in the Blue, an Autobiography* (New York: Macmillan, 1952), 18.

3 *Land Without Justice* (New York: Harcourt, Brace, 1958), 23.

4 Sylvia Sprigge, *Berenson: A Biography* (London: Allen & Unwin, 1960).

5 D. Horton, "The Function of Alcohol in Primitive Societies: A Cross-Cultural Study." *Quarterly Journal for the Study of Alcoholism* 4 (1943):199.

6 Hesketh Pearson, *G. B. S.: A Full Length Portrait* (New York: Harper, 1942), 6.

7 Maurice Chevalier, *With Love* (London: Cassell, 1960).

8 The eminent men and women in our study whose fathers were alcoholic were: Fred Allen, Sherwood Anderson, Louis Armstrong, Ethel Barrymore, John Barrymore, Lionel Barrymore, Enrico Caruso, Charlie Chaplin, Maurice Chevalier, Irvin S. Cobb, Kahlil Gibran, Kenneth Grahame, A. E. Housman, Laurence Housman, James Joyce, Gertrude Lawrence, Stephen Leacock, G. E. Rasputin, Eleanor Roosevelt, George Bernard Shaw, Joseph Stalin, Joseph Broz Tito, Thomas Wolfe, and Alexander Woollcott.

9 Eleanor Roosevelt, *This Is My Story* (New York: Harper,1937). 21.

End Notes: Chapter 4

1 Robert Magidoff, *Yehudi Menuhin: The Story of the Man and the Musician* (London: Robert Hale, 1956).

2 James Roosevelt and Sidney Shalett, *Affectionately, F.D.R.: A Son's Story of a Lonely Man* (London: Harrap, 1960).

3 John Gunther, *Roosevelt in Retrospect, a Profile in History* (London: Hamish Hamilton, 1950).

4 Roosevelt and Shalett, *op. cit.*

5 Gunther, *op. cit.*

6 Roosevelt and Shalett, *op. cit.*

7 Siao-Yu, *Mao Tse-Tung and I Were Beggars* (Syracuse, N.Y.: Syracuse University Press, 1959), 216.

End Notes: Chapter 5

1 *Sex and Personality* (New York: McGraw-Hill, 1936).

2 Anthony R. E. Rhodes, *D'Annunzio, the Poet as Superman* (New York: McDowell, 1959).

3 Tommaso Antongini, *D'Annunzio* (London: Heinemann, 1938), 484, 486.

4 Christine Gamier, *Salazar, an Intimate Portrait* (New York: Farrar, 1954).

5 Alfred Nobel, who left his fortune to promote world peace, was also an excessively mother-smothered boy who hated his father intensely for no apparent reason. Both father and son were manufacturers and inventors of munitions. Nobel wrote a long poem justifying parricide. He was never able to introduce his mistress to his mother. When his mistress bore a child, he paid another man to marry her.

6 *Maternal Overprotection* (New York: Columbia University Press, 1945).

7 *Old Men Forget: The Autobiography of Duff Cooper* (London: Hart-Davis, 1953), 29.

8 Lawrence and Elizabeth Hanson, *The Tragic Life of Toulouse-Lautrec* (London: Seeker & Warburg, 1956).

9 Syngman Rhee, *the Man Behind the Myth* (New York: Dodd, Mead, 1954), 15.

10 Textbooks describing gifted children often speak of their tendency to create fantasy worlds and have imaginary playmates. Leo and Gertrude Stein had a secret world and a secret language. Vera Brittain and her brother Edward invented a community called "The Dicks." From the ages of six to eleven, Vera kept the story alive, and the characters involved were very real to both the teller and the listener. Betty MacDonald, American humorist, kept alive for "years and years" the exciting tale of Nancy and Plum, who escaped from an orphanage, were kidnapped by bank robbers, captured by gypsies, and who finally adopted a baby who turned out to be a prince. She used these characters in published material. The Tolstoy children had a secret world initiated by the oldest brother Stephen, which involved pretending to be Moravian brothers who were creating a perfect world. In this imaginary world, no man could have any misfortune. Quarreling was taboo among the "brothers." They huddled together under chairs, hid themselves under cloth tents, and cuddled in the dark, practicing "love one another." Interestingly, Leo always thought they were being "ant-brothers," because the Russian words for "Moravian" and "ant" are similar. Sheila Kaye-Smithe, who had a rich fantasy life, imagined lengthy novels long before she wrote one. She was an only child and had an imaginary playmate who never washed or went to bed and wore dresses made of gold or flower petals.

11 Boris Souvarine, *Stalin* (London: Seeker & Warburg, 1939).

12 Blanche E. C. Dugdale, *Arthur James Balfour, First Earl of Balfour* (London: Hutchinson, 1936).

13 John Berryman, *Stephen Crane* (London: Methuen, 1951).

14 *Mrs. Eddy, the Biography of a Virginal Mind* (New York: Scribner's, 1929).

End Notes: Chapter 6

1 *New York Times* (May 12, 1961).

2 Samuel C. Webster, ed., *Mark Twain Business Man* (Boston: Little, Brown, 1946), 43, 44.

3 *Ibid.*, 40.

4 John DeLancey Ferguson, *Mark Twain: Man and Legend* (Indianapolis: Bobbs-Merrill, 1943).

5 Writers who came from broken homes were: Ilka Chase, Hart Crane, William Gilbert, Lafcadio Hearn, Edna St. Vincent Millay, "Ouida," Maria Rilke, George Santayana, Alexander Woollcott, and Richard Wright.

Actors whose parents were divorced or separated were: Maude Adams, Ethel Barrymore, John Barrymore, and Lionel Barrymore, Charlie Chaplin, Maurice Chevalier, Douglas Fairbanks, Jr., and Douglas Fairbanks, Sr. The dancers Agnes de Mille, Isadora Duncan, and Nijinsky came from broken homes.

Among musicians and those who sought artistic expression, those from broken homes were: Louis Armstrong, Maria Callas, Eisenstein, Arshile Gorki, Bill Mauldin, Prokofiev, Rachmaninoff, Toulouse-Lautrec, and Frank Lloyd Wright.

Jackie Robinson, athlete, came from a broken home.

Politicians and scientists are the least likely to have parents who live apart. The thirty-two homes which are broken by divorce or separation are very few when compared with the one in four divorced homes of the 1960s. In the time in which these families lived, to be divorced was to risk social ostracism. In the homes of the Four Hundred, there was more constant quarreling and estrangement than separation or divorce. It was the unconventional homes that tended to produce the children who chose unconventional occupations.

6 Homes which produced the Four Hundred were checked for constantly quarreling, rejecting, dominating, and overpossessive parents; for anxiety about money; for the death of one or both parents; for physically handicapped children; for broken homes; and for parents who were dissatisfied with the child's school progress or choice of profession. On this basis, the percentage of troubled homes in descending order is as follows: Actors, 100%; Authoritarian Politicians, 95%; Novelists and Playwrights, 89%; Composers and Musicians, 86%; Military Leaders, 86%; Poets, 83%; Artists, 70%; Explorers, Adventurers, and Athletes, 67%; Humanitarians and Reformers, 62%; Singers, 62%; Psychologists, Philosophers, and Religious Leaders, 61%;

Non-Fiction Writers and Educators, 59%; Non-Authoritarian Politicians, 56%; Lawyers, Doctors, and Scientists, 53%; Financiers, 25%; Inventors, 20%. (There are too few financiers and inventors among the Four Hundred to make these percentages reliable.)

End Notes: Chapter 7

1 Alpheus T. Mason, *Brandeis: A Free Man's Life* (New York: Viking, 1946), 28.

2 Kenneth E. Anderson, ed., *Research on the Academically Talented Student* (Washington, D.C.: National Education Association, 1961), 47.

3 *The Autobiography of William Carlos Williams* (New York: Random House, 1951), 11, 12.

4 Helen B. Clapesattle, *The Doctors Mayo* (Minneapolis: University of Minnesota Press, 1941), 180.

End Notes: Chapter 8

1 Sean O'Casey, *Mirror in My House* (London: Macmillan, 1956).

2 Rudyard Kipling, *Something of Myself* (London: Macmillan, 1937).

3 Jonathan Daniels, *The Man of Independence* (Philadelphia; Lippincott, 1950).

4 Arthur William Mann, *La Guardia* (Philadelphia: Lippincott, 1959), 28.

5 Arthur Koestler, *Arrow in the Blue: An Autobiography* (London: Collins & Hamish Hamilton, 1952).

6 Francis O. Matthiessen, *The James Family* (New York: Knopf, 1947), 116.

7 Diana Cooper, *The Rainbow Comes and Goes* (London: Hart-Davis, 1958).

8 There are forty-three children among the Four Hundred who described themselves or are described as having been rejected by one or both parents.

9 Samuel Foster Damon, *Amy Lowell: A Chronicle* (Boston: Houghton Mifflin, 1935), 92.

10 Carleton Putnam, *Theodore Roosevelt, Vol. I: The Formative Years* (New York: Scribner's, 1958).

11 *Theodore Roosevelt: An Autobiography* (New York: Macmillan, 1913).

12 Corinne Roosevelt Robinson, *My Brother, Theodore Roosevelt* (New York: Scribner's, 1921).

13 *Edwin Arlington Robinson* (New York: Macmillan, 1938), 10.

14 Mildred R. Bennett, *World of Willa Cather* (New York: Dodd, Mead, 1951).

15 John Alfred Atkins, *George Orwell* (London: Calder, 1954).

End Notes: Chapter 9

1 The living children in these families did not seem to understand that it is customary to not speak ill of the dead. They were sincerely convinced that the child they replaced was actually never thought troublesome or naughty or stupid.

2 Leonardo da Vinci is only one of the famous illegitimate children.

3 *The Owl of Minerva: The Autobiography of Gustav Regler* (London: Hart-Davis, 1959).

End Notes: Chapter 10

1 Amiya Chakravarty, ed., *A Tagore Reader* (New York: Macmillan, 1961).

2 Henry T. Fink, *Grieg and His Music* (London: John Lane, 1929), 8.

3 *The Bicycle Rider in Beverly Hills* (New York: Scribner's, 1952), 36.

4 Stanley J. Kunitz and Howard Haycraft, eds., *Twentieth Century Authors* (New York: Wilson, 1942), 1432.

5 Matthew Josephson, *Edison: A Biography* (New York: McGraw-Hill, 1959), 20.

6 Antonina Vallentin, *The Drama of Albert Einstein* (New York: Doubleday, 1954), 34.

7 Paul A. Schlipp, ed., *Albert Einstein: Philosopher-Scientist* (New York: Tudor, 1951), 17.

8 Martha Marquardt, *Paul Ehrlich* (New York: Schuman, 1951).

9 *And They Shall Walk: The Life Story of Sister Elizabeth Kenny* (New York: Dodd, Mead, 1943), 14.

10 Victor I. Seroff, with Nadejda Galli-Shohat, *Dmitri Shostakovich* (New York: Knopf, 1943).

11 Rene Kraus, *Young Lady Randolph* (New York: Putnam, 1943), 352.

12 *My Early Years* (London: Odhams, 1930).

13 Frank Harris, *Contemporary Portraits, Third Series* (New York: Frank Harris, 1920), 92.

14 Eli Ginsberg, ed., *The Nation's Children*, published for the Golden Anniversary of the White House Conference (New York: Columbia University Press, 1960).

End Notes: Chapter 11

1 Donald W. MacKinnon, "Genvs Architectvs Creator Varietas Americanvs," *Journal of the American Institute of Architects* (Sept. 1960).

2 E. Paul Torrance, *Status of Knowledge Concerning Education and Creative Scientific Talent* (Salt Lake City: University of Utah Press, 1961).

3 "Family Environment and Cognitive Style: A Study of the Sources of Highly Intelligent and Creative Adolescents," *American Sociological Review* 26 (1961): 3.

4 Lewis M. Terman and Melita H. Oden, *The Gifted Group at Midlife* (Stanford University, Calif.: Stanford University Press; Oxford: Oxford University Press, 1959).

End Notes: Chapter 12

1 Mildred, Victor, and Ted Goertzel, *Three Hundred Eminent Personalities* (San Francisco: Jossey-Bass, 1978). Ted Goertzel, *Turncoats and True Believers* (Buffalo: Prometheus, 1992).

2 Dean Keith Simonton, "Significant Samples: The Psychological Study of Eminent Individuals," *Psychological Methods* (1999): 425-452. Dean Keith Simonton, *Genius Creativity and Leadership: Historiometric Inquiries* (Cambridge: Harvard University Press, 1984).

3 Jane Piirto, *Understanding Those Who Create,* 2nd. ed. (Scottsdale, Ariz.: Great Potential Press, 1998).

4 Arnold Ludwig, *The Price of Greatness* (New York: Guilford Press, 1995).

5 Abraham Maslow, *Motivation and Personality* (Harper and Brothers, 1954), 203.

6 Clive James, *Fame in the Twentieth Century* (New York: Random House, 1993).

7 *Great People of the Twentieth Century* (New York: Time Books, 1996).

8 James, *Op. cit.*

9 Arnold Ludwig, *The Price of Greatness* (New York: Guilford Press, 1995), 25-26.

10 Dean Keith Simonton, "President's Wives and First Ladies: On Achieving Eminence with a Traditional Gender Role," *Sex Roles* 35 (1996): 309-336.

11 Paula Olszewski-Kubilius, "The Transition from Childhood Giftedness to Adult Creative Productiveness," *Roeper Review* 23 (December 2000): 65-72. William Therivel, "Why Mozart and Not Salieri," *Creativity Research Journal* 12 (1999): 67-76.

12 See Sharon Lind, "Overexcitability and the Gifted," on the Supporting Emotional Needs of the Gifted website at: www.sengifted.org/lind.htm.

13 James T. Webb, "Mis-Diagnosis and Dual Diagnosis of Gifted Children: Gifted and LD, ADHD, OCD, Oppositional Defiant Disorder," on the Supporting Emotional Needs of the Gifted website at: www.sengifted.org/mis_diag.htm. Jane Piirto, *Understanding Those Who Create* (Scottsdale, Ariz.: Great Potential Press, 1998). This book discusses the origins of the concept of overexcitability and has questionnaires for measuring it.

14 Eric Lax, *Woody Allen: A Biography* (Da Cappo Press, 1991), 77.

15 *Linus Pauling: A Life in Science and Politics* (New York: Basic Books, 1995). Their biography of chemist Linus Pauling was completed by Ted Goertzel and Ben Goertzel. The children's version was rewritten by Florence White, but Mildred and Victor removed their names from it because they thought that her version was too adulatory. Florence White, *Linus Pauling: Scientist and Crusader* (Walker, 1980).

16 "100 Most Important People of the Twentieth Century," *Life* 13, no. 12 (fall 1990). *Great People of the Twentieth Century* (New York: Time, Inc, 1996); posted at: www.time.com/time/time100. We included only those with a full page in the Time book, not those on a "Gallery" page. The lists in the Time book and on the Time.com website are not identical.

17 William Shakespeare, *Twelfth Night*, Act II, Section 5, Line 159.

18 David Frum, *The Right Man: The Surprise Presidency of George W. Bush* (New York: Random House, 2003), 272, 274.

19 *Ibid.*

20 George H. W. Bush, with Doug Wead, *George Bush: Man of Integrity* (Eugene, Ore.: Harvest House, 1988), 132.

21 Skip Hollandsworth, "Born to Run," *Texas Monthly* 22, no. 5 (May 1994): 94.

22 Ray Kroc, *Grinding It Out: The Making of McDonald's* (Chicago: Regnery, 1977), 17.

23 Therivel, *Op. cit.*, 70.

24 James Wallace and Jim Erickson, *Hard Drive: Bill Gates and the Making of the Microsoft Empire* (New York: Wiley, 1992), 10, 38.

25 Michael White and John Gribbin, *Stephen Hawking: A Life in Science* (New York: Dutton, 1992), 9.

26 John Dawson, *Logical Dilemmas: The Life and Work of Kurt Gödel* (Wellesley, Mass: A. K. Peters, 1997).

27 Thomas Merton, "Perry Street Journal" (unpublished), quoted in William Shannon, *Silent Lamp: The Thomas Merton Story* (New York: Crossroad, 1992).

28 Rafael Tilton, *Mother Teresa* (San Diego, Calif.: Lucent Books, 2000), 15.

29 James Spada, *Streisand: Her Life* (New York: Crown, 1992), 18.

30 Benita Eisler, *O'Keeffe and Steiglitz: An American Romance* (New York: Doubleday, 1991), 15.

31 Richard Schickel, *The Disney Version: The Life, Times, Art and Commerce of Walt Disney* (New York: Simon & Schuster, 1968), 49.

32 Allison L. Teague, *Prince of the Fairway: The Tiger Woods Story* (Greensboro, N.C.: Avisson Press, 1997), 36.

33 Derek Jeter, *The Life You Imagine: Life Lessons for Achieving Your Dreams* (New York: Crown Publishers, 2000), 5.

34 James Beckett, ed., *The Definitive Word on Michael Jordan* (Dallas, Tex.: Beckett Publications, 1998), 57.

End Notes: Conclusion

1 The "self-actualizing" concept is from Maslow, *Op. cit.* The other concepts are developed by Theresa Amabile, *The Social Psychology of Creativity* (New York: Springer-Verlag, 1983); and *Growing Up Creative* (New York: Crown, 1989). This is summarized well in Jane Piirto, *Understanding Those Who Create*, 2nd ed. (Scottsdale, Ariz.: Great Potential Press, 1998).

2 Maslow, *Op. cit.*, 202-203.

3 Quoted in Hollandsworth, *Op. cit.*

4 Piirto, *Op. cit.*, 376.

5 Victor and Mildred G. Goertzel, Cradles of Eminence: A Provocative Study of the Childhoods of Over 400 Famous Twentieth Century Men and Women (Boston: Little, Brown and Company, 1962).

Appendix A
Bibliography and Biographical Notes—1962 *Cradles of Eminence* Sample

This section identifies the subjects included in the 1962 survey and gives some biographical information about each one. It lists some of the books used as source material to serve as a guide to readers interested in further information about particular men or women. When a book speaks strongly to a given point or in our opinion has unusual merit, it is starred.

Illustrative materials were selected in order to present families that reared children who became eminent in various occupations: writers, artists, scientists, military leaders, and so forth. The method of selection of subjects (biographies in the public library) resulted in an overwhelming number of writers being included but very few scientists, financiers, or inventors. Consequently, though very interesting, some of the writers' families could not be described. A family that is not described in detail is not necessarily less eminent or less interesting than are other families treated at length. The book could be rewritten several times with different but equally powerful examples.

The number of books listed does not reflect the number of books published about a person or his or her importance in the eyes of the authors. We attempted to include as many books as necessary to describe the significant childhood influences in the life of each subject. Sometimes one book does this adequately; sometimes several are required. In every case, the person qualified for inclusion in this survey by having at least one biographical book for foreign-born and two for American-born subjects.

The notes in parentheses are intended to indicate to which section of our discussion the individual would probably have been assigned had it been possible to use an anecdote from each person's life.

The following information is given for each subject: field of eminence, b = birthplace, f = father's occupation, m = mother's occupation. The subject's educational level is coded: c+ = education beyond college, c = graduated from college, c- = some college, s = secondary school, g = grade school, M = military training, S = special training (e.g., art or music). A "+" or "–" immediately following some of these designations for a subject's educational level means that the individual either had some educational experiences beyond that level or that the level was not completed, respectively. Asterisks, as noted above, suggest unusual merit or a notable issue.

Adams, Brooks, historian, b Quincy, Mass., f historian, c+.

Anderson, Thornton. *Brooks Adams, Constructive Conservative.* Cornell University Press, 1951. (thought dull by his family)

Beringause, Arthur F. *Brooks Adams: A Biography.* Knopf, 1955.

Adams, Henry, historian, b Boston, f historian, c+.

*Adams, Henry. *The Education of Henry Adams.* Constable, 1935. (a classic on school rejection)

Stevenson, Elizabeth. *Henry Adams: A Biography.* New York: Macmillan, 1955.

Adams, Maude, actress, b Salt Lake City, f businessman, m actress, g (was child actress).

Robbins, Phyllis. *Maude Adams: An Intimate Portrait.* Chapman, 1956.

———. *Young Maude Adams.* Jones, Marshall, 1959.

Addams, Jane, Nobel Peace Prize winner, founder of Hull House, b Cedarville, Ill., f wealthy mill owner, c.

Addams, Jane. *Twenty Years at Hull House with Autobiographical Notes.* New York: Macmillan, 1916. (opinionated family)

Linn, J. W. *Jane Addams: A Biography.* Appleton-Century, 1935.

Adenauer, Konrad, statesman, b Cologne, f civil servant, c.
Weymar, Paul. *Adenauer: His Authorized Biography*. André Deutsch, 1957.

Adler, Alfred, psychiatrist, b Vienna (reared in small town), f grain merchant, c+.
Bottome, Phyllis. *Alfred Adler: A Biography*. Faber, 1957. (excellent study in sibling rivalry)

Aleichem, Sholem (Rabinowitz), writer, b Pereyaslev, Russia, f kept general store, ran inn, s.
*Aleichem, Sholem. *The Great Fair: Scenes from My Childhood.* Vision Press, 1958. (sensitive study of failure-prone father)

Allen, Fred, actor, b Cambridge, Mass., f bookbinder, s.
Allen, Fred. *Much Ado about Me*. Little, Brown, 1956.
———. *Treadmill to Oblivion*. Little, Brown, 1954. (an impoverished home)

Allenby, Edmund, military leader, b Suffolk, England, f inherited wealth, M.
Wavell, Sir Archibald. *Allenby: A Study in Greatness*. Oxford, 1941. (thought dull)

Anderson, Marian, singer, b Philadelphia, f worked in refrigerator room, sold coal and ice, m housemaid, s & S.
Anderson, Marian. *My Lord, What a Morning*. Viking, 1956.
Vehanen, Kosti. *Marian Anderson: A Portrait*. McGraw-Hill, 1941.

Anderson, Sherwood, poet, novelist, story writer, b Camden, Ohio, f harness maker, odd jobs, m washerwoman, c.
Howe, Irving. *Sherwood Anderson*. Methuen, 1952.
Schevill, James. *Sherwood Anderson: His Life and his Work*. University of Denver Press, 1951.

Angell, Norman, author, lecturer, b Holbeach, England, f department store owner, s.
*Angell, Norman. *After All: The Autobiography of Norman Angell.* Hamish Hamilton, 1951.

Anthony, Susan B., woman suffrage advocate, b Adams, Mass., f textile mill owner; after reverses, innkeeper, c.
Anthony, Katherine Susan. *Susan B. Anthony: Her Personal History and her Era*. Doubleday, 1954.

Dorr, Rheta L. *Susan B. Anthony: The Woman who Changed the Mind of a Nation*. Stokes, 1928. (opinionated family)

Lutz, Alma. *Susan B. Anthony: Rebel, Crusader, Humanitarian*. Beacon, 1959.

Armstrong, Louis, jazz musician, b New Orleans, f laborer, g.

Armstrong, Louis. *Satchmo: My Life in New Orleans*. Peter Davies, 1955.

Baton, Jeanette. *Trumpeter's Tale: The Story of Louis Armstrong*. Morrow, 1955.

McCarthy, Albert J. *Louis Armstrong*. Cassell, 1960.

Atherton, Gertrude, novelist, b San Francisco, f wealthy businessman, grandfather secretary of Bank of America, s-.

Atherton, Gertrude. *Adventures of a Novelist*. Liveright, 1932.

———. *My San Francisco: A Wayward Autobiography*. Bobbs-Merrill, 1946. (rejected, precocious girl)

Attlee, Clement, labor leader, politician, b Putney, London, f wealthy solicitor, c.

Attlee, Clement. *As It Happened*. Heinemann, 1954. (liked school)

Clemens, Cyril. *The Man from Limehouse: Clement Richard Attlee*. J. P. Didier, 1946.

Austin, Mary, novelist, b Carlinville, Ill., f lawyer (died young), m nurse (as widow), c.

*Austin, Mary. *Earth Horizon: Autobiography*. Literary Guild, 1932. (precocious child, rejecting mother)

Doyle, Helen. *Mary Austin, Woman of Genius*. Gotham House, 1939.

Baden-Powell, Robert Stephenson, military leader, founder of Boy Scouts, b Paddington, London, f mathematics professor, writer, lecturer, m artist, clubwoman, s & M.

Baden-Powell, Robert. *Lessons from the Varsity of Life*. Pearson, 1934.

Reynolds, Ernest E. *Baden-Powell: A Biography*. Oxford, 1942. (study in extension of parental interests)

Baldwin, Stanley, politician, b Bewdley, England, f industrialist, c.

Baldwin, Arthur Windham. *My Father: The True Story*. Allen & Unwin, 1955. (strong school rejection)

Young, George M. *Stanley Baldwin*. Hart-Davis, 1952.

Balfour, Arthur J., philosopher, politician, b Whittingehame, East Lothian, Scotland, f inherited income, c.
Dugdale, Blanche E. G. *Arthur James Balfow, First Earl of Balfow.* Hutchinson, 1936.

Barkley, Alben W., politician, b Graves County, Ky., f sharecropper, c.
Barkley, Alben W. *That Reminds Me.* Doubleday, 1954. (exceptionally supportive home)
Barkley, Jane Hadley. *I Married the Veep.* Vanguard, 1958.

Barrie, James Matthew, novelist, dramatist, b Kirriemuir, Scotland, f weaver, c+.
Barrie, James Matthew. *Margaret Ogilvy, by her Son.* Scribner's, 1896. (intruder complex)
Mackail, Denis George. *Barrie: The Story of J.M.B.* Peter Davies, 1941.

Barrymore, Ethel, actress, b Philadelphia, f actor, m actress, s.
Barrymore, Ethel. *Memories: An Autobiography.* Hulton, 1956. (neglected girl)

Barrymore, John, actor, b Philadelphia, f actor, m actress, s-.
Barrymore, John. *Confessions of an Actor.* Bobbs-Merrill, 1926.
Fowler, Gene, *Good-Night, Sweet Prince.* H. Hammond, 1949.

Barrymore, Lionel, actor, b Philadelphia, f actor, m actress, s-.
Barrymore, Lionel. *We Barrymores.* Appleton-Century-Crofts, 1951.

Bartok, Bela, composer, pianist, b Nagyszentmiklos, Hungary, f director of agricultural school, pianist, cellist, m teacher, s & S.
*Fassett, Agatha. *The Naked Face of Genius.* Houghton Mifflin, 1958.
Stevens, Halsey. *The Life and Music of Beta Bartok.* Oxford, 1953.

Barton, Clara, founder American Red Cross, b North Oxford, Mass., f farmer, soldier, c-.
Barton, William Eleazer. *Life of Clara Barton.* Houghton Mifflin, 1922.
Ross, Ishbel. *Angel of the Battlefield.* Harper, 1956.
Williams, Blanche C. *Clara Barton, Daughter of Destiny.* Lippincott, 1941.

Baruch, Bernard M., businessman, statesman, b Camden, S.C., f physician, agricultural expert, c.

*Baruch, Bernard M. *Baruch, My Own Story*. Holt, 1957. (supportive, learning-centered home)

Coit, Margaret Louise. *Mr. Baruch*. Houghton Mifflin, 1957.

Beecham, Thomas, conductor, impresario, b St. Helens, England, f wealthy manufacturer, c & S.

Beecham, Thomas. *A Mingled Chime: An Autobiography*. Hutchinson, 1944.

Reid, Charles. *Thomas Beecham*. Dutton, 1962,

Behan, Brendan F., writer, b Dublin, Ireland, f housepainter, s-.

Behan, Brendan. *Borstal Boy*. Hutchinson, 1958. (revolutionary-opinionated family)

Behan, Dominic. *Tell Dublin I Miss Her*. Putnam, 1962.

Behave, Vinobe, reformer, b Baroda, India, f textile merchant, c.

Tennyson, Hallam. *Saint on the March*. Gollancz, 1955.

Bell, Alexander Graham, inventor, b Edinburgh, Scotland, f speech teacher, s.

Costain, Thomas Bertram. *The Cord of Steel*. Doubleday, 1960.

Mackenzie, Catherine D. *Alexander Graham Bell, the Man who Contracted Space*. Houghton Mifflin, 1928.

Bell, Gertrude, traveler, administrator, b Washington Hall, Co. Durham, f inherited wealth, c.

Bell, Gertrude. *The Letters of Gertrude Bell*. Benn, 1927.

Kamm, Josephine. *Gertrude Bell: Daughter of the Desert*. Bodley Head, 1956. (talented girl encouraged by stepmother)

Belloc, Hilaire, author, b La Celle, St. Cloud, France, f barrister, c.

Lowndes, Marie A. *The Young Hilaire Belloc*. Kenedy, 1956. (product of international, intercultural marriage)

Speaight, Robert. *The Life of Hilaire Belloc*. Hollis & Carter, 1957.

Bellows, George, artist, b Columbus, Ohio, f architect, builder, c.

Boswell, Peyton. *George Bellows*. Crown, 1942. (supportive, middle-class home)

Eggers, George William. *George Bellows*. Whitney Museum of American Art, 1931.

Ben Gurion, David (Green), politician, b Polnsk, Poland, f lawyer, c-.

Litvinoff, Barnet. *Ben Gurion of Israel*. Vallentine Mitchell, 1960.

St. John, Robert. *Ben Gurion: The Biography of an Extraordinary Man*. Doubleday, 1959.

Bennett, Arnold, novelist and dramatist, b Hanley, Staffordshire, England, f pawnbroker, lawyer, m draper's assistant, s.

Allen, Walter Ernest. *Arnold Bennett*. Arthur Barker, 1950. (highly opinionated, intellectually striving father)

Pound, Reginald. *Arnold Bennett: A Biography*. Heinemann, 1952.

Bercovici, Konrad, novelist, short-story writer, b Braila, Rumania, f cattle breeder, trader, s-.

Bercovici, Konrad. *It's the Gypsy in Me*. Prentice-Hall, 1941. (opinionated, multilingual family)

Berenson, Bernard, art critic, author, b Butremans, Lithuania, f peddler, c.

Berenson, Bernard. *Rumour and Reflection*. Constable, 1952.

Sprigge, Sylvia. *Berenson: A Biography*. Allen & Unwin, 1960.

Bernadotte, Count Folke, diplomat, b Stockholm, f inherited wealth, M.

Bernadotte, Count Folke. *Instead of Arms: Autobiographical Notes*. Bonniers, 1948.

Hewins, Ralph. *Count Folke Bernadotte: His Life and Work*. Denison, 1950. (sternly fundamentalist upbringing)

Bernhardt, Sarah, actress, b Paris, f law student, S.

Bernhardt, Sarah. *Memories of My Life*. Appleton, 1907.

Berton, Mme. Therese. *The Real Sarah Bernhardt, Whom her Audiences Never Knew*. Boni & Liveright, 1924.

Vemeuil, Louis. *The Fabulous Life of Sarah Bernhardt*. Harper, 1942.

Besant, Annie, theosophist, political leader, b London, f unsuccessful businessman, privately educated.

Nethercot, Arthur Hobart. *The First Five Lives of Annie Besant*. University of Chicago, 1960. (story of a girl reared by a wealthy spinster with ideas about teaching gifted children)

Williams, Gertrude L. *The Passionate Pilgrim*. Coward-McCann, 1931. (failure-prone, intellectual father; ineffectual mother)

Bevan, Aneurin, politician, b Tredegar, Monmouthshire, f coal miner, g-.

Brome, Vincent. *Aneurin Bevan*. Longmans, Green, 1953.

Bevan, Aneurin. *In Place of Fear*. Heinemann, 1952. (stammering son of widow)

Beveridge, William, social reformer, b Rangpur, India, f British administrator in India, c+.
Beveridge, William. *India Called Them.* Allen & Unwin, 1947.

Bevin, Ernest, labor leader, b Winsford, Somerset, England, f agricultural laborer, g.
Evans, Trevor. *Bevin.* Allen & Unwin, 1946.
Williams, Francis. *Ernest Bevin: Portrait of a Great Englishman.* Hutchinson, 1952.

Black, Hugo L., politician, jurist, b Harlan, Ala., f farmer and general storekeeper, c+.
Frank, John Paul. *Mr. Justice Black: The Man and his Opinions.* Knopf, 1949. (strong dominating mother, supportive home)
Williams, Charlotte. *Hugo L. Black: A Study in the Judicial Process.* Oxford: Johns Hopkins, 1950.

Bok, Edward, editor, b Den Holder, Holland, f translator, g.
Bok, Edward. *The Americanization of Edward Bok.* Scribner's, 1924. (school rebel, aided by father, wins battle over penmanship)
*———. *Twice Thirty: Some Short and Simple Annals of the Road.* Scribner's, 1925.

Bottome, Phyllis, novelist, short-story writer, b Rochester, Kent, England, f minister, privately educated.
*Bottome, Phyllis. *The Challenge.* Faber, 1952. (a divided family)
*———. *Search for a Soul.* Faber, 1947. (excellent study in sibling rivalry)

Brandeis, Louis D., jurist, b Louisville, Ky., f businessman, c+.
Mason, Alpheus Thomas. *Brandeis: A Free Man's Life.* Viking, 1946.
*———. *The Brandeis Way.* Oxford: Princeton University Press, 1938.

Briscoe, Robert, politician, b Dublin, f owner of furniture business, c.
Briscoe, Robert, and Alden Hatch. *For the Life of Me.* Longmans, 1958.

Brittain, Vera, journalist, lecturer, b Newcastle-Under-Lyme, Staffordshire, England, f wealthy pottery manufacturer, c-.
*Brittain, Vera. *Testament of Youth: An Autobiographical Study of the Years 1900-1925.* Gollancz, 1933. (interesting description of lack of sex education)

*———. *Testament of Experience: An Autobiographical Story of the Years 1925-1950*. Gollancz, 1957.

Bromfield, Louis, writer, b Mansfield, Ohio, f poor dirt farmer, c-.
*Bromfield, Louis. *From My Experience*. Harper, 1955.
*———. *Pleasant Valley*. Harper, 1945.
Brown, Morrison. *Louis Bromfield and his Books*. Cassell, 1956.

Brooke, Rupert, poet, b Rugby, England, f schoolmaster, c.
Stringer, Arthur J. A. *Red Wine of Youth*. Bobbs-Merrill, 1948. (sickly boy with extremely dominating mother)

Brooks, Van Wyck, essayist, critic, translator, b Plainfield, N.J., f Wall St. broker, c.
*Brooks, Van Wyck. *From the Shadow of the Mountain*. Dutton, 1961.
*———. *Days of the Phoenix: The Nineteen-Twenties I Remember*. Dent, 1957. (details mental illness)
———. *Scenes and Portraits: Memories of Childhood and Youth*. Dent, 1954.

Buck, Pearl, novelist, b Hillsboro, W.Va., f missionary, c+.
*Buck, Pearl. *The Exile*. Methuen, 1938. (account of a mother who tutored her own children)
*———. *Fighting Angel: Portrait of a Soul*. Methuen, 1939. (account of a rejecting father with strong drives for achievement)
*———. *My Several Worlds*. Methuen, 1955.

Burbank, Luther, horticulturist, b Lancaster Township, Mass., f farmer (friend of Agassiz), s.
Beeson, Emma B. (sister). *Early Life and Letters of Luther Burbank*. Wagner, 1927. (a study in evasion, omits relevant details)
Burbank, Luther, and Wilbur Hall. *The Harvest of the Years*. Houghton Mifflin, 1927.
Howard, W. L. *Luther Burbank*. Ronald, 1946. (effect of dominating mother on marriages of son)
Williams, Henry Smith. *Luther Burbank: His Life and Work*. Hearst, 1915.

Byrd, Richard E., polar explorer, b Winchester, Va., f editor of *Winchester Star*, s & M.
Byrd, Richard E. *Alone*. Putnam, 1938.
———. *Skyward*. Putnam, 1928.
Steinberg, Alfred. *Admiral Richard E. Byrd*. Putnam, 1960.

Cabrini, Sister Frances Xavier, social worker, b St. Angelo, Lombardy, Italy, f prosperous farmer, older sister spinster school teacher, g.

Borden, Lucille. *Francesca Cabrini: Without Staff or Scrip*. Macmillan, 1945.

Mayard, Theodore. *Too Small a World*. Bruce, 1945. (sister-dominated, sickly girl is tireless adult)

Callas, Maria, singer, b New York City, f chemist, g & S.

Callas, Evangelia. *My Daughter Maria Callas*. Fleet, 1960. (mother describes her rejection of daughter)

Jellinek, George. *Callas: Portrait of a Prima Donna*. Ziff-Davis, 1960.

Cantor, Eddie, comedian, b New York City, f unsuccessful violinist, grandmother ran illegal employment agency for immigrant girls, g-.

* Cantor, Eddie. *My Life Is in Your Hands*. Harper, 1928. (the bitter story of a disadvantaged childhood)

———. *Take My Life*. Doubleday, 1957. (an unusual grandmother, tireless and imaginative)

———. *The Way I See It*. Prentice-Hall, 1959.

Cárdenas, Lázaro, soldier, politician, b Jiquilpan, Mexico, f weaver, proprietor of pool hall, g.

Townsend, William C. *Lazaro Cardenas, Mexican Democrat*. Wahr, 1952.

Weyl, Nathaniel. *The Reconquest of Mexico*. Oxford, 1939.

Cardozo, Benjamin N., jurist, b New York City, f jurist, lawyer after forced resignation, c+.

Hellman, George Sidney. *Benjamin N. Cardozo, American Judge*. McGraw-Hill, 1940.

Pollard, Joseph Percival. *Mr. Justice Cardozo: A Liberal Mind in Action*. Yorktown, 1935. (son spends lifetime "making up" for father's failure)

Carnegie, Andrew, industrialist and philanthropist, b Dunfermline, Scotland, f unemployed weaver, m kept grocery store, g-.

Alderson, Bernard. *Andrew Carnegie, the Man and his Work*. Doubleday, Page, 1902.

Carnegie, Andrew. *Autobiography*. Houghton Mifflin, 1920.

Hendrick, Burton J., and Henderson D. MacIntyre. *Louise Whitfield Carnegie: The Life of Mrs. Andrew Carnegie*. Hastings House, 1951. (effect of dominating mother)

Caruso, Enrico, operatic tenor, b Naples, Italy, f skilled mechanic, S.
Caruso, Dorothy. *Enrico Caruso: His Life and Death.* Werner Laurie, 1946. (one of the three living children of twenty-one)
Ybarra, Thomas R. *Caruso: The Man of Naples and the Voice of Gold.* Cresset Press, 1954. (a rejecting father, helped by stepmother)

Carver, George Washington, botanist, b near Diamond Grove, Mo., f slave, foster f prosperous farmer, c+.
Holt, Rackham. *George Washington Carver.* Phoenix House, 1947.
Means, Florence C. *Carver's George.* Houghton Mifflin, 1952.

Casals, Pablo, cellist, composer, conductor, b Vendrell, Spain, f village organist, g & S.
*Corredor, J. M. *Conversations with Casals.* Hutchinson, 1956.
Littlehales, Lillian. *Pablo Casals.* Dent, 1949.

Casella, Alfredo, pianist, composer, b Turin, Italy, f music teacher, m private income, tutored & S.
Casella, Alfredo. *Music in My Time.* University of Oklahoma, 1955. (mother was his only teacher until he went to conservatory)

Cather, Willa, novelist, b Winchester, Va., f real estate, loans, c.
*Bennett, Mildred R. *World of Willa Cather.* Dodd, 1951. (detailed account of Willa as "William" Cather)
Brown, Edward K. *Willa Cather: A Critical Biography.* Knopf, 1953.
Lewis, Edith. *Willa Cather Living: A Personal Record.* Knopf, 1953.

Cecil, Edgar, politician, b Stamford, Lincolnshire, England, f inherited wealth, c.
Cecil, Edgar. *A Great Experiment, an Autobiography by Viscount Cecil.* Oxford, 1941. (permissive, supportive home)

Cézanne, Paul, painter, b Aix-en-Provence, France, f well-to-do hat dealer who became a banker, s & S.
Rewald, John. *The Ordeal of Paul Cézanne.* Phoenix House, 1950.

Chagall, Marc, painter, b Vitebsk, Russia, f worker in herring factory, c- & S.
*Chagall, Marc. *My Life.* Orion, 1960. (an opinionated, warm, imaginative family)
Venturi, Lionello. *Chagall: Biographical and Critical Study.* Skira, 1956.

Chamberlain, Austen, politician, b Birmingham, f screw manufacturer, politician, c.

Chamberlain, Joseph, politician, b London, f manufacturer, s.

Chamberlain, Neville, politician, b Birmingham, f screw manufacturer, politician, c.

Hodgson, Stuart. *The Man Who Made the Peace*. Christophers, 1938.

Petrie, Sir Charles A. *The Chamberlain Tradition*. Peter Davies, 1938. (excellent account of cohesiveness in a home maintained despite death of two young mothers)

Chaplin, Charles, actor, producer, b London, f popular ballad singer, m actress, g-.

Chaplin, Charles, Jr. *My Father, Charlie Chaplin*. Random House, 1960.

Cotes, Peter and Thelma Niklaus. *The Little Fellow*. John Lane, 1952.

Payne, Pierre S. R. *The Great God Pan*. Hermitage, 1952.

Tyier, Parker. *Chaplin, Last of the Clowns*. Vanguard, 1948.

Chase, Ilka, writer, b New York City, m editor of *Vogue*, s.

Chase, Edna Woolman, and Ilka Chase. *Always in Vogue*. Doubleday, 1954. (broken homes in three successive generations)

Chase, Ilka. *Free Admission*. Doubleday, 1948.

———. *Past Imperfect*. Doubleday, 1942. (amusing description of lack of sex education in home)

Chase, Mary Ellen, educator, b Blue Hill, Maine, f municipal court judge, state legislator, farmer, m ex-schoolteacher, c+.

Chase, Mary Ellen. *A Goodly Fellowship*. New York: Macmillan, 1939.

———. *A Goodly Heritage*. Holt, 1932.

———. *Recipe for a Magic Childhood*. New York: Macmillan, 1952.

*———. *White Gate*. Collins, 1955.

Chekhov, Anton, playwright, fiction writer, b Taganrog, Russia, f small storekeeper, warehouse employee, c+.

Magarshack, David. *Chekhov*. Faber, 1952.

Saunders, Beatrice. *Tchekov, the Man*. Centaur Press, 1960.

Chesterton, Gilbert K., journalist, writer, b Kensington, London, f house agent in own father's business, s & S.

Chesterton, Gilbert K. *The Autobiography of G. K. Chesterton*. Hutchinson, 1936.

Ward, Maisie. *Return to Chesterton*. Sheed & Ward, 1952.

Wills, Garry. *Chesterton: Man and Mask*. Sheed & Ward, 1961.

Chevalier, Maurice, actor, singer, b Paris, f housepainter, m lacemaker, g.

Chevalier, Maurice. *Man in the Straw Hat: My Story*. Odhams, 1950.

*———. *With Love*. Cassell, 1960. (mother's boy)

Chiang Kai-Shek, general, politician, b near Ningpo, China, f owner of salt house, m did needlework as widow, s & M.

Chang, Hsin-Hai. *Chiang Kai-Shek, Asia's Man of Destiny*. Doubleday, 1944.

*Hahn, Emily. *Chiang Kai-Shek*. Doubleday, 1955.

Church, Richard, writer, b London, f post-office employee, m elementary-school teacher.

*Church, Richard. *Golden Sovereign*. Heinemann, 1957.

*———. *Over the Bridge*. Heinemann, 1955. (literary classic on the possessive mother and son with psychosomatic problems)

Churchill, Jennie Jerome, writer, b New York City, f journalist, Wall Street speculator, quarter owner of *New York Times*, tutored.

Cornwallis-West, Mrs. George. *The Reminiscences of Lady Randolph Churchill*. Century, 1909. (does not describe herself as a mother)

Kraus, Rene. *Young Lady Randolph*. Putnam, 1943. (home-tutored)

Churchill, Winston, politician, author, b Blenheim Palace, Woodstock, England, f inherited income, politician, s & M.

Bocca, Geoffrey. *Adventurous Life of Winston Churchill*. Julian Messner, 1958. (school experiences)

*Churchill, Winston. *Lord Randolph Churchill*. Macmillan, 1906. (account of father's illness)

*———. *My Early Life*. Odhams, 1930. (school rebel)

Cowles, Virginia. *Winston Churchill: The Era and the Man*. H. Hamilton, 1953.

Eade, Charles, ed. *Churchill by his Contemporaries*. Hutchinson, 1953. (experiences at Harrow)

Leslie, Anita. *Fabulous Leonard Jerome*. Hutchinson, 1954. (American family background)

Rowse, A. L. *The Churchills: From the Death of Marlborough to the Present.* Harper, 1958. (traumatic family background)

Clemens, Samuel, writer, b Florida, Mo., f justice of peace, merchant, land speculator, g-.

Clemens, Clara. *My Father Mark Twain.* Harper, 1931.

Clemens, Samuel. *The Autobiography of Mark Twain.* Harper, 1959.

Meltzer, Milton. *Mark Twain Himself.* Crowell, 1960.

*Webster, Samuel C., ed. *Mark Twain, Business Man.* Little, Brown, 1946. (anecdotes about family)

Cleveland, Grover, politician, b Caldwell, N.J., f minister, s.

Lynch, Denis Tilden. *Grover Cleveland: A Man Four Square.* Liveright, 1932.

McElroy, Robert McNutt. *Grover Cleveland: The Man and the Statesman.* Harper, 1923.

Nevins, Allan. *Grover Cleveland: A Study in Courage.* Dodd, Mead, 1923.

Cobb, Irvin S., humorist, journalist, b Paducah, Ky., f employee of steamboat company, s.

Cobb, Elizabeth. *My Wayward Parent.* Bobbs-Merrill, 1945.

*Cobb, Irvin S. *Exit Laughing.* Bobbs-Merrill, 1941.

Cody, Bill (William Frederick), scout and showman, b Scott County, Iowa, f farmer, politician, organizer of emigrant societies, g-.

Croft-Cooke, Rupert, and William Meadmore. *Buffalo Bill: The Legend, the Man of Action, the Showman.* Sidgwick & Jackson, 1952.

Muller, Dan. *My Life with Buffalo Bill.* Reilly & Lee, 1948.

*Russell, Donald. *The Lives and Legends of Buffalo Bill.* University of Oklahoma, 1960.

Conrad, Joseph (Teodor Josef Konrad Korzeniowski), novelist, b Berdichev, Ukraine, f land agent, unpublished poet, s.

Alien, Jerry. *The Thunder and the Sunshine.* Putnam, 1958.

Aubry, Jean. *Sea Dreamer.* Doubleday, 1957.

Conrad, Jessie. *Joseph Conrad as I Knew Him.* Doubleday, Page, 1926.

Retinger, J. H. *Conrad and his Contemporaries.* Minerva, 1941.

Cooper, Diana, actress, b London, f inherited wealth, m artist, tutored.

*Cooper, Diana. *The Light of Common Day.* Hart-Davis, 1959.

*———. *The Rainbow Comes and Goes.* Hart-Davis, 1958.

———. *Trumpets from the Steep*. Hart-Davis, 1960.

Cooper, Duff, politician, b London, f successful surgeon, c.
*Cooper, Duff. *Old Men Forget: The Autobiography of Duff Cooper*. Hart-Davis, 1953.

Copland, Aaron, composer, b Brooklyn, N.Y., f department store owner, m partner to father in store, s.
Copland, Aaron. *Our New Music*. McGraw-Hill, 1941.
Smith, Julia. *Aaron Copland: His Work and Contribution to American Music*. Dutton, 1955.

Coward, Noel, actor, playwright, b Teddington, England, f traveler for piano firm, m ran boarding house, g-.
Coward, Noel. *Future Indefinite*. Heinemann, 1956.
*———. *Present Indicative: Autobiography*. Heinemann, 1937.

Craig, Edward Gordon, actor, stage designer, b Bristol, England, f architect, m actress, g.
Craig, Edward Gordon. *Index to the Story of Days: Some Memoirs of Edward Gordon Craig*. Vista, 1960. (neglected, overweight child).

Crane, Hart, poet, b Garrettsville, Ohio, f chocolate manufacturer, s-.
Weber, Brom. *Hart Crane*. Hermitage House, 1948. (division between parents distresses son)
———, ed. *Letters of Hart Crane*. Hermitage House, 1952.

Crane, Stephen, writer, b Newark, N.J., f Methodist minister, m freelance journalist, c-.
Beer, Thomas. *Stephen Crane*. Knopf, 1923.
Berryman, John. *Stephen Crane*. Methuen, 1951.

Cripps, Stafford, lawyer and Socialist leader, b London, f wealthy lawyer, c+.
Cooke Colin. *Richard Stafford Cripps*. Hodder & Stoughton, 1957.
Estorick, Eric. *Stafford Cripps, Master Statesman*. Heinemann, 1949.
Strauss, Mrs. Patricia. *Cripps, Advocate Extraordinary*. Duell, 1942.

Cronin, Archibald Joseph, writer, b Cardross, Scotland, f businessman, c+.
Cronin, A. J. *Adventures in Two Worlds*. Gollancz, 1952.

Cunningham, Andrew, British admiral, b Dublin, Ireland, f professor of anatomy at Dublin and Edinburgh, s & M.
Cunningham, Andrew. *A Sailor's Odyssey: The Autobiography of the Admiral of the Fleet*. Hutchinson, 1951. (a mother's boy who feared his father for reasons poorly defined)

Curie, Marie, physical chemist, b Warsaw, Poland, f science teacher in secondary school, m headmistress in own girls' school, c+.
*Curie, Eve. *Madam Curie*. Heinemann, 1938. (supportive but troubled home, good sibling relationships)

Cushing, Harvey, surgeon, b Cleveland, Ohio, f, grandfather, and great-grandfather physicians, c+.
Fulton, John F. *Harvey Cushing*. Blackwell, 1947.
Thompson, Elizabeth H. *Harvey Cushing*. Schuman, 1950.

D'Annunzio, Gabriele, author, soldier, b Pescara, Italy, f Mayor of Pescara, unsuccessful businessman, c.
Antongini, Tommaso. *D'Annunzio*. Heinemann, 1938.
Rhodes, Anthony R. E. *D'Annunzio: The Poet as Superman*. McDowell-Obolensky, 1960.
Winwar, Frances. *Wings of Fire*. Redman, 1957.

Daiches, David, critic, b Northern England, f rabbi, c+.
*Daiches, David. *Two Worlds: An Edinburgh Jewish Childhood*. Macmillan, 1957. (exceptionally sensitive account of revolt of youth against father's religious ideology; love for learning and opinionatedness in family; sibling rivalry)

Dalí, Salvador, painter, b Figueras, f lawyer, g & S.
Cowles, Fleur. *The Case of Salvador Dalí*. Heinemann, 1959. (account of emotionally disturbed boy)
*Dalí, Salvador. *The Secret Life of Salvador Dalí*. Vision Press, 1948. (description of artist's sensitivity to sensory stimuli)

Darrow, Clarence, lawyer, b Kinsman, Ohio, f minister (resigned), then carpenter and furniture maker, c+.
*Darrow, Clarence. *The Story of My Life*. Watts, 1932. (opinionated, intellectual, failure-prone father)
Stone, Irving. *Clarence Darrow for the Defense*. Lane, 1950.

Day Lewis, Cecil, poet, b Ballintogher, Ireland, f Anglican curate, c.
*Day Lewis, Cecil. *The Buried Day*. Chatto & Windus, 1960. (precocious child in conflict with overpossessive widower-father)

De Gaulle, Charles, soldier, politician, b Lille, France, f professor of philosophy and literature, s & M.
Barres, Philippe. *Charles de Gaulle*. Doubleday, 1941.
Clark, Stanley F. *The Man Who is France*. Harrap, 1960.
Hatch, Alden. *The de Gaulle Nobody Knows*. Hawthorne, 1960.

De La Ramee, Mary Louise ("Ouida"), novelist, b Bury St. Edmunds, England, f French teacher in England, thought to be a spy, g.

Bigland, Eileen. *Ouida, the Passionate Victorian.* Jarrolds, 1950. (mother, English girl from small town, was deserted by mysterious French intellectual)

Ffrench, Yvonne. *Ouida, a Study in Ostentation.* Cobden-Sandreson, 1938.

Stirling, Monica. *The Fine and the Wicked.* Gollancz, 1957.

De Mille, Agnes, dancer, b New York City, f Hollywood producer, c.

de Mille, Agnes, *And Promenade Home.* Little, Brown, 1958.

*———. *Dance to the Piper.* Little, Brown, 1952. (opinionated family)

De Mille, Cecil, movie producer, b Ashfield, Mass., f playwright, m teacher, c.

Koury, Phil A. *Yes, Mr. de Mille.* Putnam, 1959.

De Valera, Eamon, politician, b New York City (left at age two), f artist, Spanish immigrant to U.S., uncle (father figure) farmer, County Limerick, Ireland, c+.

MacManus, M. J. *Eamon de Valera.* Talbot Press, 1944. (opinionated uncle reared boy)

Debs, Eugene, socialist leader, b Terre Haute, Ind., f kept grocery store, g.

*Ginger, Ray. *The Bending Cross.* Rutgers University Press, 1949. (strongly supportive family, good sibling relationships)

Morals, Herbert M. *Gene Debs: The Story of a Fighting American.* International, 1948.

Debussy, Claude, composer, b St. Germain-en-Laye, France, f kept china shop, s.

Harvey, Harry B. *Claude of France.* Allen, Towne & Heath, 1948.

*Seroff, Victor. *Debussy, Musician of France.* Calder, 1957. (neglected, rejected boy, probably illegitimate, spent holidays in luxurious, stimulating surroundings, his winters in poverty and intellectual isolation)

Delius, Frederick, composer, b Bradford, England, f export merchant, c-.

Beecham, Sir Thomas. *Frederick Delius.* Hutchinson, 1959.

* Delius, Clare. *Frederick Delius: Memories of My Brother.* Nicholson & Watson, 1935. (dominating father, indefatigable mother)

Dewey, John, philosopher, educator, b Burlington, Vt., f general store-keeper, c+.
*Eastman, Max. *Great Companions.* Farrar, 1942.
Edman, Irwin, ed. *John Dewey, his Contribution to the American Tradition.* Bobbs-Merrill, 1955.
Geiger, John R. *John Dewey in Perspective.* Oxford, 1958.
*Huff, Warren and Edna, eds. *Famous Americans.* Webb, 1941. (store-keeper father had strong literary tastes; son, small, frail, was omnivorous reader; mother was from family more distinguished than father's family, was twenty years her husband's junior)

Dewey, Thomas E., lawyer, politician, b Owosso, Mich., f publisher *Owosso Times*, postmaster of Owosso, c+.
Hughes, Rupert. *Attorney for the People: The Story of Thomas E. Dewey.* Houghton Mifflin, 1940.
Walker, Stanley. *Dewey, an American of this Century.* McGraw-Hill, 1944.

Djilas, Milovan, writer, former Yugoslav Communist party official, b near Kolasin, Montenegro, f farm owner, c.
*Djilas, Milovan. *Land Without Justice.* Methuen, 1958. (unusual, detailed, valuable account of literary and psychological merit; opinionated family; criticism of teacher)

Douglas, William O., jurist, b Maine, Minn., f Presbyterian minister, c+.
*Douglas, William O. *Of Men and Mountains.* Gollancz, 1954.
*———. *Strange Lands and Friendly People.* Harper, 1951.

Doyle, Arthur Conan, detective-story writer, b Edinburgh, f clerk, architect, builder, c+.
Carr, John Dickson. *The Life of Sir Arthur Conan Doyle.* Murray, 1949. (failure-prone father whose father and brothers were successful)
Doyle, Adrian Conan. *The True Conan Doyle.* Murray, 1945.

Dreiser, Theodore, editor, writer, b Terre Haute, Ind., f mill-owner, then day laborer after business failure, c-.
Dreiser, Helen. *My Life with Dreiser.* World, 1951.
Dreiser, Theodore. *Dawn: A History of My Life.* Constable, 1931.
Kazin, Alfred. *The Stature of Theodore Dreiser.* Indiana University Press, 1955.
Matthiessen, Francis. *Theodore Dreiser.* Methuen, 1951.

Dubinsky, David, labor leader, b Brest-Litovsk, Russian Poland, f baker, owner of small shop, g.

Danish, Max D. *World of David Dubinsky.* World, 1957.

Dewey, John. *David Dubinsky,* Inter-Allied, 1951. (father failure—good stepmother)

Duncan, Isadora, dancer, b San Francisco, f businessman, g-.

Desti, Mary. *The Untold Story: The Life of Isadora Duncan.* Liveright, 1920. (exceptionally permissive mother)

Duncan, Isadora. *My Life.* Gollancz, 1928. (father wealthy but failure-prone business man, separated from family)

Duse, Eleonora, actress, b Vigevano, Italy, factor, m actress.

Harding, Bertita. *Age Cannot Wither.* Harrap, 1950.

Duveen, Joseph, art connoisseur and dealer, b Hull, England, f art dealer, g-.

Behrman, Samuel. *Duveen.* Hamish Hamilton, 1952.

Duveen, James. *The Rise of the House of Duveen.* Knopf, 1957. (family shares interest in collecting for three generations)

Dvorák, Antonín, composer, director, b Muhlhousen, Bohemia, f butcher, s & S.

Robertson, Alee. *Dvorák.* Dent, 1945. (supportive but nonintellectual, nonmusical home)

Stefan-Gruenfeldt. *Antonín Dvorák.* Greystone, 1941.

Earhart, Amelia, aviatrix, b Atchison, Kans., f lawyer, s.

Briand, Paul L. *Daughter of the Sky.* Duell, Sloan & Pearce, 1960.

Putnam, George P. *Soaring Wings: A Biography of Amelia Earhart.* Harcourt, Brace, 1939.

Eddy, Mary Baker, founder of Christian Science Church, b Bow, N.H., f prosperous farmer, s-.

d'Humy, Fernand. *Mary Baker in a New Light.* Library Publishers, 1952.

*Dakin, Edwin F. *Mrs. Eddy: The Biography of a Virginal Mind.* Scribner's, 1929.

Johnston, Julia M. *Mary Baker Eddy, her Mission and Triumph.* Boston Science Publishers, 1946.

Powell, Lyman P. *Mary Baker Eddy, a Life Size Portrait.* Nisbet, 1930.

Eden, Anthony, politician, b Windlestone Hall, Durham, England, f inherited wealth, avocation painting, c+.

Campbell-Johnson. Alan, *Eden: The Making of a Statesman.* Washburn, 1955.

Eden, Anthony. *Full Circle: Memoirs of Anthony Eden.* Cassell, 1960.

Churchill, Randolph S. *The Rise and Fall of Sir Anthony Eden.* MacGibbon & Kee, 1958.

Edison, Thomas A., inventor, b Milan, Ohio, f innkeeper, grain business, m ex-schoolteacher, g-.

Edison, Thomas Alva. *The Diary and Sundry Observations of Thomas Alva Edison.* Philosophical Library, 1948.

*Josephson, Matthew. *Edison: A Biography.* McGraw-Hill, 1950.

Ehrlich, Paul, bacteriologist, b Silesia, Germany, f innkeeper, c+.

Marquardt, Martha. *Paul Ehrlich.* Schuman, 1951.

Einstein, Albert, theoretical physicist, b Ulm, Germany, f electrical engineer, set up small factory, c+.

Frank, Philip. *Einstein: His Life and Times.* Cape, 1948.

Schlipp Paul A. *Albert Einstein: Philosopher-Scientist,* Tudor, 1951.

Vallentin, Antonina. *Drama of Albert Einstein.* Doubleday, 1954.

Eisenhower, Dwight D., military leader, politician, b Denison, Tex., f storekeeper, mechanic, plant manager, s & M.

Childs, Marquis W. *Eisenhower, Captive Hero: A Critical Study of the General and the President.* H. Hammond, 1959.

Davis, Kenneth S. *Soldier of Democracy: A Biography of Dwight Eisenhower.* Doubleday, 1945.

Gunther, John. *Eisenhower: The Man and the Symbol.* H. Hamilton, 1952.

*Komitzer, Bela. *Great American Heritage: Story of the Five Eisenhower Brothers.* Farrar, Straus, 1955.

Kunigunde, Duncan. *Earning the Right to Do Fancy Work.* University of Kansas, 1957.

Eisenstein, Sergei, motion picture producer, b Riga, Latvia, f prosperous shipbuilder, m inherited wealth, c.

Seton, Maria. *Sergei M. Eisenstein.* J. Lane, 1952. (separated parents, rejected child).

Elgar, Edward, composer, b Broadheath, Worcestershire, f organist, s.

McVeagh, Diana M. *Edward Elgar: His Life and Music.* Dent, 1955.

Newman, Ernest. *Elgar.* Lane, 1922.

*Young, Percy. *Elgar*. Collins, 1955. (opinionated mother)

Ellis, Havelock, scientist, man of letters, b Croydon, Surrey, f sea captain, c.
Calder-Marshall, Arthur. *Havelock Ellis*. Hart-Davis, 1959.
Collis, John Stewart. *Havelock Ellis: Artist of Life*. Cassell, 1959.
Ellis, Havelock. *My Life*. Houghton Mifflin, 1940.

Fairbanks, Douglas, Jr., actor, b New York City, f successful actor, s.

Fairbanks, Douglas, Sr., actor, b Denver, Colo., f lawyer, speculator in silver, m kept boarding house, s.
Connell, Brian. *Knight Errant*. Hodder, 1955.
Hancock, Ralph. *Douglas Fairbanks, the Fourth Musketeer*. Holt, 1953.

Farson, Negley, writer, b Plainfield, N.J., grandfather adopted him at age two, unsuccessful speculator, c-.
*Farson, Negley. *A Mirror for Narcissus*. Gollancz, 1956.
———. *The Way of a Transgressor*. Gollancz, 1937. (accident-prone boy)

Faulkner, William, novelist, b New Albany, Miss., f ran livery stable, also treasurer of University of Miss., c-.
Coughlan, Robert. *Private World of William Faulkner*. Harper, 1954.
Howe, Irving. *William Faulkner: A Critical Study*. Random House, 1952.
Miner, Ward L. *The World of William Faulkner*. Evergreen, 1959.

Fermi, Enrico, physicist, b Rome, f division head on railway, m ex-elementary school teacher, c+.
*Fermi, Laura. *Atoms in the Family*. Allen & Unwin, 1955. (rejected child of dominating mother)

Ferrier, Kathleen, singer, b Higher Walton, Lancashire, f village schoolmaster, s & S.
Ferrier, Winifred. *Life of Kathleen Ferrier*. H. Hamilton, 1955.
Rigby, Charles A. *Kathleen Ferrier: A Biography*. Hale, 1956. (an all-around student)

Fessenden, Reginald, physicist, b Milton, Canada, f minister, c+.
Fessenden, Mrs. Helen May. *Fessenden, Builder of Tomorrows*. Coward McCann, 1940. (all-around student)

Fitzgerald, F. Scott, fiction writer, b St. Paul, Minn., f wholesale grocery salesman (unsuccessful), c-.

Kazin, Alfred. *F. Scott Fitzgerald: The Man and his Work.* World, 1951. (marked influence of father failure)

Mizener, Arthur M. *The Far Side of Paradise.* Eyre & Spottiswoode, 1951.

*Turnbull, Andrew. *Scott Fitzgerald.* Scribner's, 1962.

Flagstad, Kirsten, operatic soprano, b Hamar, Norway, f court stenographer by day, conductor in evenings, m vocal coach at Oslo Opera, c.

Biancolli, Louis. *The Flagstad Manuscript.* Putnam, 1952. (failure-prone father, dominating mother)

Fleming, Alexander, bacteriologist, b Lochfield, Ayrshire, f farmer, m managed farm with help of stepson after f's death, c+.

Ludovici, Laurence J. *Fleming, Discoverer of Penicillin.* Dakers, 1952. (supportive family, good sibling relationship)

Maurois, André. *Life of Sir Alexander Fleming.* Cape, 1959.

Flesch, Karl, violinist, teacher, b Wieselburg, Hungary, f surgeon, s & S.

Flesch, Karl. *Memoirs.* Barric & Rockliff, 1957. (a record of congenial parents)

Flexner, Abraham, lawyer, educator, b Louisville, Ky., f wholesale merchant to peddlers, c+.

Flexner, Abraham. *Abraham Flexner: An Autobiography.* Simon & Schuster, 1960. (record of good sibling relationship)

Flexner, Abraham. *I remember.* Simon & Schuster, 1940. (a strong mother—father's business failed)

Ford, Ford Madox, writer, teacher, b Merton, Surrey, f (a German citizen) musical editor of *London Times*, c.

Goldring, Douglas. *Trained for Genius.* Dutton, 1949. (opinionated family background)

Ford Henry, automobile manufacturer, b Greenfield, Mich., f farmer, g.

Garrett, Garet. *The Wild Wheel.* Pantheon, 1952.

Nevins, Allan. *Ford: The Times, the Man, the Company.* Scribner's, 1954. (boy thought dull by father)

Richards, William C. *The Last Billionaire.* Scribner's, 1948.

Forster, Edward Morcan, novelist, b London, f architect, c.

Forster, E. M. *Hill of Devi.* E. Arnold, 1953. (woman-smothered sickly boy)

———. *Marianne Thornton: A Domestic Biography, 1797-1887.* E. Arnold, 1956. (biography of great-aunt in whose home he lived)
Trilling, Lionel. *E. M. Forster.* Hogarth, 1944.

France, Anatole, novelist, critic, poet, b Paris, f bookseller, c.
Axelrad, Jacob. *Anatole France: A Life Without Illusions.* Harper, 1944.
Cerf, Barry. *Anatole France: The Degeneration of a Great Artist.* Dial, 1926.

Franco, Francisco, soldier, dictator, b El Ferrol, Spain, f naval officer (paymaster), s & M.
Arraras, Joaquin. *Francisco Franco: The Times and the Man.* Bles, 1938. (a rejected child, unhappy childhood)
Coles, Sydney F. A. *Franco of Spain.* Spearman, 1954. (account of unhappy childhood)

Frank, Anne, writer, b Frankfurt, Germany, f businessman s.
Frank, Anne. *Diary of a Young Girl.* Doubleday, 1952.
Schnabel, Ernst. *The Footsteps of Anne Frank.* Longmans, 1958. (Record Of A Child Thought Less Capable Than Brilliant Sister)

Freud, Sigmund, founder of psychoanalysis, b Freiburg, Moravia, f owner of small textile mill, c+.
Freud, Martin. *Glory Reflected: Sigmund Freud, Man and Father.* Vanguard, 1958. (extremely dominating mother, son rejects elderly father)
*Fromm, Erich. *Sigmund Freud's Mission.* Allen & Unwin, 1959. (provocative analysis of son's relationship with parents)
Jones, Ernest. *Life and Work of Sigmund Freud* (Vol. I). Hogarth, 1953.

Frost, Robert, poet, b San Francisco, f editor the *San Francisco Bulletin*, m teacher, c-.
Cook, Reginald L. *Dimensions of Robert Frost.* Rinehart, 1958.
Cox, Sidney H. *Swinger of Birches.* New York University Press, 1957.
Sergeant, Elizabeth S. *The Trial by Existence.* Holt, 1960. (rebellious, ineffectual father; opinionated mother)

Gag, Wanda, painter, author, b New Ulm, Minn., f artist (woodcarver in Bohemia prior to emigration), s & S.

*Gag, Wanda, *Growing Pains: Diaries and Drawings for the Years 1908-1914*. Coward-McCann, 1940.

Scott, Alma D. *Wanda Gag, the Story of an Artist*. University of Minnesota, 1949. (adaptation to being orphaned)

Galsworthy, John, novelist, playwright, b Coombe, Surrey, f lawyer, c.

Marrot, Harold V. *The Life and Letters of John Galsworthy*. Heinemann, 1935. (son rejects mother, favors opinionated father)

Gandhi, Mohandas K., political leader, b Porbandar, India, f prime minister of Porbandar, c+.

Fischer, Louis. *The Life of Mahatma Gandhi*. Cape, 1951.

*Gandhi, Mohandas K. *Gandhi's Autobiography: The Story of My Experiments with Truth*. Luzac & Probsthain, 1951. (mother's boy)

Stern, Elizabeth G. *The Women in Gandhi's Life*. Dodd, Mead, 1953. (dependent on women for most satisfying relationships)

Garland, Hamlin, writer, b West Salem, Wis., f farmer (poor), c.

Garland, Hamlin. *A Son of the Middle Border*. New York: Macmillan, 1917. (son rejects farmer-father, favors mother)

Halloway, Jean. *Hamlin Garland*. University of Texas, 1960.

Gauguin, Paul, painter, b Paris, f journalist (unsuccessful), s.

Estienne, Charles. *Gauguin*. Skira, 1953.

*Gauguin, Pola. *My Father, Paul Gauguin*. Cassell, 1937.

*Hanson, Lawrence and Elizabeth. *Noble Savage*. Chatto & Windus, 1954. (boy-in-manhood re-enacts happiest days of boyhood as lived in tropical Peru with native nurse)

Gershwin, George, composer, b Brooklyn, N.Y., f various small businesses, s-.

Armitage, Merle. *George Gershwin: Man and Legend*. Duell, Sloan & Pearce, 1958. (close sibling relationship)

Ewen, David. *Journey to Greatness*. Holt, 1946.

Jablonski, Edward. *Gershwin Years*. Doubleday, 1958.

Gibran, Kahlil, poet, painter, b Bechari, Lebanon, f small business, s.

Naimy, Mikhail. *Kahlil Gibran*. Philosophical Library, 1950. (record of mother-smothered, eccentric youth)

Young, Barbara. *A Study of Kahlil Gibran, This Man from Lebanon*. Knopf, 1945.

Gide, André, writer, b Paris, f wealthy law professor, c.
Ames, Van Meter. *André Gide*. New Directions, 1947.
Gide, André. *The Journals of André Gide*. Seeker, 1947.
Guerard, Albert Joseph. *André Gide*. Harvard University Press: O.U.P., 1951.

Gilbert, William S., playwright, b London, f naval surgeon (also novelist), c.
*Pearson, Hesketh. *Gilbert: His Life and Strife*. Methuen, 1957. (separated parents, son had father's personality problems)

Gissing George R., novelist, b Wakefield, England, f shopkeeper and chemist, c-.
Donnelly, Mabel C. *George Gissing, Grave Comedian*. Harvard University Press, 1954.
Ward, A. C. *Gissing*. Longmans, Green, 1959. (a delinquent boy)

Glasgow, Ellen, novelist, b Richmond, Va., f businessman, g-.
Glasgow, Ellen. *Letters*. Harcourt, Brace, 1958.
*———. *The Woman Within*. Eyre & Spottiswoode, 1955. (description of psychosomatic symptoms in mother and daughter)

Goebbels, Joseph Paul, politician, b Rheydt, Germany, f plant manager, c+.
Goebbels, Joseph. *Goebbels' Diaries, 1942-43*. H. Hamilton, 1948.
Riess, Curt. *Joseph Goebbels*. Hollis, 1949.

Gompers, Samuel, labor leader, b London, f cigarmaker, g-.
Gompers, Samuel. *Seventy Years of Life and Labor*. Dutton, 1957.
Harvey, Rowland Hill. *Samuel Gompers: Champion of the Toiling Masses*. Stanford University Press: O.U.P., 1935.

Gorki, Arshile (Vosdanig Adoian), artist, b Khorkom Vari, Hayotz Dzore, Turkish Armenia, f trader, carpenter, c.
Schwabacher, Ethel. *Arshile Gorki*. Macmillan, 1957.

Gorky, Maxim (Alexei Peshkov), writer, b Nizhni Novgorod, Russia, f dyemaker in father-in-law's establishment, g-.
*Gorky, Maxim. *Autobiography*. Eiek, 1953.
———. *Reminiscences*. Dover, 1946.
Roskin, Aleksandr I. *From the Banks of the Volga*. Philosophical Library, 1946.

Grahame, Kenneth, writer, b Edinburgh, f lawyer, s.
Green, Peter. *Kenneth Graham*. Murray, 1959.

Grenfell, Wilfred, physician and missionary, b Moslyn House School, Parkgate, England, f headmaster, missionary, c+.

*Grenfell, Wilfred. *Forty Years for Labrador*. Hodder, 1923.

———. *A Labrador Doctor*. Hodder, 1920.

Kerr, James L. *Wilfred Grenfell: His Life and Work*. Harrap, 1959. (an exceedingly permissive family)

Grieg, Eduard, composer, b Bergen, Norway, f British consul, s-.

Johansen, David M. *Eduard Grieg*. American-Scandinavian Foundation, 1938.

Hardy, Thomas, novelist, b Higher Beckhampton, Dorset, England, f stonemason, s & S.

Hardy, Evelyn. *Thomas Hardy*. Hogarth, 1954. (sickly boy, dominating mother)

* Hardy, Florence Emily. *Early Life of Thomas Hardy*. Macmillan, 1928.

Weber, Carl J. *Hardy of Wessex*. Columbia University Press, 1940.

Hearn, Lafcadio, writer, b Santa Maura (Greek island), f army officer, s-.

McWilliams, Vera S. *Lafcadio Hearn*. Houghton Mifflin, 1946. (severely rejected, handicapped child)

Hearst, William Randolph, newspaper publisher, b San Francisco, f mining magnate, c-.

Hearst, William Randolph. *William Randolph Hearst: A Portrait in his Own Words*. Simon & Schuster, 1952. (overindulged only son)

Swanberg, W. A. *Citizen Hearst*. Scribner's, 1961. (parents who did not agree)

Tebbel, John W. *The Life and Good Times of William Randolph Hearst*. Dutton, 1952.

Winkler, John K. *William Randolph Hearst: A New Appraisal*. Hastings House, 1955.

Hemingway, Ernest, writer, b Oak Park, Ill., f physician, s.

Fenton, Charles A. *The Apprenticeship of Ernest Hemingway*. Vision Press, 1955. (parents with different goals for son)

Hemingway, Leicester. *My Brother, Ernest Hemingway*. World, 1962.

Lania, Leo. *Hemingway*. Viking, 1961.

McCaffery, John K. M. *Ernest Hemingway: The Man and his Work*. World, 1950.

*Sanford, Marcelline Hemingway. *At the Hemingways*. Little, Brown, 1962. (mother had unusual musical talent, not fulfilled; father demanding, highly opinionated)

Herzl, Theodor, politician, b Budapest, f wealthy businessman, c.
Herzl, Theodor. *Theodor Herzl: A Portrait for this Age*. World, 1955.
Patai, József. *Star Over Jordan*. Philosophical Library, 1946.

Hess, Rudolph, politician, b Alexandria, Egypt, f merchant, c.
Rees, John R., ed. *The Case of Rudolph Hess*. Norton, 1948.

Hewart, Gordon, jurist, b Bury, Lancashire, f draper, c+.
Jackson, Robert. *The Chief: The Biography of Gordon Hewart, Lord Chief Justice of England*. Harrap, 1959. (supportive home)

Hillman, Sidney, labor leader, b Zagare, Lithuania, f unsuccessful grain and flour merchant, m small shopkeeper, g+.
Josephson, Matthew. *Sidney Hillman, Statesman of American Labor*. Doubleday, 1952. (son rebels against parental dogmatism in religion)
Soule, George Henry. *Sidney Hillman, Labor Statesman*. Macmillan, 1939.

Hitler, Adolf, politician, b Braunau, Austria, f customs official, s-.
Hitler, Adolf. *Mein Kampf*. Tr. Murphy, Hurst & Blackett, 1939.
*Kubizek, August. *The Young Hitler*. Wingate, 1954. (valuable documentary on a mother-smothered, emotionally disturbed boy)

Holmes, Oliver Wendell, jurist, b Boston, f physician, poet, c+.
Biddle, Francis B. *Mr. Justice Holmes*. Scribner's, 1952.
Howe, Mark de Wolfe. *Justice Oliver Wendell Holmes*. Harvard University Press: O.U.P., 1957. (strong father-son conflict in personal philosophy)

Hoover, Herbert, engineer, politician, b West Branch, Iowa, f blacksmith, c.
Hinshaw, David. *Herbert Hoover, American Quaker*. Farrar, Straus, 1950. (family cohesiveness, opinionated mother goes on speaking tours)
Hoover, Herbert. *Memoirs*. Macmillan, 1951. (self-sufficient orphan)

Houdini, Harry, magician, b Appleton, Wis., f rabbi, g-.
Gresham, William L. *Houdini*. Gollancz, 1960.
Kellock, Harold. *Houdini: His Life Story*. Harcourt, Brace, 1928. (a mother's boy)

Housman, Alfred Edward, poet, b Fockbury, Worcestershire, f solicitor, unsuccessful inventor, c-.

Hawkins, Maude M. *A. E. Housman: Man Behind a Mask.* Regnery, 1958.

Symons, Katharine, and others. *Recollections.* Holt, 1937.

Housman, Laurence, writer, illustrator, b Bromsgrove, Worcestershire, f solicitor, unsuccessful inventor, s & S.

*Housman, Laurence. *A. E. Housman.* Cape, 1937. (examination failure)

———. *The Unexpected Years.* Cape, 1937.

Howells, William Dean, writer, b Martin's Ferry, Ohio, f newspaper editor, printer, g-.

Brooks, Van Wyck. *Howells: His Life and World.* Dent, 1959.

Cady, Edwin Harrison. *The Road to Realism.* Syracuse University Press, 1956.

Howells, Mildred, ed. *William Dean Howells.* Doubleday, 1928.

Howells, William Dean. *Years of My Youth.* Harper, 1916.

Hudson, William Henry, naturalist, author, b Quilnes, Argentina, f farmer, brewery worker, tutored.

*Hudson, William Henry. *Far Away and Long Ago.* Dent, 1918. (handicapped boy)

Tomalin, Ruth. *W. H. Hudson.* Witherby, 1954.

Hughes, Charles Evans, jurist, b Glens Falls, N.Y., f Baptist minister, c+.

Perkins, Dexter. *Charles Evans Hughes.* Black, 1956.

Pusey, Merio John. *Charles Evans Hughes.* New York: Macmillan, 1951. (extremely precocious only child)

Hughes, Langston, writer, b Joplin, Mo., f successful businessman and rancher in Mexico, c-.

*Hughes, Langston. *The Big Sea: An Autobiography.* Knopf, 1940. (sensitive description of a divided family

———. *I Wonder as I Wander: An Autobiographical Journey.* Rinehart, 1956.

Huxley, Aldous, novelist, critic, b Godalming, Surrey, f editor, biographer, historian, c.

Atkins, John. *Aldous Huxley.* Calder, 1956.

Brooke, Jocelyn. *Aldous Huxley.* Longmans, 1954.

Ibsen, Henrik, poet, dramatist, b Skien, Norway, f merchant (unsuccessful), s.
Koht, Halvdan. *The Life of Ibsen.* Alien & Unwin, 1931.
Zuker, Adolph E. *Ibsen the Master Builder.* Holt, 1929. (rejected religious beliefs of family)

Ickes, Harold L., political reformer, b Frankstown Township, Pa., f proprietor of store, c +.
Ickes, Harold L. *Autobiography of a Curmudgeon.* Reynal & Hitchcock, 1943.
———. *Secret Diary of Harold L. Ickes.* Simon & Schuster, 1933. (rejected his failure-prone father)

James, Henry, novelist, b New York City, f lifelong student of religion, inherited income, c+.
Edel, Leon. *Henry James: The Untried Years, 1843-1870.* Hart-Davis, 1953.
James, Henry. *A Small Boy and Others.* Scribner's, 1913.
Le Clair, Robert C. *Young Henry James.* Bookman, 1955.

James, William, psychologist, philosopher, b New York City, c+.
*Matthiessen, Francis O. *The James Family.* Knopf, 1947.
Perry, Ralph B. *The Thought and Character of William James.* Harvard University Press, O.U.P., 1948.

John XXIII, Pope (Angello Roncalli), b Sotto il Monte, Italy, f farmer, s & S.
Aradi, Zsolt, and others. *Pope John XXIII.* Farrar, Straus, 1959.
Perrotta, Paul Christopher. *Pope John XXIII: His Life and Work.* Nelson, 1959.

Jones, Ernest, psychiatrist, b Rhosfelyn-Llwchwr, Wales, f colliery engineer, secretary of steel works, c+.
*Jones, Ernest. *Free Associations: Memoirs of a Psycho-Analyst.* Basic Books, 1959. (a candid story of his own childhood by Freud's biographer, strong rejection of school)

Jones, Rufus, Quaker philosopher, b South China, Maine, f farmer, c.
Hinshaw, David. *Rufus Jones, Master Quaker.* Putnam, 1951.
Jones, Rufus M. *A Small Town Boy.* New York: Macmillan, 1941.
Vining, Elizabeth. *Friend of Life.* Michael Joseph, 1959.

Joyce, James, writer, b Dublin, f doctor, actor, singer, commercial secretary, political secretary (unsuccessful), c.
*Ellmann, Richard. *James Joyce*. Oxford, 1959.
Joyce, Stanislaus. *My Brother's Keeper: James Joyce's Early Years*. Faber, 1958.

Kafka, Franz, poet, writer, b Prague, f wholesale drygoods business, c+.
Eisner, Paul. *Franz Kafka and Prague*. Arts Inc., 1950.
Janouch, Gustav. *Conversations with Kafka*, Praeger, 1953.
*Kafka, Franz. *Dearest Father: Stories and Other Writings*. Schocken Books, 1954. (extreme expression of dislike for father)
———. *The Diaries of Franz Kafka* (2 vols.). Seeker, 1948 and 1949.

Kagawa, Toyohiko, social reformer, evangelist, b Kobe, Japan, f diplomat and merchant, c+.
Axling, William. *Kagawa*. S.C.M., 1932.
Davey, Cyril. *Kagawa of Japan*. Epworth, 1960.

Kaye-Smith, Sheila, novelist, b St. Leonards-on-Sea, Sussex, f surgeon, tutored.
Kaye-Smith, Sheila. *Three Ways Home: An Experiment in Autobiography*. Harper, 1937.

Keith, Arthur, physical anthropologist, b Quarry Farm, near Aberdeen, Scotland, f farmer, c+.
Keith, Arthur. *Autobiography*. Watts, 1950. (driving, encouraging mother)

Keller, Helen, author, lecturer, b Tuscumbia, Ala., f editor, c.
*Brooks, Van Wyck. *Helen Keller: Sketch for a Portrait*. Dent, 1956.
Keller, Helen. *The Story of My Life*. Harrap, 1903.
———. *Teacher: Anne Sullivan Macy*. Gollancz, 1956.

Kennedy, John F., politician, b Boston, f politician, c+.
Burns, James M. *John Kennedy, a Political Profile*. Harcourt, Brace, 1960.
*Dinneen, Joseph F. *The Kennedy Family*. Little, Brown, 1959.

Kenny, Elizabeth, nurse, b Warrialda, New South Wales, Australia, f potato and onion rancher, tutored & S.
Kenny, Elizabeth. *And They Shall Walk*. Dodd, Mead, 1943.

Kent, Rockwell, artist, b Westchester County, N.Y., f lawyer, c-.
Kent, Rockwell. *It's Me, Oh Lord*. Dodd, Mead, 1955. (widow's son)

———. *This is My Own*. Duell, Sloan & Pearce, 1940.

Kern, Jerome, composer, b New York City, f president of streetcar association, c & S.

Ewen, David. *The Story of Jerome Kern*. Holt, 1953. (permissive, wealthy parents, musical mother)

———. *The World of Jerome Kern, a Biography*. Holt, 1960.

Khrushchev, Nikita, politician, b Kalinovka, Ukraine, Russia, f blacksmith, g.

Alexandrov, Victor. *Khrushchev of the Ukraine*. Gollancz, 1957.

Paloczi-Horvath, George. *Khrushchev*. Seeker, 1960.

King, Martin Luther, minister, social reformer, b Atlanta, Ga., f Baptist minister, c+.

King, Martin Luther. *Stride Toward Freedom: The Montgomery Story*. Gollancz, 1959. (supportive family, all-around good student)

Reddick, Lawrence D. *Crusader Without Violence*. Harper, 1959.

King, William L. Mackenzie, politician, b Kitchener, Ontario, Canada, f unsuccessful lawyer, c+.

Dawson, Robert MacG. *William Lyon Mackenzie King, Vol. I*. Methuen 1959.

Hardy, Henry R. *Mackenzie King of Canada*. Oxford, 1949.

*Hutchinson, Bruce. *The Incredible Canadian*. Longmans, Green, 1952.

Kipling, Rudyard, writer, b Bombay, India, f teacher of art, s.

Beresford, George C. *Schooldays with Kipling*. Putnam, 1936.

Carrington, Charles Edward. *The Life of Rudyard Kipling*. Macmillan, 1955.

*Kipling, Rudyard. *Something of Myself, for My Friends Known and Unknown*, Macmillan, 1937.

Kitchener, Horatio Herbert, soldier, b Ballylongford, Ireland, f army officer, Irish administrator, s & M.

Ballard, General C. R. *Kitchener*. Dodd, Mead, 1930.

Magnus, Philip M. *Kitchener: Portrait of an Imperialist*. Murray, 1958.

Klee, Paul, painter, b Berne, Switzerland, f teacher, s & S.

di San Lazzarro, Gualtieri. *Klee: A Study of his Life and Work*. Thames & Hudson, 1957.

Grohmann, Will. *Paul Klee.* Lund, Humphries, 1958.
Ponente, Nello. *Paul Klee—Biographical and Critical Study.* Skira, 1960.

Kleiber, Erich, conductor, b Vienna, Austria, f teacher of Greek, Latin, and German, s & S- (expelled Prague Conservatoire).
Russell, John. *Erich Kleiber: A Memoir.* Deutsch, 1957.

Koestler, Arthur, writer, b Budapest, f manufacturer, c-.
Atkins, John Alfred. *Arthur Koestler.* Spearman, 1956.
*Koestler, Arthur. *Arrow in the Blue.* Collins & Hamish Hamilton, 1952. (illuminating description of the development of guilt and fear in small son of speculative father and anxious mother)

Kreisler, Fritz, violinist, b Vienna, Austria, f physician and ichthyologist, c.
Lochner, Louis Paul. *Fritz Kreisler.* Barrie & Rockliff, 1951.

Kreuger, Ivar, financier, b Kalmar, Sweden, f match-factory owner, c.
Shaplen, Robert. *Kreuger, Genius and Swindler.* Knopf, 1960. (a rejected child).

La Farge, John, priest, editor, b Newport, Maine, f artist, s & S.
*La Farge, John. *An American Amen.* Farrar, Straus, 1958.
*———. *The Manner Is Ordinary.* Harcourt, Brace, 1954. (famous father is unable to endure tensions of family life)

La Follette, Robert, Jr., politician, b Madison, Wis., f politician, c.

La Follette, Robert, Sr., politician, b Primrose, Wis., f farmer, c+.
Doan, Edward N. *The La Follettes and the Wisconsin Idea.* Rinehart, 1947.
La Follette, Belle and Fola. *Robert M. La Follette, Vol. I.* New York: Macmillan, 1953.

La Guardia, Fiorello, politician, b New York City, f army musician, c+.
Cunco, Ernest. *Life with Fiorello.* Macmillan, 1955.
Mann, Arthur William. *La Guardia.* Lippincott, 1959.

Lardner, Ring, humorist, writer, b Niles, Mich., f businessman, s.
Elder, Donald. *Ring Lardner.* Doubleday, 1956. (handicapped boy, dominating mother, failure-prone father)
Lardner, Ring. *The Story of a Wonder Man.* Scribner's, 1927.

Laski, Harold J., political scientist, b Manchester, f cotton shipper, philanthropist, c+.
Martin, Kingsley. *Harold Laski.* Gollancz, 1953. (small, precocious boy)

Lauder, Harry, singer, b Portobello, Scotland, f laborer, g-.

Lauder, Harry. *Roamin' in the Gloamin'.* Lippincott, 1928. (poverty, dominating, driving widow)

Malvern, Gladys. *Valiant Minstrel.* Messner, 1943.

Lawrence, D. H., novelist, b Eastwood, near Nottingham, f collier, m teacher, s.

Aldington, Richard. *D. H. Lawrence: Portrait of a Genius But....* Heinemann, 1950. (an exceptionally maladjusted youth, mother-smothered)

Bynner, Witter. *Journey with Genius.* Peter Nevill, 1951.

Fay, Eliot G. *Lorenzo in Search of the Sun.* Vision Press, 1955.

Moore, Harry Thornton. *The Intelligent Heart.* Heinemann, 1955.

Lawrence, Gertrude, actress, b London, f actor, g-.

Aldrich, Richard S. *Gertrude Lawrence as Mrs. A.* Greystone, 1954.

Lawrence, Gertrude. *A Star Danced.* Doubleday, 1945. (child actress from a divided home)

Lawrence, Marjorie, dramatic soprano, b Dean's Marsh, Victoria, Australia, f prosperous farmer, s & S.

Lawrence, Marjorie. *Interrupted Melody: The Story of My Life.* Appleton-Century-Crofts, 1949. (a runaway girl, persistent toward goal)

Lawrence, Thomas E., archaeologist, soldier, writer, b Tremadoc Caernarvonshire, Wales, f inherited income, c+.

Armitage, Flora. *The Desert and the Stars.* Faber, 1956, (withdrawn, emotionally maladjusted youth)

Carrington, Charles E. *T. E. Lawrence (of Arabia).* Appleton-Century, 1936.

Lawrence, Thomas E. *The Home Letters of T. E. Lawrence and his Brothers.* Blackwell, 1954.

Leacock, Stephen B., humorist, economist, b Swanmoor, Hampshire, England, f farmer, c+.

*Leacock, Stephen B. *The Boy I Left Behind Me.* John Lane, 1947.

Lehmann, Lotte, singer, b Perleberg, Germany, f small town official, s & S- (sent home from music school, unsuccessful)

Lehmann, Lotte. *My Many Lives.* Boosey & Hawkes, 1948. (parents did not wish her to be a singer)

Lenin, Nikolai, Communist leader, b Simbirsk, Russia, f superintendent of rural schools, c.
Trotsky, Leon. *Nikolai Lenin.* Doubleday, 1955. (opinionated brother is executed)
Wolfe, Bertram D. *Three Who Made a Revolution.* Thames & Hudson, 1956.

Lewis, John L., labor leader, b Lucas, Iowa, f coal miner, s.
Alinsky, Saul David. *John L. Lewis: An Unauthorized Biography.* Putnam, 1949.
Sulzberger, Cyrus Leo. *Sit Down with John L. Lewis.* Random House, 1938.
Wechsler, James A. *Labor Baron.* Morrow, 1944.

Lewis, Sinclair, novelist, b Sauk Center, Minn., f physician, c.
Lewis, Grace H. *With Love from Gracie.* Harcourt, Brace, 1956.
*Schorer, Mark. *Sinclair Lewis: An American Life.* McGraw-Hill, 1961. (peer-rejected, pimply-faced object of derision)
Smith, Harrison, ed. *From Main Street to Stockholm: Letters of Sinclair Lewis.* Harcourt, Brace, 1952.

Lindbergh, Charles A., aviator, b Detroit, Mich., f politician, c-.
Davis, Kenneth S. *The Hero.* Doubleday, 1959. (social isolate in adolescence)
Haines, Lynn and Dora B. *The Lindberghs.* Vanguard, 1931. (detailed information about father's stoicism under pain and reference to his belief in the superiority of the white races)

Lindsay, Vachel, poet, b Springfield, Ill., f physician, c-.
Masters, Edgar L. *Vachel Lindsay: A Poet in America.* Scribner's, 1935.
Ruggles, Eleanor. *West-Going Heart.* Norton, 1959.

Litvinov, Maxim, diplomat, b Belostok, Russia, f produce merchant, c.
Pope, Arthur U. *Maxim Litvinoff.* Fischer, 1943. (learning-centered, liberal household)

Lloyd George, David, politician, b Ghorlton-on-Medlock, Manchester, f headmaster in National School; after father's death, uncle was father figure (Church of the Disciples minister), s & law study.
George, William. *My Brother and I.* Eyre & Spottiswoode, 1958.
Jones, Thomas. *Lloyd-George.* Harvard University Press, O.U.P., 1951.
Lloyd-George, Richard. *My Father.* Lloyd George, Muller, 1960.

*Owen, Frank. *Tempestuous Journey*. Hutchinson, 1954. (extreme drive toward goals)

London, Jack, writer, b San Francisco, foster-father common laborer, f itinerant astrologer, m professional medium, s-.

London, Joan. *Jack London and his Times*. Doubleday, 1939.

*Stone, Irving. *Sailor on Horseback: The Biography of Jack London*. Collins, 1938.

Long, Huey P., politician, b Winfield, La., f farmer, s- & c-.

Kane, Harnett T. *Louisiana Hayride: The American Rehearsal for Dictatorship, 1928-1940*. Morrow, 1941.

Martin, James. *Dynasty*. Putnam, 1960. (there was money for the older children's college expenses, none for Huey's)

Opotowsky, Stan. *The Longs of Louisiana*. Dutton, 1960. (best account of youthful exploits, rejected by siblings)

Smith, Webster. *The Kingfish: A Biography of Huey P. Long*. Putnam, 1933.

Lowell, Amy, poet, critic, b Brookline, Mass., f wealthy mill-owner, s.

Damon, S. Foster. *Amy Lowell*. Houghton Mifflin, 1935. (account of reaction to being overweight)

Gregory, Horace. *Amy Lowell: A Portrait of the Poet in her Time*. Nelson, 1958. (rich, neglected girl; turned to coachman and elder brother)

MacArthur, Douglas, army officer, b Little Rock, Ark., f general, s & M.

*Gunther, John. *The Riddle of MacArthur*. Harper, 1951.

Hunt, Frazier. *The Untold Story of Douglas MacArthur*. Devin-Adair, 1954.

MacDonald, Betty, humorist, b Boulder, Colo., f mining engineer, m dress designer, c-.

*MacDonald, Betty. *Anybody Can Do Anything*. Hammond & Hammond, 1950.

———. *The Plague and I*. Hammond & Hammond, 1948.

*———. *Who, Me?* Hammond & Hammond, 1960.

MacDonald, James Ramsay, politician, b Lossiemouth, Scotland, f laborer, m servant girl, g.

Hamilton, Mary Agnes. *J. Ramsay MacDonald*. Cape, 1939.

MacDonald, James R. *Wanderings and Excursions*. Cape, 1925. (fine tribute to gifted teacher)

MacDonald, Ramsay. *Margaret Ethel MacDonald*. Seltzer, 1924.

Weir, L. McNeill. *Tragedy of Ramsay MacDonald.* Secker, 1938.

Magsaysay, Ramon, politician, b Iba, Philippines, f teacher, c.
Romulo, Carlos. *The Magsaysay Story.* Day, 1956. (opinionated father)

Mahler, Gustav, composer, conductor, b Kalischt, Bohemia, f proprietor of small vegetable store, g & S.
Mahler, Alma Maria. *Gustav Mahler: Memories and Letters.* Murray, 1945.
*Mitchell, Donald. *Gustav Mahler: The Early Years.* Barrie & Rockliff, 1958. (unhappy home, mother hated father).

Mann, Erika, author, actress, b Munich, Germany, f successful author, s & S.

Mann, Klaus, author, b Munich, Germany, f successful writer, s.

Mann, Thomas, author, b Lubeck, Germany, f wealthy grain merchant who went bankrupt, c-.
Brennan, Joseph G. *Thomas Mann's World.* Columbia University Press, 1942.
Mann, Erika. *Last Fear.* Seeker, 1958.
Mann, Klaus. *The Turning Point.* Fischer, 1942.
*Mann, Monika. *Past and Present.* St. Martin's, 1960. (permissive home, much love of learning)
*Mann, Thomas. *A Sketch of My Life.* Knopf, 1960. (strongly influenced by unconventional, foreign mother)

Manolete, Manuel, matador, b Cordoba, Spain, f butcher.
Conrad, Barnaby. *Death of a Matador.* Michael Joseph, 1956. (fearful mother's boy)

Mansfield, Katherine, writer, b Wellington, New Zealand, f chairman of Bank of New Zealand, c-.
Alpers, Antony. *Katherine Mansfield.* Cape, 1954.
Berkman, Sylvia. *Katharine Mansfield: A Critical Study.* Yale University Press, O.U.P., 1952.
Mansfield, Katherine. *Journal of Katherine Mansfield.* Constable, 1927.

Mao Tse-Tung, communist leader, b Shao-Shan, China, f rice merchant (hired labor), c.
Payne, Pierre. *Mao Tse-Tung, Ruler of Red China.* Schuman, 1950.
*Siao-Yu. *Mao Tse-Tung and I Were Beggars.* Syracuse University Press, 1957. (boys take time-out)

Stevenson, William. *Yellow Wind.* Cassell, 1959.

Marconi, Guglielmo, inventor, electrical engineer, b Bologna, Italy, f wealthy silkworm farmer, s-.

Dunlap, Orrin E. *Marconi: The Man and his Wireless.* New York: Macmillan, 1937. (shy boy)

Jacot de Boinod, Bernard L. *Marconi—Master of Space.* Hutchinson, 1935.

Marconi, Degna. *My Father, Marconi.* McGraw-Hill, 1963. (rejecting father destroyed boy's experiments; accepting Irish mother assisted boy to fulfill talent)

Marsh, Edward, secretary to Churchill, b London, f surgeon, c.

*Hassall, Christopher. *Edward Marsh: A Biography.* Longmans, 1959. (handicapped boy with restrictive, religious mother)

Marshall, George C., soldier, politician, b Uniontown, Pa., f wealthy coal operator, s & M.

Frye, William. *Marshall, Citizen Soldier.* Bobbs-Merrill, 1947. (a father's boy)

Marshall, Katherine. *Together: Annals of an Army Wife.* Blandford, 1948.

Payne, Pierre S. R. *The Marshall Story.* Prentice-Hall, 1951.

Masaryk, Jan, diplomat, b Prague, f philosopher, politician, c.

Lockhart, Robert. *Jan Masaryk: A Personal Memoir.* Putnam, 1956. (international family)

Masaryk, Thomas, philosopher, politician, b Hodonin, Moravia, f coachman, m cook, c+.

*Capek, Karcl. *President Masaryk Tells his Story.* Allen & Unwin, 1935. (gifted boy from disadvantaged home)

Matisse, Henri, painter, b Le Cateau, France, f grain merchant, c.

Escholier, Raymond. *Matisse: A Portrait of the Artist and the Man.* Faber 1960. (started painting during time-out period due to illness)

Lassaigne, Jacques. *Matisse: Biographical and Critical Study.* Skira, 1959.

Maugham, W. Somerset, novelist, playwright, b Paris, f diplomat, c+.

Cordell, Richard A. *Somerset Maugham: A Biographical and Critical Study.* Indiana University Press, 1961.

Maugham, W. Somerset. *Mr. Maugham Himself.* Doubleday, 1954.

Pfeiffer, Karl G. *W. Somerset Maugham.* Gollancz, 1959. (school rejection, trauma over mother's death)

Mauldin, William H., cartoonist, b Mountain Park, N.M., f farmer, businessman, miner, s.

Mauldin, William H. *Back Home.* Sloan, 1947.
*———. *A Sort of Saga.* Sloan, 1949. (father-failure is a central theme of this whimsical narrative)

Maurois, André (Emile Herzog), writer, b Elbeuf, Alsace, f textile manufacturer, c+.

Maurois, André. *I Remember, I Remember.* Harper, 1942. (father made bitter by failure)

Mayo, Charles Horace, surgeon, b Rochester, Minn., f physician, c+.

Mayo, William James, surgeon, b Le Sueur, Minn., f physician, c+.

*Clapesattle, Helen B. *The Doctors Mayo.* University of Minnesota Press, 1941.
Hammontree, Marie. *Will and Charlie Mayo.* Bobbs-Merrill, 1954.

McCarthy, Joseph, politician, b farm near Grande Chute, Wis., farmer, c+.

Anderson, Jack, and Ronald W. May. *McCarthy: The Man, the Senator, the "ism."* Beacon, 1952. (three mother figures—mother and two land-ladies; disliked father).
Rovere, Richard H. *Senator Joe McCarthy.* Methuen, 1960.

Mehta, Ved, writer, b Delhi, India, f municipal health officer, c.

*Mehta, Ved. *Face to Face.* Little, Brown, 1957. (parents differ on proper attitude to take with blind son)
Mehta, Ved. *Walking the Indian Streets.* Little, Brown, 1959.

Mencken, Henry Louis, editor, satirist, b Baltimore, Md., f tobacco merchant, s.

Angoff, Charles. *H. L. Mencken.* Yoseloff, Thomas, 1956.
Kemler, Edgar. *The Irreverent Mr. Mencken.* Little, Brown, 1950.
Manchester, William. *Disturber of the Peace.* Harper, 1950.
Mencken, Henry L. *Minority Report.* Knopf, 1956.

Mendes-France, Pierre, politician, b Paris, f wealthy dress-manufacturer, c+.

Werth, Alexander. *The Strange History of Pierre Mendes-France.* Barrie & Rockliff, 1957. (precocious youth, received doctorate in law at eighteen; highly supportive, cohesive home)

Menninger, Karl, psychiatrist, writer, b Topeka, Kans., f physician, c+.

Menninger, William, psychiatrist, b Topeka, Kans., f physician, c+.
*Menninger, Flo V. *Days of My Life: Memories of a Kansas Mother and Teacher*. Smith, 1939.
Winslow, Walker. *The Menninger Story*. Doubleday, 1956.

Menuhin, Yehudi, violinist, b New York City, f teacher, tutored & S.
Gavoty, Bernard. *Yehudi Menuhin and Georges Emsco*. Barrie & Rockliff, 1955.
*Magidoff, Robert. *Yehudi Menuhin: The Story of the Man and the Musician*. Hale, 1956. (mother interpreted any disobedience as rejection of her)

Millay, Edna St. Vincent, poet, b Rockport, Maine, f school superintendent, m nurse, c.
MacDougall, Allan Ross, ed. *Letters,* by Edna Millay. Harper, 1952.
Shafter, Toby. *Edna St. Vincent Millay: America's Best Beloved Poet.* Messner, 1957. (conflict between parents over father's gambling described; also mother's conflict with school authorities)

Milne, A. A., poet, playwright, b London, f teacher, c.
*Milne, Alan A. *Autobiography*. Dutton, 1939. (exceptionally cohesive and permissive home, father made learning pleasurable)

Modigliani, Amedeo, painter, sculptor, b Livorno, Italy, f banker, s- & S.
Modigliani, Amedeo. *Modigliani: A Memoir*. Putnam, 1961.
* Modigliani, Jeanne. *Modigliani: Man and Myth*. Deutsch, 1959. (intellectual, opinionated mother)

Molnar, Ferenc, playwright, novelist, b Budapest, f physician, c+.
Molnar, Ferenc. *Companion in Exile*. Gaar, 1950.

Monet, Claude, painter, b LeHavre, France, f grocer (unsuccessful), g- & S.
Rouart, Denis. *Claude Monet.* Skira, 1958.
Weekes, C. P. *The Invincible Monet.* Appleton-Century-Crofts, 1960. (school truant)

Montessori, Maria, physician, educator, b Chiaravalle, Italy, f military man, c+.
Standing, E. Mortimer. *Maria Montessori: Her Life and Work*. Hollis & Carter, 1957. (a precocious child who fulfilled her mother's ambitions for her)

Montgomery, Bernard Law, soldier, b Kennington, London, f Episcopalian minister, s & M.

Montgomery, Bernard L. *Memories of Field-Marshal the Viscount Montgomery of Alamein.* World, 1958. (home tensions, school problems, intense mother-rejection)

Moorehead, Alan. *Montgomery, a Biography.* Hamilton, 1946. (mother seen as an indefatigable adult)

Moore George, novelist, b Moore Hall, County Mayo, Ireland, f country gentleman, politician, s & S.

Brown, Malcolm J. *George Moore: A Reconsideration.* University of Washington Press, 1955.

Hone, Joseph M. *The Life of George Moore.* Gollancz, 1936. (appallingly ugly son of opinionated father who suffered for his ideas)

Mott John R., YMCA leader, b Livingston Manor, N.Y., f lumber merchant, c.

Fisher Galen M. *John R. Mott, Architect of Cooperation and Unity.* Association Press, 1952.

Matthews, Basil J. *John R. Mott, World Citizen.* Harper, 1934.

Murry, John Middleton, writer, b London, f civil servant, c.

Lea, Frank Alfred. *The Life of John Middleton Murry.* Oxford University Press, 1960. (driving, dominating father)

Mussolini, Benito, politician, b Dovia, Forii, Italy, f blacksmith, m teacher, c.

*Hibbert, Christopher. *Il Duce: The Life of Benito Mussolini.* Little, Brown, 1962.

Megaro, Gaudens. *Mussolini in the Making.* Allen & Unwin, 1938.

Monell, Pavlo. *The Intimate Life of a Demagogue.* Vanguard.

* Mussolini, Rachele. *My Life with Mussolini.* Hale, 1959. (description of mother's complaining in her classroom of her loss of income because of husband's political views)

Seldes, George. *Sawdust Caesar.* Harper, 1935. (describes his youthful delinquencies, his grandiose ways, his love of martial poetry)

Nansen, Fridtjof, explorer, zoologist, humanitarian, b Froen, Norway, f lawyer, c-.

Hall, Anna Gertrude. *Nansen.* Viking. 1940.

Shackleton, Edward. *Nansen, the Explorer.* Witherby, 1959.

Nasser, Gamel Abdel, politician, b Alexandria, Egypt, f postmaster, s & M.
*St. John, Robert. *The Boss: The Story of Gamel Abdel Nasser.* McGraw-Hill, 1960. (father-rejection, a mother's boy).

Nehru, Jawaharlal, politician, b Allahabad, India, f statesman, c.
Morales, Francis Robert. *Jawaharlal Nehru: A Biography.* Macmillan, 1956.
Nehru, Jawaharlal. *Autobiography.* John Lane, 1936.

Niebuhr, Reinhold, theologian, b Wright City, Mo., f minister, c+.
Davies, David R. *Reinhold Niebuhr, Prophet from America.* Clarke, 1945. (supportive home)
Harland, Gordon. *The Thoughts of Reinhold Niebuhr.* Oxford University Press, 1960.

Niemoller, Martin, theologian, b Westphalia, Germany, f Lutheran minister, c.
Davidson, Clarissa S. *God's Man: The Story of Pastor Niemoller.* Washburn, 1959. (relatively untroubled home)

Nietzsche, Friedrich W., philosopher, poet, b Rocken, Saxony, f Lutheran pastor, c+.
*Forster-Nietzsche, Elisabeth. *The Life of Nietzsche.* Sturgis & Walton, 1912. (tense, woman-dominated household)
Nietzsche, Friedrich W. *My Sister and I.* Boar's Head, 1959. (bitter attack on mother, sister, and sweetheart; written in mental hospital)
Reyburn, Hugh Adam. *Nietzsche: The Story of a Human Philosopher.* Macmillan, 1948.

Nijinsky, Vaslav, dancer, b Kiev, Russia, f & m dancers, S.
Bourman, Anatole. *The Tragedy of Nijinsky.* Hale, 1937. (father, mother, and only sister talented ballet dancers; only brother mentally ill)
Nijinsky, Romola. *The Last Years of Nijinsky.* Simon & Schuster, 1952. (love for dancing helps in recovery from mental illness)
———. *Nijinsky.* Gollancz, 1933.

Nixon, Richard M., politician, b, Yorba Linda, Calif., f laboring man and storekeeper, c+.
Costello William. *The Facts about Nixon: An Unauthorized Biography.* Hutchinson, 1960.
De Toledano, Ralph. *Nixon.* Sidgwick & Jackson, 1960. (good all-around student, excelled in debating)

Kornitzer, Bela. *The Real Nixon: An Intimate Biography.* Rand, 1960.

Nkrumah, Kwame, politician, b Ankroful, Nzima, Gold Coast, f gold miner, c+.

Nkrumah, Kwame. *Ghana: The Autobiography of Kwame Nkrumah.* Nelson, 1957. (happily functioning polygamous household)

Norris, George W., politician, b Sandusky County, Ohio, f farmer, c.

Neuberger, Richard Lewis, and Stephen Kahn. *Integrity: The Life of George W. Norris.* Vanguard, 1937. (mother divorces second husband, who is unkind to her children)

O'Casey, Sean, playwright, b Dublin, f Protestant church official, g-.

Krause, David. *Sean O'Casey: The Man and his Work.* MacGibbon & Kee, 1960.

O'Casey, Sean. *Mirror in My House: The Autobiographies of Sean O'Casey, Vol. II.* Macmillan, 1956.

O'Neill, Eugene, playwright, b New York City, f actor, c-.

Boulton, Agnes. *Part of a Long Story.* Peter Davies, 1958.

Bowen, Croswell (with Shane O'Neill). *Curse of the Misbegotten.* McGraw-Hill, 1959. (childhood resentment of being born as replacement for deceased brother, and of being told that it was the pain of his birth that resulted in his mother becoming a drug addict)

Oppenheim, E. Phillips, novelist, b London, f merchant, s-.

Oppenheim, E. Phillips. *The Pool of Memory.* Little, Brown, 1945. (school rejection; supportive, congenial parents)

Oppenheimer, J. Robert, physicist, b New York City, f textile manufacturer (wealthy), c+.

Alsop, Joseph and Stewart. *We Accuse!* Simon & Schuster, 1954.

Kugelmass, J. Alvin. *J. Robert Oppenheimer and the Atomic Story.* Messner, 1953.

Orozco, José Clemente, painter, b Zapotlan, Mexico, f editor, c.

Helm, MacKinley. *Man of Fire.* Harcourt, Brace, 1953.

Orwell, George, writer, b Motihari, India, f British civil servant, s.

Atkins, John Alfred. *George Orwell.* John Calder, 1958.

*Orwell, George. *Such Were the Joys.* Harcourt, Brace, 1953. (strong denunciation of his boarding school, brutal bed-wetting cure described)

Osler, William, physician, humanitarian, author, bibliophile, b Bondhead, Ontario, Canada, f minister, c+.

Gushing, Harvey W. *The Life of Sir William Osier.* Oxford University Press, 1925.

Reid, Edith. *The Great Physician.* Oxford University Press, 1934.

Paderewski, Ignace Jan, pianist, politician, b Kurylowaka, Poland, f manager of estates, g & S.

Paderewski, Ignace Jan, and Mary Lawton. *The Paderewski Memoirs.* Collins, 1939.

Phillips, Charles J. M. *Paderewski: The Story of a Modern Immortal.* Macmillan, 1934. (school rebel)

Pasternak, Boris, writer, b Moscow, f painter, m musician, c+ & S.

Pasternak, Boris. *Essay in Autobiography.* Harwill-Collins, 1959. (strong school rejection, love for home)

———. *Safe Conduct: An Autobiography.* Elek, 1959. (supportive intellectual parents)

Ruge, Gerd. *Pasternak: A Pictorial Biography.* Thames & Hudson, 1959.

Patton, George S., soldier, b San Gabriel, Calif., f lawyer, s & M.

Mellor, William B. *Patton, the Fighting Man.* Putnam, 1946.

Semmes, Harry H. *Portrait of Patton.* Appleton, 1955.

Wellard, James H. *General George S. Patton, Jr., Man under Mars.* Dodd, Mead, 1946.

Paul, Elliot, writer, b Maiden, Mass., f farmer, c-.

Paul, Elliot. *A Ghost Town on the Yellowstone.* Cresset, 1949. (anecdotal boyhood memories, ribald, nostalgic)

———. *Linden on the Saugus Branch.* Cresset, 1948. (exercise in total recall by precocious, mother-tutored boy; never one to praise the classroom)

———. *My Old Kentucky Home.* Cresset, 1950. (covers the writer during his eighteenth year; this is one in series of autobiographical books)

Pavlov, Ivan P., physiologist, b Ryazan, Russia, f Greek Orthodox priest, c+.

Babkin, Boris P. *Pavlov.* University of Chicago, 1949. (time-out period established him as scholar)

Peary, Robert E., arctic explorer, b Cresson, Pa., f lumberman, c.

Peary, Robert Edwin. *Letters to Mother.* Channel, 1959.

*Stafford, Marie (Peary). *Discoverer of the North Pole.* Morrow, 1959. (widowed mother tried to make resistant boy effeminate, made him wear sunbonnets, accompanied him to college)
Weems, John Edward. *Race for the Pole.* Holt, 1960.

Peron, Eva T., dictator's wife, b Los Toldas, Argentina, f business, g-.
Flores, Maria. *The Woman with the Whip.* Doubleday, 1952. (a rejected girl)
Peron, Eva. *My Mission in Life.* Vantage, 1953.

Picasso, Pablo, painter, sculptor, b Malaga, Spain, f art teacher, g-.
Penrose, Roland. *Picasso: His Life and Work.* Gollancz, 1958.
Raynal, Maurice. *Picasso: Biographical and Critical Studies.* Skira, 1953.
*Sabartes, Jaime. *Picasso: An Intimate Portrait.* W. H. Alien, 1949.

Pire, Father Dominique, humanitarian, b Dinant, Belgium, f small-town official, c+.
Vehenne, Hughes. *Story of Father Dominique Pire.* Dutton, 1961.

Pius XII, Pope (Eugenio Pacelli), b Rome, f specialist in church law, s & S.
Doyle, Charles H. *Life of Pope Pius XII.* Didier, 1945.
Halecki, Oscar. *Eugenia Pacelli, Pope of Peace.* Creative Age, 1951. (scholarly, supportive family)
Hatch, Alden, and Seamus Walshe. *Crown of Glory.* Heinemann, 1957.
Smit, Jan Olav. *Pope Pius XII.* Burns Oates, 1950.

Powys, John Cowper, writer, poet, critic, b Shirley, Derbyshire, England, f clergyman, s-.
Coombes, H. *T. F. Powys.* Barrie & Rockliff, 1960. (concise and reasoned account of a tense household which produced four novelists)
* Powys, John Cowper. *Autobiography.* Bodley Head, 1934.
Powys, Littleton. *Still the Joy of It.* Macdonald, 1956.

Prokofiev, Sergei, composer, b Sontzovka, Exaterinoslav, Russia, f agronomist, estate manager, S.
Nestyev, Israel V. *Prokofiev.* Stanford University Press, 1960. (mother left home with boy to seek training, parents separated)

Proust, Marcel, novelist, b Paris, f professor of medicine, s.
March, Harold. *The Two Worlds of Marcel Proust.* University of Pennsylvania: O.U.P., 1948.
Maurois, André. *Quest for Proust.* Cape, 1950.

*Painter, George D. *Marcel Proust: A Biography*. Chatto, 1959. (asthmatic boy, smothering mother, rejecting father)

Puccini, Giacomo, operatic composer, b Lucca, Italy, f musician, village organist, as were paternal ancestors for four generations, g & S.
Garner, Mosco. *Puccini: A Critical Biography*. Duckworth, 1958.
Marek, George R. *Puccini: A Biography*. Simon & Schuster, 1951.
Specht, Ricard. *Giacomo Puccini: The Man, his Life, his Work*. Dent, 1933.

Pyle, Ernie, newspaperman, b farm near Dana, Ind., f farmer, c-.
Miller, Lee Graham. *An Ernie Pyle Album*. Sloan, 1946.
*———. *Story of Ernie Pyle*. Viking, 1950. (supportive home, good peer relationships, mediocre school record)

Quezon, Manuel, politician, b Baler, Philippines, f schoolteacher, c+.
Quezon, Manuel. *Good Fight*. Appleton-Century, 1946.
Quirino, Carlos. *Quezon, Man of Destiny*. McCullough, 1935.

Quiller-Couch, Arthur T., man of letters, b Polperro, Cornwall, f physician, c+.
Brittain, Fred. *Arthur Quiller-Couch*. Cambridge University Press, 1947.
*Quiller-Couch, Arthur T. *Memories and Opinions*. Macmillan, 1945. (opinionated, affectionate family)

Rachmaninoff, Sergei, pianist, composer, b Novgorod, Russia, f estate manager (unsuccessful), tutored & S (conservatory at age nine).
Bertensson, Sergei, and Leyda Jay. *Sergei Rachmaninoff*. NewYork University, 1956.
Seroff, Victor. *Rachmaninoff*. Simon & Schuster, 1950.

Rama Rau, Santha, writer, b Madras, India, f diplomat, c+.
*Rama Rau. *Gifts of Passage*. Harper, 1961.
*———. *Remember the House*. Harper, 1956. (a girl reared in many countries, participant in world cultures, an intellectual mother with organizing abilities)

Rasputin, Grigori E., politician, b Pokrovskoye, Siberia, f farmer, g-.
Liepman, Heinz. *Rasputin—A New Judgment*. Muller, 1959.
Rasputin, Maria. *My Father*. Cassell, 1934.

Ravel, Maurice, composer, b Ciboure, France, f mining engineer, S.
Myers, Rollo H. *Ravel: Life and Works*. Duckworth, 1960.
Seroff, Victor I. *Maurice Ravel*. Holt, 1953.

Regler, Gustav, author, b Merzig, Germany, f bookseller, c+.
*Regler, Gustav. *The Owl of Minerva*. Hart-Davis, 1959. (a dreaming, opinionated father; gentle, fearful mother)

Reuther, Walter, labor leader, b Wheeling, W.Va., f factory worker, union official, c-.
Dayton, Eldorous L. *Walter Reuther: The Autocrat of the Bargaining Table*. Devin-Adair, 1958.
Howe, Irving, and B. J. Widick. *The UAW and Walter Reuther*. Random House, 1949.

Rhee, Syngman, politician, b Nung-an-go, Korea, f inherited wealth, c+.
Oliver, Robert T. *Syngman Rhee, the Man behind the Myth*. Dodd, Mead, 1954. (sickly child of elderly smothering mother and rejecting father)

Rhodes, Cecil, administrator, financier, b Bishop's Stortford, England, f curate, c+.
Gross, Felix. *Rhodes of Africa*. Cassell, 1956. (poor sibling relationships; irritable, eccentric father)
Maurois, André. *Cecil Rhodes*. Collins, 1953.
Millin, Sarah G. *Cecil Rhodes*. Chatto, 1933.

Rilke, Rainer Maria, poet, writer, b Prague, f railway official, c-.
Peters, H. Frederick. *Rainer Maria Rilke: Masks and the Man*. University of Washington, 1960.
Rilke, Rainer Maria. *Letters to a Young Poet*. Sidgwick & Jackson, 1945.
———. *Selected Letters*. Macmillan, 1946.

Rivera, Diego, painter, b Guanajuato, Mexico, f town official, public health officer, s & S.
*March, Gladys, ed. *My Art, My Life: An Autobiography*. Citadel, 1960.
Wolfe, Bertram D. *Diego Rivera: His Life and Times*. Hale, 1939.

Robinson, Edwin Arlington, poet, b Head Tide, Maine, f ship's carpenter, storekeeper, c-.
Hagedorn, Hermann. *Edwin Arlington Robinson*. Macmillan, 1938.
Neff, Emery E. *Edwin Arlington Robinson*. Methuen, 1949.

Robinson, Jackie, baseball player, b Cairo, Ga., f farmer, city laborer, m domestic worker, c.
*Robinson, Jackie. *Jackie Robinson: My Own Story*. Greenberg, 1948.

Rowan, Carl Thomas. *Wait till Next Year*. Random House, 1960.

Rockefeller, John D., Jr., philanthropist, b Cleveland, Ohio, f financier, c.

Flynn, John Thomas. *God's Gold: The Story of Rockefeller and his Times*. Harcourt, Brace, 1932.

Fosdick, Raymond. *John D. Rockefeller, Jr.* Harper, 1956.

Morris, Joe Alex. *Those Rockefeller Brothers: An Informal Biography of Five Extraordinary Young Men*. Harper, 1953.

Nevins, Allan. *Study in Power*. Scribner's, 1953.

Rockefeller, John D., Sr., oil magnate, b Richford, N.Y., f cancer-cure salesman, s & S.

*Chase, Mary Ellen. *Abby Aldrich Rockefeller*. New York: Macmillan, 1950. (child-centered home well described)

*Manchester, William. *A Rockefeller Family Portrait*. Little, Brown, 1959. (author describes a physical vitality persisting through three generations)

Poling, James. *The Rockefeller Record*. Crowell, 1960.

Rockefeller, Nelson, politician, b Bar Harbor, Maine, f philanthropist, c.

Morris, Joe Alex. *Nelson Rockefeller: A Biography*. Harper, 1960.

Rodin, Auguste, sculptor, b Paris, f police inspector, s-.

Cladel, Judith. *Rodin: The Man and his Art*. Kegan Paul, 1917.

Lawton, Frederick. *The Life and Work of Auguste Rodin*. Unwin, 1906.

Ludovici, Anthony. *Personal Reminiscences of Auguste Rodin*. Murray, 1926.

Rogers, Will, actor, humorist, b Oologah, Indian Territory, s-.

Croy, Homer. *Our Will Rogers*, Duell, Sloan & Pearce, 1953. (incorrigible son of well-to-do widower)

Rogers, Will. *Autobiography*. Houghton Mifflin, 1949.

Rolland, Romain, man of letters, lecturer, b Clamecy, France, f notary, c+.

Rolland, Remain. *Journey Within*. Philosophical Library, 1947. (a most over-possessive mother, disliked father)

Zweig, Stefan. *Romain Rolland: The Man and his Work*. Cassell, 1938.

Romulo, Carlos, statesman, author, b Camiling, Philippines, f mayor, governor, c+.

Romulo, Carlos. *I Saw the Fall of the Philippines*. Doubleday, 1942.

———. *I Walked with Heroes*. Holt, 1961.

Spencer, Cornelia. *Romulo, Voice of Freedom.* Day, 1953.

Roosevelt, Eleanor, lecturer, writer, leader in social and international affairs, b New York City, f businessman, s.

*Roosevelt, Eleanor. *Lady of the White House.* Hutchinson, 1938.
*———. *This I Remember.* Hutchinson, 1950.
Steinberg, Alfred. *Mrs. R.: The Life of Eleanor Roosevelt.* Putnam, 1958.

Roosevelt, Franklin D., politician, b Hyde Park, N.Y., f financier (often unsuccessful), c+.

Burns, James M. *The Lion and the Fox.* Seeker & Warburg, 1956.
Gunther, John. *Roosevelt in Retrospect: A Profile in History.* H. Hamilton, 1950.
*Roosevelt, James, and S. Shallet. *Affectionately, F.D.R.: A Son's Story of a Lonely Man.* Harrap, 1960.
Schriftgiesser, Karl. *The Amazing Roosevelt Family.* Funk, 1942.

Roosevelt, Theodore, politician, b New York City, f glass importer, volunteer social worker, c.

*Putnam, Carleton. *Theodore Roosevelt, Vol. I: The Formative Years.* Scribner's, 1958.
Riis, Jacob A. *Theodore Roosevelt, the Citizen.* Outlook, 1904.
Robinson, Corinne Roosevelt. *My Brother, Theodore Roosevelt.* Scribner's, 1921.
Roosevelt, Theodore. *Theodore Roosevelt: An Autobiography.* Macmillan, 1913.

Russell, Bertrand, mathematician, philosopher, social reformer, b Trelleck, Monmouthshire, f politician, inherited wealth, c+.

Leggett, H. W. *Bertrand Russell.* O. M., Lincolns, 1949.
*Wood, Alan. *Bertrand Russell, the Passionate Skeptic.* Allen & Unwin, 1957.

Rutherford, Ernest, physicist, b Nelson, New Zealand, f farmer, c+.

Rowland, John. *Ernest Rutherford, Atom Pioneer.* Werner Laurie, 1955.

Salazar, António De Oliveira, politician, b Santo Comba-Dao, Portugal, f bailiff, innkeeper, c+.

Ferro, Antonio. *Salazar: Portugal and her Leader.* Faber & Faber, 1939.
Gamier, Christine. *Salazar: An Intimate Portrait.* Farrar, Straus, 1954.

Sandburg, Carl, author, b Galesburg, Ill., f railroad laborer, c.
Detzer, Karl W. *Carl Sandburg: A Study in Personality and Background.* Harcourt, Brace, 1941.
*Sandburg, Carl. *Always the Young Strangers.* Cape, 1953.
———. *Prairie-Town Boy.* Harcourt, Brace, 1955.

Sanger, Margaret, social reformer, b Corning, N.Y., f stonecutter, s & S.
Lader, Lawrence. *Margaret Sanger Story.* Doubleday, 1955.
Sanger, Margaret. *Margaret Sanger: An Autobiography.* Gollancz, 1939.

Santayana, George, philosopher, poet, b Madrid, f lawyer, c+.
Howgate, George W. *George Santayana.* Oxford, 1938. (a rejected boy)
Santayana, George. *Persons and Places: The Background of My Life.* Constable, 1944.

Saroyan, William, fiction writer, playwright, b Fresno, Calif., f Protestant minister, grape grower, m day worker as widow, s-.
*Saroyan, William. *The Bicycle Rider in Beverly Hills.* Scribner's, 1952. (description of school rejection and of feelings of rejection because of nationality)
———. *The Twin Adventures.* Harcourt, Brace, 1950.

Schnabel, Artur, pianist, b Lipnick, Austria, f wool merchant, g & S.
Saerchinger, César. *Artur Schnabel.* Cassell, 1957.

Schreiner, Olive, writer, b Wittebergen Mission Station, Basutoland, South Africa, f Methodist missionary, tutored.
Cronwright-Schreiner, S. C., ed. *Letters of Olive Schreiner.* Benn, 1924.
Gregg, Lyndall. *Memories of Olive Schreiner.* Chambers, 1957.
Hobman, Daisy L. *Olive Schreiner: Her Friends and Times.* Watts, 1955. (failure-prone father who loved his wife and children with infinite tenderness)

Schumann-Heinke, Ernestine, operatic contralto, b Lieberri, Bohemia, f Austrian army officer, g.
Lawton, Mary, ed. *Schumann-Heink, the Last of the Titans.* Macmillan, 1928.

Schweitzer, Albert, philosopher, physician, musician, b Kayersburg, Alsace, f Lutheran minister, c+.
Cousins, Norman. *Dr. Schweitzer of Lambarene.* Harper, 1960.

Langley, Nina. *Dr. Schweitzer.* O. M., Harrap, 1956.
Payne, Pierre. *Three Worlds of Albert Schweitzer.* Nelson, 1957.
Schweitzer, Albert. *Memoirs of Childhood and Youth.* Allen & Unwin, 1950.
*———. *My Life and Thought.* Allen & Unwin, 1933.

Shaw, George Bernard, playwright, novelist, critic, b Dublin, f manufacturer (unsuccessful), m music teacher, s.

Ervine, St. John. *Bernard Shaw.* Constable, 1956.
Harris, Frank. *Bernard Shaw.* Gollancz, 1931.
Irvine, William. *The Universe of G.B.S.* McGraw-Hill, 1949.

Shostakovich, Dmitri, composer, b St. Petersburg, f worked in patent office, m as widow worked in patent office, s- & S.

Martynov, Ivan I. *Dmitri Shostakovich: The Man and his Work.* Philosophical Library, 1947.
*Seroff, Victor I. *Dmitri Shostakovich: The Life and Background of a Soviet Composer.* Knopf, 1943. (written in collaboration with sister of subject's mother; an account of a smothering and dominating mother who could not be happy when her son persisted in his attempts to free himself from her)

Sibelius, Jean, composer, b Hameenlinna, Finland, f physician, s & S.

Ekman, Kari. *Jean Sibelius: His Life and Personality.* Wilmer, 1937.
*Johnson, Harold E. *Jean Sibelius.* Faber, 1960. (describes Sibelius as a naive, shy, dreaming boy with keen perceptions of both eye and ear; disliked discipline as a student; supportive home)
Ringbom, Nils E. *Jean Sibelius: A Master and his Work.* University of Oklahoma, 1954.

Sitwell, Edith, poet, critic, novelist, b Scarborough, f inherited income, unsuccessful (at times) financier, tutored.

Sitwell, Osbert, poet, playwright, novelist, b London, f inherited wealth, S.

Sitwell, Sacheverell, poet, critic, b Scarborough, f inherited income, c.

Sitwell, Osbert. *Great Morning!* Macmillan, 1947.
———. *Laughter in the Next Room.* Macmillan, 1949.
———. *Left Hand, Right Hand!* Macmillan, 1945. (a delightful, eccentric, but very dominating father, three talented, highly individual youngsters)
———. *Noble Essences: A Book of Characters.* Macmillan, 1950.
———. *Scarlet Tree.* Macmillan, 1946. (cutting commentary on schools; a family album of uncommon interest, skillfully told)

Smith, Alfred E., politician, b New York City, f trucker, g-.
Handlin, Oscar. *Al Smith and his America.* Little, Brown, 1958.
Warner, Emily (Smith). *Happy Warrior: A Biography of My Father, Alfred E. Smith.* Doubleday, 1956.

Smith, Lillian, writer, b Jasper, Fla., f manufacturer, c- & S.
*Smith, Lillian. *The Journey.* Cresset, 1956.
*———. *Killers of the Dream.* Norton, 1949.

Smuts, Jan Christiaan, soldier, politician, b Riebeck West, South Africa, f prosperous farmer, legislator, c.
Kraus, Rene. *Old Master.* Dutton, 1944.
Millin, Sarah G. *General Smuts.* Faber, 1939.

Sousa, John Philip, bandleader, composer, b Washington, D.C., f bandmaster, cabinetmaker, g- & S.
Berger, Kenneth W. *The March King and his Band.* Exposition, 1957.
Lingg, Ann M. *John Philip Sousa.* Holt, 1954.

Spender, Stephen, poet, critic, b London, f journalist, novelist, c-.
* Spender, Stephen. *World Within World.* H. Hamilton, 1951.

Stalin, Joseph, politician, b near Tiflis, Georgia, U.S.S.R., f shoemaker, s-.
Fischer, Louis. *Life and Death of Stalin.* Harper, 1952.
Svanidze, Budu. *My Uncle, Joseph Stalin.* Putnam, 1953.

Stanislavski (Constantine Alexeev), actor, producer, b Moscow, f inherited wealth, mill owner, tutored.
Gorchakov, Nikolai M. *Stanislauski Directs.* Funk, 1954.
Stanislavski, Constantine. *My Life in Art.* Bles, 1937.

Stanley, Henry Morton, explorer, b near Denbigh, Wales, adopted, g-.
Anstruther, Ian. *I Presume: Stanley's Triumph and Disaster.* Bles, 1956.
Stanley, Dorothy, ed. *The Autobiography of Sir Henry Morton Stanley.* Houghton Mifflin, 1909.

Stefansson, Vilhjalmur, arctic explorer, b Arnes, Manitoba, Canada, f farmer, c+.
Hanson, Earl P. *Stefansson, Prophet of the North.* Harper, 1941.

Steffens, Lincoln, journalist, f prosperous merchant, c+.
*Steffens, Lincoln. *Autobiography of Lincoln Steffens.* Harcourt, Brace, 1931. (congenial parents; supporting, permissive, stimulating home)

*———. *The Letters of Lincoln Steffens*. Harcourt, Brace, 1938.

Stein, Gertrude, writer, b Allegheny, Pa., f vice-president streetcar company (unsuccessful), c-.

Brinnin, John M. *The Third Rose*. Weidenfeld & Nicolson, 1960.

Rogers, William G. *When This You See, Remember Me: Gertrude Stein in Person*. Rinehart, 1948.

Sprigge, Elizabeth. *Gertrude Stein*. H. Hamilton, 1957.

Stein, Gertrude. *Everybody's Autobiography*. Heinemann, 1938.

Steinmetz, Charles P., electrical engineer, b Breslau, Germany, f engineer, c.

Hammond, John W. *Charles Proteus Steinmetz: A Biography*. Century, 1924.

Lavine, Sigmund A. *Steinmetz, Maker of Lightning*. Dodd, Mead, 1955.

Leonard, J. N. *Loki: The Life of Charles Proteus Steinmetz*. Doubleday, 1929.

Stevenson, Adlai E., politician, b Los Angeles, f farm manager, c.

Busch, Noel F. *Adlai E. Stevenson of Illinois*. Farrar, Straus, 1952.

Davis, Kenneth S. *Prophet in his Own Country*. Doubleday, 1957.

Ives, Elizabeth. *My Brother Adlai*. Morrow, 1956.

Martin, John B. *Adlai Stevenson*. Harper, 1952.

Stravinsky, Igor, composer, b Oranienbaum, Russia, f singer, c & S.

Stravinsky, Igor. *Chronicle of My Life*. Gollancz, 1936.

Strobel, Heinrich. *Stravinsky: A Classic Humanist*. Merlin, 1955.

Tansman, Alexander. *Igor Stravinsky: The Man and his Music*. Putnam, 1949.

Stuart, Jesse, writer, b Cedar Riffles, Ky., f farmer, c+.

Stuart, Jesse. *Beyond Dark Hills: A Personal Story*. Hutchinson, 1938.

*———. *God's Addling: Story of Mick Stuart, My Father*. McGraw-Hill, 1960. (an energetic father who wanted schooling for his children)

———. *Thread that Runs so True*. Scribner's, 1949.

Sullivan, Arthur S., composer, b London, f army bandmaster, S.

Darlington, William A. *The World of Gilbert and Sullivan*. Peter Nevill, 1950.

Power-Waters, Alma. *The Melody Maker*. Dutton, 1959. (school truant, home tutored)

Sullivan, Herbert. *Sir Arthur Sullivan: His Life, Letters and Diaries.* Doran, 1927. (parents were in love to the end of their days, encouraged son's early evidenced talent)

Sun Yat-Sen, politician, b Chou-Hung, Macao, f rice farmer, c+.
Chen, Stephen. *Sun Yat-Sen: A Portrait.* Day, 1946.
Hahn, Emily. *The Soong Sisters.* Doubleday, 1941.

Taft, Robert A., politician, b Cincinnati, Ohio, f politician, c+.
Harnsberger, Charles T. *A Man of Courage: Robert A. Taft.* Wilcox & Follett, 1952.
Taft, Helen. *Recollections of Full Years.* Dodd, Mead, 1914.
White, William S. *The Taft Story.* Harper, 1954.

Tagore, Rabindranath, poet, artist, composer, b Calcutta, India, f wealthy merchant, c-.
Chakravarty, Amiya, ed. *A Tagore Reader.* Macmillan, 1961.
Tagore, Rabindranath. *My Reminiscences.* Macmillan, 1917.
Thompson, Edward John. *Rabindranath Tagore: Poet and Dramatist* (2nd ed.). Oxford, 1948.

Thomas, Dylan, poet, b Carmarthenshire, Wales, f teacher, s.
Brinnin, John M. *Dylan Thomas in America.* Dent, 1956.
Thomas, Caitlin. *Leftover Life to Kill.* Putnam, 1957.

Tito (Joseph Broz), politician, b Kumrovec, Croatia, f horsetrader.
Dedijer, Vladimir. *Tito.* Simon & Schuster, 1952.
Maclean, Fitzroy. *The Heretic: The Life and Times of Joseph Broz-Tito.* Harper, 1957.

Tolstoi, Leo N., novelist, philosopher, b Yasnaya Polyana, Russia, f estate manager, c-.
Dole, Nathan Haskell. *The Life of Count Tolstoi.* Crowell, 1911.
Simmons, Ernest J. *Leo Tolstoy.* Little, Brown, 1946.
*Tolstoi, Alexandra. *Tolstoy: A Life of My Father.* Gollancz, 1954.
Tolstoi, Count Ilya. *Reminiscences of Tolstoy.* Century, 1914.

Toscanini, Arturo, conductor, b Oleorrente, Italy, f tailor, S.
Chotzinoff, Samuel. *Toscanini: An Intimate Portrait.* H. Hamilton, 1956.
Ewen, David. *Story of Arturo Toscanini.* Holt, 1951.
Haggin, Bernard H. *Conversations with Toscanini.* Doubleday, 1959.
Taubman, Hyman H. *The Maestro.* Simon & Schuster, 1951.

Toulouse-Lautrec, Henri, painter, b Aibi, France, f inherited wealth, c.
Gauzi, François. *My Friend: Toulouse-Lautrec.* Spearman, 1957.
Hanson, Lawrence. *Tragic Life of Toulouse-Lautrec.* Seeker & Warburg, 1956.
Lassaigne, Jacques. *Lautrec.* Skira, 1953.
Perruchot, Henri. *Toulouse-Lautrec.* Perpetua, 1960.

Trotsky, Leon, Communist leader, b Yanovka, Russia, f well-to-do farmer, c.
Trotsky, Leon. *Diary in Exile.* Faber, 1959.
*———. *My Life: An Attempt at an Autobiography.* Scribner's, 1930.

Trujillo Molina, Rafael, army officer, politician, b San Cristobal, Dominican Republic, f laborer, g-.
de Besault, Laurence. *President Trujillo: His Work and the Dominican Republic.* Washington, 1936. (neglected boy)
Hicks, Albert C. *Blood in the Streets: The Life and Rule of Trujillo.* Creative Age, 1946.
Ornes, German E. *Trujillo: Little Caesar of the Caribbean.* Nelson, 1958.

Truman, Harry, politician, b Lamar, Mo., f farmer, s.
Daniels, Jonathan. *The Man of Independence.* Lippincott, 1950.
Hillman, William. *Mr. President.* Farrar, Straus, 1952. (early reader; read Bible through twice before he was twelve; an upwardly mobile home; parents were community leaders; father had strong physical drive, worked from daylight to dark)
McNaughton, Frank, and Walter Hehmeyer. *This Man Truman.* Harrap, 1945.

Undset, Sigrid, novelist, b Kalundborg, Denmark, f archaeologist.
Larsen, H. A. "Sigrid Undset." *American-Scandinavian Review* (1929).
Winsnes, Andreas H. *Sigrid Undset.* Sheed & Ward, 1953.

Van Paassen, Pierre, journalist, author, b Gorcum, Holland, f business, c+.
*van Paassen, Pierre. *Days of Our Years.* Heinemann, 1939.
*———. *Visions Rise and Change.* Dial, 1955.

Verne, Jules, writer, b Nantes, France, f lawyer, c+.
Allotte de la Fuye, M. *Jules Verne.* Macmillan, 1941.
Waltz, George H. *Jules Verne: The Biography of an Imagination.* Holt, 1943.

Von Ribbentrop, Joachim, diplomat, b Wessel-am-Rhine, f business, s & S.
Schwarz, Paul. *This Man Ribbentrop.* Messner, 1943.

Waksman, Selman, bacteriologist, b Novaia-Priluka, Ukraine, f carpenter, landlord, m storekeeper, c+.
*Waksman, Selman. *My Life with the Microbes*. Simon & Schuster, 1954.

Wallace, Henry A., agriculturalist, politician, b Adair County, Iowa, f editor, Wallace's Farm Journal, Secretary of Agriculture, c.
Kingdon, Frank. *An Uncommon Man: Henry Wallace and 60 Million Jobs*. Readers Press, 1945.
Lord, Russell. *The Wallaces of Iowa*. Houghton Mifflin, 1947.
Macdonald, Dwight. *Henry Wallace: The Man and the Myth*. Vanguard, 1948.

Walpole, Hugh, novelist, b Auckland, New Zealand, f Episcopal minister, c.
Hart-Davis, Rupert. *Hugh Walpole*. Macmillan, 1952.
Walpole, Hugh. *Roman Fountain*. Doubleday, 1940.

Washington, Booker T., educator, b Franklin County, Va., f unknown, m did housework, c.
Mathews, Basil J. *Booker T. Washington: Educator and Interracial Interpreter*. S.C.M., 1949.
Spencer, Samuel R. *Booker T. Washington and the Negro's Place in American Life*. Little, Brown, 1955.
Washington, Booker T. *Up from Slavery*. Harrap, 1909.

Webb, Beatrice, writer, b Standish House, Gloucester, f wealthy manufacturer (prone to reverses), s- & tutored.
Cole, Margaret I. *Beatrice Webb*. Longmans, 1945.
Webb, Beatrice. *Our Partnership*. Longmans, 1948.

Weizmann, Chaim, chemist, politician, b Motol, Russia, f lumber business (dramatic ups and downs), c+.
Berlin, Isaiah. *Chaim Weizmann*. Weidenfeld & Nicolson, 1958.
Weizmann, Chaim. *Trial and Error: An Autobiography*. H. Hamilton, 1949.

Wells, H. G., writer, b Bromley, Kent, f gardener, shopkeeper, m housekeeper, c+.
Brome, Vincent. *H. G. Wells: A Biography*. Longmans, 1951.
Vallentin, Antonina. *H. G. Wells: Prophet of Our Day*. Day, 1950.
*Wells, H. G. *Experiments in Autobiography: Discoveries and Conclusions of a Very Ordinary Brain*. Gollancz, 1934.

Wharton, Edith Newbold, novelist, b New York City, f engineer, also inherited wealth, tutored at home.
Lubbock, Percy. *Portrait of Edith Wharton*. Cape, 1947.
Wharton, Edith. *A Backward Glance*. Appleton-Century, 1934.

Whistler, James A. McNeill, painter, etcher, b Lowell, Mass., f engineer (failure-prone, personality problems), s & M (expelled).
Mumford, Elizabeth. *Whistler's Mother*. Little, Brown, 1939. ("Jaime" perpetually tardy, unable to submit to routine)
Parry, Albert. *Whistler's Father*. Bobbs-Merrill, 1939. (mother described as a woman who was obnoxiously dominating)
Pearson, Hesketh. *The Man Whistler*. Methuen, 1952.

White, Walter Francis, author, secretary NAACP, b Atlanta, Ga., f postman, c.
Cannon, Poppy. *Gentle Knight: My Husband, Walter White*. Rinehart, 1956.
White, Walter Francis. *Man Called White: The Autobiography of Walter White*. Viking, 1948. (race riot turned boy's mind toward becoming champion of the African-American)

White, William Allen, editor, writer, b Emporia, Kans., f doctor (without degree), hotelkeeper, c-.
Hinshaw, David. *A Man from Kansas: The Story of William Allen White*. Putnam, 1945.
*White, William Allen. *Autobiography of William Allen White*. New York: Macmillan, 1946.

Wiener, Norbert, mathematician, writer, b Columbia, Mo., f professor, c+.
* Wiener, Norbert. *Ex-Prodigy: My Childhood and Youth*. Simon & Schuster, 1953. (parents differed in sense of values)
*———. *I Am a Mathematician: The Later Life of a Prodigy*. Gollancz, 1956.

Wilde, Oscar, poet, wit, dramatist, b Dublin, f physician, c+.
Byrne, Patrick. *The Wildes of Merrion Square*. Staples Press, 1953.
Harris, Frank. *Oscar Wilde*. Constable, 1938.
Holland, Vyvyan. *Son of Oscar Wilde*. Hart-Davis, 1954.
Pearson, Hesketh. *Life of Oscar Wilde*. Methuen, 1950.

Williams, William Carlos, physician, writer, b Rutherford, N.J., f engineer, c+.

*Williams, William Carlos. *The Autobiography of William Carlos Williams*. Random House, 1951. (love for learning, unconventional home)

———. *Yes, Mrs. Williams: A Personal Record of My Mother*. McDowell, Obolensky, 1959.

Willkie, Wendell, politician, b Elwood, Ind., f lawyer, m lawyer, c+.

Barnes, Joseph. *Willkie*. Simon & Schuster, 1952.

Dillon, Mary. *Wendell Willkie*. Lippincott, 1952.

Hatch, Alden. *Young Willkie*. Harcourt, Brace, 1944.

Wilson, Woodrow, professor, politician, b Staunton, Va., f minister, c+.

Baker, Ray Stannard. *Woodrow Wilson: Life and Letters*. Heinemann, 1927.

Day, Donald, ed. *Woodrow Wilson's Own Story*. Little, Brown, 1952.

McAdoo, Eleanor Wilson. *The Woodrow Wilsons*. Macmillan, 1937.

Wolfe, Thomas, writer, b Asheville, N.C., f stonecutter, c+.

Holman, Clarence Hugh. *Thomas Wolfe*. University of Minnesota: O.U.P., 1960. (an all-round student)

Nowell, Elizabeth. *Thomas Wolfe: A Biography*. Doubleday, 1960.

Wheaton, Mabel Wolfe, and LeGette Blythe. *Thomas Wolfe and his Family*. Doubleday, 1961. (father described as an irritable man with a gift for narrative, loved his children, liked to set an extravagant table, resented wife's real estate deals; mother was a driving, "needling" woman)

Woolf, Virginia, writer, b London, f editor of *Dictionary of National Biography*, home-tutored.

Pippett, Aileen. *The Moth and the Star*. Little, Brown, 1955. (delicate, home-tutored girl)

Woolf, Leonard, ed. *A Writer's Diary*. Harcourt, Brace, 1954.

Woollcott, Alexander, journalist, writer, b The Phalanx, New Journal, f unsuccessful expatriated lawyer, c.

Adams, Samuel Hopkins. *A. Woollcott: His Life and his World*. H. Hamilton, 1946.

Kaufman, Beatrice, and Joseph Hennessey, eds. *The Letters of Alexander Woollcott*. Viking, 1944.

Wright, Frank Lloyd, architect, b Richland Center, Wis., f minister, m teacher, c-.
*Wright, Frank Lloyd. *An Autobiography*. Faber, 1945.
———. *A Testament*. Architectural Press, 1959.
Wright, John Lloyd. *My Father Who Is on Earth*. Putnam, 1946.
Wright, Olgivanna Lloyd. *Our House*. Horizon, 1959.

Wright, Orville, aviation pioneer, b Dayton, Ohio, f minister.
Kelly, Fred C. *The Wright Brothers*. Harcourt, Brace, 1943.

Wright, Richard, writer, b near Natchez, Miss., mill worker, s-.
Wright, Richard. *Black Boy*. Harper, 1945. (strong opinions about religion and learning in the family)
———. *Black Power*. Dobson, 1956.

Wright, Wilbur, aviation pioneer, b Millville, Ind., f minister, s-.
Wright, Wilbur and Orville. *Miracle at Kitty Hawk: The Letters of Wilbur and Orville Wright*. Farrar, Straus, 1951.

Yeats, William Butler, poet, dramatist, b near Dublin, f artist, s & S.
Ellmann, Richard. *Yeats—The Man and the Masks*. Macmillan, 1949.
Yeats, J. B. *Yeats: Letters to his Son*. Dutton, 1946.
Yeats, William Butler. *Autobiographies: Reveries over Childhood and Youth*. Macmillan, 1955. (his aunts and uncles thought him dull, his teachers found him slow and annoying, only his father enjoyed him)

Zinsser, Hans, bacteriologist, b New York City, f chemist, c-.
Wagenknecht, Charles, ed. *When I Was a Child*. Dutton, 1946.
*Zinsser, Hans. *As I Remember Him*. Little, Brown, 1940.

Zola, Emile, novelist, b Paris, f engineer, s.
Hemmings, Frederick W. *Emile Zola*. Clarendon Press, 1953.

Zweig, Stefan, writer, b Vienna, f successful businessman, c+.
Zweig, Friderike M. W. *Stefan Zweig*. Crowell, 1946.
Zweig, Stefan. *World of Yesterday*. Cassell, 1943.

Collective Biographies

Bolton, Sarah K. *Famous American Authors.* Crowell, 1954.

Bradford, Gamaliel. *American Portraits.* Houghton Mifflin, 1922.

Churchill, Winston. *Great Contemporaries.* Butterworth, 1938.

Cooper, A. C., and Charles A. Palmer. *Twenty Modern Americans.* Harcourt, Brace, 1954.

Eastman, Max. *Great Companions.* Museum Press, 1960.

Huff, Warren, and Edna L. W. Huff. *Famous Americans.* Charles Webb, 1941.

Kornitzer, Bela. *Famous Fathers and Sons.* Hermitage, 1952.

Kunitz, Stanley J. *Twentieth Century Authors.* H. W. Wilson, 1942.

Law, Frederick H. *Modern Great Americans.* Century, 1926.

Ludwig, Emil. *Three Portraits: Hitler, Mussolini, Stalin.* Alliance, 1940.

Madison, Charles A. *Critics and Crusaders: A Century of American Protest.* Holt, 1947.

Riedman, Sarah R. *Men and Women Behind the Atom.* Abelard, Schuman, 1958.

Untermeyer, Louis. *Makers of the Modern World.* Simon & Schuster, 1955.

Wilson, H. W. (publisher), *Current Biography,* 1940-1961 (published annually)

Wolfe, Bertram D. *Three Who Made a Revolution.* Thames & Hudson, 1956.

Professional References Cited

Anderson, Harold H., ed. *Creativity and Its Cultivation.* H. Hamilton, 1959.

Anderson, Kenneth E., ed. *Research on the Academically Talented Student.* National Education Association, 1961.

Brandewein, P. F. *The Gifted Student as Future Scientist.* Harcourt, Brace, 1955.

Getzels, Jacob W., and Phillip W. Jackson. "Family Environment and Cognitive Style: A Study of the Sources of Highly Intelligent and Creative Adolescents," *American Sociological Review* 26, no. 2 (1961).

Ginsberg, Eli. *The Nation's Children.* Teachers College, Columbia University, 1961.

Hollingworth, Leta S. *Children Above 180 IQ.* World Book Company, 1942.

Knapp, R. H., and H. B. Goodrich, *Origins of American Scientists.* University of Chicago Press, 1952.

Levy, David M. *Maternal Overprotection.* Columbia University Press: O.U.P., 1945.

McClelland, David C., Alfred L. Baldwin, Urie Bronfenbrenner, and Fred L. Strodtbeck. *Talent and Society.* Van Nostrand, 1958.

MacKinnon, Donald W. "Genus Architectus; Creator Varietas Americanus," *Journal of the American Institute of Architects* (Sept. 1960).

Murphy, Gardner. *Human Potentialities.* Allen & Unwin, 1958.

Roe, Anne. *Making of a Scientist.* Dodd, Mead, 1953.

Rubin, Louis J., ed. *Nurturing Classroom Creativity.* Ventura County (CA) Secondary Schools, 1960.

Taylor, Calvin W., ed. *Research Conference on the Identification of Creative Scientific Talent.* University of Utah Press, 1959.

Terman, Lewis M., and C. C. Miles. *Sex and Personality.* McGraw-Hill, 1936.

Terman, Lewis M., and Melita H. Oden. *The Gifted Group at Mid-Life.* Stanford University Press: O.U.P., 1959.

Torrance, E. Paul, *Status of Knowledge Concerning Education and Creative Scientific Talent.* Bureau of Educational Research, University of Minnesota, June 1961.

Witty, Paul. *One Hundred Gifted Children.* Kansas University Publications, 1930.

Wolfe, Dael. *America's Resources of Specialized Talent.* Harper, 1954.

Appendix B
Individuals Discussed in *Three Hundred Eminent Personalities: A Psychosocial Analysis of the Famous* (1978)

Activists
Angelou, Maya
Bates, Daisy
Bethune, Mary
Booth, Evangeline
Chavez, César
Davis, Angela
Devlin, Bernadette
Dolci, Danilo
Du Bois, W. E. B.
Ehrenburg, Ilya
Fanon, Frantz
Gerstein, Kurt
Goldman, Emma
Gramsci, Antonio
Guevara, Ernesto
Nader, Ralph
Odinga, Odinga
X, Malcolm

Actors
Bergman, Ingrid
Brando, Marlon
Chaplin, Michael
Coleman, Ronald
Dietrich, Marlene
Fonda, Henry
Fonda, Jane
Fonda, Peter
Garbo, Greta
Garland, Judy
Hayes, Helen
Hepburn, Katherine
Jolson, Al
Langtry, Lillie
Lillie, Beatrice
Maclaine, Shirley
Monroe, Marilyn
Muni, Paul
Negri, Pola
Olivier, Lawrence
Quinn, Anthony

Robinson, Edward
Taylor, Elizabeth
Ustinov, Peter
von Stroheim, Eric
Williams, Emlyn

Architects
Fuller, R. Buckminster

Artists
Bufano, Beniamino
Calder, Alexander
Cassatt, Mary
Epstein, Jacob
Gris, Juan
John, Augustus
Kokoschka, Oskar
Kollwitz, Kathe
Lipchitz, Jacque
Miró, Joan
Mondrian, Piet
Moore, Henry
Moses, Anna
O'Keeffe, Georgia
Pollock, Jackson
Renoir, Auguste
Sloan, John
Soyer, Moses
Soyer, Raphael
Utrillo, Maurice
Wood, Grant
Wyeth, Andrew
Zorach, William

Athletes
Ali, Muhammad
Gehrig, Lou
Koufax, Stanley
Mantle, Mickey
Mays, Willie
Naismith, James
Namath, Joe
Pele, Edson
Ruth, Babe

Business Leaders
Arden, Elizabeth
Chanel, Coco
Hughes, Howard
Jellinek-Mercedes, Emil
Renault, Louis
Rubinstein, Helena
Sarnoff, David

Criminals, Assassins, and Spies
Cohen, Elie
Genet, Jean
Hari, Mata

Dancers and Choreographers
Astaire, Fred
Dunham, Katherine
Fonteyn, Margot
Graham, Martha
Nureyev, Rudolph

Diplomats
Casement, Roger
Dulles, John F.
Hammarskjöld, Dag
Kissinger, Henry
Lodge, Henry Cabot
Nicolson, Harold

Editors and Publishers
Beaverbook, William
Luce, Henry
Meynell, Francis
Northcliffe, Alfred
Patterson, Eleanor
Woolf, Leonard

Explorers and Adventurers
Chichister, Francis
Heyerdahl, Thor
Shipton, Eric

Film Makers
Bergman, Ingmar
Capra, Frank
Korda, Alexander

Journalists
Cunard, Nancy
Leitch, David
Pearson, Drew
Thompson, Dorothy

Judges and Lawyers
Frankfurter, Felix
Warren, Earl

Labor Leader
Hoffa, James

Law Enforcement
Hoover, J. Edgar

Military Leaders
Dayan, Moshe
Zukhov, George

Musicians and Composers
Aznavour, Charles
Barbirolli, John
Bernstein, Leonard
Britten, Benjamin
Dylan, Bob
Ives, Charles
Joplin, Janis
Piaf, Edith
Porter, Cole
Robeson, Paul
Rubinstein, Arthur
Schoenberg, Arnold
Shankar, Ravi
Sinatra, Frank
Varèse, Edgard
Waters, Ethel
Welk, Lawrence

Photographers
Beaton, Cecil
Modotti, Tima
Steichen, Edward

Physician
Barnard, Christian

Pilot
Richtofen, Manfred

Political Leaders
Adler, Friedrich
Agnew, Spiro
Asquith, Herbert
Astor, Nancy
Ayub Kahn, Mohommod
Azikiwe, Nnamidi
Bond, Julian
Brandt, Willy
Brezhnev, Leonid
Bukharin, Nikolai
Carter, Jimmy
Castro, Fidel
Chisholm, Sidney
Chou En Lai
Dubèek, Alexander
Duvalier, François
Eban, Abba
Eichmann, Adolf
Ford, Gerald
Fulbright, William
Gandhi, Indira
Health, Edward
Ho Chi Minh
Humphrey, H. H.
Hussein, King of Jordan
Johnson, Lyndon
Kazantzakis, Nikos
Kefauver, Estes
Kennedy, Edward
Kennedy, Robert
Kenyatta, Jomo
McCarthy, Eugene
McGovern, George
Meir, Golda
Mosley, Sir Oswald
Muskie, Ed
Quisling, Vidkun
Regan, Ronald
Selaisse, Haile
Sukarno, Ahmed
Thomas, Norman
Trudeau, Pierre
Wallace, George
Weisgal, Meyer

Psychics and Hypnotists
Cayce, Edgar
deLouise, Joseph
Dixon, Jeane
Dykshoorn, M. B.
Ford, Arthur
Garrett, Eileen
Geller, Uri
Hurkos, Peter
Leek, Sybil

Psychotherapists
Deutsch, Helene
Erikson, Erik
Jung, Carl G.
Masserman, Jules
Reich, Wilhelm

Religious and Spiritual Leaders
Pope Paul V
Riou, Roger
Yoganda, Paramahansa

Scientists, Scholars, and Educators

Bohr, Niels
Bonhoeffer, Dietrich
Buber, Martin
de Chardin, Teilhard
Franklin, Rosalind
Gamow, George
Hahn, Otto
Huxley, Julian
Kinsey, Alfred
Krishnamurti, Jiddu
Lawrence, Earnest
Leakey, Louis
Mead, Margaret
Neill, Alexander
Sartre, J. P.
Tillich, Paul
Ulam, Stanislaw
von Frisch, Karl

Wives, Family Members, and Socialites

Alliluiyeva, Svetlana
Dayan, Ruth
Fitzgerald, Zelda
Johnson, Lady Bird
Kahn, Aly
Kennedy, Rose
Krupskaya, Nadezhda
Morrell, Ottoline
Onassis, Jacqueiline
Rachewiltz, Mary
Rasmussen, Anna-Marie
Reich, Pater
Renoir, Jean

Writers

Agee, James
Andreas-Salomé, Lou
Auden, W. H.
Babel, Isaac
Bagnold, Enid
Baldwin, James
Beauvoir, Simone
Bentley, Phyllis
Brecht, Bertolt
Brenan, Gerald
Breton, André
Carson, Rachel
Cary, Joyce
Céline, Louis F.
Cloete, Stuart
Cocteau, Jean
Codrescu, Andrei
Colette
Cookson, Catherine
cummings, ee
de la Roche, Mazo
Dinesen, Isak
Eliot, T. S.
Ferber, Edna
Forester, C. S.
Ginsberg, Allen
Giraudoux, Jean
Greene, Graham
Hellman, Lillian
Hesse, Hermann
Hoffer, Eric
Isherwood, Christopher
Kaufman, George
Lardner, Ring

Lawrence, Frieda
Leduc, Violette
Lehmann, John
Lessing, Doris
Lindbergh, Anne
Lowry, Malcolm
Malraux, André
Maugham, Robert
Mayakovsky, Vladimir
McCullers, Carson
Miller, Henry
Mishima, Yukio
Mitford, Nancy
Moraes, Dom
Myrdal, Jan
Nabokov, Vladimir
Narayan, R. K.
Nîn, Anaïs
O'Conner, Flannery
O'Connor, Frank
O'Faolain, Sean
O'Hara, John
Plath, Sylvia
Pound, Ezra
Priestly, John
Pritchett, Victor
Radclyffe-Hall, Marguerite
Roethke, Theodore
Sachs, Maurice
Sackville-West, Vita
Saint-Exupery, Antoine
Simenon, George
Sinclair, Upton
Singer, Isaac
Solzhenitsyn, Alesandr
Steinbeck, John
Strachey, Lytton
Suyin, Han
Thurber, James
Vining, Elizabeth
Watts, Alan
Waugh, Evelyn
West, Jesamyn
White, T. H.
Williams, Tennessee
Wodehouse, P. G.
Yevtushenko, Yevgeny

Appendix C
Individuals Discussed in *Turncoats and True Believers: The Dynamics of Political Belief and Disillusionment* (1992)

Agee, Philip
Bellamy, Edward
Boulding, Kenneth
Brittain, Vera
Burnham, James
Bush, George W.
Butz, Arthur
Castro, Fidel
Churchill, Winston
Cleaver, Eldridge
Comte, Auguste
Donnelly, Ignatius
Eastman, Max
Einstein, Albert
Engels, Friedrich
Freud, Sigmund
Friedan, Betty
Gandhi, Mohandas
Gorbachev, Mikhail
Greer, Germaine
Harrington, Michael
Hayden, Tom
Hess, Karl
Hitler, Adolf
Hoffman, Abbie
Horowitz, David
Hussein, Saddam
Jones, Jim
Lenin, V. I.
Marx, Karl
Mead, Margaret
Mill, John Stuart
Millett, Kate
Muste, Abraham
Pauling, Linus
Rand, Ayn
Schlafly, Phyllis
Smith, Bradley
Stalin, Joseph
Wilson, Woodrow

Note: *Turncoats and True Believers* has a different theoretical focus than *Cradles of Eminence* or *Three Hundred Eminent Personalities,* but it also includes some childhood information. There is some overlap in the individuals discussed.

Appendix D
Biographical Sources for the *Cradles of Eminence*, *Second Edition* 2003 Update Sample

Since biographical references on the individuals in the update sample are available online, there is no need to list two references for each of them in this Appendix. The names we chose came from four sources, which are readily available to readers:

1. The Montclair Public Library, which is at www.montlib.com. Most readers, at least in the United States, may find it more convenient to consult their own online public library catalog. We have found that most American public libraries have good collections on our subjects.

2. *Life* magazine's special issue "The 100 Most Influential Americans of the Twentieth Century," Vol. 13, No. 12, Fall 1990. This issue is only available in the back issue departments of selected libraries.

3. *Time* magazine's website, "100 Most Important People of the Twentieth Century," available at: www.time.com/time/time100.

4. The *Time* book titled *Time, Great People of the Twentieth Century*, New York, Time, Inc, 1996. The lists in this book and on the Time.com website are not identical.

The *Life* and *Time* lists were helpful for sampling, but they do not include much childhood information. More of this type of information is sometimes available at www.biography.com, although the comprehensiveness of the biographies on that site is quite variable. It is especially useful for minorities, musicians, actors, athletes, and recent celebrities. There is also a good deal of information of highly varying quality on the World Wide Web.

The following is a list of some books and other sources that we found useful in writing the update in Chapter 12, listed by the name of the individual.

Allen, Woody

Allen, Woody. *A Biography.* Da Cappo Press, 1991.

Meade, Marion. *The Unruly Life of Woody Allen.* New York: Scribner, 2000.

Berners Lee, Tim

www.computerweekly.com/Article25873.htm

Bush, George W.

Hollandsworth, Skip. "Born to Run." *Texas Monthly* 22, no. 5 (May 1994).

Minutaglio, Bill. *First Son: George W. Bush and the Bush Family Dynasty.* New York: Times Books, 1999.

http://users.bigpond.net.au/wmontagu/Family%20Tree/index.html

Clinton, Hillary Rodham

Clinton, Hillary Rodham. *Living History.* New York: Simon & Shuster, 2003.

Radcliffe, Donnie. *Hillary Rodham Clinton: A First Lady for Our Time.* New York: Warner Books, 1993.

Crick, Francis

Crick, Francis. *What Mad Pursuit.* New York: Basic Books, 1988.

Disney, Walt

Schickel, Richard. *The Disney Version: The Life, Times, Art and Commerce of Walt Disney.* New York: Simon & Schuster, 1968.

Thomas, Bob. *Building a Company: Roy O. Disney and the Creation of an Entertainment Empire.* New York: Hyperion, 1998.

Friedman, Milton

Friedman, Milton and Rose. *Two Lucky People: Memoirs.* Chicago: University of Chicago Press, 1998.

Goodall, Jane

Peterson, Dale, ed., *Africa in My Blood: An Autobiography in Letters, The Early Years*, by Jane Goodall. Boston: Houghton Mifflin, 2000.

Jane Goodall Institute, biography at www.janegoodall.org/jane

Hawking, Stephen

White, Michael, and John Gribbin. *Stephen Hawking: A Life in Science.* New York: Dutton, 1992.

Hendrix, Jimi

Shapiro, Harry, and Caesar Glebbeek. *Jimi Hendrix: Electric Gypsy.* New York: St. Martin's, 1991.

Jeter, Derek

Craig, Robert. *Derek Jeter: A Biography*. New York: Pocket Books, 1999.

John Paul II

Kwitny, Jonathan. *Man of the Century: The Life and Times of Pope John Paul II.* New York: Holt, 1997.

Wiegel, George. *Witness to Hope.* New York: Cliff Street, 1999.

Jordan, Michael

Greene, Bob. *Hang Time: Days and Dreams with Michael Jordan.* New York: Doubleday, 1992.

Naughton, Jim. *Taking to the Air: The Rise of Michael Jordan.* New York: Warner Books, 1992.

Kahlo, Frida

Tibol, Raquel. *Frida Kahlo: An Open Life.* Albuquerque: University of New Mexico Press, 1983.

Kroc, Ray

Kroc, Ray. *Grinding It Out: The Making of McDonald's.* Chicago: Regnery, 1977.

Love, John F. *McDonald's: Behind the Arches.* New York: Bantam, 1986.

Lauder, Estée

Israel, Lee. *Estée Lauder: Beyond the Magic.* New York: MacMillan, 1985

Lauder, Estée. *Estée: A Success Story.* New York: Random House, 1985.

Mandela, Nelson

Meredith, Martin. *Nelson Mandela: A Biography.* New York: St Martin's, 1998.

Sampson, Anthony. *Mandela: The Authorized Biography.* New York: Knopf, 1999.

McCardell, Claire

Yohannan, Kohle, and Nancy Nolf. *Claire McCardell: Redefining Modernism.* New York: Harry Abrams, 1998.

McGwire, Mark

McNeill, William. *Ruth, Maris, McGwire and Sosa: Baseball's Single Season Home Run Champions.* Jefferson, N.C.: McFarland & Company, 1999.

Rains, Rob. *Mark McGwire: Home Run Hero.* New York: St. Martin's Press, 1998.

Merton, Thomas

Mott, Michael. *The Seven Mountains of Thomas Merton.* Boston: Houghton Mifflin, 1984.

Sussman, Cornelia and Irving. *Thomas Merton.* Garden City: Doubleday, 1980.

Mother Teresa

Sebba, Anne. *Mother Teresa: Beyond the Image.* New York: Doubleday, 1997.

Spink, Kathryn. *Mother Teresa: A Complete Authorized Biography.* New York: Harper Collins, 1997.

O'Keeffe, Georgia

Eisler, Benita. *O'Keeffe and Steiglitz: An American Romance.* New York: Doubleday, 1991.

Robinson, Roxana. *Georgia O'Keeffe, a Life.* New York: Harper & Row, 1989.

Parks, Rosa

Brinkley, Douglas. *Rosa Parks.* New York: Penguin Group, 2000.

Friese, Kay. *Rosa Parks: The Movement Organizes.* Englewood Cliffs, N.J.: Silver Burdett Press, 1990.

Greenfield, Eloise. *Rosa Parks.* New York: Thomas Y. Crowell, 1973.

Pauling, Linus

Goertzel, Ted and Ben. *Linus Pauling: A Life in Science and Politics.* New York: Basic Books, 1995.

Stanton, Elizabeth Cady

Banner, Lois W. *Elizabeth Cady Stanton: A Radical for Woman's Rights.* Boston: Little, Brown, 1980.

Oakley, Mary Ann B. *Elizabeth Cady Stanton.* New York: Feminist Press, 1972.

Steiglitz, Alfred

Eisler, Benita. *O'Keeffe and Steiglitz: An American Romance.* New York: Doubleday, 1991.

Whelan, Richard. *Alfred Steiglitz: A Biography.* Boston: Little, Brown, 1995.

Steinem, Gloria

Heilbrun, Carolyn. *The Education of a Woman: The Life of Gloria Steinem.* New York: Dial, 1995.

Streisand, Barbra

Spada, James. *Streisand: Her Life.* New York: Crown, 1992.

Walton, Sam

Trimble, Vance. *Sam Walton: The Inside Story of America's Richest Man.* New York: Dutton, 1990.

Walton, Sam, with John Huey. *Sam Walton: Made in America.* New York: Doubleday, 1992.

Watson, James

Watson, James. *A Passion for DNA.* Cold Spring Harbor: Cold Spring Harbor Laboratory Press, 2000.

Wells, Ida

Sterling, Dorothy. *Black Foremothers.* Old Westbury, N.Y.: Feminist Press, 1979.

Wilder, Laura Ingalls

Miller, John E. *Becoming Laura Ingalls Wilder: The Woman Behind the Legend.* Columbia, Mo.: University of Missouri Press, 1999.

Wilson, Bill

Hartigan, Francis. *Bill W.: A Biography of Alcoholics Anonymous Cofounder Bill Wilson.* New York: St. Martin's, 2000.

Winfrey, Oprah

King, Norman. *Everybody Loves Oprah*. New York: William Morrow, 1987.

Woods, "Tiger"

Owen, David. *The Chosen One: Tiger Woods and the Dilemma of Greatness*. New York: Simon & Schuster, 2001.

Rosaforte, Tim. *Tiger Woods: The Making of a Champion*. New York: St. Martin's Press, 1997.

Index

About the Authors

Victor Goertzel, Ph.D., a psychologist specializing in group and individual psychotherapy, lived in Palo Alto and San Jose, California. After receiving his B.A. and M.A. degrees in psychology from the University of California, Berkeley, he was awarded a Ph.D. degree in clinical psychology from the University of Michigan in 1953. He was a member of the American Psychological Association, the Society for the Psychological Study of Social Issues, the American Orthopsychiatric Association, and was a Past President of the National Association for Gifted Children.

Mildred George Goertzel, formerly a high school teacher, became director of the Forum School for Emotionally Disturbed Children in Paterson, New Jersey, but later devoted full time to writing. She received her bachelor's degree in English from Ball State University in Muncie, Indiana

and did graduate work in English at the University of Chicago and Northwestern University, as well as in child development at the University of California at Berkeley.

Mildred and Victor met in the late 1930s and traveled to Mexico, where they became acquainted with the painters Diego Rivera and Frida Kahlo, and also where they discovered Quakerism. They both subsequently spent a lifetime working on peace and social justice issues, and both were intrigued with early influences on children who later became famous people. In 1962, Victor and Mildred George wrote *Cradles of Eminence*, which soon became recognized as a classic. Other jointly authored books followed, including *Three Hundred Eminent Personalities*, published in 1978, and *Linus Pauling: A Life in Science and Politics*, published in 1995. Victor died in 1999, and Mildred died in 2000.

Ted George Goertzel, a son of Mildred and George, has continued the family tradition of studying people, particularly as they are involved in social or political change. He has published six books and numerous professional papers primarily concerning social movements, generational conflict, and social class and political attitudes. Ted currently is professor and former chairperson in the Department of Sociology at Rutgers University in Camden, New Jersey. He received his B.A. degree from Antioch College in Yellow Springs, Ohio with a major in sociology and anthropology. Both his M.A. degree in sociology and Latin American studies and his Ph.D. degree in sociology were awarded by Washington University in St. Louis. Prior to teaching at Rutgers, Ted taught at the University of Oregon and the University of São Paulo.

Ariel M. W. Hansen is a science writer living in Portland, Oregon. A fifth-generation Pacific Northwesterner, she was born and raised on an island in Washington's Puget Sound. Her early education included home schooling and the Evergreen School for Gifted Children in Seattle. Ariel attended high school at Westtown School in Westtown, Pennsylvania and obtained her B.A. in English from Haverford College in Haverford, Pennsylvania. A step-niece of Ted, she is pursuing a career in science journalism, with particular focus on astrophysics and cosmology.